GORDON IN CHINA

AND

THE SOUDAN

GORDON IN CHINA

AND

THE SOUDAN

BY

A. EGMONT HAKE

DARF PUBLISHERS LIMITED
LONDON
1987

FIRST PUBLISHED 1896
NEW IMPRESSION 1987

ISBN 978 1 85077 165 4

Printed and bound in Great Britain
by A. Wheaton & Co. Ltd, Exeter, Devon

"*One honest man, one wise man, one peaceful man commands a hundred millions, without a baton and without a charger. He wants no fortress to protect him; he stands higher than any citadel can raise him, brightly conspicuous to the most distant nations, God's servant by election, God's image by beneficence.*"—LANDOR.

CONTENTS

THE STORY OF CHINESE GORDON

---◆---

CHAPTER I

THE GORDONS AND THE ENDERBYS

THIS book would be interesting to many if its object were merely to set forth a detailed account of the varied and splendid exploits of Charles Gordon, and to sound his praise. Such, however, is not its only aim. The history of Christ has been recorded, to the end that men might have before them the example of a perfect life. This example Charles Gordon followed, perhaps as closely as mortal may do. To show his achievement step by step is to place the actions of such a man in a light wherein they may serve as a beacon to others; with this intention it is that the story of Chinese Gordon is given to the world.

His one aim in life was to do his duty, and that without incurring the penalty of fame, the displeasure of being called a hero. He always abhorred publicity, he never courted renown; yet now his is among the most renowned of names, and to the peoples of three continents is a household word. Though fully conscious of irresistible strength of purpose, he claimed no merit for himself. He, "with celestial vigour armed, and plain heroic magnitude of mind," regarded no feat of war as due to efforts of his own; no peril he surmounted as due to daring; no victory he won as due to prowess or to skill. Whatever his triumphs, he held them none of his, but the triumphs of a higher cause, whose instrument he was, and whose flag he bore.

In him were united the genius of action and the genius of morality. He had the unalterable simplicity of a character whose primary elements were the capacities of faith and love. A Lieutenant of Engineers in 1852, he became a Major-General in

I

the service of his own country, a Mandarin of the highest order in the service of China, a Pasha in the service of the Porte, and a Viceroy under the British and the Egyptian Governments. Yet his letters from South Africa, the scene of some of his latest exploits, were written in a spirit as fresh and modest as those he penned in the trenches before Sebastopol. In his retreat at Jerusalem he worked at his self-imposed task—the reconstructive survey, half mystical, half scientific, of the Holy Sepulchre—with an intelligence as untiring and an interest as boyish and frank as he bestowed upon the boundaries of Bessarabia and Armenia close on thirty years before.

In every walk of life there are those whose aim it is to do their highest duties to their fellows. Examples of self-sacrifice are thickly scattered through the annals of religion, government, and war: but it has been in the power of few to bear themselves so congruously as he in the midst of incongruities; to be as gentle in times of strife as in times of peace; to vanquish so many, to condemn so few; to accept so little, and to give so much. His story, indeed, is the story of a swordless conqueror; of a true disciple of the Divine Master, who laid down His life for humanity; of a complete Christian in thought, word, and deed. The man must be peculiarly endowed who, wholly devoid of personal ambition, finds himself sought out as fittest for the highest tasks, and only accepts the position when the service demanded of him is in the cause of humanity. This, however, was the case with Gordon. Never did he look to being great; and when, after almost miraculous achievements, greatness was thrust upon him, he ignored the honour implied, and declined the proffered reward. From first to last he was content in the belief that he had done his best. This perfect disinterestedness was consistently maintained throughout a career which teemed with temptations and the sorest trials; which was made up of incidents the most romantic and adventures the most desperate. This was the characteristic in one gifted with a mysterious power of fascinating his fellow-men, whether of the Western or the Eastern world. It is small wonder if to many its possessor was not merely heroic, but unique, among men.

Before recounting his adventures, it will be interesting to say something of the family to which he belonged, if only to trace to their source the qualities which contributed to the making of his strange and brilliant career. His father, the late Lieutenant-General Henry William Gordon, of the Royal Artillery, left a memoir of his family. Scanty as it is, it contains some facts worth noting. General Gordon relates, for instance, that his grandfather, David Gordon (born in 1715), a Highlander and a soldier, was taken prisoner at Prestonpans while serving under Sir John Cope in Lascelles' Regiment (late 47th Regiment); his kinsman, Sir William Gordon of Park, fighting on the same field under the Pretender. David was released upon parole through the influence of the Duke of Cumberland, whom he had met at Edinburgh, and to whom he was previously known, the Duke having some six years before stood sponsor for his son—Charles Gordon's grandfather — and given him his name of William Augustus. After Culloden, David Gordon, with his son, embarked for North America. There he died from an accident, and was buried at Halifax in 1752. His son, the "Butcher's" namesake, entered the British army, and served successively in the 40th, 72nd, and 11th Regiments of infantry. He fought at Minorca—also with distinction at the siege of Louisburgh in 1758; and in 1759 he was with Wolfe on the Plains of Abraham. In 1762 he witnessed the attack and surrender of the Moro Castle. On his return to England he was sent to Hexham, in Northumberland, where he met his future wife, Anna Maria Clarke, at the house of her brother, the Reverend Slaughter Clarke. To this lady he was married in 1773. By her he had four daughters and three sons. Of his sons, the eldest, William Augustus, was a captain of the 95th Regiment; he died from a fall from his horse while on duty at the Cape. The second, Augustus Henry, was educated at the Royal Military Academy, and died a Lieutenant of the Royal Engineers. The third, Henry William, born in 1786, entered the Royal Artillery, and was the only male survivor of his family in that generation. He married Elizabeth, a daughter of the late Samuel Enderby, of Blackheath, and had issue five sons and six daughters. Three of the sons entered the army. The youngest of these was the Captain of the Ever-Victorious Army—Chinese Gordon. It will be seen from this that for a century and a half the family had been a family of soldiers, and that without threatening extinction, for there is a new generation in the service; and that it has culminated in the genius of Charles Gordon, the most famous of his adventurous and distinguished clan.

Charles Gordon's father, whom many still recollect, was a man of marked individuality. He was a good and complete soldier, with a cultivated knowledge of his profession. He will be long remembered by those who served under him, as well as by his family and his friends, for his firm yet genial character, and his very striking figure. He was of a peculiar type. Those who knew him can never forget his lively and expressive face; his great round head—bald, and surrounded by short curly hair, black in his best days; his robust playfulness of manner; and above all, the twinkle of fun in his clear blue eyes. In his company it was not possible to be dull; he had a look which diffused cheerfulness, and an inexhaustible fund of humour. On occasions he could be stern; for the essence of his character was a decision which turned to severity when others deviated from their duty, or did it amiss. He lived by the "code of honour": it was the motive of all his actions, and he expected those with whom he dealt to be guided by its precepts. It is said that no man succeeds in his calling unless he considers it the best and highest. This was General Gordon's feeling for the army. So deeply did he revere the ideal of the British officer, that Charles Gordon's acceptance of a foreign command, despite its singular and momentous results, gave him no pleasure: he was proud of his son, but he did not like to think that he was serving among foreigners, and not, as a Gordon should, with the men of his own race and faith. He was greatly beloved; for he was kind-hearted, generous, genial in his nature, always just in his practice and in his aims. He spent a long life in the service, and, like his son, was less fitted to obey than to command. More than once, well as he knew the value of discipline, it was his to resist his superiors, and to protest against dictates which he would hold to be superfluous and unjust. No portrait[1] left of him does him justice, or in the least recalls a face which all who knew it remember as noble and commanding.

His wife, Charles Gordon's mother, was no less remarkable a character. She possessed a perfect temper; she was always cheerful under the most trying circumstances, and she was always thoughtful of others; she contended with difficulties without the slightest display of effort; and she had a genius for making the best of everything. During the Crimean War her anxieties were interminable: she had three sons and several near kinsmen at the front. She was perfectly equal to the strain. Her hopefulness remained unclouded; all day long did she busy herself with the

---

[1] One which pictures him as a cadet of the Royal Woolwich Academy, by Dr. Walcott (Peter Pindar), is in possession of Lady Gordon, the widow of his eldest son.

wants of others at home and in the field; while a duty remained to do, or a kindness to bestow, her sunny energy maintained her at her work. She came of a family—originally from Leicestershire —of merchants and explorers : a family which presented a marked contrast with that race of the "gay Gordons" with which in her person it was allied. Her father, Samuel Enderby, made himself in connection with geographical research a name which still has a conspicuous place on the map of the world. A London merchant for many years, he took a prominent part in opening up the resources of the Southern Hemisphere. Previous to the War of Independence, he worked and traded much in America. There he trafficked in the whale fishery, the ships engaged in it being his own, and their crews in his pay. The produce he sent on to England in vessels also his own property. Two of these, outward bound for Boston from the Thames, were chartered by the English Government to carry the tea which proved the occasion of the Revolution. Their arrival in Boston harbour is matter of history. Both were boarded by the rebels. They broke open the chests of tea, and emptied them over the side; and so was struck the first blow for American independence.

In those days colonial ships were not often permitted to sail from England with British registers. Samuel Enderby was a favoured exception among owners. The bottoms he owned in America, and in which he traded between that colony and his own country, were specially licensed—for the whaling traffic only— to sail from London as well as from Boston or New York, and to pursue adventure in all quarters of the ocean. The practice of this privilege had some important results. Under the terms of the East India Company's charter, it was unlawful for any ship to go east of the Cape without the Company's licence, or to trade in those waters except under conditions in the Company's gift. Such a licence was not easily obtained, the H.E.I.C. being in the enjoyment of a monopoly of the largest and richest type, which it was bent upon working entirely to its own advantage. As the ways of the Southern Ocean were very little known, except to such bold and hardy navigators as Cook and La Perouse, whose aims were purely geographical and scientific, and as there was no trade to be done in them by private owners, they were practically no more than a vast whaling-ground, frequented only by fisher-men in search of oil and spermaceti, and closed and barren to all the world besides. Samuel Enderby, as I have said, was one of the boldest of all the whaling owners; and it is thanks to his enterprise and constancy, and to those of the men who followed in his wake, that the Southern Hemisphere was opened up so soon. This was particularly the case with Australia and New Zealand. They lay outside the limits of the H.E.I.C.'s adventure, and they offered the H.E.I.C. no inducement either to traffic or explore; so that but for the Enderby whalers they might have remained in idleness and desolation much longer than they did.   It was on the occasion of the foundation of our first penal settlement that the Enderby fleet became directly useful.   It had been decided that such an establishment should be essayed; and it had been found that the expense of carrying convicts out in bottoms for which there was no chance of finding a return freight was an almost insurmountable objection.   The practice of the Enderby whalers removed the difficulty.   They were in the habit of going out to the fishing-grounds in ballast, and of picking up a return freight at the voyage-end.   It was seen that they might as well be laden with men as with casks of water; and the issue was that they took out to Botany Bay the first batch of convicts ever settled on Australian shores.   The communication thus established was by their means continued : they took out settlers as well as "lags"; more than once they saved the community of exiles from starvation ; they may certainly be said to have borne no unimportant part in the settlement of our greatest dependency.   And their presence in Southern waters was fraught with issues hardly less momentous for New Zealand than Australia.   It was mainly by runaways from them and their sisters and rivals that the two islands were first settled.   The habits and customs of these gentry—who plied the Maoris with firearms and rum, and cheated them in return of great expanses of territory—obliged the Home Government to interfere.   To put a stop to their depredations, it was found necessary to annex the whole country ; and this—although the British Government was loth to do it—is what was actually done.

Nor is this all.   The Enderby whalers were the first to frequent the Pacific round the dreadful Horn, and abolish the bugbear that for centuries had perched upon its cliffs.   To the southward they explored the Antarctic Ocean, and under the command of Briscoe and of Bellamy discovered the Auckland Islands, with Enderby and Graham's Lands.   Their initiative has since been followed up by the English, French, and American Governments, under Sir James Ross, Admiral d'Urville, and Commodore Wilkes, who—it may be added—have done little more than confirm the correctness of their researches.   To the northward they made themselves useful to Pitt, and were active in the contraband trade with the Western States of South America, which the Heaven-Born Minister designed and encouraged to the prejudice of the natural enemy.[1] They were the first to attempt the whale fishery in Japanese waters; and they did their best to open trade with the Middle Kingdom. It will be seen that they were the primary cause of our acquaintance with and settlement of all the important colonies in the Southern Ocean, from Australia to the Fijian Archipelago.

Gordon was educated at Taunton, and at the Royal Military Academy, Woolwich. There is but little to say about his early life. He was not strong, and this may account for his doing nothing really noteworthy either at school or in his later examinations. In this part of his story there was always humour, and now and then there were flashes of that resolution and energy which afterwards showed themselves in so many ways, and to such splendid purpose. Once, for instance, during his cadetship at the Academy, he was rebuked for incompetence, and told that he would never make an officer; whereupon he tore the epaulets from his shoulders and flung them at his superior's feet.

On leaving the Royal Academy of Woolwich for service as an officer of Engineers, he was ordered to Pembroke. Here he was engaged in making plans for forts at the entrance of the Haven. This was in August 1854, and in November in the same year he got orders for Corfu. These were in one sense disappointing to him, for he had lived in the hope of being sent to the Crimea; on the other hand, he was in fear of being drafted to the West Indies or to New Zealand, and thus of being removed out of reach of the war. It was natural that he should display no great eagerness to revisit the Ionian Islands, inasmuch as his father had commanded the artillery for some years at Corfu during Charles Gordon's boyhood. He therefore asked two months' leave, to be spent on duty at Pembroke. This he obtained; and early in December his route was changed, and he was making arrangements to leave for the Crimea.

[1] The story goes that the Spanish Government had issued a proclamation to the effect that any ship caught within fifty miles of these coasts should be confiscated. The prohibition pressed hard upon Enderby's undertakings, and he complained of it to Pitt. Pitt asked him, "What distance would satisfy you?" and was told that he would be content with twenty miles. "Make it five," says Pitt; "and if you are caught within that limit, say you are short of water and need a supply."

CHAPTER II

HE left England in company with the Honourable F. Keane, afterwards Major-General Keane, C.B., who was then in charge of a battery.

At Constantinople, he saw, for the first time, blows struck in real earnest, as he was present at a serious *fracas* between the native police and the French troops, in which some of the latter were badly wounded. On January 1st, 1855, he reached Balaclava in the *Golden Fleece*, and reported himself at headquarters; but as he was not detailed for any duty for some weeks, he had plenty of time to look about him. His letters home gave a vivid picture of the position of affairs. He tells us that, though the French were advancing on their works, the English were at a standstill. Supplies were short, and officers and men were engaged in foraging expeditions, as the Commissariat had completely broken down. The streets and villages were crowded with a military rabble. English cavalry and artillery, Turks, Zouaves, and camp-followers of every description, mingled with the sickly troops of Omar Pasha, who were nearly as ill-fed as their own half-starved camels that helped to block the roads. The cold, which was intense, was fatal to many, while others were perishing of suffocation by the fumes of charcoal fires. Everything was in confusion, and everybody more or less despondent. Food, how and where to get it, was the one absorbing interest; and no one seemed to know—or to be anxious to learn —what progress was being made in the siege.

So things went on for nearly a month, when Gordon was detailed for duty in the trenches before Sebastopol. His letter home, dated February 14th, describes accurately the kind of work he had to do; and gives an account of how, after being fired upon first by the English sentries, and then by the Russian pickets,

8

and how, after the working party and sentries under his command had bolted, he was able to carry out his first definite order on active service. This was to effect a junction by means of rifle-pits between the French and English sentries who were stationed in advance of the trenches.

The manner and the circumstances of this, Gordon's first important duty, are in some sort typical of his whole achievement. As will be seen later on, he was frequently fired upon by friends as well as by foes, and several of his most notable conquests were made almost single-handed, after those whom he had under his command had mutinied or deserted him.

The siege of Sebastopol extended over a period of nearly eleven months, as it was begun in October 1854, and only completed in September 1855. Balaclava was fought on October 25th, 1854, and Inkerman on November 5th in the same year. Gordon's first experience of active service was in February 1855; and it is with affairs from that date up to the final assault upon Sebastopol on September 8th, that I have now to deal.

Evidence of military capacity is not wanting, even at this early period of his soldiering, and the serene, earnest, and religious fervour which has since been characteristic of the man, was at this time distinctly marked. Years only served to strengthen, not to change it.

From February 28th to April 9th, Gordon's duty was limited to the making of new batteries in the advance trenches. During the whole of this time active operations against the enemy seemed to have almost ceased, save for a prolonged and feeble duel between the French rocket battery and the Russian artillery, the effect of which was very slight on either side. Now and then the wearisome work of throwing up battery after battery was relieved by the excitement of a dropping fire, either from the enemy's trenches or from the heights in the rear, and this was returned by the working party under the command of the Engineer officers.

It was during this time that Gordon met with a very narrow escape, from a bullet fired at him from one of the lower Russian rifle-pits, some 180 yards away. The missile passed within an inch of his head; but, in referring to the incident in one of his letters home, his only comment is: "They (the Russians) are very good marksmen; their bullet is large and pointed."

A few days after this, one of his captains, named Craigie, was killed by a splinter from the enemy's shells, and Gordon, writing home of the casualty, winds up by saying: "I am glad to say that he (Captain Craigie) was a serious man. The shell burst above him, and *by what is called chance* struck him in the back, killing him at once." The words italicised are noteworthy. They are the words of a fatalist; and they furnish the first written evidence we have of the religious convictions which controlled the writer's actions. That all things are ordained by God is the belief he held even when he wrote of Craigie's death. That it was greatly strengthened by strange personal adventures in later years there is no doubt; but through all its development it has remained essentially the same. Milton's lines,

"Necessity or chance
Approach not me, and what I will is fate,"

are applicable to Gordon's belief in himself. His will he held to be identical with God's—with God's, whose instrument he feels and knows he is.

At the time of the Czar's death, which took place in March 1855, the number of French troops in the Crimea was 80,000, the number of the English 23,000. Of the former Gordon speaks in rather disparaging terms, for he says in one letter: "The Russians are brave, better, I think, than the French, who begin to fear them"; and again, in another letter of a later date: "I cannot say much for our allies; they are afraid to do anything, and consequently quite cramp our movements. The Russians certainly are inferior to none; their work is stupendous, and their shell-practice beautiful."

On April 9th heavy firing was resumed on both sides, and continued, with short intervals of cessation, up to the 30th inst. During this time the casualties in the trenches were many, with a large proportion of officers to men among the killed. Gordon was untouched, though actively engaged during the whole time, and present at several sorties in front of the Redan, in one of which several officers and 70 men were killed and wounded. Writing on April 20th, he refers to the weakness of our ally. He says: "I think we might have assaulted on Monday, but the French do not seem to care about it. The garrison is 25,000, and on that day we heard afterwards that only 800 men were in the place, so the rest had gone to repel an attack (fancied) of ours at Inkerman." And on April 30th he says: "We are still pushing batteries forward as much as possible, but cannot advance our trenches until the French take the Mamelon, as it enfilades our advance works. Until that occurs, things are at a stand-still."

This was on April 30th. Thenceforward, until early in the month of June, active operations ceased; and though innumerable councils of war were held, nothing definite was done or decided upon. Gordon's letters home during this time have no special interest. I shall make but a single extract, which is certainly worth reading: " We have a great deal to regret in the want of good working clergymen, there being none here that I know of who interest themselves about the men."

On the 6th of June the English opened fire from all their batteries, and there ensued a tremendous artillery duel, in which 1000 guns were engaged. The casualties on the Russian side were numerous, while our own were few. Gordon, who was in the trenches during the whole time, was returned as among the wounded, but his injury was such that he was able to continue his duty. A stone thrown up by a round shot stunned him for a second, but did him no further hurt. On the following day the French attacked the Mamelon, and the redoubts of Selinghinck and Volhynia. The Russians retreated towards the Malakoff, and were rapidly followed by the French; but the latter were so punished by the guns from the tower that they had to retire, pursued by the very enemy they had been pursuing. However, they attacked again, and while we secured the quarries they carried the Mamelon, as well as the redoubts before named. " Only a few lines," writes his brother from the scene of action, " to say Charley is all right, and has escaped amidst a terrific shower of grape and shells of every description. You may imagine the suspense I was kept in until assured of his safety. He cannot write himself, and is now fast asleep in his tent, having been in the trenches from 2 o'clock yesterday morning during the cannonade until 7 last night, and again from 12.30 this morning until noon." Gordon, in his account of this successful assault, says: "I do not think the place (Sebastopol) can hold out another ten days; and once taken, the Crimea is ours." Sebastopol did hold out for nearly ten times ten days, but many officers in high command have since expressed their belief that the siege might have been brought to an end in June instead of in September. When Gordon wrote, the allied armies numbered nearly 165,000; the French were erecting a battery on the Mamelon; the Russian works had been completely ruined; and their fleet—its old position made untenable by the capture of the redoubts—had moved out into the middle of the harbour. There was an armistice for a few days, for the burial of the dead; and had it been succeeded by a bold assault upon the Malakoff Tower, the Redan, and the Central Bastion, the probability is that Gordon's impression as to the duration of the siege would have proved correct. Instead of this, however, there ensued a period of inactivity, during which Gordon, in his letters home, for the first and only time, alludes to his wants,—a map of the Crimea and a bottle of Rowland's Odonto. From this time forth to the evacuation of Sebastopol on September 8th, the siege operations were proceeded with slowly and deliberately, but with a lack of energy and activity that was wearisome and irritating. Gordon's duty kept him in the trenches during the whole time ; but beyond stating that his officers speak of his zeal and intelligence in terms of admiration and affection, I can say little or nothing definite of his actions. I am, however, disposed to select from his letters home the following paragraphs, inasmuch as they will enable the reader to gain some insight into the further progress of the siege, as well as into the character and disposition of the writer.

"*June* 15*th*.—The Russians are down-hearted, although determined ; they are much to be admired, and their officers are quite as cool as our officers under fire."

"*June* 30*th*.—Lord Raglan died on the evening of the 26th, of tear and wear, and general debility. He was universally regretted, as he was so kind. I am really sorry for him, his life has been entirely spent in the service of his country. *I hope he was prepared, but do not know.*"

"*August* 3*rd*.—We are disappointed that General Jones did not mention Brown in the attack on the Quarries. I, for one, do not care about being 'lamented' after death. I am tired of the inactivity, but when we move again in advance or assault it will break the monotony."

"*August* 17*th*.—Sebastopol is now in every part under our fire, but the caves underground protect the men to a great degree. They have fired shot into, around, and over our camp from guns placed or slung as the guns were in the Baltic, at a high elevation of 35° or 40°. Two shots went within three yards of my pony, which, however, Government would repay if killed. I am not ambitious, but what easy-earned C.B.'s and Majorities there are in some cases ; while men who have earned them, like poor Oldfield, get nothing. I am sorry for him. He was always squabbling about his batteries with us, but he got more done by his perseverance than any man before did. I am obliged to conclude, but can tell you that this opening fire is only to reduce the fire from the place, so that they may not annoy us by shell or shot for a few days."

"*August* 24*th.*—Our fire has ceased again after four days, and now we are still in uncertainty as to what is to be done. I think the French will go in at the Malakoff Tower in a fortnight, they have been working up pretty close during our firing. The Redan looks very sickly as we fire platoons of musketry to prevent the Russians repairing it, and give them shells all night. The Russians repay us by baskets of shells, perhaps twelve at a time, $5\frac{1}{2}''$ each, fired from a big mortar; it requires to be lively to get out of their way. What a consolation it will be to get the place. I have now been thirty-four times twenty-four hours in the trenches, more than a month straight on end; it gets tedious after a time, but if anything is going on one does not mind. The Russian prisoners taken the other day seem to say that they are obliged to attack us as they have no provisions, and also say that their army is desperate. From what I can hear, I imagine that if (as I do not think likely) we fail this next assault, we shall make some great effort elsewhere."

"*August* 31*st.*—The Russians still keep us on the *qui vive*, but they have not much chance, as we are quite awake to their endeavours, and have entrenched ourselves well on every side. How I should like a week in September partridge-shooting! it is very tedious here, with nothing going on. The French still continue to sap into the Malakoff. I expect the Russians have had almost enough of it, as their work must be very hard. I send a sketch of the Mamelon; it will be a well-known place in after years. Captain Du Cane [1] has gone sick to Corfu, and Captain Wolseley [2] (90th Regiment), an assistant Engineer, has been slightly wounded with a stone."

"*September* 7*th.*—I hope by the time this reaches you, you will have received the news of our having taken the south side of Sebastopol. We attempt it to-morrow, and I think with better chance of success than last time. We opened fire on the 5th, and have continued it ever since. I have nothing more to tell until next mail, when I do hope to give you good news."

The day after this letter was written the Malakoff was taken

[1] Now Sir E. Du Cane, K.C.B.
[2] Now Lord Wolseley, who, although a captain in the army, served under lieutenants of Engineers in the trenches, and did excellent service, being twice wounded, and yet no promotion.

by the French, at noon, when the Tricolor was hoisted on the
tower as a signal for us to attack the Redan. Our men went
forward in high spirits, and with comparatively small loss
succeeded in planting their ladders in the ditch and entering the
Redan, which they held for half-an-hour, but were then driven
out with terrible loss by an enormous Russian reserve. At the
same time the French were repulsed in their assault on the
Central Bastion, when they lost four general officers. Thus,
the immediate result of the day's work was the taking of the
Malakoff only. In the evening it was decided that the Redan
should be stormed next morning by the Highlanders. This
operation, however, was not undertaken, for the Russians
evacuated Sebastopol before it could be carried into effect.

Gordon had been, as usual, detailed for the trenches on the
morning of the 9th, and his account of what he saw at daybreak
is best given in his own words. He says : "During the night of
the 8th I heard terrific explosions, and on going down to the
trenches at four the next morning I saw a splendid sight. The
whole of Sebastopol was in flames, and every now and then
terrible explosions took place, while the rising sun shining on
the place had a most beautiful effect. The Russians were leaving
the town by the bridge ; all the three-deckers were sunk, the
steamers alone remaining. Tons and tons of powder must have
been blown up. About 8 o'clock I got an order to commence
a plan of the works, for which purpose I went to the Redan,
where a dreadful sight was presented. The dead were buried in
the ditch—the Russians with the English—Mr. Wright reading
the Burial Service over them." The fires in the town continued
until the following day, so that it was not safe for the English troops
to attempt to effect an entry until the evening of the 10th.

Shortly after the surrender of Sebastopol, Gordon joined the
force that laid siege to Kinburn, and was present at the capture
of that fortress. He then returned to the Crimea, and from that
time until February 1856, a period of four months, was engaged,
almost without interruption, in destroying the dockyard, forts,
quays, barracks, and storehouses of the fallen stronghold. With
this work of demolition — a work as uninteresting as it was
arduous—his duties in the Crimea came to an end.

What I have written has been taken chiefly from private
letters sent by Gordon to his friends and relatives. From such
documents it is quite impossible to learn how he stood in the
estimation of others, or what were his real deserts as regards

the performance of his duties in the trenches and elsewhere. But, fortunately, there is other testimony at hand, and in quoting that of one officer, I am quoting the substance of that of many others. Colonel C. C. Chesney, in writing on Gordon's after-career in China, says:

"Gordon had first seen war in the hard school of the 'black winter' of the Crimea. In his humble position as an Engineer subaltern he attracted the notice of his superiors, not merely by his energy and activity, but by a special aptitude for war, developing itself amid the trench work before Sebastopol in a personal knowledge of the enemy's movements *such as no other officer attained.* We used to send him to find out what new move the Russians were making."

General Jones especially mentioned him as an officer who had done gallant service, but who, from the constitution of the corps, wherein promotion goes by seniority, could not be promoted. Add to this that he was decorated with the Legion of Honour—a special mark of distinction not often conferred upon so young an officer—and the proof of his valour and conduct are complete. It will be seen that, young as he was, he had made his mark, and had begun to do the best that was in him.

In May 1856, Gordon was appointed Assistant Commissioner, and ordered to join Major Stanton[1] in Bessarabia, to help in the work of laying down the new frontiers of Russia, Turkey, and Roumania. To go about in the summer days and nights, with Eastern cities to visit and a new and delightful country to explore, was no unpleasant change for two young fellows, war-worn and weary with a year's service in the Crimea, and with month after month of bitter work in the trenches. Gordon enjoyed himself greatly, and was keenly interested in all he saw. There was great variety in the life he led, and with his inquiring mind and sunny temper he was not the man to let time hang heavily on his hands; yet, when the survey came to an end, he was sorry to find himself ordered to undertake similar duties in another country. Indeed, in April 1857, when he received instructions to join Colonel Simmons[2] for delimitating the boundary in Asia, he sent a telegram home asking whether it were possible for him to exchange. But his value was already known, and the answer said: "Lieutenant Gordon must go."

[1] Now Lieutenant-General Sir E. Stanton.
[2] Now General Sir Lintorne Simmons, G.C.B.

After six months spent in Armenia, he went back to Constantinople to be present at a Conference of the Commission. Here he remained longer than he expected, to nurse his chief, who had fallen ill.   This done, he was not sorry to return to England after his three years' absence.   Another six months in England, and he was once more sent to Armenia as Commissioner. Here he remained from the spring of 1858 until nearly the end of the year, employed in verifying the frontier he had taken so active a part in laying down, and in examining the new road between the Russian and Turkish dominions.

During the next year he was engaged at Chatham as Field-work Instructor and Adjutant.

CHAPTER III

In the middle of July 1860, he left home for China, travelling by Paris and Marseilles, and visiting in turn Malta, Alexandria, Aden, Ceylon, Singapore, and Hong-Kong. On his arrival at the last-named place, the mail from the north came in, bringing the news of the capture of the Taku Forts. As, however, no counter-orders arrived relative to the stopping of officers going north, he was ordered a passage, and left on the 11th of September for Shanghai, whence, after one day's stay, he continued his journey for Tientsin, having travelled in all sixty-eight days. He had not been there long before he learned that his colleague, De Norman, with Mr. Parkes, Mr. Loch, Captains Anderson and Brabazon, Mr. Bowlby, and fourteen others, had been taken prisoners by San-ko-lin-sin. In consequence of this outrage, the Allies marched on Peking in October, and the city was invested. Gordon took part in the operations, and was present at the sacking and the burning of the Summer Palace on October the 12th.

The following is an account he gives of the part he took in that famous affair:

"On the 11th October we were sent down in a great hurry to throw up works and batteries against the town, as the Chinese refused to give up the gate we required them to surrender before we would treat with them. They were also required to give up all the prisoners. You will be sorry to hear that the treatment they have suffered has been very bad. Poor De Norman, who was with me in Asia, is one of the victims. It appears that they were tied so tight by the wrists that the flesh mortified, and they died in the greatest torture. Up to the time that elapsed before they arrived at the Summer Palace they were well treated,

but then the ill-treatment began.   The Emperor is supposed to
have been there at the time.

"To go back to the work—the Chinese were given until
twelve on the 13th to give up the gate.   We made a lot of
batteries, and everything was ready for the assault of the wall,
which is battlemented, and forty feet high, but of inferior
masonry.   At 11.30 P.M., however, the gate was opened, and we
took possession; so our work was of no avail.   The Chinese had
then until the 23rd to think over our terms of treaty, and to pay
up £10,000 for each Englishman and £500 for each native
soldier who died during their captivity.   This they did, and the
money was paid and the treaty signed yesterday.   I could not
witness it, as all officers commanding companies were obliged to
remain in camp.   Owing to the ill-treatment the prisoners experienced at the Summer Palace, the General ordered it to be
destroyed, and stuck up proclamations to say why it was ordered.
We accordingly went out, and, after pillaging it, burned the
whole place, destroying in a Vandal-like manner most valuable
property, which could not be replaced for four millions.   We got
upwards of £48 a-piece prize-money before we went out here;
and although I have not as much as many, I have done well.
Imagine D—— giving 16s. for a string of pearls which he sold
the next day for £500. . . . The people are civil, but I think
the grandees hate us, as they must after what we did to the
Palace.   You can scarcely imagine the beauty and magnificence
of the places we burnt.   It made one's heart sore to burn them;
in fact, these palaces were so large, and we were so pressed for
time, that we could not plunder them carefully.   Quantities of gold
ornaments were burned, considered as brass.   It was wretchedly
demoralising work for an army.   Everybody was wild for plunder.

"You would scarcely conceive the magnificence of this
residence, or the tremendous devastation the French have committed.   The throne and room were lined with ebony, carved in
a marvellous way.   There were huge mirrors of all shapes and
kinds, clocks, watches, musical boxes with puppets on them,
magnificent china of every description, heaps and heaps of silks
of all colours, embroidery, and as much splendour and civilisation
as you would see at Windsor; carved ivory screens, coral screens,
large amounts of treasure, etc.   The French have smashed everything in the most wanton way.

"It was a scene of utter destruction which passes my
description."

On November the 8th, the two armies left for Tientsin, there to take up their winter quarters; and Gordon, with his regiment, went as Commanding Royal Engineer. His stay there was prolonged, however, over a much longer period than he had expected; for, with the exception of a few excursions, he remained there till the spring of 1862. During this time he was engaged in providing for the wants of his troops, in surveying the neighbouring country in parts where no European had ever been seen, and in occasional rides to the Taku Forts and back, a distance of 140 miles; indeed, his longest absence from Tientsin did not exceed two months, and this was on the occasion of an expedition he made on horseback to the Outer Wall with his comrade, Lieutenant Cardew—a tour full of adventure, and for which they gained great credit, having visited, in the course of their journeys, regions before unknown to Europeans.

Beyond this excursion, his many rides and surveying expeditions, there is little to record of his doings at Tientsin. An account he gives, however, of a terrific dust-storm in which he was caught on April 5th, 1862, is not without interest:—

"We had a tremendous dust-storm on the 26th at 3 P.M. The sky was as dark as night; huge columns of dust came sweeping down, and it blew a regular hurricane, the blue sky appearing now and then through the breaks. The quantity of dust was indescribable. A canal about 50 miles long, and 18 feet wide and 7 feet deep, was completely filled up; and boats which had been floating merrily down to Tientsin found themselves at the end of the storm on a bank of sand, the canal having been filled up, and the waters absorbed. They will have to be carried to the Peiho, and have already commenced to move. The canal was everywhere passable, and will have to be re-excavated. The boat-owners looked very much disgusted at their predicament, which was not pleasant. The storm lasted sixteen hours, and the vibrations of the aneroid barometer were very extraordinary. I, of course, was caught in it coming from Taku, and, after vainly attempting to get on, was obliged to stop at a village. The darkness was such that it enforced candles being lighted at 3 P.M., and it came on very suddenly. I left my house for a few yards, and could not find it again for ten minutes. . . . Of course I came in for it, because I am peculiarly lucky in this way in my rides from Taku. Numbers of junks were lost, and forty-five Chinamen drowned, at Taku. Two officers of the 31st Regiment were *en route* for Taku by boat, and one of them started to get a coat when the storm began. He lost his way, fell into every ditch he could find in the neighbourhood (and there are not a few), and had to sleep in a grave all night. He was brought in quite wild and blind the next morning. The thermometer fell to 25° from 60° during the night, so we did- not have a comfortable time of it."

In May 1862, the Tai-ping rebels becoming troublesome in the neighbourhood of Shanghai, it was considered necessary to undertake some operations against them. Seven hundred of the 31st Regiment and two hundred of the 67th Regiment were consequently ordered up to that port, and Gordon, having despatched them from the Taku Forts, himself followed in a few days. He was at once appointed to the command of the district, and was given the charge of the Engineers' part in an expedition against the rebels. He led his men to Singpoo, stormed and entered it, taking a number of rebels prisoners; and thence he moved to other parts in the possession of the Tai-pings, and drove them from their strongholds. The towns were stored with rice stolen from the neighbouring peasants, and their misery was intense. For some months no further steps were taken to keep off the rebels, and Gordon returned to Shanghai to resume his official duties there. In October, however, he started for Kahding, on a more difficult enterprise than his previous ones, for in order to reach it broken bridges had to be repaired. Five thousand rebels had taken refuge in the town, and on the first night of attack they made some resistance; but the walls being escaladed by the English troops, the Tai-pings made their escape to Taitsan, an important stronghold on the road to Soochow. This was the last of the attacks made on these marauders, with the view to clearing a radius of thirty miles round Shanghai for the protection of its citizens. The step was indeed necessary, for, when least expected, these robbers made raids on the outlying suburbs, forcing the peasants to take refuge in the city.

"We had a visit from the marauding Tai-pings the other day," Gordon says. "They came close down in small parties to the settlement and burnt several houses, driving in thousands of inhabitants. We went against them and drove them away, but did not kill many. They beat us into fits in getting over the country, which is intersected in every way with ditches, swamps, etc. . . . You can scarcely conceive the crowds of peasants who come into Shanghai when the rebels are in the neighbourhood—upwards of 15,000, I should think, and of every size and age—many strapping fellows who could easily defend themselves come running in with old women and children.

"The people on the confines are suffering very greatly, and are in fact dying of starvation. It is most sad, this state of affairs, and our Government really ought to put the Rebellion down. Words could not depict the horrors these people suffer from the rebels, or describe the utter desert they have made of this rich province."

During the next few months he was engaged on a survey of the thirty miles radius round Shanghai, a task fraught with the greatest difficulty and danger, owing to the disturbed state of the country; but its prosecution, as will be afterwards seen, turned out to be of infinite value to Gordon a little later.

"I have been now in every town and village in the thirty miles radius," he says, on the completion of the work. "The country is the same everywhere—a dead flat, with innumerable creeks and bad pathways. The people have now settled down quiet again, and I do not anticipate the rebels will ever come back; they are rapidly on the decline, and two years ought to bring about the utter suppression of the revolt. I do not write what we saw, as it amounts to nothing. There is nothing of any interest in China; if you have seen one village, you have seen the whole country. I have really an immensity to do. It will be a good thing if the Government support the propositions which are made to the Chinese.

"The weather here is delightful: a fine, cold, clear air, which is quite invigorating after the summer heats. There is very good pheasant-shooting in the half-populated districts, and some quail at uncertain times. It is extraordinary to see the quantities of fishing-cormorants there are in the creeks. These cormorants are in flocks of forty and fifty, and the owner, in a small canoe, travels about with them; they fish three or four times a day, and are encouraged by the shouts of their owners to dive. I have scarcely ever seen them come up without a fish in their beaks, which they swallow; but not for any distance, for there is a ring to prevent it going down altogether. They get such dreadful attacks of mumps, their throats being distended by the fish, which are alive, when the birds seem as if they were pouter pigeons; they are hoisted into the boats, and there are very sea-sick. Would you consider the fish a dainty?"

We now approach the most romantic incidents of Gordon's career—the incidents which won him the name of Chinese Gordon. But before following the young Commander in his desperate onslaught upon the Tai-ping rebels, it will be necessary for me to state, in a few words, the causes which led to the then disturbed state of China, and to sketch the attempts of others before him to grapple with the now vast power that threatened dominion over the whole empire.

The Tai-ping Rebellion was the outcome of an egoism such as the world has rarely seen—the egoism of one man who, assisted by the accidents of general discontent, gathered to him millions of adherents, and, deluding them into the belief that they were the soldiers of a Divine cause, spread ruin, fire, and famine over the length and breadth of the Flowery Land.

At a time when the province of Kwang-tung was infested by pirates, bandits, and secret societies; when discontent was rife, and, in the Opium War of 1842, the discontented had learned the use of arms, a village schoolmaster named Hung-tsue-schuen declared himself to be inspired—inspired to the usurpation of the Dragon throne. Some thought him mad; but as his clansmen numbered 20,000, and the means he employed to convert them were masterly to a degree, he soon collected about him a band of followers not unlike an army. He was a seer of visions, a prophet of vengeance and freedom, an agent of the Divine wrath, a champion of the poor and the oppressed. To the persecuted Hakkas[1] he gave out that his mission was the extermination of the hated Manchu race and the glorious reinstatement of the Mings. He had seen God, and the Almighty had Himself appealed to him as the Second Celestial Brother. So he said, and so his lieges were mad enough to believe. What he really had seen was a missionary in flowing robes, who gave him a bundle of tracts, and told him that he should attain to the highest rank in China. Thus it is not the least curious point in this man's history that his ideas originated in certain tracts which were given him by a European missionary—that, in fact, the Tai-ping Rebellion, of which Hung was the leader, was in some sort the outcome of an attempt to spread the Gospel among the Chinese.

[1] The Hakka, or "Stranger."

The Mandarins were more insolent than ever to the oppressed race of Hung, and the future rebel king was incensed at not passing certain examinations which would give him a worthy place among the *literati*. With his little army of converts he traversed his province on a proselytising tour, breaking the idols and effacing the Confucian texts from the walls of schools and temples. The doctrine of extermination, thus early practised by the Tai-pings, soon brought them into collision with the mandarins, and many disturbances arose, in which sometimes the authorities, and sometimes the Tai-pings, gained the day. Hung's tactics the while were worthy so great and able a trickster. Once, for example, finding himself and his followers hard pressed, and obliged to shift their ground for want of provisions, he left his quarters secretly, while a squadron of boys and women went on drumming within the walls. His enemy believed him still on the ground, when he and his men were miles away.

Defeat and victory alike drew new recruits to his following; and in 1851, having got together an army some hundreds of thousands strong, he proclaimed himself the Heavenly King, the Emperor of the Great Peace. Then, with five Wangs, or warrior kings, chosen from among his kinsmen, he marched through China, devastating the country and augmenting his legions as he went. He brought over not only the piratical bands which infested the seaboard of Kwang-tung, but even such ancient and powerful secret societies as the Triad; while two desperate women brought 4000 warriors, all of whom bowed to his authority, and adopted his creed. Their tawdry dress, their many-coloured banners and flags, their long, lank hair, lent to these predatory hordes a fierce barbaric air, so that, as they passed from city to city and from province to province, armed with cutlasses and knives, the quiet, docile, clean-shorn Chinese were terror-stricken at the sight of these monsters—at these land-pirates, who robbed them of their rice-harvests and the products of their farms. A march of nearly 700 miles brought his huge army to Nanking, which fell, and became the capital of the Heavenly King.

Here, under the shadow of the Porcelain Tower, he established himself in royal state. He gave to his kinsmen who had most distinguished themselves in the campaign against the reigning dynasty, the titles of Wangs, or kings. There were the Chung Wang, or Faithful King; the Eastern King and the Western King; the Warrior King and the Attendant King. Many had gained for themselves nicknames in addition to their high-sounding titles; the soubriquets of the Yellow Tiger, the One-Eyed Dog, and Cock Eye, were famous among their ranks. Both titles and names alike had been won in battle, and were often the records of deeds of valour. These kingships at last became so numerous that they numbered several hundreds, and Tien Wang, the Emperor of the Great Peace, found himself constrained to cease conferring them on his great adherents. One of the amusements of the chief, who soon developed a tyranny almost without parallel, was to kick his many wives and concubines to death. The wonder is that the Wangs, who were all desperate leaders of armies, continued their allegiance to one who never hesitated to behead them for even a trivial offence. But so it was. They believed him to be the Junior Lord, come down to earth to save the suffering Mings. One of the Wangs, more ambitious than his comrades, did venture on an occasion to assert himself—to call himself the Holy Ghost—and for this he was sent straightway to his grave. It is almost inconceivable that in this latter half of the nineteenth century such an organised imposture as this of Hung-tsue-schuen's could exist. It must not be forgotten, however, that his pseudo-religious tenets appealed to a people saturated with superstition, and that the methods he employed to impress himself upon them were of a kind singularly suited to their moods. It is not easy to give an idea of this huge harlequinade of worship and war, of which much will be said hereafter in these pages. Meanwhile, it may be well to read the impressions of a missionary—Mr. J. L. Holmes—who visited Nanking, and saw how these warlike devotees of the so-called Great Peace comported themselves in their palaces and the palace of their Emperor :—

" At night," says this authority, " we witnessed their worship. It occurred at the beginning of their Sabbath, midnight of Friday. The place of worship was the Chung Wang's private audience-room. He was himself seated in the midst of his attendants—no females were present. They first sang, or rather chanted ; after which a written prayer was read and burned by an officer, upon which they rose and sang again, and then separated. The Chung Wang sent for me again before he left his seat, and asked me if I understood their mode of worship. I replied that I had just seen it for the first time. He asked what our mode was. I replied that we endeavoured to follow the rules laid down in the Scriptures, and thought all departure therefrom to be erroneous. He then proceeded to explain the ground upon which they departed from this rule. The Tien Wang had been to heaven, he said, and had seen the Heavenly Father. Our revelation had been handed down for 1800 years. They had received a new, additional revelation; and upon this they could adopt a different mode of worship. I replied that if the Tien Wang had obtained a revelation, we could determine its genuineness by comparing it with the Scriptures. If they coincided, they might be parts of the same; if not, the new revelation could not be true, as God did not change. He suggested that there might be a sort of *disparagement*, which was yet appropriate, as in the Chinese garment, which is buttoned at one side. To this comparison I objected, as comparing a piece of man's work with God's work. Ours were little and imperfect; His great and glorious. We should compare God's works with each other. The sun did not rise in the east to-day, and in the west to-morrow. Winter and summer did not exchange their respective characters. Neither would the Heavenly Father capriciously make a law at one time and contradict it at another. His Majesty seemed rather disconcerted at thus being carried out of the usual track in which he was in the habit of discoursing, and we parted, proposing to talk further upon the subject at another time.

"At daylight we started for the Tien Wang's palace. The procession was headed by a number of brilliantly coloured banners, after which followed a troop of armed soldiers; then came the Chung Wang in a large sedan, covered with yellow satin and embroidery, and borne by eight coolies; next came the foreigner on horseback, in company with the Chung Wang's chief officer, followed by a number of other officers on horseback. On our way several of the other kings who were in the city fell in ahead of us with similar retinues. Music added discord to the scene, and curious gazers lined the streets on either side, who had no doubt seen kings before, but probably never witnessed such an apparition as that. . . . Reaching at length the palace of the Tien Wang, a large building resembling very much the best of the Confucian temples, though of much greater size than these generally are, we entered the outer gate, and proceeded to a large building to the eastward of the palace proper, and called the "Morning Palace." Here we were presented to the Tsau Wang and his son, with several others. After resting a little while, during which two of the attendants testified their familiarity with, and consequent irreverence for, the royal place by concluding a misunderstanding in fisticuffs, we proceeded to the audience-hall of the Tien Wang. I was here presented to the Tien Wang's two brothers, two nephews, and son-in-law, in addition to those whom I had before met at the "Morning Palace." They were seated at the entrance of a deep recess, over the entrance of which was written, "Illustrious Heavenly Door." At the end of this recess, far within, was pointed out to us His Majesty Tien Wang's seat, which was as yet vacant. The company awaited for some time the arrival of the Western King, whose presence seemed to be necessary before they could proceed with the ceremonies. That dignitary, a boy of twelve or fourteen, directly made his appearance, and, entering at the "Holy Heavenly Gate," took his place with the royal group. They then proceeded with their ceremonies as follows : First they kneeled with their faces to the Tien Wang's seat, and uttered a prayer to the Heavenly Brother ; then, kneeling with their faces in the opposite direction, they prayed to the Heavenly Father; after which they again kneeled with their faces to the Tien Wang's seat, and in like manner repeated a prayer to him. They then concluded by singing in a standing position. A roast pig and the body of a goat were lying with other articles on tables in the outer court, and a fire was kept burning on a stone altar in front of the Tien Wang's seat, in a sort of court which intervened between it and the termination of the recess leading to it. He had not yet appeared, and, though all waited for him for some time after the conclusion of the ceremonies, he did not appear at all. He had probably changed his mind, concluding that it would be a bad precedent to allow a foreigner to see him without first signifying submission to him ; or it may be that he did not mean to see me after learning the stubborn nature of our principles ; but, anxious to have us carry away some account of the grandeur and magnificence of his court, had taken this mode of making an appropriate impression, leaving the imagination to supply the vacant chair which his own ample dimensions should have filled. We retired to the "Morning Palace" again, where kings, princes, foreigner, and all were called upon to ply the "nimble lads" upon a breakfast which had been prepared for us, after which we retired in the order in which we came.

"In the course of the afternoon, after our return, the Chung Wang invited me in to see him privately. I was led through a number of rooms and intervening courts into one of his private sitting-rooms, where he sat clothed loosely in white silk, with a red kerchief round his head and a jewel in front. He was seated in an easy-chair, and fanned by a pretty slipshod girl. Another similar chair was placed near him, on which he invited me to be seated, and at once began to question me about foreign machinery, etc. He had been puzzled with a map with parallel lines running each way, said to have been made by foreigners, which he asked me to explain. He then submitted to my inspection a spy-glass and a music-box, asking various questions about each, evidently supposing every foreigner to be an adept in the construction of such articles. After this he became quite familiar, and was ready to see me at any hour. At the next interview, which occurred on the day following, I referred him to various passages in the New Testament which conflicted with the doctrines of Tien Wang. I found it impossible to gain his attention to these matters. He was ready enough to declaim in set speech about all men being brethren, but it was easy to perceive that his religion, such as it was, had little hold upon his heart. He confessed carelessly that the revelation of Tien Wang did not agree with the Bible, but said that of Tien Wang, being later, was more authoritative. I found him but little disposed to have his faith tested, either by reason or revelation, or indeed to think about it at all when it was abstracted from public affairs.

"The two days which yet elapsed before our departure were spent mostly in conversation with various persons connected with the establishment of the Chung Wang and other kings. These conversations, informal and desultory, gave me an opportunity to ascertain something of the practical working of Hung-tsue-schuen's principles upon the masses of his adherents. I could not perceive that there was any elevation of character or sentiment to distinguish them from the great mass of the Chinese population; indeed, the effect of his pretensions to a commission to "slay the imps" appears to have annihilated in their minds all consciousness of crimes committed against those who are not of their own faith. To rob and murder an adherent of the Manchu dynasty is a virtuous deed. To carry away his wife or daughter for infamous purposes, or his son to train up for the army, are all legitimate acts. We questioned some of the boys who were sent to wait upon us as to their nativity; some were from Ngang-hu-ai, some from Hupeh, some from Honan, and others from Kiang - si. Wherever their armies had overrun the country, they had captured the boys and led them away with them. The large proportion of comely-looking women to be seen looking out at the doors and windows showed the summary way in which these celestial soldiers provided themselves with wives."

Up to the year 1860 this monstrous civil war was waged solely between the followers of the Heavenly King and the Imperial Government. There had been rumours of foreign aid being given to the one and to the other; but there was an odd prejudice in favour of Hung on account of the mad impossible Christianity of his pretensions and ambitions; a feeling prevailed that the Tai-pings might after all be in the right; and, owing to our hostile relations with the Chinese Government, our representatives refused to take arms against the rebels, though our aid was invited on the very eve of a battle between the allied forces of England and France and the army of San-ko-lin-sin. The tactics of the Imperialist leaders had all along been to drive the rebels towards the sea. The consequence was that Shanghai and other consular ports were menaced by the insurgents, and had become, as well, the refuge of distracted and destitute peasants, whose villages were burned and whose lands were laid waste by the ruthless Tai-pings. These tactics on the part of the Imperial authorities were the worst possible, for the rebels had everything to gain from being driven towards the wealthy cities along the coast, which contained sufficient war material to supply all their armies. Before long the Chinese Government were awakened to their folly; but they nevertheless clung to their policy, for they counted on the frightened foreign community to protect the ports, if only to save themselves and their property. Seeing, at a critical juncture, that nothing was being done, two great Chinese officials applied to the Allies for certain help. The English and French Ambassadors considered the request; and it was decided that, without taking any part in the civil contest or expressing any opinion on the rights of the contending parties, we might protect Shanghai from attack and assist the authorities in preserving tranquillity within its walls, on the ground that it was an open port, and that there was a complete community of interest between the town and the foreign settlement. In the meantime, as was expected, the wealthy traders of Shanghai had taken the alarm, and the more influential among them had subscribed for a foreign force to keep the enemy at bay. Two American ci-devant filibusters named Ward and Burgevine were commissioned to raise a contingent. A reward was offered to them for the capture of a place called Sung-kiang—some twenty miles from the city—held by the rebels. About a hundred seamen were got together, and Ward, who had been a sailor and had served under Walker in Nicaragua, led them to the attack and was repulsed with considerable loss. He, however, made another attempt, and, with the help of an Imperialist force, succeeded in taking the city. Then, encouraged by the reward he had won, and with his force augmented by a bevy of rowdies, he proceeded to make further raids on the rebels. But the Faithful King, one of the Tai-ping leaders, hearing of his people's defeat, led a new army against Ward and his "foreign devils," as they were termed, and drove them back into Sung-kiang; to keep Ward in durance and in check he left a part of his force before the city, and with the rest of his troops marched on Shanghai, ravaging the intervening country as he went.

But at this time the war was not to be entirely between the Imperialists and the rebels ; for, when the Faithful King advanced upon Shanghai, the allied French and British troops that were in the city joined the Imperialists, and drove the rebels back with heavy loss. This was on the 18th of August 1860, and upon the following day the Faithful One renewed his attack, but was again repulsed, and had to retire to Soochow. From this place he was summoned to Nanking by the Heavenly King ; and from that city, in October 1860, four great armies were sent forth under four mighty Wangs, to drive the Imperialists from the cities immediately north and south of the Yangtze river, over a district extending from Nanking to Hankow, a distance of about 400 miles. No sooner, however, had these four armies been set in motion, than the British naval Commander-in-Chief, Admiral Sir James Hope, thought it necessary to visit those ports on the Yangtze which had been opened up to foreign trade by the Convention of Peking. In February 1861, therefore, the Admiral sailed up the river, and, anchoring at Nanking, entered into communication with the Heavenly King. The result of his negotiation was that an arrangement was agreed upon by which the Yangtze trade was not to be interfered with, nor was Shanghai to be in any way molested by the Armies of the Great Peace for the space of one year. The rebel leader kept his word, and during the whole of 1861 his followers were actively engaged in endeavouring to take Hankow, and to re-establish themselves in the Yangtze valley. They met with constant reverses ; and, after a year of defeats, were driven back into the neighbourhood of Shanghai. The Heavenly King then informed the British

Admiral that he intended to attack Shanghai as soon as the year's truce had expired. Sir James Hope warned him against any such proceeding; but the warning was disregarded, and the Faithful King was ordered to march on Shanghai in January of 1862. This led to the allied forces co-operating with Ward, who was then at Sung-kiang with a thousand drilled Chinese; and it is from this that British interference in the Tai-ping Rebellion may be said to date. From February to June the allied forces assisted Ward and the Imperialists; and in May, Captain Dew, R.N., was appointed to a naval command, and drove the Tai-pings from Ning-po. In September, Ward was killed, and Burgevine succeeded him in the command of the Ever-Victorious Army; but in January 1863 the new commander was cashiered for corrupt practices, and the British Government was formally applied to, and requested to provide the army with a captain in his stead.

CHAPTER IV

THE Governor-General of the Kiang provinces was Li-Futai, better known as Li-Hung-Chang—the Chinese Bismarck, as he has since been called—the most famous soldier and statesman of modern China. He had been sent by Tseng Kwo-fan,[1] General- issimo of the Imperialists, to Shanghai, to take the command there, and to crown his ten years' service against the rebels by saving that port from them, and so in some sort reversing the foolish policy which, as I have shown, was insisted upon at Peking. On his arrival, he was told by General Staveley that, though the French and English would continue to guard the frontier up to a radius of thirty miles round Shanghai, the actual treatment of the rebellion must be given over to the Chinese; so, like a skilful commander, he at once began to train the native troops to the use of foreign arms.

Neither he, however, nor any other Chinese, was competent to assume the command of Ward's adventurers. Burgevine, too, was wholly unsuited to the work which was now in his hands. On his arrival at Shanghai with a bodyguard of a hundred picked men, armed with rifles, he had entered the premises of a mandarin, who was the local treasurer of the Government, and demanded money for arrears of pay. This demand not being immediately complied with, Burgevine struck the treasurer with his fist, led his men into the treasury, and ordered them to carry off 40,000 dollars. For this insult, the authorities, under the seal of Li-Hung-Chang, degraded him, as I have said, and dismissed him their service.

This outrage and its consequences led to a vacancy in the command of the Ever-Victorious Army, and Li-Hung-Chang—

---

[1] The famous Tseng Kwo-fan was the father of the even more famous Marquess Tseng.

always in sympathy with foreigners—at once evinced his capacity as a statesman and his understanding of the true position of affairs, by soliciting General Staveley to appoint a British officer to the post. With a kindly feeling towards the Chinese, Staveley entertained the request conditionally. It was necessary first to refer the matter to the Horse Guards ; meantime he had not far to look for the right man. His choice fell on Gordon, one who had never commanded ; but who above all other men had impressed those who knew him with a sense of his great abilities. The reputation he had won before Sebastopol, and which had accompanied him into Bessarabia and Armenia, he had more than sustained before Peking and at Shanghai. Wherever he had been he had improved his opportunities and made the most of his talents. Even now, when the tempting offer of this command was made him, such was his desire to be thoroughly competent for its duties, that instead of rushing upon the task, and trusting wholly to fortune, as so many had done before him, he modestly asked that his appointment might be deferred until he had finished the military survey of the thirty miles round Shanghai which he had in hand, on the ground that it would be of the utmost service to him on the campaign. This was conceded him, and Captain Holland, of the Marine Light Infantry, by the advice of Sir James Hope, Admiral of the naval forces in China, took temporary command.

Holland believed in himself, and with a mixed force of men, 2500 of all arms, two pieces of ordnance, and an Imperial brigade about 5000 strong, he at once laid siege to the walled city of Taitsan. For information as to its defences he depended solely on the mandarins. They had assured him that the city was surrounded by a dry ditch—which proved to be a deep moat thirty yards wide—and no means of crossing it were at hand. He contrived to breach the walls. But the bamboo ladder, over which the storming party managed to cross the moat, broke down ; a repulse ensued, under a galling fire from the walls ; 300 men and 4 foreign officers were killed and wounded, and the two 32-pounders, which had been placed "in the open" without cover, got imbedded in the mud, and had to be abandoned.

This defeat — the greatest triumph the Tai-pings had yet attained — showed that the Ever-Victorious Army, as it was obligingly called, still wanted a leader. At this juncture Gordon left his survey unfinished, and took command of it at Sungkiang on the 25th of March. From this time it lacked a leader no longer—a leader, too, who could perpetuate and justify its name.

"I am afraid you will be much vexed at my having taken the command of the Sung-kiang force, and that I am now a Mandarin," he says, writing home on the 24th March 1863. "I have taken the step on consideration. I think that anyone who contributes to putting down this Rebellion fulfils a humane task, and I also think tends a great deal to open China to civilisation. I will not act rashly, and I trust to be able soon to return to England; at the same time I will remember your and my father's wishes, and endeavour to remain as short a time as possible. I can say that if I had not accepted the command I believe the force would have been broken up and the Rebellion gone on in its misery for years. I trust this will not now be the case, and that I may soon be able to comfort you on this subject. You must not fret on this matter; I think I am doing a good service. . . . . I keep your likeness before me, and can assure you and my father that I will not be rash, and that as soon as I can conveniently, and with due regard to the object I have in view, I will return home."

There was a great deal of eagerness to avenge the defeat at Taitsan. But it is clear, judging from what followed, that Gordon, with his concentrated experience of war, listened to no one : he looked only to the grand result, and exercised his military genius in determining at once on the best and surest means of striking the Rebellion at its very heart, and restoring as speedily as possible the provinces to the Imperial power. He had learned enough from the past history of the war to see that the petty operations of defence and skirmish against the Tai-pings—such as clearing Shanghai from their raids over a circle of thirty miles' radius, and attacking strongholds like Taitsan, with doubtful and often disastrous results—were merely calculated to prolong the Rebellion. He could see, too—what was even more to the purpose—that by rapidly changing his ground, and striking sudden blows at points where he was least expected, he would not only hearten and inspire his followers, but constrain the rebels in all their holds to adopt an attitude of defence, and leave them neither time nor courage to molest Shanghai, or threaten Imperial ports.

His mind once made up, it was not many days ere he was

steaming into the Yangtze estuary towards Fushan, which lies on its southern bank. He carried with him some 200 of his artillery, also as many of his infantry—about 1000 in all—as the two steamers he had at his command would transport. An Imperialist force was entrenched not far from Fushan; and under cover of this he landed unopposed, though a large body of Tai-pings watched his movements in the open field. On the 3rd of April he reached Fushan with all his force, and went at once to its attack.

The little place had a history. It had long been a haunt of pirates; but it had submitted to the rebel arms, had freed itself, and had been recaptured and garrisoned with Tai-pings. It was important as commanding the river as far as Chanzu, a loyal city ten miles inland, hard pressed by a Tai-ping force.

The motive of Gordon's advance on Chanzu is clear. Its object was twofold: to carry the war into the enemy's own country, and to relieve a suffering garrison in danger of falling a second time into the merciless hands of the rebel king. Gordon lost no time in planting his guns among the deserted ruins, which afforded excellent cover during the bombardment. He opened fire from his 32-pounder and from four 12-pounder howitzers, on a strong stockade built by the rebels on the left bank of the creek towards Chanzu. The fire of another 12-pounder howitzer was directed at the same time against a second stockade on the opposite bank. The creek was bridged with boats; and, after three hours' bombardment, a storming-party, under Captain Belcher, advanced to the assault, and carried the position. The rebels, receiving large reinforcements from the direction of Chanzu, then showed so threatening a front that Gordon drew into his stockade for the night. Next morning, however, the enemy was abandoning his positions and retreating towards Soochow, a great rebel centre on the Grand Canal, lying inland about thirty miles to the south-west.

This vigorous action, the work of a single day, enabled Gordon with equal celerity to relieve Chanzu itself. As far as that place, the country was now open along both sides of the creek, and Gordon's force, together with a large body of Mandarin troops, made their way unmolested up to its gates. Its crowded population, swelled by multitudes of refugees from the surrounding villages, were rejoiced at their relief. The Mandarins received Gordon and his officers in state. "I saw the young rebel chiefs who had come over," he says; "they are very intelligent, and splendidly dressed in silks, and with big pearls in their caps. The head man is about thirty-five years old; he looked worn to a thread with anxiety. He was so very glad to see me, and chin-chinned most violently, regretting his inability to give me a present, which I told him was not the custom with us people." The young General left 300 men to garrison a stockade, and returned inland by the river to his headquarters at Sung-kiang.

When Gordon took on himself the command of his little army, he found its discipline extremely bad. This he almost instantly improved; he had the great commander's capacity of making men both love and obey him. Nothing at this time could have gratified him more than the circumstance that on his appointment, several applications were made by British officers to General Brown (who had succeeded General Staveley) for leave to join Gordon's force, and enter the Chinese service under him. These would have been no doubt more numerous but for the terms of the Order in Council placing such officers on half-pay. A certain number of permits were given, subject to Gordon's approval. One of the officers who thus joined the force, and the only one who served from first to last, was Surgeon Moffitt, of the 67th Regiment, who proved himself to be of invaluable aid. So, surrounded by his brother - officers, who knew his high qualities, and greatly strengthened, Gordon was able to purge his staff of incompetent men. The general confidence had been fully justified and confirmed by his brilliant march on Fushan and Chanzu, an achievement which won him, by Imperial decree, the grade of Tsung - Ping, or Brigadier-General.

At Sung-kiang he went at once to work upon his army and his plans. He took forthwith a high place in the estimation both of his men and of Li-Hung-Chang. The latter, a Mandarin of the Yellow Button, he treated loyally, and without the aristocratic airs which had rendered his predecessors offensive to native authority. When Burgevine was intriguing at Peking to get reinstated in his command, Li had warmly advocated Gordon's appointment, and Burgevine's intrigues had thus been brought to an end. After being degraded and dismissed, that American adventurer had gone to the capital, and it was made to appear for the moment that Prince Kung himself was in his favour. This arose out of two very curious circumstances : one was that the American Minister warmly advocated Burgevine's cause, and gave a history of his past career, which, however, did not coincide with facts; the other, that our own Ambassador, Sir Frederick Bruce, was under the diplomatic feeling that it would be discourteous to refuse his support to the claims of a man about whom he knew nothing, save that he had impressed him favourably. Under these circumstances, Prince Kung had played a very pleasant part by appearing to listen to the ambassadors, at the same time stating that the final settlement of the matter rested with Li, the Governor of the Province, and that it should be formally referred to him. Burgevine's conduct, infamous in many ways, and crowned by his assault on the Treasury, had made, as Prince Kung well knew, his pardon impossible. Li would not consent to his reinstalment on any terms whatever, and in this way the filibuster's career was broken and ended.

After all this it will easily be understood that Li was anxious to forward Gordon's views on his return to headquarters. In truth, there was much to be done. The young Captain was determined upon re-organising his little army on the English model; and his first move in this direction was to establish regular pay on a liberal scale, and to abolish the abominable practice of rewards for captures. Under Burgevine and Ward, it had been customary to bargain with the troops for the perform-ance of special service : they on their side were to do the work, and when it was done they were to have as much as they could make by looting the fallen city. Gordon saw at once that it was impossible to maintain the morality of a body of men under circumstances such as these ; and by securing them a regular fee for their services, and absolutely breaking them off the habit of plunder, he made the work of re-organisation on which he had resolutely set his heart a mere matter of time.

His force was from 3000 to 4000 strong. It consisted of five or six infantry regiments, four siege-batteries, and two field-batteries. Its men were, for the most part, armed with smooth-bore muskets, while a chosen few were entrusted with Enfield rifles ; the uniforms consisted of dark serge, with green turbans. Its Colonels or Lieutenant-Colonels were to receive from £75 to £85 a month, while the pay of Majors, Captains, and Adjutants was in a diminishing ratio between these sums and the pay of its Lieutenants, which was fixed at £30 a month. The pay of its privates, who were all Chinese, was from £4, 10s. downwards, according to grade, certain rations being allowed while in the field. The pay of the Commander himself was high. "It is £260 per month, or £3120 per annum," says Gordon; "but that is a minor consideration."

It is to be remarked that the commissioned officers were all foreigners—Englishmen, Americans, Germans, Frenchmen, and Spaniards; and that, as a rule, they were brave, reckless, quick in adapting themselves to circumstances, steady in action, but greatly given to quarrelling among themselves.

Payment was made monthly by a Chinese official of high civil rank, named Kah, a good man of business and very popular. He was well educated, honest, and of pleasant manners, and he paid the force in the presence of the Commander. The monthly cost to the Government was from fourteen to twenty-six thousand pounds, and it is said that the men were never kept in arrears more than ten days. The army had a uniform which the men at first greatly objected to, as it exposed them to the satire of their countrymen, who called them "Imitation Foreign Devils." Gordon's purpose was to make the rebels imagine that they had foreign soldiers to fight. When the troops became victorious, their uniform was a source of pride to them; they would have strongly objected to change it for a native dress. Woo, the Tautai of Shanghai, was so full of the idea that the very footprints of the disciplined Chinese impressed the rebels with fear, that he purchased, for general distribution, some thousands of pairs of European boots, such as were worn by Gordon's troops, that their marks might be everywhere visible.

But Gordon did more than feed and pay and discipline his men. He provided himself with a heavy force of artillery, amply supplied with ammunition, and with every means of transport in the way of gun-carriages and boats. He had mantlets to protect his gunners; a pontoon equipment, bamboo ladders, planks for short tramways, and many other provisions for rapid movement in a country abounding in water. And he trained up his men in the drill of Her Majesty's army. He practised his artillery both in breaching fortifications and in covering storming-parties. He instituted a system of punishments for the native force, and one for the foreign officers, who were subject even to instant dismissal, but this only by the order of the Commander himself. With an army thus organised, and with a flotilla of steamers and Chinese gunboats, he was soon prepared again to take the field.

Nearly to the north of Shanghai, and of Gordon's headquarters at Sung-kiang, lies Taitsan, from which a road runs

south-westward through Quinsan and Soochow. These were then
three rebel centres, of which the last was the chief. It was the
natural capital of the country which was to be the seat of war.
Towards the district of which it was the chief place, Gordon,
before the end of April, proceeded with his force, but without
communicating to anyone which of the centres was the aim of his
first onset. It was presently seen that his object was to reduce
Quinsan, which was of the greatest strategical importance in
relation both to Soochow and Taitsan. The approaches to
Soochow on the eastern side met at the city; Taitsan was equally
dependent upon it; it was also the rebel arsenal and shot manu-
factory. As Gordon was making straight for his mark, the news
reached him that the commander of Taitsan had made proposals
of surrender to Governor Li; that accordingly an Imperialist
column had been marched to occupy the place; that the men so
sent had been treacherously made prisoners, and 200 beheaded.
He therefore abandoned his scheme, and moved swiftly upon
Taitsan.

This was a great undertaking, and full of peril. The place
was garrisoned by 10,000 men, of whom 2000 were picked braves,
with several English, French, and American renegades serving at
the guns; while his own force numbered only 3000 of all arms.
That, however, mattered little to him. He laid siege to the city
forthwith. He took some outlying stockades, and established his
army in the west suburb, about 1500 yards from the gate; he
then seized upon the two bridges of the main canal. Working
round the town, and keeping out of gunshot, he captured some
small forts which protected the Quinsan road, and so cut the two
centres asunder. At a distance of 600 yards from the walls he
placed his guns in position, each covered with a portable wooden
mantlet, and flanked with riflemen. Thus prepared, he advanced
with his artillery to within 100 yards, when he opened a
scorching fire upon the battlements, rapidly owerpowering the
fire of the enemy, which was brisk, but not as yet damaging. He
bridged the moat with gunboats from headquarters. In two
hours he breached the walls, and his stormers crossed to the
attack. Suddenly the wall was manned; a tremendous fire was
poured down upon the heads of the column; the bridge was
pelted with fire-balls; and, in the confusion, one of the gunboats
was captured. Still, Captain Bannen gallantly led on his column,
and succeeded in mounting the breach. The enemy, headed by
the foreigners in his service, met the assault with spears; and

the stormers, after a short and bloody conflict, were compelled to retire. Gordon now cannonaded the breach for twenty minutes, over the heads of his stormers. They mounted it once more, when the energy of those in front, and the impetus of the men in the rear, broke through all obstacles, and the breach was crowned. All resistance ceased, the city was captured, and the enemy fled in the utmost confusion, the men trampling each other to death in their eagerness to escape pursuit.

Gordon's loss in this brief and desperate struggle was unusually heavy, amounting to between eight and nine per cent. of his force. Among the dead was the brave Captain Bannen, who led the assault, and several other officers. Of the column whose treacherous capture had induced Gordon to turn aside towards Taitsan, 300 remained alive in the city, with two Mandarins. On the Tai-ping side the loss had been less heavy.

The following is Gordon's own account of the affair, in a letter to his mother, written on his return to headquarters:—

"I left Sung-kiang with some 3000 men, on 24th April, and intended to attack Quinsan, a large town between Taitsan and Soochow. However, before I had arrived at the place, intelligence reached me that the Tai-ping forces at Taitsan, who professed to come over to the Imperialists, had treacherously seized the party sent to take possession. I immediately changed my route, and marched on Taitsan, attacked the two large stockades on one day, and the town on the next. The rebels made a good fight, but it was no use, and the place fell. Taitsan was very important, and its capture well merited, after the treachery shown by the head chief, who was wounded in the head. It opens out a large tract of country; and the Chinese generals were delighted, and have said all sorts of civil things about the force. I am now a Tsung-Ping Mandarin (which is the second highest grade), and have acquired a good deal of influence. I do not care about that overmuch. I am quite sure I was right in taking over the command, as you would say if you saw the ruthless character of the rebels. Taitsan is a large place, and was strongly held. It is a Fu, or capital city."

Seven among the prisoners taken later by the Imperialists were condemned to the punishment of slow and ignominious death. The execution took place near Waikong. They were tied up and exposed to view for about five hours previous to decapitation, with an arrow or two forced through the skin in various parts of the body, and a piece of skin flayed from one arm. This business—of which Gordon was wholly innocent, which was the work of Mandarins quite independent of his command, and against which he protested in the strongest terms —is noticed in connection with the victory at Taitsan, because it gave rise to a curious piece of fiction, which—first promulgated in China, and, through the instrumentality of an English Bishop whose see was Victoria, handed on to Earl Russell, then Foreign Secretary, took, through the press, a strong hold on the sentimental section of the British public. In excuse it was stated that the unlucky seven were special offenders; that they had been guilty of that act of bloody treachery which sacrificed the lives of half the Chinese column entrapped in Taitsan; and that they had no claim to be treated as prisoners of war. It was added that, according to Chinese notions, the punishment inflicted on them was extremely mild. The account of these executions as above given was strictly verified by General Brown, who commanded Her Majesty's forces in China. When he had ascertained the facts of the case, he at once told the Futai, Li, that if any similar cases were reported to him he should withdraw his troops, and cease to encourage the Imperialist cause.

But the account did not seem sufficiently horrible for the public, and fiction was made stranger than truth—at any rate, more terrible. The story, communicated to the press under a string of plausible signatures (such as "Eye-Witness," "Justice and Mercy," etc.), was that, from personal observation, the prisoners were tortured with the most refined cruelty; that arrows had been forcibly driven into their heads, breasts, stomachs, and so forth; and that strips of flesh had been hacked from all parts of them. The colonial Bishop above alluded to gave a private interview to the "Eye-Witness" of the legend, and liked his story so well that he sent it at once to the Foreign Secretary, though by communicating with General Brown, which would have been usual, he might have got at the facts. He himself preferred, however, to address Lord Russell, to whom he stated that there was no doubt as to the truth of his report.

At this time there was a brisk business done in China by persons who sat down to invent stories of Imperialist cruelties for the press. These dismal epics, always about "unmentionable atrocities," were, on examination, found to be false; but, unfortunately, they reached the sentimentalists at home before their contradictions. They thus accomplished all the mischief that was desired, doing not a little momentary harm to Gordon's position and the cause that he had espoused. On this subject Gordon wrote a letter somewhat later to the *Shanghai Shipping News*, which runs thus:—

"*June 15th*, 1863.

"I am of belief that the Chinese of this force are quite as merciful in action as the soldiers of any Christian nation could be; and, in proof of this, can point to over 700 prisoners, taken in the last engagement (Quinsan), who are now in our employ. Some have entered our ranks, and done service against the rebels since their capture. But one life has been taken out of this number, and that one was a rebel who tried to induce his comrades to fall on the guard, and who was shot on the spot. It is a great mistake to imagine that the men of this force are worthless. They will, in the heat of action, put their enemies to death, as the troops of any nation would do; but when the fight is over, they will associate as freely together as if they had never fought. . . . If 'Observer' and 'Eye-Witness,' with their friend 'Justice and Mercy,' would come forward and communicate what they know, it would be far more satisfactory than writing statements of the nature of those alluded to by the Bishop of Victoria. And if anyone is under the impression that the inhabitants of the rebel districts like their rebel masters, he has only to come up here to be disabused of his idea. I do not exaggerate when I say that upwards of 1500 rebels were killed in their retreat from Quinsan by the villagers, who rose *en masse*."

It could hardly be expected that the introduction of English discipline into a Chinese army, officered by so many nationalities, could be immediately successful, though whatever Gordon once determined on he always ended by accomplishing. His soldiers at Taitsan had been guilty of plunder, which was contrary to his articles of war; but the moment after the splendid victory they had won for him, and the heavy losses they had sustained, was scarcely the time for punishment. Punished, however, they were, in being marched off to the siege of Quinsan before opportunity of selling their loot was allowed them. There Gordon ordered the Mandarins to front the walls with strong stockades, and man them with their own soldiers; while, on his side, he took back his troops to Sung-kiang to be re-organised. He then issued a general order, thanking the officers and men for their gallantry at Taitsan. He added, at the same time, that he was compelled to find fault with his officers for their laxity of discipline; and to improve the force in this respect, he filled the places of those who had been killed, or who had resigned, by certain officers from Her Majesty's 99th Regiment, then quartered at Shanghai, who had been allowed to volunteer for the service.

He was now ready again to advance on Quinsan, when a new difficulty arose. He had found it necessary to place over the Commissariat and the military stores an officer of rank, who might speak with authority to the majors in command of the different regiments, who were apt to be troublesome in the matter of rations. To this post accordingly he appointed the Deputy-Assistant Commissary-General Cooksley, of the English army, with the rank of Lieutenant-Colonel. This met with a violent opposition from his majors, which threatened to pass into open mutiny. Hardly was the force under marching orders for Quinsan, when they all requested an interview with their Commander, at which they complained of the appointment, impudently insisting that they should receive the same rank and pay as the new Lieutenant-Colonel. Gordon refused point-blank, and they retired to send in their resignations, with a request that these should be at once accepted, but that they should be allowed to serve on the pending expedition. Gordon accepted their resignations, and declined their proffered service. The force was to march at daybreak the next morning, and as late as 8 A.M. Gordon's body-guard only had fallen in. The officers in command came to report that none of their men would move. At this juncture the majors, finding that there was only one Commander in that army, thought better of their conduct, and submitted.

Thereupon Gordon started, with 600 artillery and 2300 infantry, to the attack of Quinsan. There he found the Imperialist force, which he had left stockaded before the place under General Ching, in some peril, for the Tai-pings were gradually encompassing it at the East Gate. At this point Gordon attacked, and drove the enemy towards the West Gate. They numbered about 12,000 ; a very large force was encamped within the walls, which were five miles round. The stone forts in the neighbourhood were in the enemy's hands. As I have shown, this stronghold was of the utmost strategical importance. Not only would its possession enable Gordon to hold the conquests he had already effected ; it was also the key to Soochow, which, once reduced, would restore the eastern half of the rebel territory to the Imperial Government. The aspect it presented was that of an isolated hill within the city walls, with a pagoda at the top; while in front was an open plain. Every manœuvre of the attacking force could be distinctly seen, and two or three guns placed on the spurs of the hill would have made it a perfect citadel. Men were stationed on the high ground to telegraph all they saw to their Commander, a skilful chief named Moh Wang; and in addition to all these qualities of defence, a ditch more than forty yards wide surrounded the city.

Gordon was not long in discovering that Quinsan, admirably situated as it was, had one weak spot. This suggested a scheme of operations which speedily led to its downfall. He saw that the only road between Quinsan and Soochow, two places all-important to each other, ran between a lake—that of Yansing— and a chain of large creeks widening out here and there into small lakes; and he at once concluded that by bringing an armed steamer to bear upon it he could cut off all communication. Accordingly, after investing the city with his own force and 7000 Imperialists, to prevent the retreat of the enemy upon Chanzu, which he held in the north, and on Soochow along the narrow way leading to it from the West Gate, he ordered up his little steamer, the *Hyson*, with its guns protected by iron mantlets.

It was the 30th of May, and at dawn the steamer was under weigh, with 300 picked riflemen of the disciplined corps, accompanied by field artillery in boats, and with about fifty small gunboats—eighty sail in all—with large white sails and variously coloured flags. On reconnoitring the country, he found that the road could be cut at Chunye, a village eight miles from Quinsan, and the key to the city. To reach this point, it was necessary for him to make a twenty miles' detour by water through the country held by the enemy. This was easily done; and the rebel garrison in the Chunye stockades was surprised and captured without the loss of a man. Leaving his 300 riflemen at Chunye, and the main body of his force at the East Gate of Quinsan, Gordon manned the *Hyson* only with her crew, well armed, under the command of Captain Davidson, an American of the greatest experience, ability, and tact, and proceeded to reconnoitre the country towards Soochow. Davidson had not gone far when he fell in with a large body of Tai-pings marching to reinforce Quinsan, little dreaming that they should meet an enemy by these solitary waters. The steamer opened fire upon them with

murderous effect, leaving them no alternative but to retreat along
the canal, of which Gordon was now master.   The steamer
followed the flying mass of men, who became jammed together upon
this single road in fearful confusion.   What increased this disorder
to the utmost was that the retreating body met fresh reinforcements coming up, with whom they became inextricably mixed,
the whole mass remaining completely at the steamer's mercy.   In
her progress the *Hyson* came to a bridge, and fears were entertained that she could not pass it.   Its arch, however, proved
sufficiently high to let the funnel through, and she continued
her cruise at easy speed.   At intervals on either bank of the canal
stockades had been erected by the Tai-pings, as well as strong stone
forts.   On the *Hyson* firing a few shots, these were evacuated,
and the fugitives were pursued.   In this manner all the fortified
posts were silenced, and Gordon steamed up to the very walls of
Soochow, which was to be the next stronghold to fall.   It was
one of the boldest and most successful feats of the campaign ; and
thenceforward the name of Gordon struck terror into the hearts
of the lieges of the Great Peace.

The steamer returned during the night, and reached Chunye
at three in the morning.   It found the 300 riflemen in a state of
great alarm : the rebel garrison of Quinsan, 7000 strong, were
trying to make their escape along the road to Soochow.   The
Hyson was again brought into action, driving back the panic-
stricken rebels up to the walls of the city, and repulsing every
advance.   The crowd of desperate Tai-pings was so great, that,
had they been well commanded, they could have swept the Ever-
Victorious Army from the face of the earth.   The Imperialists
themselves, surrounded by the enemy, were given over to terror,
and were beginning to abandon their gunboats, when the arrival
of the *Hyson* changed the aspect of affairs.   By firing into the
Quinsan garrison she obliged it to retire, with great slaughter.
The shelling went on till half-past two in the morning, and, at
a later hour, the force which had been left at the East Gate
entered Quinsan unopposed.

During this series of engagements the number of Tai-pings
met and dealt with could not have been less than 15,000.   Of
these, 5000 were either shot or drowned, or afterwards murdered
by the villagers, who had suffered the utmost cruelty at their
hands, and who rose *en masse* against them.   Gordon had made
it a condition with the Imperialists that there should be no
barbarity nor decapitation of prisoners, but that these should be

treated as having surrendered to a British officer. The effect of this was to turn enemies into friends, and greatly to increase the strength of the disciplined force. About 2000 prisoners were taken, 700 of whom then entered the ranks of the Ever-Victorious Army. In fact the whole garrison of Quinsan was lost to the rebels. The casualties on Gordon's side were only two killed and five drowned. The prisoners taken were very fine big men. Most of them had been impressed by the enemy.

Here is a hurried letter, written by Gordon after the capture of Quinsan, which will give some idea of the state of things :—

"The rebels certainly never got such a licking before, and I think that there will not be much more severe fighting, as we have such immense advantages in the country in the way of steamers. Quinsan is a large city 4½ miles round, and has a hill in the centre some 600 feet high, from which the flat country around can be seen for upwards of 50 miles. It is a wonderful country for creeks and lakes, and very rich. My occupying this city enables the Imperial Government to protect an enormous district rich in corn, etc., and the people around are so thankful for their release that it is quite a pleasure. They were in a desperate plight before our arrival, as their way lay between the rebels and Imperialists; but they had the sharpness to have two head men or chiefs in each village—one was Imperialist and the other a rebel; these paid the various taxes to both sides. In order to put you *au fait* as to my position, I must tell you something perhaps egotistical; but I suppose you want to hear what is the case. The Governor of the Province, Prince Kung, and nearly all the Mandarins, are extremely satisfied with my appointment. I rejoice in the rank of Tsung-Ping, or Red Button Mandarin, but I do not wear the dress, as you may suppose. They write me very handsome letters, and are very civil in every way. I like them, but they require a great deal of tact, and getting in a rage with their apathy is detrimental, so I put up with it. I have no doubt of my having been able to take Soochow the other day, if the Mandarins had been able to take advantage of our success. . . . You may hear of cruelties being committed, do not believe them. We took nearly 800 prisoners, and they have some of them entered my body-guard and fought since against their old friends the rebels. If I had time I could tell such extraordinary stories of the way men from distant provinces meet one another, and the way villagers recognise in our ranks old

rebels who have visited their villages for plunder; but I really
have no time for it. I took a Mandarin, who had been a rebel
for three years, and have him now; he has a bullet in his cheek,
which he received when fighting against the rebels. The rebels
I took into my guard were snake-flag bearers of head chiefs, and
they are full of the remarks of their old masters. The snake-
flags are the marks of head men in both armies. Whenever they
are seen there is a chief present. When they go, you know the
rebels will retire. At Taitsan the snake-flags remained till the
last, and this accounted for a very severe fight. The rebel
Wangs or kings knew that 'a new English *piecée* had come
when Fushan was taken, but did not expect him at Taitsan.'
Some of the reports spread are most amusing; one is that 'the
rebels gave me £2000 not to attack Quinsan' when I advanced
on that place after the capture of Taitsan. All the Mandarins
have heard of this; but it must have slightly upset their story
when we came up again against Quinsan. Bu Wang and ten
other Wangs were drowned in the retreat; the former was head
man of Soochow, and wrote a very important letter to General
Staveley, saying we were a nation of traders, and that his armies
were as sand on the seashore. I never did think the rebels were
as strong as people said; they do not number many fighting men.
Chung Wang, the Faithful King, is away, and is said not to intend
returning to Soochow. The Soochow people have removed their
wives and property to the lakes behind Soochow; but I think
the Wangs will be sadly put out when they see the three
steamers we have in the lakes, which I hope they will do shortly.

"Knowledge of the country is everything, and I have studied
it a great deal. Chanzu is within forty miles. I have been
several times to see the city; it now feels quite relieved at the
capture of Quinsan. The horror of the rebels at the steamer is
very great; when she whistles they cannot make it out. I
suppose Sherard Osborne will be out in a mail or two, but his
steamers will draw too much water for these creeks and lakes.
We have several personal servants of the Bu Wang among the
prisoners; they, of course, can retail their masters' remarks on the
past affairs, and are very amusing. They issued a proclamation
ordering powder to be put under the steamer, and for her to be
thus blown up. The query was, Who should do it? which was
not answered."

Gordon had seen, with the intuition of a true general, that

Quinsan was the key to his future military operations. It was now within gunshot of his little war steamer, with her 32-pounder, from every side, and he determined to make it his headquarters. There the men would be more under his control than at Sung-kiang, where they had been in a measure demoralised by the lax systems and the old traditions of Ward and Burgevine. By the mere fact of their presence they paralysed the Tai-pings, and restored the peasantry to confidence. But when this change of headquarters was communicated to the troops, it went sufficiently against the grain of the rowdy class of officers and the Chinese rank-and-file, to make them imagine once more that they must have a hand in determining what was right and wrong. At Sung-kiang they could dispose of their loot, of which, all regulations to the contrary, they doubtless had plenty on hand. Thus it came to pass that a mutinous spirit was again aroused. The artillery refused to fall in, and threatened to blow the officers to pieces, both European and Chinese. The intimation of this serious mutiny was conveyed to Gordon in a written proclamation, and he at once took measures that showed it was no easy task to shake him in his absolute command. Convinced that the non-commissioned officers were at the bottom of the affair, he called them up and asked who wrote the proclamation, and why the men would not fall in? They had not the courage to tell the truth, and professed ignorance on both points. With quiet determination Gordon then told them that one in every five would be shot, an announcement which they received with groans. During this manifestation, the Commander, with great shrewdness, determined in his own mind that the man whose groans were the most emphatic and prolonged was the ringleader. This man was a corporal: Gordon approached him, dragged him out of the rank with his own hand, and ordered two of the infantry standing by to shoot him on the spot. The order was instantly obeyed. Gordon then sent the remaining non-commissioned officers into confinement for one hour, with the assurance that within that time, if the men did not fall in, and if the name of the writer of the proclamation was not given up, every fifth man among them would be shot. This brought them to their senses. The files fell in ; the writer's name was disclosed. Gordon had done justice to him some hours before : it was the loud-voiced corporal.

Troubles of this sort were not the only ones with which the young Captain had at this time to contend. In General Ching he found a difficult and expensive coadjutor—a man eager to obtain credit with his own Government, sometimes by taking steps contrary to Gordon's advice, at others by showing his jealousy of the Englishman's successes. Thus, Gordon's modes of reducing Quinsan he visited with complete disapproval, writing to his colleague Li that if he had had artillery at the East Gate he could himself have taken the city by storm. Just now his anger made itself manifest in a manner altogether intolerable. Of set purpose, without doubt, some of his gunboats opened fire on 150 men of the Ever-Victorious Army under Majors Kirkham and Lowden. He affected to treat the matter as a jest. He was forcibly informed that it was nothing of the kind, but he protested his ignorance of the flag on which his troops had fired. This gave rise to a correspondence between Gordon and Li, and led to Gordon starting for the scene of action, determined upon fighting Ching as well as the rebels, if that General should permit his sense of humour to get the better of him again. Then Mr. McCartney was sent up by Li to arrange matters, and a humble apology was wrested from Ching; in this way the difficulty was arranged.

And now arose another danger. Burgevine, smarting under the disgrace of his dismissal, was enlisting rowdies and renegades for sinister purposes of his own, and service with the armies of the rebel King. He had some influence still with men who had served under him; they admired his system of plunder and his desperate methods. His present movement, therefore, was alarming; and it unsettled the minds of some of Gordon's foreign officers. Their discontent became apparent just as the Commander was starting for Wokong, with a view to the destruction of Soochow. The artillery officers, unwilling to serve under Major Tapp, a new commander imposed upon them by their General, while concealing their ringleaders in the old-fashioned formula of a round-robin, refused to accompany the expedition. Gordon had not the power to shoot an officer, but he had all the inclination to make an example of one or two. He therefore left them to their own devices, and by his personal influence collected men to serve the guns and to get the artillery started without the officers. At dusk, however, a letter came from the offenders, begging that their conduct might be overlooked. This, as their place could not be effectively supplied, was granted; and, after all, they were gallant men, who had evinced much ability, and were quick in acquiring a knowledge of the country.

CHAPTER V

AT this time the reduction of Soochow, the capital of the province, was the great object of the Imperial Government. There was much confusion of tongues, and much darkening of counsel, over the matter among the Imperial captains. Gordon had, however, his own particular idea as to the ways and means by which the city should be taken, and he was not long in putting it into practice. Soochow, the famous City of Pagodas, is situate on the Grand Canal, and, the centre of a splendid system of water-ways, is by water approachable on every side. By water, therefore, and from every side, did Gordon determine on attacking it: to isolate it from all possible assistance, to cut and master all its communications and approaches. Ten miles south of it lies Kahpoo, where the rebels had two strong forts. These it was of especial importance to take—first, because they secured a good junction between the Grand Canal and the Taho, a lake some fifty miles across; and next, because they commanded the direct road from Soochow to the Tai-ping cities of the south. At Kahpoo, therefore, and at Wokong, three miles south of Kahpoo, and like it a key to the rebel positions, did Gordon resolve to strike a first blow.

With about 2200 men, infantry and artillery, in boats, with the armed steamers *Firefly* and *Cricket*, he stormed Kahpoo, and next day advanced upon Wokong. On his march he came upon a rebel fort which had been left unoccupied. The Tai-pings, seeing the approach of the enemy, made a rush for the abandoned hold; and Gordon at once pushed forward his 4th and 6th Regiments to cut them off. They got in first; but so close was the race that the 6th Regiment entered almost on their heels, and drove them out, and not without loss. Leaving the 6th in occupation, Gordon went on his way, took certain other stockades

4

which commanded Wokong, and by 10 o'clock that evening had beleaguered it on every side. The panic-stricken garrison made some futile attempts to force a passage, but was soon compelled to surrender. The leader himself, Yang Wang, had escaped the night before. But 4000 prisoners were taken, among whom were many chiefs, including the second in command. On the march back to Quinsan, Gordon, finding that at Kahpoo there were not sufficient men to hold the stockades, resolved to remain there himself with 100 of the Ningpo battalion and a good supply of ammunition.

In the midst of these successes, Gordon had much to disturb that equanimity which is essential to a commander. In the first place, his colleague Ching had arrived, and was anxious to get hold of the prisoners and turn them into soldiers. Some 1500 were given up to him, under his promise that they should receive good treatment. It was not long, however, before Gordon heard that five had been beheaded. He saw that it was useless to protest against these abominable proceedings. The non-payment of his force, too, preyed heavily on his mind. Heartily sick of the business, he determined to throw up his command; and to this end he left for Shanghai.

A man who had proved himself to be possessed of the highest military instincts, who had succeeded in all his undertakings, who had exposed himself to so many dangers, deserved the ungrudging support of the Government whose cause he had adopted, even as he deserved the affection of an army he had led from victory to victory. Nevertheless, some of his officers were disaffected towards him, because he insisted on the maintenance of discipline, while his troops regarded him with disfavour because he steadily refused to gratify their lust of plunder. Indeed, the capture of Quinsan, which would have set a European force on fire with ardour and confidence, was followed by the desertion of nearly half the Ever-Victorious Army; so that Gordon had been compelled to recruit from the rebel prisoners, who, fortunately, had proved much better men than the deserters. Moreover, on one ground and another, many influential persons in his own country were urging him to resign. Had the Chinese Government frankly supported him in any measure proportionate to the dictates of their own interests, he certainly would not have entertained the thought of abandoning his command; for he perceived the difference it would make to the people and the country if he left this iniquitous Rebellion to drift back into its former triumph, and if he left it crushed and broken beyond the power of revival.

Governor Li, who presently became his warm friend and admirer, had not at that time learned to appreciate his great and commanding qualities. He had probably never seen a type of complete disinterestedness before, so that he was naturally slow to acknowledge Gordon, whom he had known but a few months. The foreigners who had hitherto served in the force had been governed only by a spirit of rapine. They were mercenaries, and with them all had been a mere question of money. Gordon had not yet had time to show that he was utterly unlike his predecessors. Li, then, having only a limited knowledge of the new man's character, took no steps to discharge the debt that weighed upon the Anglo-Chinese army. What was worse, in less than three months he pledged his word to Gordon and broke it. The consequences of this were so serious, that, but for certain pressing contingencies, Gordon would have left the Empire to its fate.

But Gordon had no sooner reached Shanghai, with the resolve to throw up his commission, than he found that Burgevine's treachery had been fully confirmed. That singular adventurer, through the instrumentality of a renegade named Jones, who had been master of the *Kiao-Chiao*, a small war-steamer belonging to the Chinese, had got together a band of foreign rowdies, and seized the vessel on his own account on August 1st. Having failed to recover command of the Ever-Victorious Army, he had avenged himself by entering into communication with the Taipings, and had succeeded, in the *Kiao-Chiao*, in reaching Soochow with a band of desperadoes of all nations, thoroughly armed. It was not for Gordon to desert his post in such a moment. He saw that the campaign had entered upon a new and desperate phase. He rode back to Quinsan, and at once resumed his command and the operations he had had in view.

The better to do his work, the more rigorously to grapple with the new peril, he had already written to Quinsan, which was now his headquarters, for information as to the humour of his officers. No unsatisfactory signs appeared; but during the day there were reports of so serious a nature, that he at once sent his siege-train to Taitsan for safety, and the principal part of his siege ammunition to Shanghai, while he despatched reinforcements to Kahpoo, his most advanced post. He had taken the decisive step of sending in his resignation to Li, and of enclosing a copy of it to General

Brown, the instant the piratical capture of the *Kiao-Chiao* and Burgevine's change of front came to his knowledge. In this letter he informed Li that he would remain in command of the force only until such time as he should receive replies from the British Minister and General. But now a crisis was imminent. To abandon the command would be to leave a suffering people not only at the mercy of the Tai-pings, but of the freebooter, whose treachery and love of violence might greatly strengthen the rebel cause. Moreover, Burgevine's popularity might draw men from the already disaffected force who had once served under the renegade Commander. His former followers had not forgotten how on an occasion he had plundered the Treasury in order to obtain funds for their pay, despoiled temples and robbed the images of their jewels. Gordon, therefore, with his own payments in arrear, was not a little anxious as to the influence of Burgevine's tactics on the rebel cause.

This situation of affairs excited general uneasiness, and the alarm was fully shared in by Colonel Hough, commanding at Shanghai, who wrote to General Brown that Burgevine's terms with the rebels whom he enlisted, some 300 in number, included, besides pay, an unrestrained licence to sack every town they took, including Shanghai itself, which he thought no idle threat, owing to the present reduced state of Gordon's force, all reported to be treacherously inclined to join Burgevine. These and yet more serious anticipations were not, however, realised. Meantime Gordon was on the alert. He left Shanghai on the 1st of August for Quinsan, and sent for reinforcements to Kahpoo, for his station was seriously threatened by the rebels. The next day he proceeded in the *Cricket* to Kahpoo, where the rebels were in great force on all sides; not less than 40,000, led by Europeans, and coming up to close quarters. Having a howitzer and shell, they blew up one gunboat; and for the protection of the steamers it was necessary to reinforce the stockades by infantry and artillery. While all these attacks were repulsed, the rebels employed themselves in burning the villages around.

Gordon resolutely held on to Kahpoo and Quinsan, feeling that if those strongholds were lost, Shanghai would soon follow. To relieve his anxiety, he was obliged to move constantly between Quinsan and Kahpoo; for he had no officer fit to undertake the defence of the latter place, or to keep the rebels in check.

Some account of his movements, and his views on the situa-

tion of affairs at this time, may be gathered from the following
letter, dated Quinsan, 12th August:—

" Since my last, Burgevine has joined the rebels, and they
have tried hard to take Kahpoo, which is on the Grand Canal.
We have, however, repulsed all their attacks, and they have now
retired into Soochow. I think the rebels will soon get very tired
of their auxiliaries and the latter of the rebels. Thirty of them
deserted the other day, and came back to Shanghai. We had a
field fight with the rebels at Kahpoo, and drove them back two
miles, burning their camp. They had become very audacious,
and had come up close to the stockades, throwing fireballs into
the same. The Mandarins are not a particularly nice set. There
is nothing interesting about them; in fact, the Chinese are much
more matter-of-fact people than Europe gives them credit for.
I dare say you may have alarming news about the rebels this
mail, but I can answer that this is exaggerated. There is no
doubt but that the accession of Burgevine will give them some
little spirit, but it cannot, in my opinion, last. The whole
country around Wokong is flat, and intersected with large creeks.
There are no roads, except the one leading to Hangchow from
Soochow ; and this one we now hold by the stockades at Kahpoo.
. . . I am in a very isolated position, and have to do most of my
work myself, which accounts for my not writing at greater length
to you. We took a large number of prisoners, and let them go,
having made soldiers of some of them. They are only too happy
to get away from the rebels."

General Brown, from his headquarters at Shanghai, lost no
time in communicating with the Secretary of War on the perilous
position of Gordon's force. In a despatch of September 14, he
describes Gordon as entirely in the hands of men formerly in the
pay of Ward and in communication with Burgevine, who had
already tampered with some of the officers and lured over many
to his side. The guns and munitions of war in Gordon's
possession, furnished to him with the sanction of the British
Government, were in peril, through treachery, of falling into the
hands of the rebels. This would render General Brown's own
position most critical at Shanghai, he having no larger description
of ordnance to contend against the rebels with than that which
might be brought against him. These circumstances decided
General Brown to visit Gordon's headquarters in person, and to

inspect his garrison. He found these in a very efficient state; nevertheless he considered it would be rash in the extreme for Gordon to hazard an attack.

Three days previous to the date of the despatch alluded to, Gordon was taking a more hopeful view of affairs, as may be seen from the following characteristic letter:—

"QUINSAN, 11th September 1863.

"I have determined not to attack Soochow till Sherard Osborne arrives, for Burgevine's defection has very much increased the strength of the rebels, and it does not do to risk anything. I expect the rebels will very soon get sick of their men, and, in fact, cannot pay them what they promise. They are quiet, and our stockades are around two-thirds of the city, distant from here some twenty miles. Burgevine's boy, who acted as his interpreter, has run out, and says that Burgevine tells the Wangs all about the settlement and about the force, etc., etc., which interests the Wangs very much. He is in good health, and very indolent; he has a nice lot with him, all the scum of Shanghai, which may be said to be celebrated for its produce in that way. He is not allowed to send money out of Soochow, so I expect the rebels intend eventually to take it all back again: this would not be the first time they had done a similar thing. An intercepted letter from Burgevine says he has thirty to forty men who are with him, and who declare they will run away at the first opportunity, and he does not know where to send them.

"I was at first rather afraid of treachery among my officers, but now have no fear. One gentleman I turned away I found had been corresponding for some time with Burgevine, but he was such an owlet that it made no difference. Burgevine wrote to me two days before he joined the rebels, saying that he would come and see me, and that I was not to believe any of the reports about him, and that he would explain everything. I believe he now regrets his conduct.

"The presence of Europeans has not in any way changed the barbarities perpetrated by the rebels; they burn away as hard as ever round the city, and this place is full of poor, destitute people, who are fed by subscriptions. They did not like the repulse at Kahpoo at all, and have not repeated it. The agents of Burgevine have been trying in vain to get the men over."

In yet more hopeful terms Gordon continues his narrative as follows :—

"CAMP, WAI-QUAIDONG, TWO MILES EAST OF SOOCHOW,
25th September 1863.

"I am now encamped in support of the Imperialists, who are stockaded some 1800 yards from the walls.   The Imperialists having moved up so close, oblige me to have part of my force nearer them for support, and the weather being delightful, it is very agreeable.   The rebels have made great efforts to drive the Imperialists away, but without success, and our present position is extremely strong.   Burgevine has been down at Shanghai, and escaped by a very little being captured.   The United States Marshal, who has a nephew in this force, was seized in a lorcha with nine others; two other boats with arms were captured, and Burgevine jumped into the river.   This shows what men these Americans are.   This United States Marshal pretended that no one was on board the boat; but the men were found below.   I do not think I told you that Kongzu was taken by the Imperialists; this is very important, as they have no place but Hangchow by which they (the rebels) can now get arms, and I expect Burgevine will lose caste by his mishap; the rebels do not generally make much allowance. . . . A great many Europeans have left him, and I think there are not more than thirty or forty there now. The Imperialists here are very good, and we get on very well with them; they make first-rate stockades, and work willingly.   We have now some native troops at Quinsan, and at Taitsan; also some of H.M.'s 67th at the latter place.   The rebel shells are very poor things, not one in twenty bursts; they have some of brass, but they are not much better.   The rebels are not in very good spirits, and are moving their things southward towards Wuchu, through the Taho Lake."

Events were now progressing more favourably for the Ever-Victorious Army, and the spirits of the Commander rose as he more clearly discerned the final success of his cause.   His next letter is written at Patachow, on the day following the capture of that place.

"STOCKADES, PATACHOW, *30th September* 1863.

"Finding that the Imperialists were incommoded by the presence of some stockades at Patachow, I determined to attack these.   The stockades were very feebly held, and the loss in capturing them nil. In repulsing an attack made to recapture them, we had five men wounded. The rebels are now threatened on the south as well as the east, and I heard to-day that the rebels had approached close to Wusieh. The Patachow bridge is a fifty-three arched bridge, 300 yards long. I am very sorry to say that twenty-six of the arches fell in yesterday like a pack of cards, killing two men; ten others escaped by running as the arches fell one after another as fast as a man could run. It made a tremendous noise, and my boat was nearly smashed by the ruins. I regret it immensely, as it was unique and very old; in fact, a thing to come some distance to see. I am afraid it was my fault, as I had commenced removing an archway to let a steamer through into the Taho Lake, and this caused the fall, as each arch rested on the other. Two men were saved, though they fell in the water. Matters go very badly for the rebels, and I expect in two or three mails to be able to announce the fall of Soochow. We are now two miles from it on the Grand Canal. The steamers do great execution. We attacked Patachow at 11 A.M., and took it by outflanking and threatening the use of the stockades; it was a very simple affair."

One evening Gordon was seated alone on the parapet of the bridge—referred to in the preceding letter—smoking a cigar, when two shots in succession struck the stone on which he sat. These shots, which were purely accidental, had come from his own camp, it not being known that he was there. On the second striking the seat he thought it time to descend, and rowed across the creek to make inquiries as to what was going on. He had not been long on the river when that part of the bridge on which he had been seated gave way, and fell into the water, nearly smashing his boat. This narrow escape from falling through with the ruins, to which he does not himself allude, is one of those incidents which added not a little to the reputation he had acquired of having a charmed life.

At Patachow negotiations were opened with him by the Europeans in the Tai-ping service; many of these had formerly been his comrades, though now serving on the other side. The communication these men had to make was that they were by no means satisfied with their position at Soochow, and that they desired him to meet and talk on the subject with Burgevine, who was of the same mind. These conferences were to take place on a bridge between the opposing lines.

Dangerous as the business was, Gordon at once agreed to it. Burgevine stated that he and his men had resolved to quit the rebel service; but that they would not do so unless they could obtain some guarantee of their not being held responsible to the Imperial Government. On this Gordon undertook that the authorities at Shanghai should let the matter drop, and even offered to take as many of the men as he could, and assist the rest to leave the country.

The repulse of his first attempt upon Gordon in the field had dispirited Burgevine, who was slow in his movements, and could not contend against the brilliant and rapid manœuvres of his opponent. The negotiations led to nothing at the moment, except that in a measure they rallied Burgevine's spirits. In his next interview with Gordon he betrayed an ambition he had long indulged in. His dream had been to found an empire for himself, and he had fixed on China as a fit country in which to fulfil it. He even proposed that Gordon should join him. They would seize on Soochow, expel both rebels and Imperialists, lay hands on the treasure contained therein, raise an army of 20,000 men, and march on Peking. Gordon indignantly dispelled these hallucinations, and curtly informed him he would entertain no such idea.

Meantime much fighting was going on, and a desperate and futile attempt was made by the rebels to retake Wokong. Though the recent negotiations had seemed to end in nothing, they were soon to bear fruit. Burgevine and his gang had convinced themselves of one thing, that they could rely on Gordon's word; and they sent him secret information to the effect that they purposed to make a sally, with a view to deserting and throwing themselves on his protection. The manner of doing this was agreed on: seeing a signal-rocket from Gordon's lines, they were to board the *Hyson* as if intent on her capture. This they did with such a show of purpose, that thousands of the Tai-ping troops rushed to their assistance, but these were repulsed with shot and shell, while the *Hyson* steamed back and safely landed the deserters in the besieging camp. Burgevine and several other of the Europeans were, however, not among them. Morton, their leader, said that the Moh Wang, the Commander, seemed to suspect them, so they thought it wise to leave at once without waiting for the rest.

The majority of these deserters were seamen who had been lured into Soochow with little idea as to their destination. Their condition was pitiable in the extreme, and their gratitude on finding themselves within Gordon's lines was hardly less touching. Nearly all of them volunteered to stay and fight for him to whom they owed their release from starvation and death. Gordon, immediately he heard of Burgevine's detention, wrote and despatched the following letter [1] to two of the principal Wangs of Soochow :—

"STOCKADES, PATACHOW, 16*th October* 1863.

"To their Excellencies, Chung Wang, Moh Wang.

"YOUR EXCELLENCIES,—You must be already aware that I have on all occasions, when it lay in my power, been merciful to your soldiers when taken prisoners, and not only been so myself, but have used every endeavour to prevent the Imperial authorities from practising any inhumanity.   Ask for the truth of this statement any of the men who were taken at Wokong, and who, some of them, must have returned to Soochow, as I placed no restriction on them whatever.

"Having stated the above, I now ask your Excellencies to consider the case of the Europeans in your service.   In every army each soldier must be actuated with faithful feelings to fight well.   A man made to fight against his will is not only a bad soldier, but he is a positive danger, causing anxiety to his leaders, and absorbing a large force to prevent his defection.   If there are many Europeans left in Soochow, I would ask your Excellencies if it does not seem to you much better to let these men quietly leave your service if they wish it; you would thereby get rid of a continual source of suspicion, gain the sympathy of the whole of the foreign nations, and feel that your difficulties are all from without.   Your Excellencies may think that decapitation would soon settle the matter, but you would then be guilty of a crime which will bear its fruits sooner or later.   In this force officers and men come and go at pleasure, and although it is inconvenient at times, I am never apprehensive of treason from within.   Your Excellencies may rely on what I say, that should you behead the Europeans who are with you, or retain them against their free will, you will eventually regret it.   The men have committed no crime, and they have done you good service, and what they have tried to do, viz. escape, is nothing more than any man, or even animal, will do when placed in a situation he does not like.

"The men could have done you great harm, as you will no doubt allow; they have not done so, and I consider that your

---

[1] Some of the words in this letter were obliterated by blood spots, under circumstances to be shown later.

Excellencies have reaped great benefit from their assistance.   As far as I am personally concerned, it is a matter of indifference whether the men stay or leave; but as a man who wishes to save those unfortunate men, I intercede.

"Your Excellencies may depend you will not suffer by letting these men go; you need not fear their communicating information.   I knew your force, men and guns, long ago, and therefore care not to get that information from them.   If my entreaties are unavailing for these men in . . . . yourself by sending down the wounded, and perform an action never to be regretted.

"I write the above with my own hand, as I do not wish to entrust the matter to a linguist; and trusting you will accede to my request, I conclude,—Your Excellencies' obedient servant,

C. G. GORDON,

Major Commanding."

Gordon feared that Burgevine would be decapitated in consequence of what had happened; and for this reason he had at once sent the letter and presents to Moh Wang, together with all the Enfields brought into camp, and entreated him to spare Burgevine's life.   It is recorded that after these events the Tai-ping chief sent Burgevine away in safety, and delivered him up to the American Consul.   At Gordon's request, all proceedings against him were waived, on condition that he left the country. When these affairs were investigated by Mr. Mayers, the acting British Consul at Shanghai, who was sent to inquire into them, the desperate character of Burgevine was fully brought to light. That gentleman stated in an official letter, that at the very moment when the interviews were proceeding in which Burgevine offered to surrender, he was planning with Jones, his lieutenant, to entrap the man on whose mercy he had cast himself and his followers.   His companion, desperate as he was, had some honesty left, and revolted against such treachery.   This, among other things, gave rise to much ill-feeling against him in his Captain's mind.   But for the fact that Gordon's frankness had no untoward result, the confidence with which, at the risk of his life, he negotiated with others, one would say, displayed a want of that common prudence which others find so necessary.

As has been said, the foreigners were most grateful to Gordon for the skill with which he had planned and carried out their escape on the *Hyson.*   Their gratitude was warmly expressed in a deposition afterwards made before the United States Consul, by

Jones, Morton, Porter, Barclay, and Whiting. This document gives a very full account of the plot and counter-plot between Burgevine and those of his friends who had not lost all confidence in him, but who had resolved on deserting him after a drunken outrage of which he was guilty in firing on his lieutenant, Jones. It is thus described by Jones himself :—

"At noon I went to Burgevine, who was lying asleep on board a 32-pounder gunboat, and asked him whether I should assist him to get ashore, as many of our officers and men were making remarks on the condition he was in. On his demanding the names of those who had made remarks, I declined giving them, and shortly afterwards again attempted to remonstrate with him, in company with another officer. On my again declining to give up names, Burgevine drew out his four-barrelled pistol, which he cocked and discharged at my head from a distance of about nine inches. The bullet entered my left cheek and passed upwards. It has not yet been extracted. I exclaimed, 'You have shot your best friend!' His answer was, 'I know I have, and I wish to God I had killed you!'"

Burgevine fully confirmed the truth of the above statement in a letter which he sent to a local paper, in which he said :—

"Captain Jones's account of the affair is substantially correct; and I feel great pleasure in bearing testimony to his veracity and candour whenever any affair with which he is personally acquainted is concerned."

Owing to the heat of the weather, there had been great inactivity in the garrison, and the men were falling sick. This determined Gordon to remove from Quinsan and encamp at Wai-Quaidong, six miles from the East Gate of Soochow, the doomed city. Meantime McCartney had been doing good service in various ways; but the Imperialists, though in certain cases they fought to some purpose, were guilty of more than one mistake. This was owing to the blundering arrogance of Ching, who, before attacking, steadily refused to consult with Gordon as to his intentions. The consequence was that, while Gordon was making the greatest efforts to effect the escape of Burgevine and his party from Soochow, Ching, on his own account, was marching a force on the East Gate of that city. Thus the foreigners, whose release was imminent, were ordered by the rebel Wang within the walls to the point of attack, and the scheme for their escape was thwarted. It was brought about later on, but only because the feint planned by Gordon was complete. When they got away, it was at the risk of their lives and of those who were forced to remain behind. It is not necessary to give in detail the diffi-culties which Gordon encountered through the clumsy manœuvres of his Chinese colleague. It will be enough to say that they were great indeed, inasmuch as it was the opinion of onlookers at Shanghai, that, with Ching on his hands, it would be impossible for him, even after the successes he had achieved, ever to take Soochow. With the overwhelming numbers in his front, the vast extent of territory he had to protect, the rough and dis-orderly condition of his men, and the little support afforded by the Imperial Government, it seemed beyond hope that even he could succeed; and many were the cries from all quarters, that, unless Gordon were given the entire command of the allied troops, defeat was inevitable, and his death a not unlikely result of the campaign. With this command he was never entrusted; and we shall presently see what were the fortunes of war in his hands, as the Captain of his mutinous and now sickly force.

His advance had been checked by various attacks of the rebels, now at Wokong, now at Wulungchiao, a village about two miles to the west of Patachow, and a mile and three-quarters only from the South Gate of Soochow. But all these had been repulsed, as well as an assault on Chanzu.

A letter written by him from Wulungchiao, in the intervals of engagements with the enemy, gives a vivid idea of what went on:—

"You will remember my having mentioned the fact of the Europeans and Burgevine having come over from the rebels. Since then the following have been our movements: We started for the Fifty-three Arch Bridge (alas! now only twenty-seven arched), Patachow, and made a great detour by the lakes to Kahpoo to throw the rebels off the scent. We left at 2 P.M., and although the place, Wulungchiao, which I wanted to attack was only 1½ miles to the west of Patachow, I made a detour of 30 miles to confuse them, on a side they were not prepared for. It turned out wet, and the night of the 23rd October was miser-able enough, cooped up in boats as we were. However, it cleared a little before dawn, and about 7 A.M. we came on the stockades.

I had asked the Imperialists, under General Ching, to delay their attack from Patachow till I had become well engaged; but as usual General Ching must needs begin at 5.30 A.M., and he got a good dressing from the rebels and was forced to retire. His loss was 19 killed and 67 wounded, while the Taho gunboat admiral, who had abetted him in his tom-fooling, lost 30 killed and wounded. We lost none; three were slightly bruised. The head chief of Soochow, Moh Wang, knew we were out, but had no idea of our going to Wulungchiao. He is greatly angered; and in addition to this has had trouble with his brother Wangs, who reproached him for having trusted the Europeans and for neglecting them. Eleven out of twenty-seven Wangs refused to go out and fight. Yesterday afternoon a European left Soochow and came over. I had met him before, and consider that he had acted in a very brave manner in remaining in Soochow. He says Moh Wang does not understand our movements, and is very much put out at the loss of this place. They tried to take it back again on the 25th at dusk, but got defeated."

"29th October 1863.

"Since my last letter an expedition went out to drive the rebels away from Wokong; they had had the temerity to return there, after their defeat on the 13th, and occupied nearly the same position. I sent a steamer this time, and the result was a most tremendous victory, almost equal to the Quinsan affair, and resulting from the same cause, namely, the rebels being driven out of their position, had to retreat along a narrow road running along the bank of the Grand Canal, and close to it. They could not leave the road, and there are innumerable large creeks passing from it at right angles into the Taho Lake, and only spanned by bridges on this road. These bridges are narrow and high, and one person or two can only pass over at one time. Thus you may imagine the delay which occurs at each bridge; frequently the road was about three or four feet wide for 200 or 300 yards, having a lake or ditch on one side and the Grand Canal on the other. I will not give details, as I have no time; suffice it to say that, after the flanks of their position were turned, the rebels began their retreat on Pingwang, and had 12 miles of the above road to traverse under fire of the steamer, and pursued by the troops. About 3000 to 4000 got away, one Wang and 1300 prisoners were taken, and one Wang and some men were drowned. The rush of the fugitives was met by a reinforcement from Pingwang on a high bridge, and the former swept the latter in one mass into the lake. The value of the victory is that we now have no fear for our rear, and I believe that the rebels in the silk districts seriously think of giving in. In the meantime I am preparing an attack on the north of the city which will take place about the 1st November. You will see all the Burgevine affair in the papers. I am afraid he is a rascal, but I acted to the best of my judgment. I told you I had been attacked here. It was Chung Wang and his son who attacked, and had to swim the creek in consequence of our having cut off their retreat."

The crowning mercy of the campaign was soon to come. After making a strong disposition of the Imperial forces, both at the outposts and on the Great Lake, Gordon swept round by the eastward of Soochow to the north with his siege-train and the *Hyson*, to reduce the remaining outposts held by the Tai-pings around the city. He carried Leeku by assault, and in the course of the next few days captured and occupied points which completed the investment of the city. Within it were 30,000 Tai-pings.

In almost all these engagements Gordon found it necessary to be constantly in the front, and often to lead in person. The officers of his force were brave men enough, but were not always ready to face their desperate antagonists. Gordon, in his mild way, would take one or other of these by the arm, and lead him into the thick of the fire. He always went unarmed himself, even when foremost in the breach. He never recognised danger ; to him a shower of bullets was no more than a hail-storm. He carried one weapon to direct his troops—he had but a little cane, and this soon won for itself the name of "Gordon's magic wand of victory." His Chinese followers, seeing him always victorious, always foremost in the fight, concluded it was his wand that ensured him protection. The idea encouraged the Ever-Victorious Army greatly, and was of more service to the young Commander than all the arms he could have borne.

Some days previously to the assault on Leeku, Gordon found a letter in the handwriting of one of his officers, Captain Perry. It informed a Tai-ping sympathiser of the intended movements of the force. Captain Perry confessed he had written the letter, but declared he thought the facts were of no importance ; it was only meant as a piece of gossip. To this statement Gordon replied : " I shall pass your fault over this time, on condition that, in order to show your loyalty, you undertake to lead the next forlorn hope." But Gordon had forgotten the severe test to which he had pledged his comrade, when, a few days later, they stood together by the ditch in front of the stockade. Both were leading a forlorn hope, when a ball struck Perry in the mouth. He fell screaming into his Captain's arms, and almost immediately expired.

"I have another report to make to you of our operations," says Gordon, in allusion to the late engagement: "We started from Wai-Quaidong on the 31st October, and slept the night at Ding-King. At 4 A.M. we left for Leeku, and, having met the Imperial forces some 15,000 strong at Chowdong, we advanced at 11 A.M. to attack. We began the action at 12.30 P.M., and got round their right flank, but as they had another road they did not move. We therefore carried it with a rush. I am sorry to say an officer, a very good one, Lieutenant Perry, was killed. Only three men were slightly wounded. The rebels fought well, and held on to the last; they lost some 40 to 60 killed, and we took three gunboats, about 40 other boats, and some 60 prisoners; I have no time to give details."

He further writes on the 3rd of November :—

"We yesterday, after a hard fight, took all the stockades up to the walls along the east face of the city, and last night four Wangs came in to negotiate a surrender. I think that this is likely, and the heaviest part of our fighting is over. The rebels are having great troubles among themselves, and have to pay largely for their food."

The next point of attack was Wanti, where, as well as at Leeku, it was Gordon's aim to station a part of the force. The surrender of Wanti meant the almost complete investment of Soochow; for so soon as stockades and forts were captured by the Ever-Victorious Army, they had been garrisoned by Imperialist troops. With this exception, then, all the water-ways and roads leading from the devoted city were now closed.

Eleven days after his arrival at and capture of Leeku, Gordon went to the attack of Wanti. The place was so strongly fortified that the heaviest shelling was of no avail. Gordon thus gives his own account of the affair :—

"Since I last wrote we have had another fight, and have happily driven the rebels out of this stockade. We left Leeku on the 11th November, and had two miles to go before we came here. We managed to completely surround the place, and took it by assault in three-quarters of an hour. I am sorry we had one officer killed and 20 men wounded. The casualties were more numerous from our men having had a cross fire from our own artillery. The rebels fought very bravely, and we took 600 prisoners, and I do not think more than 10 got away. Their loss was heavy, some 350; this was owing in a great measure to the fire of the artillery. I had men fighting here who had fought against us a week ago at Leeku. They behaved very well. From what the prisoners say, the rebels are much disheartened. We took all their head men prisoners. You will see a place called Tajowka on the map; this stockade was the one attacked by Burgevine and Chung Wang, and where the *Kajow* steamer was blown up. I do not know if I mentioned that Lai Wang, who was in charge of the northern stockades, had offered to come over with his force, some 20,000 men. Unfortunately he was killed in one of the skirmishes which took place after the capture of Leeku, and thus his defection did not take place. The head men here say the rebels almost despair of holding the city. I hope sincerely they will leave it, as it ruins the soldiers to plunder after the capture. The Burgevine party are a nice lot, but their defection has been a great thing for the Imperials, and has caused a corresponding depression on the side of the rebels. I think a map explains the advantages of a position far better than any description; it will suffice to say that there is only one stockade to take to cut off the rebel retreat, which we hope to have in a few days. The investment of the city will be then complete, and dissension may work the fall of the place when they have only two months' rice. I sent an expedition into the Taho Lake about the time I started for the attack on Leeku, and the steamer has just returned, having captured six gunboats, four high chiefs and some hundred prisoners, and two stockades; another expedition will start in a day or two of two steamers and infantry. The place I propose to attack is Mouding, on the Grand Canal; it is only four miles from there to the lake, and the rebels there have no option but to surrender. The Imperialists will guarantee their safety, and more than three-fourths of them would jump at the chance."

We shall presently see how guarantees, when assured by the Imperialists, were disregarded, and what fatal consequences ensued from their violation.

5

CHAPTER VI

In the investment of Soochow there were employed some 13,000 to 14,000 men, of which between 3000 and 4000 were under Gordon's orders. But in the neighbourhood there were 25,000 Imperialists besides, whose centre was at Fushan, and who were under General Ching. The Tai-pings had 40,000 men at Soochow and the suburbs alone, with 20,000 more in the city of Wusieh, and 18,000 in Mahtanchiao, a place between Wusieh and Soochow, whence Chung Wang, the Faithful King, could attack on the flank any advance on the Grand Canal.

Gordon knew all this, and was alive to the danger of such overwhelming forces. But he had made his calculations. He knew the Faithful King could only approach Soochow on the east of his outlying armies, at the imminent risk of exposing Nanking, and of losing Hangchow, as well as the city actually under siege. On his part, the Tai-ping leader knew that Nanking was hard pressed, and that, should that capital be wrested from him, the Rebellion could no longer be sustained. The works around the Kaiachiao Gate of Nanking had been already evacuated, and the city was beleaguered. This intelligence was in Gordon's possession; it had been intercepted by the Imperialists at the very moment when the action of the Faithful King was paralysed, and his forces could move neither one way nor the other without danger of rout and destruction. Gordon determined on a vigorous assault upon the north-east angle of the Soochow wall. First of all, however, he tried to capture a formidable inner line of the outer defences, and he accordingly made a night attack. This resulted in defeat, for the place was extraordinarily strong and well guarded. About one o'clock in the morning the young Commander himself, with Majors Howard and Williams, advanced to the outer stockade, leaving the remainder of his force under orders to come on at a given signal. All were dressed in white turbans, in order that they might not mistake each other for the enemy in the dark. Everything seemed quiet, and an advance-guard succeeded in climbing the breastwork. Scarcely were the troops at the front engaged on the stockade to support their Commander, when the Tai-pings opened a tremendous fire of grape and musketry. The rebel line seemed one line of fire, while the attacking party were throwing rockets and shell. The leading files, with Gordon at their head, held gallantly on at the breastwork, but those detailed to support them failed to move up, and Gordon was compelled to retire. The rebels, though they had the best of it, did not seem to like fighting in the dark. The exception was Moh Wang, who was in the front stockade, without shoes or stockings, and who fought like a private soldier, with twenty Europeans at his side. The attack, though unsuccessful, made a strong impression. The rebel loss, the work of twenty guns which during three hours poured out shot and shell, was enormous. Of the Ever-Victorious Army, 50 rank-and-file were killed, and 130 wounded, besides a large number of officers.

Next morning General Ching had an interview with the Faithful King, and learned that there was great dissension among the Wangs in Soochow. It appeared that, with the exception of Moh Wang and 35 other chiefs, these were anxious to come over to the Imperialists with 30,000 men. It had become evident to the leaders that, in spite of their success of the night before, the fall of their city was only a work of time, and they therefore proposed that Gordon should make another attack on the East Gate, when they would shut Moh Wang out of the city, and so get liberty to make terms for themselves.

Accordingly, Gordon brought siege guns and all his force into action, opened a tremendous fire on the stockades, and quickly reduced them to ruins. The advance was sounded, and the stockades were taken by assault. Gordon, accompanied only by a few men, was cut off from his main body by a large party of the enemy, and, being unable to fall back, deemed it the safer course to press forward. He found the stockades on his right almost empty. He pushed through them, and seized the nearest stone fort. The stockades he had passed happened to be occupied by some of his own men, who followed up his advance and completed the victory. It cost the young Captain 50 privates, and many of the officers of his body-guard, chiefly his own countrymen. Many others were wounded, among them Major Kirkham, the Adjutant-General, whose energetic services could ill be spared.

The following general order, dated Low-mün, Soochow, November 30, 1863, was issued at this time by Gordon:—

"The Commanding Officer congratulates the officers and men of the force on their gallant conduct of yesterday. The tenacity of the enemy, and the great strength of their position, have unfortunately caused many casualties, and the loss of many valuable officers and men. The enemy, however, has now felt our strength, and, although fully prepared and animated by the presence of their most popular chiefs, have been driven out of a position which surpasses in strength any yet taken from them. The loss of the whole of the stockades on the east side of the city, up to the walls, has already had its effect, and dissension is now rife in the garrison, who, hemmed in on all sides, are already, in fact, negotiating defection. The Commanding Officer feels most deeply for the heavy loss, but is convinced that the same will not be experienced again. The possession of the position of yesterday renders the occupation of the city by the rebels un-tenable, and thus victualling the city is lost to them."

Gordon, accompanied by Ching, now had an interview with the Wangs. They wished him to assault the city itself, promis-ing not to assist in its defence, provided they were protected on the entry of the Imperialists. The arrangement presented many and great difficulties. Little more than 5500 men were available for the attack. The walls were circumvallated by a ditch of an appalling width; while north of the East Gate there were lines of stockades as far as the eye could reach. But the city was completely commanded from without, and was so cut off from all communication that it could have held out but little longer. When the Nar Wang appealed to Gordon to carry it by assault, Gordon told him that if Soochow was thus taken, it would be impossible to prevent his force from sacking and burning it. He added, that if the Wangs were sincere in their wish to surrender, their course should be to give over a gate as a warranty of their good faith; that if they could not do this, they might either vacate the place, or fight it out. They agreed to hand over a gate, and the arrangement of the terms of capitulation were left to General Ching, Gordon himself starting off to see Li, to negotiate for the safety of any prisoners.

Meantime Moh Wang, who was obstinate, and resolved to hold out to the very last, had learned something of these parleys, and had his suspicions thoroughly aroused. He sent for his six brother kings that he might speak with them on the subject. After certain ceremonies, they adjourned to the reception-hall, where Moh Wang seated himself at the head of a table, which was on a dais. Unfortunately for the rebel cause, the chiefs thus collected together in council had each a separate command, and were therefore able to enforce their differences of opinion. Moh Wang was captain of the city. He was not wise, but he was brave as a lion, and would have shed the last drop of his blood rather than surrender. Gordon knew this, and had a great respect for his character. He had in person extorted a pledge from Governor Li that Moh Wang's life should be spared, but this pledge he was never to call upon Li to keep. The council was the last at which Moh Wang was ever to preside. The question of capitulation was raised and discussed : Moh Wang and another voted against surrender; all the rest were loud in its favour. Hot words ensued, when Kong Wang jumped up, threw aside his robes, drew out a dagger, and stabbed Moh Wang nine times in the back. Assisted by the others, he then bore his victim into the outer court, and severed his head from his body. This was the story told to Gordon on his return to the lines before Soochow, after pleading the cause of Moh Wang and his followers with Li.

Soochow surrendered that very night. Gordon, to prevent looting, withdrew his troops to some distance, and went a second time to confer with Li. To him he applied for two months' extra pay for officers and men, as a reward for what they had gone through, as compensation for their abstaining from plunder, and as an inducement for them to push on with him for the attack of Wusieh. This boon, small as it was, was denied him. Later on, General Ching came to him with an offer from Li of one month's extra pay. This meanness disgusted the men, who were by this time almost mutinous, and would rather have had a day's loot than four months' pay. Gordon, unable to trust them in the neighbourhood of a fallen city, marched them at once to Quinsan.

Nearly all the fighting which led to the capitulation had been done, as all knew, by Gordon and Gordon's men. He little thought that the influence he had so brilliantly acquired would be set aside so soon in favour of Chinese principles. It was fully understood by Li-Hung-Chang and by Ching, that humanity, as practised by the nations of the West, must be observed so long as Gordon was in command. The English leader had been promised as much, and looked to his Chinese comrades that the promise should be kept. But no sooner had Soochow surrendered, than he found himself completely betrayed. He had exposed himself to danger with the coolness and daring of one who believed himself invulnerable, and he might well think that in thus perilling his life, he had earned a right to plead for the lives of others. Though he does not appear to have had any emphatic and express promise from Li that the rebel Wangs should be spared, it is quite certain, as will be seen, that Li so far acquiesced in his views and wishes as to leave him in the belief that the Wangs would be humanely treated. This may be said to have amounted to a complete understanding, which was unhesitatingly confirmed on every occasion by General Ching, who, as far as can be gathered from the various accounts, was conscious of Gordon's just expectations in regard to what should happen when Soochow was given up to the Imperialists. What actually happened was this. Returning from Quinsan, Gordon entered the city for the first time and alone. He was met by Ching, who informed him that Li had extended mercy to all. This pleased and satisfied Gordon, for in his negotiations with the Wangs he had made them the promise, endorsed by Li, that they should receive honourable treatment. The next day, December 6, Gordon again went into Soochow, to the house of Nar Wang, which he reached before noon. He then found that the Wangs were to go out to Li, and formally give over the keys of the city. Gordon, proceeding alone towards the East Gate, met a large party of Imperialists, who were yelling and firing their muskets into the air. He remonstrated with them, saying that their conduct would frighten the rebels, and lead to mis-understandings. Immediately after this, Ching came in at the gate, and on seeing Gordon became much agitated, and turned pale. The time of the interview between Li and the chiefs had passed. Gordon anxiously inquired what had been the result; but Ching only equivocated, and would give him no definite information. Gordon, who was on horseback, unaccompanied by anyone but his interpreter, at once suspected that something had gone wrong, and rode towards Nar Wang's palace to see what he could learn there. On his arrival he found the place gutted; the Imperialists had already begun their plunder. An uncle of Nar Wang entreated him to go along with him to his house, and to help him in escorting thither the ladies of Nar Wang's family. Matters already looked so threatening that Gordon hesitated, as he was unarmed. At length he yielded, purposing first to see the women safe, and then to go out for some of his own troops, and put a stop to the looting of his allies.

So ill-organised was the local Chinese Government, and so independent was Li of the military commanders, to whom he owed the supremacy he enjoyed, that he not only executed his own plans without reference to others, but did not even intimate to Gordon—who was, he may possibly have believed, in quarters at' Quinsan—the danger of entering the city. By this time he had beheaded the principal Wangs, and given up Soochow to plunder. Gordon's situation was most perilous; what made it worse was that he was wholly ignorant of the massacre which had been secretly effected outside the town, and of which Ching had not had the courage to inform him. It is not surprising, therefore, that when he entered the courtyard of the house with Nar Wang's uncle and his family, he at once was surrounded by some thousands of armed Tai-pings, who shut the gates on him as he went in, and declined to allow him to send out his interpreter with a message to his troops. Fortunately it happened that the Tai-pings no more knew than Gordon himself that their chiefs had been put to death. Had they done so, they would have held Gordon responsible, and might have put him to torture. As it was, they held him as a hostage for the good treatment of their leaders. He was kept powerless in the palace from the afternoon of the 6th till the morning of the next day, surrounded by Tai-pings, who knew that the city was being plundered contrary to treaty, and who must have surmised that bloodshed was going on, and that some untoward fate had overtaken the Wangs who had gone out to Governor Li. Such a suspicion might have made Gordon their victim; but he was left unharmed, probably from the forlorn hope that his presence might yet be a protection to themselves. Few men have looked upon death under circumstances so intricate and so threatening. But Gordon's life was to be preserved for other times and other events.

By two in the morning he had prevailed on his captors to let his interpreter take out a letter to his boat, which lay at anchor under the South Gate. It is characteristic of him that his message contained no reference to himself, but consisted of an order to the captain of his flotilla to seize on the Governor's person and lay him by the heels until the Wangs were given up. This was a fine stroke of policy, and perfectly sincere ; but it failed. The guide in charge returned alone, stating that the interpreter had been seized by the Imperialists, and the letter taken and torn up. At three o'clock the Tai-pings were so far persuaded as to allow Gordon himself to go out in search of the missing interpreter. He reached the South Gate, where some Imperialist soldiers, not knowing probably who he was, took him prisoner for being in the company of rebels. From them he made his escape, and found his way round to the East Gate, where his body-guard was camped under Major Brookes. True to his purpose and to his word, he sent the guard at once to the protection of the Tai-pings he had quitted an hour before. Soon after, General Ching made his appearance ; but Gordon, after all that had happened to himself, and all that he had witnessed in the city, refused to hold communication with him. Ching then sent an artillery officer named Bailey to explain matters. But this gentleman had not courage to tell the truth ; and when Gordon asked him what had become of the Wangs, and if they were still prisoners, he replied that he did not know, but that he would bring in Nar Wang's son, who was in his tent.

The interview which followed opened Gordon's eyes. He learned that the Wangs had been executed on the previous day, and was so deeply moved at the intelligence that he burst into tears. He at once crossed the creek, on the other banks of which the Wangs had been murdered, and there he was not long in discovering their bodies, headless and frightfully gashed.

It was probably the most trying moment of his life, and never perhaps had he before given way to so angry an outburst of sorrow. Not only was this butchery needless and brutal, but the feeling came bitterly home to him that his own honour was at stake. He had not pledged himself for their safety, but he had negotiated with them on the understanding, as a primary condition, that their lives would be spared. As we have seen, he had refused to hold any parley with Ching. That General, however, had seen enough of his state of mind to greatly fear the consequences, and to feel that the Governor's life was in danger should Gordon come in contact with him. Not the least offence to Gordon, a very flagrant one in itself—and this had not even been notified to him—was that the Imperialists had sacked the city. Owing to this discourtesy, the man through whose daring and skill Soochow had fallen, saw himself made a prisoner and in peril of his life. It is not to be wondered at if Gordon was enraged beyond bounds ; it is not surprising that for the first time during the war he armed himself and went out to seek the life of an enemy. He took a revolver, and sought the Governor's quarters, fully resolved to do justice on his body, and accept the consequences.

But Ching was on the alert. He was scared at the terrible form of Gordon's anger, and contrived to give the Governor the alarm. Gordon boarded Li's boat, only to find that Li had taken refuge in the plundered city. Thither he hastened in pursuit. Li,[1] however, went into hiding, and, though Gordon was "hot and instant in his trace" for many days, he never came up with him. He had ordered up his troops to assist him in running the fugitive to earth ; but when he found his efforts were in vain, he marched them back into quarters at Quinsan. There, with the deepest emotion, he read them an account of what had happened. He intimated to his officers that it was impossible for a British soldier to serve any longer under Governor Li ; that he did not purpose to disband his force, but that he should hand it over to General Brown, the commander of the troops at Shanghai, until such time as the Government at Peking should inflict on Li the punishment that was his due.

In his official investigation into the details of the massacre, Mr. Mayers discovered that it was doubtful whether the Futai and Ching ever intended to keep the engagement entered into. Whilst Li was panic-stricken about the numbers of rebel troops in the city, his colleague was secretly fearful lest Nar Wang should eventually supplant him as Commander, and had resolved to destroy him. It appears, says Mr. Mayers in his despatch of December 14th, to Acting-Consul Markham, that the chiefs, on reaching the camp on the 6th instant, were received with friendly demonstrations by Li, who mentioned to each the decoration and rank he was to expect from the throne, and then handed them over to General Ching, who held them in colloquy until the executioners suddenly rushed upon them. No sooner was this act committed than the order was given for the troops to rush into the city on the east side, in the hope of terrifying the rebels

---

[1] It will be remembered that Li, or Li-Futai, is the Li-Hung-Chang of the present day.

and driving them—as actually occurred—in panic through the Western Gates.[1]

The following is Gordon's own account of the circumstances :—

"On the morning of the 28th November, the headquarters were moved up from Wai-Quaidong to General Ching's stockades, and General Ching came to see me ; he said that Kong Wang had been to see him, and that he had proposed to come over with Nar Wang, Pe Wang, Ling Wang, and Such Wang, thirty-five Tiench Wangs, and three-fourths of the garrison of Soochow. General Ching asked me if I thought it a good thing ; I told him that, with the small force at my disposal, it would be a far safer mode, and one more likely to bring the Rebellion to a close, than if we had to take the city by assault. . He said that Kong Wang was desirous to get Moh Wang out of the way with his troops, and proposed to shut him out of the city, if we renewed our attack on the stockades from which we had been repulsed in our night attack.

"The attack of the 29th November has already been reported. After it General Ching came to me and told me that Nar Wang had sent him a message to say that Chung Wang had arrived at 2 o'clock A.M. on the 29th November, and had by his presence prevented the execution of their designs. General Ching came to me again on the 1st December, to tell me that Chung Wang had left the city at 3 o'clock A.M., and that Nar Wang would send out three Tiench Wangs to him (General Ching) that evening. General Ching asked me to see them, which I did that evening in his boat, they having come into our lines. Some desultory conversation of no importance took place, and I left. On the morning of the 2nd December, General Ching came to me again, and asked me if I would see Nar Wang, whom he had agreed to meet that night; I said not unless there was any necessity for my doing so. He said he thought it would be a good thing, and finally urged me to go with him that night. I agreed to do so, and went up to the evacuated stockades off the North Gate. Nar Wang arrived at 9 o'clock P.M., and saw General Ching first. General Ching then asked me to come, which I did, and found Nar Wang and two Tiench Wangs whom I had previously seen in Ching's boat. Nar Wang was a man of medium height, dark complexion, and about thirty years of age, with a very intelligent and pleasing countenance. He was a

[1] Blue Book, " China," No. 3.

native of Woopoo, and dressed simply in silk, with a black handkerchief on his head. His first expression after seeing me was that he wished me to help him, to which I replied that I should be most happy if he could inform me of the way I could do so.

"I should have mentioned previously that General Ching had told me that Nar Wang had some difficulty about the Moh Wang and his soldiers, and had proposed to General Ching that we should attack the city, and had promised that his men should remain neutral, and wear white turbans, if their property and lives were spared. I therefore at once entered into this question with Nar Wang, and told him that the proposition General Ching had spoken to me of was impracticable; that if the city was assaulted and taken, the pillage would be universal, and I should be only deceiving him if I told him I could maintain the terms; that it would be better for him and his men to fight if they could arrange no other means; and that if they were desirous of coming over, and could make their terms with the Imperialists, they could give over one gate as a guarantee.

"He said he would consult the other Wangs, and see what could be done with respect to Moh Wang and his men. I then asked him to delay as little as possible. He said he wanted to the 6th instant, and I told him that if General Ching asked me to wait I would do so. I then asked Nar Wang to settle with Ching the terms of the compact. After having told him what I thought of the prospects of the Rebellion, how anxious the foreign Governments were for the cessation of hostilities which led to nothing but misery to the inhabitants, how I longed to make the rebels and Imperialists good friends, etc., etc., I took leave, and left Nar Wang and General Ching to settle matters.

"I may here remark that the Imperialists had behaved very well in their negotiations with the rebels. The city of Chanzu had faith strictly kept with it, and the Mandarin camps were full of chiefs who had come over from time to time.

"I had, therefore, not the very remotest idea but that perfect faith would be kept with the Wangs. I expressed to Nar Wang a hope that the negotiations might not be of much length, as I was apprehensive that Moh Wang might hear of it. He replied that his men were sufficient to protect him, and that he did not care.

"On the morning of the 3rd December General Ching came to me. He was in high spirits, and told me that my interview with Nar Wang had been most successful, and he thought there was do doubt of their coming out. He came to me again in the afternoon, and I told him that, after my heavy loss in officers and men on the 27th and 28th November, it could not be looked on as a certainty that I could take the city, as any hitch with the bridge, which was 70 yards long, might cause a repulse, and that therefore I looked on the Futai as bound to aid the negotiations with all his means. I saw the Futai immediately after, and told him he must show mercy to these people, to which he gladly assented. I was the more anxious for this, as I knew the disorders which were sure to arise if we took the city, many Mandarins having been to me to request that the women, etc., might be protected, as they were so numerous.

"The morning of the 4th December, General Ching came to me and told me that Nar Wang had sent out to say that he had arranged with the other Wangs to get Moh Wang on the wall to see our preparations for the attacks which were daily going on, and that they would then throw him down, and have a boat with an escort to convey him to our side. I told General Ching that Moh Wang must be my prisoner, to which Ching, who knew Moh Wang before, gladly assented. I then went to the Futai, who was out. I saw Paon, the Mandarin, who owns most of the property around Soochow, and who is of very high rank; he said he would tell the Futai, and I then told him I had asked what I had power to take, and that he must not refuse. I had not returned to my boat five minutes before General Ching sent me two Frenchmen who had ridden out of Soochow. This was at 4 P.M. They said that an assembly of all the Wangs had taken place at Moh Wang's palace at 11 o'clock A.M., and that, after a great dinner, they had offered up prayers and adjourned to the great hall of reception. They had all put on their crowns and robes of ceremony, and taken their seats on the raised dais. Moh Wang mounted his throne and commenced a long discourse, expatiating on their difficulties, and praising the Cantonese and Kwangzi rebels, saying the others were not trustworthy (it appeared afterwards that Moh Wang had some idea of what was going on, and was anxious to try a *coup d'état* himself). Another Wang then got up, and the altercation became hotter and hotter, till Kong Wang got up and took off his robes. Moh Wang asked him what he was doing. He drew a short dagger and stabbed Moh Wang in the shoulder. Moh Wang called out and fell over the table; the other Wangs seized him and dragged him down from the dais, and a Tiench Wang cut off his head. The chiefs then mounted their horses and rode off to their troops. The head of Moh Wang was afterwards sent to General Ching.

"The Frenchmen said that Moh Wang had been most anxious to see me for several days, that he had asked them to write to me and ask for an interview, he coming to see me in disguise.

"Nar Wang told General Ching afterwards that my letters which I had written to him respecting coming to terms, fell out from his (Moh Wang's) pockets when they seized him, and I found them myself near the raised dais.

"I should have mentioned before that Nar Wang had told General Ching, the night of the 3rd December, that Chung Wang had assembled the chiefs after his defeat on the 29th November, and had proposed to them to vacate Soochow and Nanking, and return to the south. Moh Wang would not accede to it, as he hoped to hold the city, and had all his property there. The other Wangs, knowing of the negotiations, did not also entertain the idea. Another reason for Moh Wang's holding out was that his father and mother were hostages at Nanking with Tien Wang.

"On the morning of the 5th December there was some musketry to be heard in the city, but it soon ceased, and General Ching advanced some of his men to the East Gate, while some of our men went to the North Gate; but I soon withdrew them, as I knew their propensities, and I then went to the Futai and asked him to give the men two months' pay, and let the force push on to Wusieh and Chan-chu-fu.

"He objected, although the troops had had no remuneration for any of the places that had fallen, and had had very hard and continuous fighting. I told him I could not keep them in hand unless he assented, and gave him until 3 o'clock P.M., and after that time I could not remain in command. This was a hard fact, but both officers and men were of the same mind, and I had no option. I then went into the city, and passed down to Nar Wang's house, and there met all the Wangs. I asked them if everything had gone on properly, and if they were content; they said yes, and appeared quite at ease. Their troops were in the streets, and everything appeared orderly. I then went down to Moh Wang's palace, and tried to get his body buried, but the people would not touch it. I then went out to the troops who were under arms, and soon after General Ching came in on the part of the Futai to arrange terms. I referred him to the officers commanding regiments, but they could not agree. Ching then

came to me and begged me to try and get the force to accept one
month's pay. After some demur, I determined on making the
force accept, as night was coming on, and I was afraid of the
troops within making an attack on the Futai, as also on the rebels
in the city.

"I therefore assembled them, and, addressing them, I let them
know that I had succeeded in obtaining one month's pay. The
men made a slight disturbance, which was quickly quelled, and
after one attempt to march down on the Futai, dismissed. I left
a guard on the Futai's boat that night, and, being apprehensive of
further trouble if the troops remained, I marched them back at
8 o'clock A.M. on the 6th December, and, anticipating no further
trouble with the men, I ordered the steamers *Tsatlee* and *Hyson*
round to Wulungchiao, directing my chop to come up to the
Pou-mün, or South Gate. I then went into the city, to Nar
Wang's house, reaching it at 11.30 o'clock A.M. I had heard that
the Wangs had to go out to the Futai at 12 o'clock noon, and
that then the city would be given over. I should mention that
General Ching had told me, on the afternoon of the 5th December,
that the Futai had written to Peking respecting the capture of
Soochow, and stating that he had amnestied the prisoners. At
the Nar Wang's house I met all the Wangs, with their horses
saddled, to leave for the Futai. I took Nar Wang aside, and
asked him if everything was all right. He said 'Yes.' I then
told him I had the intention of going to the Taho Lake to look
for the *Firefly*. He said he was coming down to see me, and
would like me to stop two or three days. I said, unless he
thought there was an absolute necessity, the business I was going
on was too important for me to stop; but that if he thought he
had any reason for wishing me to stay, I would do so. He said
'No,' and I bid him and the other Wangs good-bye, and they
all passed me a few minutes afterwards, with twenty attendants,
going towards the Low-mün, or East Gate, on their way to the
Futai.

"I went down to Moh Wang's palace, and saw General
Ching's men come down to bury Moh Wang's body, according to
my request. I then went on the East Gate, or Low-mün, to
while away the time until the steamers got round to Wulungchiao, intending to go round the wall to the Pou-mün, or South
Gate. Just as we arrived at the gate, I saw a large crowd on the
bank opposite the Futai's boat, and soon afterwards a large force
of Imperialists came into the city and ran off to the right and

left along the wall and into the city, yelling, as they usually do when they enter a vacated stockade, and firing off their muskets in the air. I remonstrated with the Mandarins and soldiers, as their conduct was liable to frighten the rebels, who might retaliate and cause a row. After a few minutes General Ching came in, and I noticed he looked disturbed. I asked him eagerly if the interview was over and had been satisfactory. He said the Wangs had never come to the Futai. I said I had seen them going, and asked him what could have become of them. He said he did not know, but thought they might have run away. I asked him what could have induced them to do so. He said they had sent out to the Futai to ask to keep 20,000 men, and to have half of the city, building a wall inside; that Nar Wang had said before that he wanted only 2500, and that at another time he said he wanted no soldiers, but merely to retire home; that the Futai had objected to his demand, and that he had told him to go to the Tch-mün, and stockade his men outside that gate, and that he supposed Nar Wang had taken alarm and gone off. He said further that Nar Wang had sent to Chung Wang for assistance. I asked him if he thought Nar Wang and the other Wangs had gone back to the rebels. He said no; but they would go back to their own homes and live there. I did not feel very well satisfied, and asked Mr. McCartney, who was by, to go to Nar Wang's house and see if he was there, and to reassure him if he was alarmed at anything. General Ching was anxious I should not go; and as I had no suspicion, I went round the wall with him to the Pou-mün, which we reached at 5 o'clock P.M. I had frequently returned to the question of Nar Wang, but found that both General Ching and my interpreter seemed to evade the questions. When I got to the Pou-mün, I told General Ching I should go no farther, as I felt uncomfortable about Nar Wang, and also heard volleys of musketry in the city, but not of any great amount. I asked General Ching what it was. He said there were some Kwangzi and Canton men who would not shave, and they were driving them out of the city, having left two gates open for their retreat; but they were only frightening them out. General Ching then left, and I asked my interpreter what he thought of the state of affairs. He said that he thought the Imperialists, having got the city, did not care about keeping their agreement. I therefore decided on riding to Nar Wang's house, and seeing him if possible. I rode through the streets with my interpreter, which were full of rebels standing to their arms, and Imperialist soldiers looting. I went to Nar Wang's palace, and found it ransacked. I met Nar Wang's uncle, a second in command, and he begged me to come to his house and protect it. He then withdrew the female household of Nar Wang and accompanied them to his house, where there were some thousand rebels under arms in a barricaded street. It was now dark, and, having seen the state of affairs, I wished much for Nar Wang's uncle to let my interpreter go, taking orders for the steamers to come round and take the Futai prisoner (as he, the interpreter, thought that the Futai had not yet beheaded the Wangs), and also an order to bring up my force. They unfortunately would not let my interpreter go, and I remained with them until 2 o'clock A.M. on the 7th, when I persuaded them to let him go and procure assistance. I had kept several bands from looting the house by my presence. About 3 A.M. one of the men who had gone out with the interpreter returned, and said that a body of Imperialists had seized the interpreter and wounded him. I was now apprehensive of a general massacre, as the man made me understand that the order I had sent had been torn up, and therefore went out to go to the Pou-mün to send by my boat additional orders, and also to look for the interpreter. I found no traces of him, and, proceeding to the Pou-mün, was detained an hour by the Imperialists. It was then 5 A.M., and I determined on proceeding for my guard to the Low-mün, or East Gate, hoping to be able to seize the Futai, and to get back in time to save the house of Nar Wang's uncle.

"I got to the Low-mün at 6 A.M., and sent on my guard to the house. It was, however, too late, it had been ransacked. I then left the city and met General Ching at the gate. I told him what I thought, and then proceeded to the stockade to await the steamers. As I was still ignorant that the Wangs had been beheaded, I thought that they were prisoners, and might still be rescued if the Futai could be secured. When awaiting the steamers, General Ching sent down Major Bailey, one of the officers I had sent him to command his artillery, who told me that General Ching had gone into the city, and sat down and cried. He then, to alleviate his grief, shot down twenty of his men for looting, and sent Major Bailey to tell me he had nothing to do with the matter; that the Futai ordered him to do what he did, and that the Futai had ordered the city to be looted. I asked Major Bailey if the Wangs had been beheaded; he said that he had heard so. He then told me he had Nar Wang's son in the boat, and had brought him to me. The son came up, and, pointing to the other side, said that his father and the Wangs had been beheaded there. I went over and found six bodies, and recognised Nar Wang's head. The hands and bodies were gashed in a frightful way, and cut down the middle. Nar Wang's body was partially buried. I took Nar Wang's head, and just then the steamers were seen coming up. The Futai, however, had received some warning, and left for Soochow by some other route. I then went to his boat, and left him a note in English informing him of what my intention had been, and also my opinion of his treachery. I regret to say that —— did not think fit to have this translated to him.

" The two steamers then left for Quinsan, and one was sent down with Prince F. de Wittgenstein to inform the General of the state of affairs ; this officer had been with the force nearly a month, and had been informed in detail by me of the whole that had passed as above related.

" On the 8th December the Futai sent —— to persuade me that he could not have done otherwise, and I blush to think that he could have got an Englishman to undertake a mission of such a nature.

" C. G. GORDON,

" Major Commanding.

" December 12th, 1863.

" P.S.—To continue. On the 8th December I started with an escort and a steamer to General Ching's stockade to obtain Nar Wang's body, and some of his family who had been retained prisoners in General Ching's stockade. These I obtained, and also the body.

" General Brown arrived on the afternoon of the 9th, and took the protection of the force under his command. I had already spoken to the officers and got them to agree to leave the solution to the British General. The disgust and abhorrence felt by all of them was and is so great, as to lead me to fear their going over en masse to the rebels ; but I have shown them that the sin would then be visited on the Chinese people, and not on the culprits who committed it. The rebels have no government at all, while the Imperialists can lay claim to some.

" C. G. GORDON."

It will be observed that Gordon, according to his wont,

6

omits all mention of the perilous position in which he was placed while in the hands of the Tai-pings during the night he passed at Nar Wang's palace.

This is what Gordon wrote home from Quinsan a fortnight after the slaughter of the chiefs :—

"You will be glad to hear we are all quietly back at Quinsan —not likely to move again for a very long time, if, in fact, we ever do.   I have not time to give you any details of our fight at the East Gate, or of the treachery at Soochow, and hope you will see the same in the papers.   I have Nar Wang's son.   He is a very sharp young fellow, and very lively—about eighteen years old.   His poor father was a very good Wang, and very far superior to any of the Imperialists I have met.   You can have little idea of the regret I have, for several reasons, on account of the last affair.   In the first place, if faith had been kept, there would have been no more fighting, as every town would have given in ; in the next, we had accomplished the suppression of the Rebellion with very little loss of life to rebels or Imperialists, and not much injury to the inhabitants, as our quick movements prevented the rebels devastating the neighbour- ing villages ; in the next, if I had not seen Nar Wang, he would not have come over ; and, in the next, I fear that all my work has been thrown away.   My only consolation is that everything is for the best.   It is quite incomprehensible to me the reason which actuated the Futai ; he must have known from his previous acquaintance with me of what a row would be pro- duced, and of what a personal risk he ran, for, when it happened, my troops were not two hours' march from him.   I have sent H—— the *Friend of China*, which is somewhat abusive, and therefore you had better not see it, as well as the *North China Herald*. . . . I have just heard from Shanghai that the mer- chants, Chinese and foreign, are very irate with the Futai, and will go a great length to get him released."

Soon after, Gordon arrived at headquarters with his force. General Brown visited him, and learnt what had happened at Soochow.   The following is the account the General forwarded to Sir Frederick Bruce and Lord de Grey of this visit, and one he paid later to Li-Hung-Chang :—

"The circumstances attending and preceding the occupation

of Soochow by the Imperialists are so calculated to produce an impression on public opinion unfavourable to the line of policy adopted by Her Majesty's Government in China, that I trust I need not apologise for entreating your most earnest consideration of the whole subject.

"I received the first intimation of events passing in Soochow, by a hurried note from Major Gordon, which reached me during the forenoon of the 8th instant; a second note, which, although written previously, did not reach me until a later period, produced the impression that affairs were proceeding favourably, consequently I was so far from apprehending the gravity of the crisis, that I decided to carry out my intention of proceeding to Hong-Kong by the mail steamer, and was on board when Prince Wittgenstein, despatched by Major Gordon in the steamer *Tsatlee*, brought a more complete and detailed narrative of events.

"The additional information thus received determined me to accede to the urgent entreaties of Major Gordon, of which the Prince was the bearer, and to proceed to Quinsan, the headquarters of Major Gordon's force, at once. I arrived at Quinsan about 3 o'clock P.M. the following day, and immediately received from Major Gordon a report which differed but slightly from the more carefully compiled narrative enclosed. Major Gordon has been unable to express in writing the intense indignation and disgust with which the infamous and dastardly conduct of the Futai had inspired him.

"You will perceive by Major Gordon's narrative that he was able to withdraw his force from before Soochow to Quinsan only under the formal promise from the Futai of one month's pay to the officers and soldiers, and that it required all his influence to prevail on them to accept these terms. The subsequent treachery of the Imperial authorities had, however, destroyed the confidence of all ranks; their cruelties had turned the sympathies of Europeans in favour of the rebels, and I found it necessary, in order to restore discipline, and to avert a perhaps total defection of the force, to take Major Gordon and his force formally under my command.

"This move on my part, I am happy to inform your Excellency, had the best effect; all ranks now express their perfect satisfaction and reliance, and every symptom of hesitation has disappeared from the force under Major Gordon's command.

"I considered it expedient to have an interview with the

Futai, with the view of hearing any explanatory statement he
might have to offer, and to communicate to him my views on
recent events, and explain the future relations between himself
and Major Gordon.

"I therefore despatched the interpreter to the Consulate
(Mr. Mayers), accompanied by two of my officers, to convey to
him my desire for an interview.

"Having thus prepared the way, I proceeded the following
day to Soochow, but was met at Ching's stockade by the Futai,
who had come out from the city to meet me.

"I speedily ascertained that, though the Futai was prepared
to take on himself the whole responsibility of the murder of
the Wangs, and sacking of the city, and fully to exonerate
Major Gordon from all blame, he was either unable or unwilling
to offer any exculpation or explanation of his conduct, and it
only remained for me to express my opinion and future intentions.

"This I did in as few words as possible. I expressed the
indignation and grief with which the English people, together
with all the civilised nations of the world, would regard his
cruelty and perfidy. I exposed to him my views on the im-
policy of a fruitless severity which paralysed his friends, and
drove the rebels to desperation, at the time when we had good
reason to believe they were prepared to capitulate and return to
their homes in peace. I then informed him that I should insist
on the promised reward of one month's pay; that I deemed it
my duty to refer the whole matter to our Minister at Peking; and
that, pending such reference, Major Gordon had received instructions from me to suspend all active aid to the Imperialist
cause, further than protecting Soochow, knowing its importance
to the safety of Shanghai; and warning the rebels to abstain
from attacking his position. I concluded by expressing my un-
hesitating conviction that after what had occurred my Government
would withdraw all assistance hitherto afforded to the Imperial
cause, recall Major Gordon and all English subjects serving under
him, and disband the Anglo-Chinese force."

For two months, pending the inquiry instituted on his
demand at Peking, Gordon remained in quarters. For many
reasons his position was endangered by the inactivity of his
troops. Governor Li in his despatches, while making highly
honourable mention of Gordon's services, had taken to himself

the credit which attached to the fall of Soochow. The truth was that the Commander of the Ever-Victorious Army, taking post after post with his own troops, had garrisoned them as he took them with Imperialist forces in Li's command, and that to him was due all the strategy and all the fighting which led to the surrender. There yet remained some half-dozen cities in the rebel occupation. But with the fall of Soochow the backbone of the Rebellion was broken ; and as the whole of the guns and munition which were captured in that siege were handed over to General Ching and put under the command of Major Bailey, one of Gordon's old officers, the Imperialists may have felt themselves now competent to reduce the remaining strongholds without assistance. This may have emboldened them to take up the independent position they assumed with regard to the causes of Gordon's wrath and the pertinence of Gordon's demand.

Matters connected with the execution of the chiefs were in the hands of Major-General Brown at Shanghai, and Sir Frederick Bruce at Peking ; but before they could take cognisance of the affair, Li had sent his despatches to Peking, and had received the congratulations of Prince Kung, together with the honour of the Yellow Jacket, which carries with it the highest military grade of the empire. This was on the 14th of December 1863. Then an Imperial decree was issued, stating that Gordon, a Tsung-Ping (a Brigadier-General) of the province of Kiang-su, in command of Li's auxiliary force, had displayed thorough strategy and skill, and put forth most distinguished exertions, and ordaining that a medal of distinction of the highest class be conferred upon him ; and further, that he receive a donation of 10,000 taels in token of the Imperial approbation. A private decree, issued on the same day, enjoins the Governor to communicate this document to Gordon, and to provide and send him the donation. It also signifies that foreign nations already possess orders of merit under the name of Stars, and that the decoration of the first class which is conferred on Gordon be arranged in accordance with their system.

This gift, with many other presents, was sent to Gordon by the Governor, together with extra pay for his troops, and sums of money for his wounded. The latter Gordon received ; the former he indignantly refused. When the treasure-bearers entered his presence, with bowls of bullion on their heads—like a train from the *Arabian Nights*—he flogged them from the chamber with his " magic wand." The consternation was extraordinary. To refuse the Imperial treasure—to batoon the Imperial envoys! If the sun had started from his sphere they would have been less frightened and less amazed. This is the answer Gordon returned to the Imperial decrees :—

"Major Gordon receives the approbation of his Majesty the Emperor with every gratification, but regrets most sincerely that, owing to the circumstances which occurred since the capture of Soochow, he is unable to receive any mark of his Majesty the Emperor's recognition, and therefore respectfully begs his Majesty to receive his thanks for his intended kindness, and to allow him to decline the same."

On writing home a little later, Gordon thus refers to the honours which the Chinese Government desired to confer on him :—

"To tell you truly, I do not want anything, either money or honours, from either the Chinese Government or our own. As for the honours, I do not value them at all, and never did. I know that I am doing a great deal of good, and, liking my profession, do not mind going on with the work under the circumstances which I have related in my letter to ——. I should have refused the 10,000 taels even if everything had gone well, and there had been no trouble at Soochow. I am fully aware of the false step I took in writing my account of the Soochow transactions to the paper—not that anyone has told me so—but must say that allowances must be made for the disgust I felt. I know you feel for my position, which is no easy one, and am sure you are glad of my success. The rebels are a ruthless lot. Chung Wang beheaded 2000 unfortunates, who ran to him from Soochow, after the execution of the Wangs by the Futai. This was at Wusieh. I have read the Futai a lesson he will not forget."

It was not difficult for Governor Li to make an impression on the Peking Government, nor was it unnatural that the Emperor, in a new decree which was to be read by his people, should, in announcing the recent victories, give the pre-eminence to his own army and his own Commander. In this document he set forth and acknowledged the services of the various high officers concerned.   Li-Hung-Chang, he says, reports that the army under his command has captured the city of Soochow ; that, acting under his orders, it has taken in succession the lines of rebel works outside the four gates of the city, and struck terror into the enemy ; that General Ching has attacked the different gates of the city incessantly, and that Gordon has established himself close to the city walls, and opened a cannonade against them.

All this may be taken as a sample of Chinese history. Its truthfulness will appear the more questionable when it is mentioned that Governor Li, while in person he was achieving all these great results before Soochow, was actually living at Shanghai, from which city he hardly ever stirred. Those who wished to know the truth, or those who wished to falsify it, held long newspaper discussions. The one set wrote history for the Chinese, the other, history for the world at large.

Defences of Li's conduct in the treatment of the Wangs were not wanting. These state that the Wangs were insolent and threatening, that the terms they proposed were such as would have imperilled the Imperialist cause, and that the Governor, as a patriot and a statesman, had nothing to do but put them to the sword. Whatever the truth of these statements of his, there is something to be said for his policy of ending the Rebellion by cutting off its chiefs. But nothing can be advanced in palliation of his behaviour in making use of Gordon as a negotiator between himself and the men he had made up his mind to massacre.

CHAPTER VII

THE massacre at Soochow had placed Gordon in a position of unparalleled difficulty. To continue the campaign he had so brilliantly carried on, would be to endorse the conduct of his colleague; while to leave the Rebellion to its fate, would be to undo all that had been done. Already his own force was showing signs of mutiny at the sudden suspension of hostilities, and sixteen of his officers had to be dismissed; while the rebel bands were fast gaining ground to the west of the fallen city. He knew that to waver was to fail; that on his action depended the lives of millions of innocent people. He therefore ignored the world's opinion, put aside his own feelings, and entered on terms of cordiality with Li-Hung-Chang once more.

The slaughter of the Wangs, unmerciful as it was and unnecessary, was an act not contrary to Chinese military law. As the excitement died away, and Gordon came to hear the Futai's explanation of what had transpired at the moment of their execution, he was so far softened by it as to reconsider his position, and to question whether he was justified in abandoning the cause of humanity. So earnest was his desire to rid China of its cruel oppressors, and to relieve the suffering millions, that he felt the more what a calamity it would prove if the work so far achieved were thrown away. His force, disciplined in the main and attached to him, was above all things mercenary and ready to desert for better pay; and he was aware that this period of inactivity was demoralising the men yet further; and that, if he dissolved his little army, many would go over to the other side.

Mr. Hart, an Englishman of high standing, who was in China at the time, penetrated Gordon's views, and accurately described them. He wrote:—

"The destiny of China is, at the present moment, in the hands of Gordon more than of any other man, and if he be encouraged to act vigorously, the knotty question of Tai-pingdom *versus* 'union in the cause of law and order' will be solved before the end of May, and quiet will at length be restored to this unfortunate and sorely-tried country.

"Personally, Gordon's wish is to leave the force as soon as he can. Now that Soochow has fallen, there is nothing more that he can do, whether to add to his own reputation or to retrieve that of British officers generally, tarnished by Holland's defeat at Taitsan. He has little or nothing personally to gain from future successes; and as he has himself to lead in all critical moments, and is constantly exposed to danger, he has before him the not very improbable contingency of being hit sooner or later. But he lays aside his personal feelings; and seeing well that, if he were now to leave the force, it would in all probability go at once to the rebels, or cause some other disaster, he consents to remain with it for a time."

To make his way clear, Gordon paid a visit to Li-Hung-Chang at Soochow. There an arrangement was entered into, that the Futai should issue a proclamation exonerating him from all participation in the massacre. His reasons for taking this step are fully explained in the following letter written to Sir Frederick Bruce after the Soochow conference :—

"Soochow, *February 6th*, 1864.

"MY DEAR SIR FREDERICK BRUCE,—In consequence of the danger which will arise by my inaction (with the force any longer in a state of uncertainty), I have arranged with the Futai to issue a proclamation (which he will send to you), clearing me of any participation in the late execution of the Wangs, and have determined to act immediately.

"The reasons which actuate me are as follows :—I know of a certainty that Burgevine meditates a return to the rebels; that there are upwards of 300 Europeans ready to join them, of no character; and that the Futai will not accept another British officer if I leave the service; and therefore the Government may have some foreigner put in, or else the force put under men of Ward's and Burgevine's stamp, of whose action at times we should never feel certain.

"I am aware that I am open to very grave censure for the

course I am about to pursue; but in the absence of advice, and knowing as I do that the Peking authorities will support the Futai in what he has done, I have made up my mind to run the risk.   If I followed my own desire, I should leave now, as I have escaped unscathed, and been wonderfully successful.   But the rabble called the Quinsan force is a dangerous body, and it will be my duty to see that it is dissolved as quietly as possible, and that while in course of dissolution it should serve to benefit the Imperial Government.

" I do not apprehend the Rebellion will last six months longer if I take the field.   It may take six years if I leave, and the Government does not support the Imperialists.   I propose to cut through the heart of the Rebellion, and to divide it into two parts, by the capture of Yesing and Liyang.

" If the course I am about to pursue meets your approbation, I shall be glad to hear; but if not, shall expect to be well rebuked. However, I know that I am not actuated by personal considerations, but merely as I think will be most conducive to the interests of our Government.

" The Futai does not want the force to move against Nanking, I imagine, as Tseng Kwo-fan has the wish to capture it himself.

" The Futai, if he is to be believed, has some extenuating circumstances in his favour for his action, and although I feel deeply on the subject, I think that we can scarcely expect the same discernment that we should from a European Governor.

" This letter will relieve you from any responsibility on this matter ; and, thanking you very much for your kind letter, which I will answer shortly,—I am, etc.

"C. G. GORDON.

"*P.S.*—If you would let the matter drop, and make me responsible for my action in the matter, I think it would be more conducive to our good relations with the Peking Government than pressing them to punish or degrade the Futai."

The proclamation referred to was issued on February 14th. In it Li not only cleared Gordon of all blame, but stated his own motives for the course he had pursued.

Prince Kung and his Government could not be made to see that Li had acted otherwise than in the interests of his country. It was not to be expected, either, that at the dictation of foreigners Kung would recommend the dismissal of a high Chinese official.

Nevertheless, Sir Frederick Bruce obtained a promise from the Chinese Government, that, when employing a foreign officer, they should strictly observe the rules of warfare as practised among foreign nations. This being done, he gave his approval and support to Gordon on his resuming operations, and wrote him as follows :—

"It would be a serious calamity and addition to our embarrassments in China, were you compelled to leave your work incomplete, and were a sudden dissolution or dispersion of the Chinese force to lead to the recurrence of that state of danger and anxiety from which, during the last two years, Shanghai has suffered. I approve of your not awaiting the result of the inquiry into the Futai's proceedings at Soochow, provided you take care that your efforts in favour of humanity are not in future defeated by Chinese authorities."

On the 19th February 1864, Gordon took the field once more. There was yet much work to be done, for the western half of the rebel country was still in the hands of the Tai-pings, and defended by hordes of broken and desperate men.

Far greater difficulties attended him than he had hitherto experienced. He was going into the enemy's country, with none of the resources which had been previously at his command. His easy communication with Shanghai had secured him an abundance of munitions and stores; supplies could now no longer be had from that quarter; and his force had to carry with them enough for their consumption in the field. With this extra encumbrance, he started from Quinsan in snow and hail. He marched to Wusieh; but the city was in so ruinous a state that no quarters could be found, and, at the recommendation of his guide, he led his men to a small village at the foot of a hill. Here he was met by an old woman, who came out from a large pagoda, and told him that, some two months before, four "barbarians" like themselves had been killed at the foot of the pagoda. She led the way to a paved yard, and there Gordon witnessed a sight as horrible as that of the headless chiefs at Soochow. In a grave—the way to which was strewn with fragments of burnt bones, a pen-knife, and rags and scraps of clothing—were four charred skeletons; and Gordon saw that the murder of the chiefs had been avenged. A mystery had for some time hung about the fate of an Imperialist steamer, the *Firefly*, officered by four

Europeans. These men, it now turned out, had fallen into the hands of Chung Wang, the Faithful King, who, it will be remembered, had played a considerable part in those consultations which led to the fall of Soochow. Before the surrender he had escaped with his army to Nanking; on his way to the city he had learned the fate of his brother chiefs, and had captured the four Europeans, tortured and burned them to death, and left their remains near the pagoda where they were now found. It was the first instance that came to light of any ill-treatment of foreigners by the rebels, and the murder may be fairly attributed to Li-Hung-Chang's treatment of the Wangs. This at least was the common opinion; and it was generally regretted that Gordon should again have taken the field in conjunction with the Futai, inasmuch as the discovery of the murdered men afforded fair ground for inferring that he was held responsible by the Tai-pings for the massacre at Soochow.

It was a melancholy march from Wusieh to Yesing. The country had been depopulated by the rebels, and the few poor wretches who still haunted its fields were dying of starvation. Yesing was a small city, about two miles in circumference, surrounded by walls and a broad, but not very formidable, ditch. A reconnoitring party which had been sent out, however, was soon driven away by an accurate fire from the ramparts. Gordon therefore determined to cross the lake on the eastern side, where the *Hyson* was expected, seize its outworks, and so cut the communications between the city and Liyang. His first step was to capture an outlying village, which, as he said, was a piteous sight to behold. Robbed by the Tai-pings of their last means of subsistence, the people had been brought to feed on the bodies of their dead. It is not surprising that, as soon as the East Gate was taken, the mass of the population instantly quitted the city, and that the rebels made no effectual resistance. A few shells were thrown in by the troops as they advanced to the assault, and many of the garrison took to their heels and ran. They fell back into some forts outside the South Gate, where they were reinforced by a contingent from Liyang. This enabled them to take the field in considerable force, and there was some sharp skirmishing outside the walls. Gordon, however, dealt with the newcomers very summarily indeed. Amusing them with a distant fire of musketry in front, he flung some 1500 men—round some neighbouring hills—upon them in the rear. The rebels fled, and were pursued with great slaughter. During the night many escaped from Yesing, which surrendered next day, those who remained shaving their heads in token of submission.

Yesing capitulated on the 1st of March—eleven days after Gordon had left Quinsan, ten of them spent on the road. A few hours after, news came in that 3000 Tai-pings in garrison at Tajowka, a town on the Taho Lake, were desirous of coming over to the Imperialists; but that the rebel captain, with 1000 desperadoes of his own temper, had sworn to fight it to the last. Gordon at once proceeded to Tajowka. There, on the 3rd of March, he completely quelled the bolder spirits among the garrison; and he brought the willing 2000 back with him to Yesing.

On March 5th he advanced against Liyang, with a repetition of the difficulties that constantly beset him in the command of troops with no heart in the cause but the heart to plunder. When he absolutely forbade his men to enter Yesing, they showed symptoms of insubordination, which had to be repressed by picking a man out and shooting him on parade. Of course the starving villagers were allowed to enter the city and to take out rice for food. At Liyang the rebels were disheartened, and they yielded almost without a protest. The commandant had intended to defend the place. On the approach of the attacking force he sallied forth to meet them with part of his army, but the others shut the gates upon him, and compelled him to surrender. Bearing in mind the disasters and confusion attendant on the sacking of Soochow, Gordon sternly refused to allow the Mandarin troops to enter the city. Posting his own guards at the gate, to prevent bloodshed and pillage, he now pursued his march northward towards Kintang. The tidings of his approach struck terror into the garrison, and it instantly prepared to surrender. Suddenly, however, it was largely reinforced from Chan-chu-fu, so that Gordon had to endure a repulse. The garrison having expressed its willingness to surrender, would have done so had the Imperialists performed their task of keeping Chan-chu-fu in check, as they had undertaken to do, while Gordon attacked Kintang; now Kintang, which would have fallen without a blow, was held by the most desperate of the rebels—men brave, but cruel beyond anything ever recorded by their opponents.

Gordon brought his forces to within 1200 yards of the walls. He fixed on the north-east angle as the best point of attack, and under cover of night he stationed near it a flotilla of heavy boats with artillery. Everything was ready, when despatches came in from Governor Li with disastrous news. Some 7000 rebels,

under Chung Wang's son, had left Chan-chu-fu, and had turned
the flank of the Imperialists; they were threatening Wusieh;
they had captured Fushan; and they were now besieging Chanzu,
only thirty miles from the headquarters and depôt of the Ever-
Victorious Army.

Startling as this news was, Gordon felt that to abandon the
attack of Kintang would be to afford great encouragement to the
rebels. He accordingly opened fire, and in three hours made a
breach in the walls; but whenever his stormers appeared, the
Tai-pings crowded to the breach, swarmed on the ramparts, and
hurled down every sort of missile. This so intimidated the crews
of Gordon's gunboats that they could not be got to advance,
and the stormers were driven back. The troops were therefore
withdrawn and re-formed. The artillery cleared the breach at
once, but a second storming party was repulsed, and Major
Kirkham was severely wounded. Gordon, who himself led the
assaults, was shot through the leg. One of his body-guard cried
out that the Commander was wounded; but Gordon silenced
him, and stood giving orders till he nearly fainted from loss of
blood. Still he would not retire, and Andrew Moffitt, principal
Medical Officer to the force, a brilliant surgeon and a loyal friend,
came out and carried him by main force into his boat. Even
then Gordon struggled to get away. The stormers sustained
heavy losses. Major Brown,[1] Gordon's aide-de-camp, headed a
third assault, and carried his Commander's flag into the breach;
but the attack failed, and he too was wounded.

Gordon, having no fresh regiments on hand with which to
make another effort, withdrew without further loss, the troops
resuming their former positions. It was found that 100 of the
assailants were killed and wounded, among them were 15
officers, two of whom, Major Taite and Captain Banning, lost
their lives.

When the news of Gordon's wound—the first and only one
he got—was known, much anxiety was naturally evinced as to
what would be its effect on the campaign. The Emperor, it
is said, was sadly grieved. He at once issued the following
proclamation :—

" Li-Hung-Chang reports that General Gordon some time
since started from Liyang to attack Kintang. He carried with
him mortars to breach the walls. At the attack he was wounded

[1] Son of General Brown, commanding H.M. forces in China.

in the leg; Li has therefore recommended him to remain at rest. Such is the despatch. Now, Gordon being excessively brave and fearless, was wounded in consequence. We are on this account deeply moved with grief and admiration. On the other hand, we are informed that the wound is not serious. We order Li-Hung-Chang to visit Gordon, and inquire for him daily, so as to keep his mind at rest, requesting him to wait until he shall be perfectly restored to health and strength. Respect this!"

Li's instructions to keep Gordon's mind at rest were more easily issued than carried out. Even Dr. Moffitt's influence was of no avail; and before long Gordon returned with his men to Liyang. Here more bad news awaited him. The Faithful King himself had occupied Fushan, his first conquest. He was bodily disabled by his wound, but on hearing this he started forthwith for Wusieh. Leaving the greater portion of his force in garrison behind him under General Li-Adong, he proceeded with his light artillery and a regiment only 400 strong, together with 600 Liyang men, all Tai-pings only a few days before, who had willingly enlisted to take part against their former masters. At this point, Dr. Wilson remarks, and Colonel Chesney echoes him, "One scarcely knows here whether most to admire the pluck or to wonder at the confidence of the wounded Commander!"

On reaching Wusieh, Gordon found despatches of a more promising kind. The enemy had been driven back from that place; Chanzu continued to hold out, though Fushan had been retaken; and the Imperialists still held the stockades before Chan-chu-fu. Advancing at once about ten miles to the south-west, he drove the rebels before him, and cut off the retreat of Chung Wang's son, who had already been defeated at Chanzu. In spite of his wound and weakness he still pushed on, through a district where not only had the wretched inhabitants been plundered and butchered, but their villages burned by their rapacious rulers. After driving the rebel force away from three of these burning villages, he halted for the night. A most anxious night it was, for until dawn the enemy was firing on his sentries, and trying hard to ride through the lines of his little force. In the morning Gordon drove the rebels out of a village in front of his position; but he had to retire in the face of a large force which came down on his boats. Of this body, however, he managed to cut off and separate a part from the rest, and these were bayoneted, while the others were driven, under fire of a howitzer, across a bridge. Reaching a range of hills near Chan-chu, he thrust the rebels over them before him, and concentrated his troops to operate against the left of the rebel line. The rapidity of these movements—which dealt with a vast expanse of country strewn with the dead and the dying—was extraordinary.

"A terrible picture is drawn of the desolation of the country, and the misery of the inhabitants," wrote one who was not far from the scene. "Hundreds of gaunt, starving wretches, with hardly any other means of sustenance than human flesh, and the few scraps of refuse they can pick up from the Imperialist troops, wander hopelessly about, more dead than alive, amid the ruins of their villages and of the suburbs. The living are too weak to bury the dead, and the latter lie about on the ground in every stage of decomposition, tainting the air and horrifying the beholder." A correspondent, writing from the camp, says : " It is horrible to relate ; it is horrible to witness. To read that people are eating human flesh is one thing ; to see the bodies from which the flesh has been cut is another. No one can eat a meal here without a certain degree of loathing. The poor wretches have a wolfish look that is indescribable, and they haunt one's boat in shoals in the hope of getting some scraps of food. Their lamentations and moans completely take away any appetite which the horrors one has witnessed may have left one. I ought to be tolerably callous by this time, but no one could witness unmoved such scenes as these. The rebels have evidently swept up everything edible, and left the unfortunate inhabitants to die."

Gordon took advantage of the water system, which was good and complete, to command from his boat. In her he lay disabled, accompanied by the flotilla which held his artillery. The Tai-pings, who had issued out of Chan-chu-fu, had taken a bend towards the shore of the Yangtze, and had resolved on getting possession of Quinsan. The centre of this movement was at Waissu. Gordon, alive to the advantage of sometimes dividing his forces, advanced by water on that place with his artillery, while he sent Colonels Howard and Rhode by land, with orders to incline to the right before reaching the rebel stockades, and there to join his boats. But new troubles were in store for him. The infantry, on the 31st of March, stumbled on the Tai-pings' camp, which was strongly stockaded and entrenched. The officers committed an unfortunate mistake in the distribution of their little force by separating it ; the consequence was that the Tai-pings, who had a large body of cavalry in ambush, came forth from their hiding-places in thousands, and struck panic among the men. The newly-raised Liyang regiment fled, together with the 4th, which was the best regiment of the Ever-Victorious Army. The greatest confusion prevailed ; 400 soldiers were either killed or taken prisoners ; 3 captains were killed or captured, and afterwards decapitated or subjected to mutilation.

When Gordon reached the enemy's position with his artillery, he found himself unsupported and in great danger, inasmuch as, when the enemy came out to the attack, owing to the steepness of the banks, he was unable to fire upon them. Nothing was left him but retreat upon his own encampment. Here everything was in the utmost disorder, the enemy having pursued his land forces up to his very tents. This calamitous affair incensed him greatly against the surviving officers, for not having kept proper reserves, and for neglecting to look to their flanks. To these mistakes they owed their defeat by a mere rabble, armed with spears and knives.

These events entailed some loss of time. Gordon had once more to re-organise his force. He did so by withdrawing to Si-yang-chow, about thirteen miles to the south-west. He then ordered up his 3rd Regiment ; and, having spent some days in working his demoralised troops into discipline and order, he encamped once more near Waissu, where he was joined by Li-Hung-Chang, who had come from Soochow with some 6000 Imperials.

Elsewhere the Imperialist forces had meanwhile being doing good service. General Ching had been operating to the south, and Tso, with the Franco-Chinese, assisted by Colonel Bailey, whom Gordon had given him for artillery instruction, had been engaged in investing Hangchow. In storming Ka-shing-fu, Ching had killed two of the chiefs, but was himself wounded in the head by a bullet, from the effects of which he died. The Franco-Chinese, under D'Aiguibelle, had made an attack on Hangchow, in combination with Tso's Imperialists, and, after some repulses, due to a bad choice of points of attack, had succeeded in capturing the city. After this the Tai-pings evacuated place after place, and finally fell back on the south-west corner of the Taho Lake, which was thus almost entirely clear of them. Many took refuge in the mountains, whither the Imperialists did not care to follow them, knowing that in those sterile regions starvation would be their certain end.

Gordon was keenly affected by the death of General Ching,

7

and shed tears when it was announced to him.   As we have seen, the relations existing between the two Commanders were not of the cordial description which characterises those of men of the same nationality.   Ching had his own part to play before his own Government; and, taking a liberal view of his conduct, much that he did to promote his own glory when he had the opportunity must be overlooked in consideration of his many high qualities.   When Gordon had successfully carried out assaults and taken stockades and fortified towns, Ching was ready at all times to garrison them with his troops, and to hold them while Gordon pressed on with his artillery and disciplined troops to make new conquests.   General Ching was a man of undaunted courage and of sound judgment in all matters relating to the conflict in which he was engaged.   He did not die immediately from the effect of his wound ; indeed, for a time he was restored to consciousness, and his mind grew perfectly clear.   According to Li-Hung-Chang, he passed this interval in earnest thoughts of what was yet to happen, though fully convinced that his death was near at hand.   Addressing his colleague, he said that, although the rebels had been defeated, their strength was still not to be despised, and he begged him to order the officers to be careful in battle.   He remarked that brave men were not easily found, and he bitterly regretted his own fate, by which he was prevented from doing his duty to his country.   Later, while gradually sinking, he called his servant, and ordered him to bring the Yellow Jacket presented to him by the Emperor, and to assist him on with it.   He then bowed his head towards the Imperial Palace.   His last act was to send the Superintendent of the Camp to his colleague Li, with a message entreating him to follow out his design and exterminate the rebels wherever he found them.

From Li's record of him, it appears that General Ching, who, having been formerly among the rebels, knew their mode of thought, had strongly urged the execution of the chiefs at Soochow.   " Cut off the heads of their leaders," he said, " and their myriads of followers will instantly subside into insignificance. You will thus secure the tranquillity of the city.   Their crimes," he said, " have been outrageous ; their punishment should be proportionately severe."   On this same authority it is stated that so highly did Gordon value General Ching, that he begged Governor Li to give him the dead captain's battle-flags, that he might bear them to his own country, and thus preserve the memory of one he loved so well. Gordon was always unwilling to converse on the past; and when a near relative of his brought him Ching's portrait, he would not look at it, but turned away in great agitation.

By the 6th of April Gordon had nearly recovered from his wound, and had brought his augmented force to bear on Waissu, taking up his position on the south-east. The Imperialist troops were well disposed on the south-west. To the north-west was Kongyin, now in the hands of the Imperialists, and on the Yangtze river, to the north, were the Imperialist fleets. Further, all the bridges past Kongyin had been broken, but in such a fashion that the rebels still imagined that the road was open for retreat. Gordon, advancing with great caution upon Waissu, found it surrounded by strong stockades and breastworks. His first step was to open fire, by way of feint, from his 24-pounder howitzers, while he moved his 4th Regiment and two mounted guns to the north, which was really the weakest side of the city. The Tai-pings were thus taken by surprise, fully believing that the direction from which the howitzers were fired was to be the only point of attack. The result of this manœuvre was that the stockades on the north were quickly taken, and the rebels, for their own safety, instantly vacated the place. They retreated as best they could into the country, where Li, now engaged in active operations, drove them towards the broken bridges. Next day Gordon took up the pursuit. Then the villagers came forth, armed with rude weapons of every kind. Their rice had been plundered, and their cottages had been burned, and they attacked the Tai-pings with the utmost fury, and slaughtered them without mercy. The town was full of stolen rice. But they had the satisfaction of knowing that two of the chief rebel Wangs had been caught and put to death.

Though these successes dealt almost a final blow to the Rebellion, there was still much to be done against forces so large. Only, indeed, by superior strategy was their complete destruction possible even at this period. The next place of attack was to be Chan-chu-fu, which the Imperialists had been beseiging for a considerable time without making any impression on it; indeed, it was thought the troops were willing to delay its capture, on the ground that with its fall the Rebellion would collapse and their services be brought to a close. Their sentiments throughout the campaign were those of mercenaries. So slow, in fact, were the military Mandarins in their operations against the place

where they had been quartered three months, that Li was fain to
threaten them with degradation.

When Gordon reached Chan-chu-fu with his 3000 disciplined
troops, he impressed upon Li the importance of wholly investing
the city. It held a large force, he urged, of the most desperate
among the rebel band ; and if these escaped, they would spread
devastation over the neighbouring districts, and develop into new
centres of revolt. But the Imperialist troops were still unwilling
to end the campaign in too great a hurry. This was shown in an
unmistakable manner at midnight on the 25th of April. There
is no way of explaining what then happened, except on the
supposition that a deep and preconcerted scheme was laid to put
an end to Gordon, who, as they knew, would take the city by a
coup de main. He and his artillery officer, Major Tapp, were
superintending the construction of a battery. The work was
being done by a party of Imperialists, supported by a strong
picket on both sides, and by a covering party in the rear. The
work was nearly completed, when the picket on the left fired into
the battery, and on this the covering party also fired into it—an
act which was followed by a second volley from the left. This
roused the Tai-pings, who in their turn directed their guns on the
same point, so that those who were engaged at the battery were
in the centre of a fire from the enemy in front and from their
own troops in flank and rear. Many of the sappers were killed
and wounded. Major Tapp received a ball in the stomach and
died in a few minutes. Gordon escaped unhurt, and proved anew
that his was a charmed life.

The loss of such a man as Major Tapp, at this pass, was a
calamity equal almost to the loss of a battle. He was a singularly
energetic and courageous man, and his influence over the force
was greater than that of any other officer.

The habitual savagery of the Tai-pings was manifested in the
preliminary fighting. Some of the soldiers who wanted to quit
the city had escaped to the walls ; they were retaken, and
beheaded on the ramparts as an example to others who might have
it in their minds to desert. Li-Hung-Chang, it is to be noted,
was most eager to distinguish himself, and to take Chan-chu-fu
for himself with his own troops. He accordingly ordered Colonel
Bailey, in command of the artillery under Ching, to open fire and
breach the wall between the South and West Gates, while
Gordon's artillery played upon the town. He then made the
assault alone, and was repulsed with great loss. The next day,

Li, finding that Gordon had completed his batteries at the south-east angle of the wall, agreed that they should open fire. He also arranged that a body of Imperialists should join the Ever-Victorious Army in the assault. But when Gordon went forward to the attack, the Imperialists were wanting. The rebels manned the walls in great numbers, led by Hu Wang, or " Cock Eye," as he was called, in person ; the resistance was desperate, and the burden fell on Gordon's men. Ten or twelve officers succeeded in mounting the breach, but the rebels outnumbered them, and the force had to be recalled. Li, deeply disappointed with the issue of his manœuvre, sent round to Gordon, entreating him to renew the assault. This was done, and a combined movement was made at the two points of the breached wall. But the Tai-pings were desperate, and set no value on their lives. The artillery played on them with shell and canister, but no sooner was one party blown away than another took its place. Colonels Cawte, Howard, and Chapman, Captain Winstanley, and other officers, reached the crest of the breach ; but the men hung back, and the retreat was sounded. The loss of officers was very great ; 19 were wounded, while Colonel Morton, Captains Rhode, Hammond, Donald, and Smith, together with Lieutenants Brown, Gibb, Chowerie, Robinson, and Williamson, were killed.

Gordon declined to expose his officers to this butchery any longer, and set to work to teach the Mandarins how to approach the wall by trenches. They took to the work, and did it well. Meanwhile Li-Hung-Chang put up proclamations in characters large enough to be read from the walls. In these he offered pardon to all who would leave the city, Hu Wang excepted. This step proved most successful; deserters came in shoals, in spite of Hu Wang's efforts to keep them in. The truth is, that Hu Wang and his following were hateful to the vast mass of the garrison ; they were Cantonese of the worst type, while the others were peasants who had been captured and pressed into the service. It is not surprising, then, that, finding the opportunity of escape, they went over to the Imperialist camp at the rate of 300 a day.

Very soon the chiefs of one party in the garrison sent Gordon a very treasonable letter. They requested him to send his troops to the breach, and make a false attack or two ; and they promised thereupon to give him up the place. The letter shows that Gordon had already been in communication with them ; for it tells how they made their signal with strips of white cloth, and lighted a fire in the city, while they threw fire-balls and rockets from the wall, without seeing anything of him, or of the "floating-bridge," up to the time of the fourth watch. They add that their signals were discovered and reported to Hu Wang, and that they had only narrowly escaped being beheaded; that they still looked to him to carry out the scheme, and that they proposed to distinguish themselves by wearing white bands, or by going with the left arms out of their sleeves. "Should you intend coming to-night," they go on to say, "hang up two lamps at the East Gate as a signal; then send troops to the North and West Gates to make false attacks, whilst another body lie in ambush near the South Gate; also open fire on the new city. The rebels will rush to defend the North and West Gates, and, on our throwing two fire-balls, you should instantly scale the walls. Our party are on guard during the fifth watch, and will assist you, our cry being 'Death to the rebels!' Should you not come, hoist one lamp to the East Gate. No future time for your attack need be fixed, as we can be guided by your signals. We are talked about as traitors, and should anything be proved against us, 2000 of us would lose our lives. Our movements will be regulated by what is going on outside the city; and after the place falls, we shall collect at the East Gate and await your Excellency. You must have no misgivings as to our sincerity. May heaven and earth conspire against us if we be found liars! Pray keep our communications quiet, lest anyone coming into the city betray us."

Nothing seems to have come of this correspondence. On the anniversary of the city's capture by the Faithful King, Governor Li proposed to celebrate it by a new assault, in which the Imperialists should take the leading part. The artillery brought down great masses of wall; the Imperialist generals crossed the ditches and crowded the ramparts, where they met with a desperate resistance. The columns began to give way. The moment was critical in the extreme, when Gordon led on a storming-party, supported by his 1st Regiment and 200 volunteers, crossed the bridges and mounted the breach. The Imperialists rallied; the Tai-pings were swept away at the point of the bayonet, and the besiegers swarmed into the city. Four of the Wangs were taken prisoners and beheaded. The rout was complete. Hu Wang came up in haste with a large body of troops. But he was driven back. He fought to the last, however. When he was taken prisoner in his palace, it took ten men to bind him. He was brought before Li-Hung-Chang, but he refused him submission. "Were it not," he said, "for aid of Gordon and his men, he defied all the Futai hosts to take the city from him." He and all the Cantonese among the prisoners were executed; the rest were spared.

The garrison was 20,000 strong. The slaughter was proportionately great.

Even before this crowning mercy, Gordon was considering the necessity of disbanding his little army. The following note, written to his mother on May 10, the day before the last assault, shows what his views were at this time:—

"I shall of course make myself quite sure that the rebels are quashed before I break up the Force, as otherwise I should incur great responsibility, but on these subjects I act for myself and judge for myself; this I have found to be the best way of getting on. I shall not leave things in a mess, I hope, but I think if I am spared I shall be home by Christmas. The losses I have sustained in this campaign have been no joke: out of 100 officers I have had 48 killed and wounded, and out of 3500 men nearly 1000 killed and wounded; but I have the satisfaction of knowing that as far as mortal can see, six months will see the end of this Rebellion, while if I had continued inactive it might have lingered on for six years. Do not think I am ill-tempered, but I do not care one jot about my promotion or what people may say. I know I shall leave China as poor as I entered it, but with the knowledge that through my weak instrumentality upwards of eighty to one hundred thousand lives have been spared. I want no further satisfaction than this. The rebels of Chan-chu-fu are the 'originals' of the Rebellion, and though there may be some innocent, still the mass of them are deserving the fate that awaits them. If you could see the horrible cruelties they have everywhere perpetrated, you would say with me that it is impossible to intercede.

"They are the runaways of Soochow, Quinsan, Taitsan, Wusieh, Yesing, and many other towns; they cut off the heads of the unfortunate country people inside at the rate of thirty to forty per diem for attempting to run away."

The following was scratched off in pencil on a small strip of paper two hours after the fall of Chan-chu-fu:—

"11th May 1864, 4 P.M.

"MY DEAR MOTHER,—Chan-chu-fu was carried by assault by

the Quinsan force and Imperialists at 2 P.M. this day, with little loss.   I go back to Quinsan on May 13, and shall not again take the field.   The rebels are now done ; they have only Tayan and Nanking, and the former will fall probably in a day or two, and Nanking in about two months.   I am happy to say I got off safe.— Your affectionate son,

"C. G. GORDON."

CHAPTER VIII

On his return to Quinsan, Gordon received information that the Order in Council which permitted British officers to take service under the Chinese Government was withdrawn. This would have been a serious blow to China, but for the extraordinary rapidity of his recent movements, which left the Rebellion so shattered that it fell to pieces almost of its own accord. Several strongholds surrendered as a mere consequence of the leaguer of Chan-chu-fu. But Nanking, though it had been long invested, and was gradually being starved, held out in a surprising manner. This made Gordon extremely anxious: the permanent success of his work was dear to him; and to see the smouldering embers of the Rebellion again bursting into flame would have been matter for a lifelong sorrow.

So, after taking the necessary steps to disband his immortal army, he visited Tseng Kwo-fan at Nanking, and had a most important interview with him regarding the best method of completing the success of the Imperial arms. On his way thither up the Yangtze he visited Kwo-tsun, the Governor of the Province of Chekiang, who commanded all the troops round the rebel capital, and resided on one of the hills behind the Porcelain Tower. He inspected the siege-works, and was greatly impressed by the perseverance of the Imperialists. From the summit of the hill above the Porcelain Tower he viewed Nanking and all its palaces. Within the walls were large empty spaces, and for miles the ramparts were completely deserted; not a flag was flying, while a death-like stillness hung about the city. The wall was 40 feet high and 30 feet thick. Some Tai-pings were being lowered from it by a rope, to gather lentils outside. They were not molested by the Imperialists, though their stockades were within 80 or a 100 yards of the spot. The Imperial lines stretched for miles, with a double line of breastworks and 140 mud forts standing 600 yards apart, each containing 500 men. No one appeared to be on the look-out, and a free-and-easy style pervaded the whole force. This is what Gordon wrote on his way to Tseng Kwo-fan :

"OFF NANKING, 19th June 1864.

"I came up here to see Tseng Kwo-fan, and also to see what chance the Imperialists had of taking Nanking.   I arrived on the 16th June, and went up to see Tsen-Kwo-jen (Tseng Kwo-fan's brother, who commands here) the next day.   He was uncommonly civil, but I found that both he and his Mandarins preferred fighting on in their own way to any change ; they did not see the advantage of big guns, and thought they could take the place by themselves.   I went round the works, and found the Imperialist lines extend some twelve miles, closing in the place most effectually, but still not proof against a determined attack on the part of the rebels.   I also visited the galleries which they are driving under the walls, some fourteen in number.   They exploded one charge two months ago, but although they got in they were driven out again.   Nanking is a large place, but seemingly deserted, no men being seen on the walls or in the city, which you can see into from the hills around.   It would be easy to capture, but I doubt if the Imperialists will manage it for some time, although they are going to try in about fourteen days.   They are badly armed, while the rebels have plenty of muskets, etc.   The Chinese are a wonderful people : they seem so apathetic about any changes that I am much afraid for them.   The only man I have seen worth anything is the Futai of Kiang-su, Li, who is stigmatised by Osborn as unprincipled, etc., etc.   That the execution of the Wangs at Soochow was a breach of faith, there is no doubt; but there were many reasons to exculpate the Futai for his action, which is not at all a bad act in the eyes of the Chinese.   In my opinion (and I have not seen Tseng Kwo-fan yet), Li-Hung-Chang is the best man in the Empire ; has correct ideas of his position, and, for a Chinaman, has most liberal tendencies.   To support him—and he has a most difficult card to play with the other Mandarins—I should say would be the best policy of our Government.

"The Imperial troops are fine men, but, as I said, most inefficiently armed.

"Burgevine has again joined the rebels; he will do no

harm inside Nanking, if he gets there, and is far safer with the rebels than when concocting conspiracy at Shanghai and seizing steamers.

"I go up to-night to see Tseng Kwo-fan, and to speak to him about the absolute necessity of attending to the re-organisation of the Imperial forces. Lord de Grey may rest assured that our Government's policy has been the best that could have been followed."

During his stay with Tseng Kwo-fan, Gordon discussed with him such military matters as affected China, and gave him his reasons for dissolving the Ever-Victorious Army. Composed as it was, he considered that it would prove a danger rather than an aid. He pointed out the importance of strengthening the Imperial force, of adopting the system of regular payments, and of instructing the natives in the use of foreign arms. He told the Chinese general that 10,000 men so trained would suffice, and that men and officers should be carefully chosen *ad hoc* for the purpose. Tseng Kwo-fan listened attentively, and accepted a memorandum of these and other matters of moment. Besides advising, Gordon lent the generals a helping hand, and assisted them considerably in their siege operations. He had seen enough to satisfy himself that Nanking must shortly fall, and, taking into detailed consideration the condition of the few remaining cities which still held out, he felt that the Rebellion was dead.

Some of the opinions he had formed of the Chinese were expressed at this very time in a letter dated Nanking, 19th June '64. They serve to show the course he had pursued in his relations with them :—

"What I think is this, that if we try to drive the Chinese into sudden reforms, they will strike and resist with the greatest obstinacy, and will relapse back again into old habits when the pressure is removed ; but if we lead them, we shall find them willing to a degree, and more easy to manage. They like to have an option, and hate having a course struck out for them as if they were of no account in the matter. They also like to see the utility of the course proposed, and to have the reasons for the same explained over and over again, and they are also quick in seeing advantages and disadvantages.

"What we have tried to do is to force them into a certain course, making them pay for the same, and thinking it not worth while discussing the matter with them at all. I have got on by proposing to them a course of action in such a way as to give them a certain option as to whether they will follow it or not, and have always endeavoured to recommend nothing which would clash utterly with their prejudices; by this means I have led them on to change many things, which I should never have succeeded in doing if I had tried to force them to do all at once. I can say that few men have so much faith put in them by the Chinese as myself. I always consider the great difficulty the Mandarins have to contend with: they may perfectly agree in everything that may be urged on them by us, but cannot carry it out; and we must confess that it is far easier to say 'go and do this or that' *than to do it.* We row the poor devils if they do not make reforms in their army, but do not consider that changes must be gradual, and palatable as far as possible. My idea is, that the change should be made in their army gradually, and on a small scale at first, and through the Futais, not through the Peking Government, who are a very helpless lot. There are 60,000 troops here, and 40 Futais, or Generals of Division. What a task it would be for Tseng to try and suddenly change the organisation of this force—with our organisation, 40 independent commanders would be impossible. But how is Tseng to get rid of them, with their troops some six months in arrears of pay? I would say much more for the Imperialists: they have many faults, but have suffered much wrong from foreigners, who have preyed on their country. The utter waste of money through Lay's fleet is quite painful to think of."

He had dissolved the Ever-Victorious Army on his own responsibility, though at the suggestion of Li, who saw that so costly a machine was no longer needed. Li, however, found great difficulty in meeting its demands. Our Ambassador was averse to its dissolution, and the foreign merchants at Shanghai were panic-stricken by Gordon's determination. But he was right in his resolve. The army might have been re-organised under its foreign officers; it might, following on the traditions of Burgevine, have formed a party of conquest on its own account. It might have gone over to the enemy and revived the Rebellion. "I can say now," writes Gordon, "that a more turbulent set of men (?) who formed the officers have not often been collected together, or a more dangerous lot, if they had been headed by one of their own style." He stipulated for rewards to his officers and men proportionate to the services they had rendered : the former to receive large sums—in fact, little fortunes—the men to have such amounts as would provide for them and take them to their homes. His terms were readily granted, the more so probably as he himself refused all pecuniary rewards, though Li had been again commissioned by the Imperial Government to vote him a large sum of money. This he refused, as on a previous occasion he had declined the smaller reward of 10,000 taels. He had spent his pay of £3120 a year in comforts for his army and in the relief of the victims of the Heavenly King. To these ends he had even taxed his own private means. It was not likely, then, that he should now do anything to give a mercenary stamp to his services, or deprive him of the reflection that he had acted in the cause of humanity alone. It might have been better, perhaps, if our Government at home had permitted him to be present when the last gun was fired over the dead Rebellion. But they were time-servers ; the shriek of the sentimentalists still reached their ears, stories of cruelties committed by the Ever-Victorious army were still afoot ; the missionary cliques were still damning and denouncing ; and a policy of good sense had to give way to one of expediency. Happily, though bigotry and ignorance had done their worst, the end had been achieved.

When Gordon went to take leave of Li, he was received with the highest distinction. The Futai had learned to recognise the greatness of his character. He had met with no man of that stamp in his own country, and his intercourse with foreigners had shown him that their ruling principle was the desire of gain. He had a new experience of human nature, and thenceforth his admiration and love of Gordon underwent no change.

Other acknowledgments of his services awaited the Captain of the Ever-Victorious Army—from the Imperial Government itself, from the merchants resident in China, and from the Press both in that country and in this. On the 12th of July 1864, our Ambassador, Sir Frederick Bruce, wrote as follows to Earl Russell :—

" I enclose translation of a despatch from Prince Kung, containing the decree published by the Emperor, acknowledging the services of Lieutenant-Colonel Gordon, Royal Engineers, and requesting that Her Majesty's Government be pleased to recognise them. This step has been spontaneously taken.

" Lieutenant-Colonel Gordon well deserves Her Majesty's

favour, for, independently of the skill and courage he has shown, his disinterestedness has elevated our national character in the eyes of the Chinese. Not only has he refused any pecuniary reward, but he has spent more than his pay in contributing to the comfort of the officers who served under him, and in assuaging the distress of the starving population whom he relieved from the yoke of their oppressors. Indeed, the feeling that impelled him to resume operations after the fall of Soochow was one of the purest humanity. He sought to save the people of the districts that had been recovered from a repetition of the misery entailed upon them by this cruel civil war."

The Prince's communication runs thus :—

"Some time has elapsed since his Excellency the British Minister, profoundly animated by the feeling of friendliness towards China entertained by the British Government, did, in view of the fact that rebellion was still rife in Kiang-su, authorise Gordon and other officers of the British army to co-operate, heart and hand, with the forces of the Chinese Government against the rebels.

"On the 11th of the 5th moon of the 3rd year of Tung-che (14th June 1864), Li, the Governor of Kiang-su, in a memorial reporting a series of distinguished services rendered in action by Gordon, now a Tsung-Ping, with the title of Ti-Tu, together with the particulars of his conduct and discipline of the Ever-Victorious Army, requested His Majesty the Emperor to be pleased to commend him ; and on the same day the Grand Secretariat had the honour to receive the following decree :—

"'On the occasion of the recovery of Chan-chu, we issued a decree conferring on Gordon, Provisional General of Division of the Army of Kiang-su, for his co-operation with the force he commanded, the title of Ti-Tu (Commander-in-Chief of a Provisional Army) ; and we further presented him with banners and decorations of honour. This was to distinguish his extraordinary merit, and Li-Hung-Chang was to address us again whenever he (Gordon) should have brought the Ever-Victorious Battalions under his command into a satisfactory state of drill and discipline, and to request us to signify our approval of his conduct in laudatory terms. Li-Hung-Chang now writes to say that, both as regards their movements and its discipline, the Ever-Victorious Battalions under Gordon are in a very satisfactory state, and requests us to signify our pleasure accordingly.

"'Since the spring of last year, Gordon has distinguished himself in a series of actions with the Ever-Victorious Force under his command; he has co-operated with the Forces of Government (with such effect that) Fushan has been recovered, the siege of Chanzu has been raised, and the sub-prefectural city of Taitsan, with the district cities of Quinsan and Wokong, have also been retaken, as well as the provincial capital of Soochow. This year he has retaken Yesing and Liyang; he has driven off the rebels who had worked their way to Yanshê, and he has recaptured Chan-chu. He has now brought the Ever-Victorious Force to such a degree of improvement that it will prove a body of enduring utility. Not only has he shown himself throughout both brave and energetic, but his thorough appreciation of that important question, a friendly understanding between China and foreign nations, is also deserving of the highest praise. We command that Gordon be rewarded with a Yellow Riding-jacket to be worn on his person, and a Peacock's Feather to be carried on his cap; also that there be bestowed on him four suits of the uniform proper to his rank of Ti-Tu, in token of our favour and desire to do him honour. Respect this.'

"A copy of the above having been reverently made and forwarded to the Tsung-Li Yamun, the Prince and the Ministers, members of it, have to observe that General Gordon, ever since he began to co-operate with the forces of the Chinese Government against the rebels, has been alike remarkable for his courage and intelligence, and displayed extraordinary energy. But the fact that he was further able to improve the drill and discipline of the Ever-Victorious Force shows him to be in very eminent degree both able and respectable, while his success in supporting the friendly policy of the British Government, whose subject he is, entitles him to the admission that he has not shown himself unworthy of the language ever held by the British Minister regarding him.

"In respectful obedience to the will of His Imperial Majesty, the Yamun is preparing the uniforms and other articles for transmission to him. The banners and decorations will be cared for by Li, the Governor of Kiang-su.

"Meanwhile it becomes the duty of the Prince to address the British Minister, that his Excellency may bring these things to the notice of Her Majesty the Queen of England, in evidence of the desire of the Chinese Government, by its consideration of (Colonel Gordon's) merits, and its bestowal of rewards, to strengthen the *entente cordiale.*

"General Gordon's title, Ti-Tu, gives him the highest rank in the Chinese army; but the Prince trusts that if, on his return home, it be possible for the British Government to bestow promotion or reward on General Gordon, the British Minister will bring the matter forward, that all may know that his achievements and his character are equally deserving of praise."

This despatch of Prince Kung, with the Imperial decree which it embodies, is unquestionably a high-minded and generous acknowledgment of Gordon's services and achievements. The rank of Ti-Tu is the highest ever conferred on a subject; for the banner and the Order of the Star we have parallels of our own; the Yellow Jacket and the Peacock's Feather are Chinese equivalents for the Garter and the Bath. The inference is obvious that in China they know a good man when they find one, and delight to honour him as he deserves.

The pigeon-holes of the Peking Administration are more promptly emptied than those in Downing Street, which must have the depth of wells. Prince Kung's despatch was acted upon to the minutest particulars; Sir Frederick Bruce's is buried to this day. All that Gordon received from his own Government was one step in the army; somewhat later he was made a Companion of the Bath. Had he been a Clive, taken all the money he could get, and entered Parliament and voted straight, perhaps the Ministers would have been kinder judges of his claims. But it was not for him to play their part; he had one of his own.

That he would have preferred to go unhonoured is certain. To him the good work done was an ample reward. Indeed, the wonder and admiration evinced at his triumphs rather pained than pleased him; his one desire was to get home and be forgotten.

"The Yellow Jacket," he says in one of his letters, "which has been conferred on me, is a regular Chinese distinction, with which some twenty Mandarins have been decorated; it constitutes the recipient one of the Emperor's body-guard. I will send you a short history of its institution, etc., as soon as I can. I do not care twopence about these things, but know that you and my father like them. I will try and get Sir F. Bruce to bring home Chung Wang's sword, which is wrapped up in a rebel flag belonging to a Tien Wang, who was killed on it at Chan-chu-fu

You will see marks of his blood on the flag. Chung Wang's sword was given by him to Lye Wang (the rebel chief of Liyang), at Wusieh in December '63, after the fall of Soochow, and at the time that Chung Wang, disgusted, determined to return on Nanking, and take for the time no further operation. It is more than an ordinary sword. The Emperor of China gave one to Tseng Kwo-fan, and this gift was accompanied with permission to Tseng Kwo-fan to execute anyone, whatever his rank might be, without reference to Peking; in fact, it was the symbol of the power of Dictator.

"I have sent my journal (of 1863) home to H——. I do not want the same published, as I think if my proceedings sink into oblivion it would be better for everyone, and my reason for this is that it is a very contested point whether we ought to have interfered or not, on which point I am perfectly satisfied that it was the proper and humane course to pursue; but I still do not expect people who do not know much about it to concur in the same. It is absurd to talk about Manchus and Chinese; the former are extinct, and the latter are in every part. And it is equally absurd to talk of the Mandarins as a class distinct from the people of the country; they are not so, but are merely the officials who hold offices which are obtainable by every Chinese, without respect to birth, I will not say money, as certainly there is some amount of corruption in the sale of offices; but Russia is equally corrupt for that matter in her distant provinces, and it is not so very long ago that we were also somewhat tainted in the same way."

As bearing on the conduct of our Goverment, however, it is worth while that a letter from " A Student of History," of a later date, addressed to and printed in the *Times*, should even now be resuscitated. The following extract from it will have a deep interest for Gordon's many admirers :—

"It has been already pointed out that Colonel Gordon's being an Engineer, no less than his peculiarly retiring character, has kept him from the employment for which his genius seemed to indicate him, and which less exploits than his might fairly have claimed. But there is probably another reason for this apparent neglect, of which I have only become aware since writing to you last week. A gentleman, himself in the public service and well acquainted with China, happening to identify at a guess the

8

writer of the *Times* letter, has just communicated to me the following account of matters intimately connected with the fall of the Tai-pings, and our share in it, which I take the liberty of introducing in his own words to your readers' notice. He states :—

"'Being at Shanghai in the summer of 1864, I met the late Sir Frederick Bruce, our Minister, on his way to England. He told me that the very day before he left Peking he was astonished at receiving a personal visit from Prince Kung, the then Regent of China, who had some days before come to say good-bye to him. The Prince said, "You will be astonished to see me again, but I felt I could not allow you to leave without coming to see you about Gordon. We do not know what to do. He will not receive money from us, and we have already given him every honour which it is in the power of the Emperor to bestow ; but as these can be of little value in his eyes, I have brought you this letter, and ask you to give it to the Queen of England, that she may bestow on him some reward which would be more valuable in his eyes." Sir Frederick showed me a translation of Prince Kung's letter. I only remember that it was couched in the most charming terms, and that it pleaded Gordon's services as to what he had done to "promote the kindly intercourse between the two nations," while fully acknowledging the immense services he had rendered to China. I went,' adds my informant, 'to Peking in the autumn of that year, where Gordon had been officially invited ; but his dislike of being made a hero of prevented his going. Had he done so, he would have been received with almost royal honours.'

"Now, sir, receiving as I have done this narrative from a man of honour, who speaks earnestly and in good faith, and coupling it with the well-known fact that when Colonel Gordon presented himself at the War Office some months later, the Minister seemed hardly to have heard of his name, and to know nothing whatever of his successes, may it not be true—as a weekly contemporary of yours seems to suggest—that the letter of Prince Kung never reached its destination at all ; indeed, never got beyond the pigeon-holes of the Foreign Office ? At least, in the interest of historical truth, I would hope that some active-minded member of Parliament may not think it too late to draw attention to the subject, and to seek the production of the missing despatch, the absence of which possibly has excused that extraordinary neglect of a great soldier with which the War Office authorities have been charged."

The fact is that Gordon, instead of allowing himself to be made the hero of official fêtes at Peking, was carrying out a new plan for the good of the country he had saved. The cry of surprise and alarm raised by the traders of Shanghai on the disbandment of the Ever-Victorious Army.had by no means been lost on him. He had conceived the idea of organising a disciplined Chinese contingent with an English officer in command. The scheme had for its object the instruction of native troops in foreign drill, that the city, in the event of a new outbreak, might possess a more trustworthy force than a Mandarin army for its protection. The advantages of the idea were at once perceived by Li-Hung-Chang, and several officers were selected from the 67th Regiment as drill instructors. But it was agreed that in the event of the corps taking the field, all these, with Gordon at their head, should be at once withdrawn. Judging from the letters which the Ever-Victorious General wrote home at this time, the enjoyment he got out of teaching his Chinese recruits the various manœuvres and exercises was not small. "I am getting on very well instructing the Chinese officers in artillery, etc., in Chinese," he says, "and they make great progress, knowing the manual, platoon, and gun drill already, and I hope will know the simple manœuvres of battalion drill shortly. It is much easier than I supposed it would be."

Nanking was by this time reduced and captured, so that the Rebellion had received its death-blow before Gordon left China. He had, indeed, done more than preside at the Councils of the Imperialists; he had advanced to far within the city wall. The rebels fought to the last, and defended themselves desperately, even when in the palace of the Heavenly King. The arch-impostor himself had been urged to escape and resign the city, when, its investment being complete over an area of thirty miles, and its inhabitants in a state of starvation, it could no longer be defended. But the man had a certain respect for the character he had assumed. He wished to be remembered by posterity as inspired of Heaven—as the Heavenly King. He scouted the suggestion that one so great as himself should fly: he had received, he said, the command of God and Jesus to come down upon earth and rule it. "I am the sole Lord of ten thousand nations," he cried; "what should I fear?" He told how he held the empire, the hills, and the streams with an iron grasp. Whether all this was mere cynicism, or the outcome of a diseased brain, is of little moment. Certain it is that he had ceased to take any account of public affairs. His subordinates might act as they pleased, except in one respect : he demanded the implicit observance of etiquette, in addressing him in theological phrase and in professing absolute submission to his decrees. He had been guilty of cruelties greater than are accredited to any other human being : flaying alive and pounding to death were his ordinary modes of punishment. When he knew the end was come, he hanged all his wives ; then, like Mokanna, he committed suicide. Thus was destroyed the horrible hope that some other fanatic might adopt and preach his hideous creed ; if there is anything that will wipe out the belief that a man is inspired by God, it is the self-slaughter of the prophet. Few atrocities were committed by the Imperialists on the surrender of the city ; this was attributed to Gordon's influence over the Mandarins. The great soldier Chung Wang, or the Faithful King, the right arm of the Rebellion, who was taken prisoner with other rebel warriors, was, however, decapitated.

"I know," says Gordon, "you will be glad to hear of the fall of Nanking, which virtually ends the Rebellion. I expect the rebels will soon run, and then disperse over the country. The city is in a very ruinous state, and looks the picture of desolation. I was only there two days, and those days were very hot. It is a grand thing the fall of Nanking, and will do a deal of good in every way. Having lost their chief, the rebels will soon disperse and break up.

"As long as it held out, my officers were ready to join the rebels if there was a chance of success ; now they will see the futility of such a course, and disperse over the globe. It is the greatest blessing for the Mandarins, who did not see their danger from these men, who do not want for talent.

"I never want anything published. I am sure it does no good, and makes people chary of writing."

Having completed his work and taken public leave of all with whom he had been associated in his duties, Gordon was now at liberty to return home. But before quitting China, the press had begun to shower on him such eulogies as are seldom the portion of the very greatest. An engrossed and illuminated address from the merchants of Shanghai was presented to him ; and this, as the expression of large and important firms of business-men, who are for the most part excellent judges of whatever affects a national interest, may be taken as a sober estimate of the good he had done. It is signed by nearly sixty firms, including the great banks; and as most of the signatories were only a year before opposed to the policy of British interference with the Rebellion, it is too significant to be omitted.   Thus it runs :—

"On the eve of your departure for your native country, we, the undersigned, mostly fellow-countrymen of your own, but also representing various other nationalities, desire to express to you our earnest wish for a successful voyage and happy return to your friends and the land of your birth.

"Your career during the last two years of your residence in the East has been, so far as we know, without a parallel in the history of the intercourse of foreign nations with China; and, without entering at all upon the political bearings of the great question with which your name must ever remain so intimately connected, we feel that we should be alike wanting towards you and towards ourselves were we to pass by this opportunity without expressing our appreciation and admiration of the line of conduct which you personally have pursued.

"In a position of unequalled difficulty, and surrounded by complications of every possible nature, you have succeeded in offering to the eyes of the Chinese nation, no less by your loyal and, throughout, disinterested line of action, than by your conspicuous gallantry and talent for organisation and command, the example of a foreign officer serving the Government of this country with honourable fidelity and undeviating self-respect.

"It is by such examples that we may trust to see many of the prejudices which warp the Chinese mind, as regards foreigners, removed, and from such experience that we may look forward with hope to the day when, not only in the art of war, but in the more peaceful occupations of commerce and civilisation, the Chinese Goverment may see fit to level the barriers hitherto existing, and to identify itself more and more with that progressive course of action which, though springing from the West, must prove ultimately of equal benefit to the countries of the East.

"Once more wishing you a prosperous voyage and a long career of usefulness and success. . . ."

This was Gordon's answer :—

"SHANGHAI, *November 25th*, 1864.

"GENTLEMEN,—I have the honour to acknowledge the receipt of your handsome letter of this day's date, and to express to you the great satisfaction which I feel at the honourable mention you have made therein of my services in China.

"It will always be a matter of gratification to me to have received your approval, and, deeply impressed with the honour you have paid me, I have the honour to be, gentlemen, yours obediently,   C. G. GORDON."

Other expressions of admiration and gratitude poured in. The press at home and abroad were loud in Gordon's praise; and when he left Shanghai for England, it was universally felt that China was parting with her greatest hero and her best friend. The following lines, written by one who well knew how deeply the Empire was indebted to him, may be taken as fairly representative of the universal feeling :—

"Can China tell how much she is indebted to Colonel Gordon? Would twenty million taels repay the actual service he has rendered to the Empire?

"While ordinary Chinese commanders were sitting down before a city, Gordon was walking round it, regardless of shots from the walls. He never permitted an hour to elapse before putting his ideas into practice, and this very rapidity quite appalled his too confident adversaries. They, accustomed to conquest, and to constant superiority, began to get confused by the coolness with which they were handled, even in the most difficult circumstances, until it came to pass that the name of Gordon paralysed their hearts, and became equivalent to the word 'surrender.' Whether this be the case or no, recent facts have since proved that the Colonel's operations have completely broken the back of the Rebellion. Chinese commanders, with all their conceit, have given ample testimony to the skill and prowess of the ever-gallant Colonel. Gordon's name alone has a weight in the province of Kiang-su which is not at all approached by any Chinaman lower than Tseng Kwo-fan himself.

"It seems like a dream to us to think that the traders in Shanghai were trembling only the other day for the safety of their lives and property, and that now they are as free from fear as if they were sitting in a Lombard Street counting-house. Again we say that the Rebellion is finished; and we do not suppose that there breathes the man who regrets it. Even to scenes of slaughter we have become callous, knowing that out of the misery will rise joy, out of chaos order, and out of depression prosperity."

Even the rebels, to whom his name was a terror, admired and loved him. A letter written by a Tai-ping chief, after the massacres of Quinsan and Soochow, shows what a splendid estimate they took of their most formidable foe :—

"Far be it from me to assert that Gordon was privy to the massacres committed. Well as we are accustomed to the ruffianly conduct of many of the low scoundrels who disgrace the name of Englishmen, and whom we know to be capable of any atrocity, we do not imagine that the great leader of the army would ever consent to the perpetration of murders so horrible. Yet never did the plains of China blush with blood more unrighteously spilled than on the day succeeding the capture of Quinsan, when the disorganised Hua contingent satiated itself with outrage. No, not even in the ancient days, when the men of Han fought valiantly with Mongol and Manchu, not even in the sanguinary but glorious days of Chu, did undisciplined and semi-barbarous troops equal the atrocities of the English-drilled army. I have heard that Gordon grieved bitterly over the cruelties which he could not prevent, and that his heart burned when he thought that in your happy and prosperous country beyond the Western Ocean, these horrors would be ascribed to him. It may gratify him to think that even amongst those who would willingly be his friends, but are forced to be his enemies, he does not receive the blame of the events he could not control. I have spent so much room already in speaking of Gordon that I may as well say a few words more. Would to Heaven that some unworthy adventurer would take command, someone that could be slain without regret, and, if necessary, slaughtered without mercy ! *Often have I seen the deadly musket struck from the hand of a dastardly Englishman (tempted by love of loot to join our ranks), when he attempted from his place of safety to kill Gordon, who ever rashly exposed himself. This has been the act of a chief— yea, of the Shield King himself. How then can we be accused of blind hatred even to our enemies ?*"

CHAPTER IX

THAT Gordon was gratified by the appreciation of those who had watched his career in China, there can be no doubt; but to be praised, courted, and called a hero for doing his duty was more than he cared to approve. The few lines announcing his intention of coming home show that his one idea on arriving in England was to enjoy the quiet of his own family circle. "The individual is coming home," he writes to his mother on the 17th November 1864, "but does not wish it known, for it would be a signal for the disbanded to come to Southampton; and although the waits at Christmas are bad, these others are worse." No sooner, however, had he set foot in this country, than invitations came in upon him from all quarters, and to have him for a guest was the season's ideal; friends and kinsmen were made the bearers of superb invitations, all of which he had the courage to decline. In truth, he was in no humour for personal congratulations from the great. He had gracefully received the acknowledgment of those whom he had served; he had read with pleasure the appreciations of the public press; but when he saw a tendency to pronounce him a hero, he ceased from reading and listening. He even implored a fellow-officer who had written a narrative of the campaign, to let the subject drop.

In his home letters he had earnestly requested that his part in putting down the Rebellion should not be made public; he had said, indeed, that the sooner it was forgotten the better, On his return, then, none save his relatives heard anything more of the campaign. By the fireside at Southampton, once more he told the strange and splendid romance of those fifteen months—a story teeming with the noblest and most lofty incidents of war, with singular encounters, disastrous chances, and moving accidents by flood and field. To listen to it was a new and unique experience; and as Gordon stood every evening for three or four hours descanting on the things he had seen, now pointing to the map before him to explain a position, now raising his voice in sudden anger at defeat, or dropping it with victory in mercy for the fallen, the company was spell-bound and amazed. The wonderful scenes he described, and the simple enthusiasm with which he described them, left the impression of a new "Arabian Nights." Never was the unrecorded better worth recording. But though nothing of it was written down, its effect on those who listened still remains—unforgettable and unforgot.

Had Gordon been touched with the ambition incident to successful men, he would have seized the opportunities so abundantly afforded him of mingling with the dignitaries of the world, whose invitations and courtesies were many. Had he accepted them, there can be little doubt that he would have been made to "shine in use" till England had cause to bless him for one of the greatest of her sons; but to push and to intrigue was impossible. The consequence was that he soon dropped out of the recollection of those in whose power it was to promote his professional and worldly interests. For his own part, he had no desire to enjoy advantages above the lot of his brother officers; he was content to rejoin his corps, and to resume his duty as a Royal Engineer.

Many circumstances tend to show that, as part of his mental constitution, he had a temper, well under control, but on occasion hasty and impatient. His anger never found such vent as against those who praised him. His mother used to show her friends a beautifully executed map, torn through the middle and pasted together again; it was a relic of Woolwich Academy. One day she was exhibiting it when her son suddenly entered the room, saw the admiration of the lookers-on, and at once took the map from her, tore it in half, and flung it on the back of the fire. The journal of the Tai-ping War, illustrated by his own hand, met, it is to be feared, with a worse fate still. He had sent it home from China, not wishing it (as has been seen by one of his letters) to be seen outside his family. A minister interested in the Rebellion heard of the manuscript, borrowed it, and was so struck by its contents that he sent it to the press, in order that his colleagues might have the benefit of reading it. Late one evening it so happened that Gordon inquired about his journal. He was told what had occurred. He rose from table, left the house, and posted off to the minister's residence. Not finding him at home, he went to the printer's, demanded his manuscript, and gave orders that what copies had been printed should be destroyed, and the type broken up. What eventually befell the manuscript is unknown; but it is certain that no one has since seen it; in fact, there is every probability of its having been destroyed.

In 1865 he received the appointment of Commanding Royal Engineer at Gravesend, where he remained until 1871. These six years, different from any other period of his career, were perhaps the happiest in his life. Among his earliest tasks, in addition to the fulfilment of his official duties—the construction of the Thames Defences—was the distribution of the various medals and rewards to such of his old comrades of the Ever-Victorious Army, as had in any way distinguished themselves. This was done for the most part by correspondence, his followers being scattered over all parts of the world. He received a great number of acknowledgments. There is not one of these but shows how reverently he was beloved by all who had served with him.

To the world his life at Gravesend was a life of self-suppression and self-denial; to himself it was one of happiness and pure peace. He lived wholly for others. His house was school, and hospital, and almshouse, in turn—was more like the abode of a missionary than of a Colonel of Engineers. The troubles of all interested him alike. The poor, the sick, the unfortunate, were ever welcome, and never did suppliant knock vainly at his door. He always took a great delight in children, but especially in boys employed on the river or the sea. Many he rescued from the gutter, cleansed them and clothed them, and kept them for weeks in his home. For their benefit he established evening classes, over which he himself presided, reading to and teaching the lads with as much ardour as if he were leading them to victory. He called them his "kings," and for many of them he got berths on board ship. One day a friend asked him why there were so many pins stuck into the map of the world over his mantelpiece; he was told that they marked and followed the course of the boys on their voyages—that they were moved from point to point as his youngsters advanced, and that he prayed for them as they went, day by day. The light in which he was held by these lads was shown by inscriptions in chalk on the fences. A favourite legend was "God bless the Kernel." So full did his classes at length become, that the house would no longer hold them, and they had to be given up. Then it was that he attended and taught at the Ragged Schools, and it was a pleasant thing to watch the attention with which his wild scholars listened to his words.

" His benevolence embraced all," writes one who saw much of him at this time. " Misery was quite sufficient claim for him, without going into the question of merit; and, of course, sometimes he was deceived. But very seldom, for he had an eye that saw through and through people; it seemed useless to try to hide anything from him. I have often wondered how much this wonderful power was due to natural astuteness, or how much to his own clear singleness of mind and freedom from self, that the truth about everything seemed revealed to him. The workhouse and the infirmary were his constant haunts, and of pensioners he had a countless number all over the neighbourhood. Many of the dying sent for him in preference to the clergy, and ever ready was he to visit them, no matter in what weather or at what distance. But he would never take the chair at a religious meeting, or be in any way prominent. He was always willing to conduct services for the poor and address a sweeps' tea-meeting; but all public speechifying, especially where complimentary speeches were made in his honour, he *loathed*. All eating and drinking he was indifferent to. Coming home with us one afternoon late, we found his tea waiting for him—a most unappetising stale loaf and a teapot of tea. I remarked upon the dryness of the bread, when he took the whole loaf (a small one), crammed it into the slop-basin, and poured all the tea upon it, saying it would soon be ready for him to eat, and in half an hour it would not matter what he had eaten. He always had dry, humorous little speeches at command, that flavoured all his talk, and I remember the merry twinkle with which he told us that many of the boys, thinking that being invited to live with the Colonel meant delicate fare and luxury, were unpleasantly enlightened upon that point when they found he sat down with them to salt beef and just the necessary food. He kindly gave us a key to his garden, thinking our children might like to walk there sometimes. The first time my husband and I visited it, we remarked what nice peas and vegetables of all kinds there were, and the housekeeper coming out, we made some such remark to her. She at once told us that the Colonel never tasted them—that nearly all the garden, a large one, was cultivated by different poor people, to whom he gave permission to plant what they chose, and to take the proceeds. She added that it often happened that presents of fine fruit and flowers would be sent to the Colonel, and that he would never so much as taste them, but take them or send them at once to the hospital or workhouse for the sick. He always thanked the donors, but never told them how their gifts had been appropriated. We used to say he had no *self*, in that following his Divine Master. He would never talk of himself and his doings. Therefore his life never can and never will be written. It was in these years that the first book about him came out. He allowed the author to come and stay at Fort House, and gave him every facility towards bringing out his book —all the particulars about the Tai-ping Rebellion, even to lending him his diary. Then, from something that was said, he discovered that personal acts of his own (bravery, possibly) were described, and he asked to see what had been written. Then he tore out, page after page, the parts about himself, to the poor author's chagrin, who told him he had spoiled his book. I tried to get at the bottom of this feeling of his, telling him he might be justly proud of these things; but was answered that no man has a right to be proud of anything, inasmuch as he has no *native* good in him—he has received it all; and he maintained that there was a deep cause for intense humiliation on the part of everyone, that all wearing of medals, adorning the body, or any form of self-glorification, was quite out of place. Also, he said, he had no right to possess anything, having once given himself to God. What was he to keep back? He knew no limit. He said to me, 'You who profess the same have no right to the gold chain you wear; it ought to be sold for the poor.' But he acknowledged the difficulty of others regarding all earthly things in the light that he did : his purse was always empty from his constant liberality. He told us the silver tea-service that he kept (a present from Sir William Gordon) would be sufficient to pay for his burial without troubling his family. But though he would never speak of his own acts, he would talk freely of his thoughts, and long and intensely interesting conversations have we had with him : his mystical turn of mind lent a great charm to his words, and we learned a great deal from him. I have often wished I had recorded at the time many of his aphorisms. We saw him very frequently, but there was a tacit understanding that we never were to invite him nor to ask him to stay longer when he rose to go. To ask him to dinner would have been a great offence. He would say, 'Ask the poor and sick; don't ask me, who have enough!'"

He had a great number of medals, for which he cared nothing. There was a gold one, however, given to him by the Empress of China, with a special inscription engraved upon it, for which he had a great liking. But it suddenly disappeared—no one knew where or how. Years afterwards, it was found out, by a curious accident, that Gordon had erased the inscription, and sent the medal anonymously to Canon Miller for the relief of the sufferers from the cotton famine at Manchester.

Thus he spent the next six years of his life—in slums, hospitals, and workhouse, or knee-deep in the river at work upon the Thames Defence. Then, in 1871, he was appointed British Commissioner to the European Commission of the Danube. In taking leave of Gravesend, he presented a number of splendid Chinese flags, of all colours—the trophies of his victories—to his "kings" at the Ragged Schools. These are still yearly exhibited on the occasion of school-treats, and the donor's name is cheered to the echo. The expressions of regret on his departure from the town were many and unanimous.

A year and a half after his departure from England, the question what to do with the Ashantees was uppermost in the public mind. The way in which they were planning an attack on Cape Coast Castle, after the destruction of a town and a couple of bad defeats at our hands, proved them an enemy not easy of conquest. A general feeling prevailed that a leader was wanted, and, as has often since happened in like emergencies, Chinese Gordon was the name that rose to many lips. Letters were written to the papers, in which his exploits were revived, and leading articles appeared in the *Times* and elsewhere, in which the Government was urged to employ the services of the matchless soldier, who had been told off to fritter away his genius as a Vice-Consul on the Danube.

Among the communications sent to the papers, was one of such deep interest that I make no apology for reproducing it. It is a letter addressed to the *Times*, from one signing himself "Mandarin," who fought with Gordon in the campaign against the Tai-pings. It throws new light on the subject. It is from the pen of one who knew the true quality of the Commander under whom it had been his fortune to serve.

"It is really surprising," says this writer, "how scanty a knowledge English people have of the wonderful feats performed not many years since by an officer whose name has lately been rather prominently mentioned — Colonel, or Chinese Gordon. Having served under him during the most eventful period of his command of the 'Ever-Victorious Army,'—an epithet, you may be sure, not given by himself,—I might fill many of your columns with traits of General Gordon's amazing activity and wonderful foresight, his indomitable energy and quiet unassuming modesty, his perseverance, kindness, cool courage, and even heroism. My individual opinion may not be worth much, but is it not notorious that every man who has ever served under or with General (as you must allow me to style him) Gordon is an enthusiastic believer in his military genius and capacity? There are not many commanders of whom the subordinates would speak with such unanimous praise. What is, perhaps, most striking in Gordon's career in China is the entire devotion with which the native soldiery served him, and the implicit faith they had in the result of operations in which he was personally present. In their eyes, General Gordon was literally a magician, to whom all things were possible. They believed him to bear a charmed life, and a short stick or rattan cane which he invariably carried about, and with which he always pointed in directing the fire of artillery or other operations, was firmly looked on as a wand or talisman. These things have been repeated to me again and again by my own men, and I know they were accepted all over the contingent. These notions, especially the men's idea that their General had a charmed existence, were substantially aided by Gordon's constant habit, when the troops were under fire, of appearing suddenly, usually unattended, and calmly standing in the very hottest part of the fire.

"Besides his favourite cane, he carried nothing except field-glasses—never a sword or revolver ; or rather, if the latter, it was carried unostentatiously and out of sight ; and nothing could exceed the contrast between General Gordon's quiet undress uniform, without sword, belts, or buckles, and apparently no weapon but a two-foot rod, and the buccaneering, brigand-like costume of the American officers, strapped, armed, and booted like theatrical banditti.

"I only know one occasion on which General Gordon drew a revolver. The contingent had been lying idle in Quinsan for three months of the summer without taking the field. This time

had been employed in drilling the men, and in laying in large
stores of war material preparatory to the approaching attack on
Soochow. The heat all this time was fearfully oppressive;
dysentery and cholera had carried off many men and officers, and
drill towards the end of the term was somewhat relaxed. This in
some measure affected the discipline of the men, and, indeed, of
the officers also. But the chief cause of the deteriorated discipline
was perhaps to be found in another direction. On the march
and in the field the men were unable to obtain opium, the officers
but slender stores of liquor; in garrison, on the contrary, they
could indulge to the full extent of their monthly pay.

"But whatever the causes, it is certain that when, towards
September, orders to prepare for an expedition against strong
forts and stockades barring the way by canal from Quinsan to
Soochow were issued, the discipline of the troops was greatly
inferior to what it had been three months earlier. The artillery,
in particular, showed decided insubordination. One company of
it refused to embark in the barges which were to take it up the
canal, the men declining to take the field before the approaching
pay-day. The officers managed to make the men 'fall in,' but
from the parade-ground they refused to move, although the
luggage was already on board the boats, lying fifty yards off. At
this juncture, General Gordon, who had been apprised by messengers of the state of affairs, arrived on the spot with his
interpreter. He was on foot, in undress, apparently unarmed,
and, as usual, exceedingly cool, quiet, and undemonstrative.

"Directly he approached the company he ordered his interpreter to direct every man who refused to embark to step to the
front. One man only advanced. General Gordon drew his
revolver from an inside breast-pocket, presented it at the soldier's
head, and desired the interpreter to direct the man to march
straight to the barge and embark. The order was immediately
complied with, and then, General Gordon giving the necessary
words of command, the company followed without hesitation or
demur. It may be said that any other determined officer might
have done likewise, and with the same results. Not so. It was
generally allowed by the officers, when the event became known,
that the success in this instance was solely due to the awe and
respect in which General Gordon was held by the men; and that
such was the spirit of the troops at the time, that had any other
but he attempted what he did, the company would have broken into
open mutiny, shot their officers, and committed the wildest excesses.

" In less than a week the spirit of the troops was as excellent as before, and gradually the whole garrison joined in a series of movements which culminated in the fall of Soochow.

" Considering the materials Gordon had to work with, the admirable state of discipline and military efficiency which his contingent eventually attained is really amazing. He certainly had a few first-rate officers—rough-and-ready ones, no doubt— perhaps half a dozen altogether, of which General Kirkham, at present in Abyssinia, is one. But as for the remainder, or the great majority of the remainder, I scarcely like to use the epithets which would be most applicable to them. This I remember ; during the month of July, when the corps was in Quinsan, out of 130 or 140 officers, 11 died of delirium tremens. There was no picking or choosing ; the General was glad to get any foreigners to fill up vacancies, and the result, especially in garrison, was deplorable. They fought well and led their men well, however, and that, after all, was the chief requisite.

" Well, notwithstanding such drawbacks, every regiment could go through the manual and platoon and bayonet exercises to English words of command with a smartness and precision to which not many Volunteer companies can attain ; could manœuvre very fairly in companies or as a battalion ; and each regiment had been put through a regular course of musketry instruction, every man firing his ninety rounds at the regular distances up to 300 yards, the scores and returns being satisfactorily kept and the good shots rewarded.

" It was a most fortunate thing for General Gordon, that, a few years before he accepted the Chinese command, he had been employed in surveying and mapping precisely that portion of the country in which his future operations were carried on. This part of China is a vast network of canals and towpaths ; there are absolutely no roads, wheeled vehicles are never used, and the bridges still remaining were scarce and precarious. It was an immense advantage to know what canals were still navigable, which choked with weeds, and what bridges were left standing ; where the ground would be likely to bear artillery, and where it was impassable swamp. Gordon knew every feature of the country better than any other person, native or foreigner—far better even than the rebels who had overrun it and been in partial possession for years.

" But even these advantages would go but a short way towards accounting for the complete and thorough success which marked

Gordon's career where his predecessors had gained merely temporary advantages, fruitless towards securing the main object in view, the expulsion of the enemy from the province. The reasons for Gordon's great successes, for his unparalleled feat, must be sought for elsewhere ; and they are, without doubt, firstly his military genius, and secondly his character and qualities, which were such as to cause all brought in contact with or serving under him to have unbounded faith in his capacity, and to feel firmly that the best means at his disposal would be used to the best purpose.

" To persons who know General Gordon, his unassuming ways and quiet retiring manners, it speaks volumes that the ignorant men and rowdy officers composing his contingent should have looked on him in the light they did, and in the manner I have attempted to describe.

" That a swaggering, ostentatious, dashing, and successful General should be looked up to by such men would be natural enough. If one were to draw inferences, one might, perhaps, say the ignorant Chinamen were better judges than certain well-educated folk nearer home."

Admirable as is the above testimony to Gordon's influence over his men, it contains a statement which is quite incorrect. Gordon knew nothing of the country he was destined to traverse, except that portion of it which represented the thirty miles radius round Shanghai, marked out by the Government as a protection against the inroads of the rebels.

The voice of the press and the voice of the public died away in an echo of the old strain, that in this country to be an Engineer is to be unfit for staff employ. When the authorities were called upon by the Khedive, however, a few months later, to allow Gordon to enter the Egyptian service and settle a question of more importance to Egypt than to England, they readily gave their consent.

9

CHAPTER X

HE left Galatz towards the end of 1873. Early next year he took service with the Khedive, and succeeded Sir Samuel Baker as Governor of the Tribes in Upper Egypt. While at Constantinople in the summer of 1872, he had been asked by Nubar Pasha, whom he had greatly impressed during the sitting of the Danubian Commission, to recommend some officer of Engineers to fill the post. A year later, he tendered his own services, subject always to the approval of the British Government. No objection was raised; so he came to London, made his preparations, and started forthwith for Central Africa, calling at Cairo on his way for final instructions.

The Khedive proposed to give him £10,000 a year; but he would not hear of it. He declined to accept more than £2000. This very unusual conduct gave rise to a great deal of comment at the time, and has since been the subject of much criticism; but to those who knew the man, and the way in which Ismail filled his treasury, the refusal was intelligible enough. In the first place, while acting as English Commissioner at Galatz, he had been in receipt of £2000 a year from his own Government; and it did not fall in with his theory of patriotism nor his sense of honour to accept a larger stipend from a foreign Government than he had been receiving from his own. He knew well, too, that the larger sum would in point of fact be blood-money wrung from the wretches under his rule. He decided, therefore, to take no more than would pay his expenses.

Egypt's advance into Central Africa since 1853 had been considerable. In that year her possessions on the Nile did not extend much farther than 100 miles south of Khartoum. Now her rule had touched the Albert and Victoria Lakes, while the conquest of Darfour had brought her western frontier within fifteen days' march of Lake Tchad, and her eastern to the lower Red Sea and the Gulf of Aden. The country south of Khartoum —Baker's Ismailia—was first opened up by European traders, whose main object was the acquisition of ivory. They were not long in finding out that " black ivory " was far more profitable than white, and they soon established fortified posts, garrisoned them with armed bands, captained them with Arab bravos, and kidnapped and sold the negroes far and near. At last the traffic grew so large and shameless, that it became the scandal of the world. There was a hue and cry, and the European traders were obliged to withdraw. This did not, however, prevent them from selling their stations to the Arabs, who paid a tax to the Egyptian Government, and so bought toleration and impunity. In less than ten years from the date of this new arrangement, the slave-trade became a Government monopoly. The suffering tribes suffered tenfold. The Arab captains, being under no control as heretofore, increased their bands by pressing the boy slaves taken in their raids. They trained them up in the arts of kidnapping and plunder ; and they set them to the very work of which they were the victims. In this way the hunters of men became a power, and their horrible traffic a dominant interest. At last the Government got at once afraid and ashamed of them. Their hordes were a standing menace to its peace, whilst the outcry against them was a blemish on its fame. Moreover, so successful and strong were they, and so confident withal in their strength, that they refused to pay the tax. One of them, indeed, a certain Zebehr Rahama—called the Black Pasha—set up as the equal and rival of the Khedive himself. He was lord of over thirty stations ; and Dr. Schweinfurth found him surrounded by a court, and living in little less than princely state.

Zebehr, indeed, was not a man to be trifled with. An officer named Bellali was sent out to humble his pride, and put him in his proper place ; but he met Bellali in battle, and routed him with great slaughter. The Khedive seems at first to have been exasperated by his defeat, but he was afterwards compelled to submit to it ; for Zebehr grew stronger year by year, and was soon confirmed in his position as the King of the Slave-dealers in Equatorial Africa. Then the Khedive grew thoroughly afraid of him. He made the scoundrel a Bey, and in his invasion of Darfour he accepted him as an ally. Zebehr marched on the enemy from the south, while Ismail Pasha Yacoob, who represented the Khedive, supported the slave-dealer from the north. The Sultan of

Darfour and his two sons were slain; the country was subdued; and Zebehr was made a Pasha. But this was not enough for him; he wanted to be Governor-General. The Khedive, who had encouraged slave-dealing while it served to increase his revenue, was converted to active and sonorous philanthropy the moment he saw his own supremacy at stake. He began to regard the traffic with a holy horror, and he gave out to the admiring world of Europe that he was determined to suppress and stamp it out. To this end (he said) he engaged the services of Sir Samuel Baker; to this end he called to his aid the genius of Gordon. The lesson must be made clear—to use his own words—even in those remote parts, that a mere difference of colour does not make men a commodity, and that life and liberty are sacred things. Under this mask of philanthropy, Gordon, who was known for one of the most philanthropic of men as well as one of the most daring and brilliant of commanders, was chosen by him as his new Governor. Under this mask of philanthropy Upper Egypt was formed into a separate Government, and the Khedive claimed as a monopoly of the State the whole of its trade with the outside world.

Gordon grew restless during his few days' sojourn at Cairo. The fact is, that before he had been many hours in the place he had, with his rapid perception, gone to the heart of the whole scheme. Almost his first words on writing home from Egypt were these: " I think I can see the true motive of the expedition, and believe it to be a sham to catch the attention of the English people." Nevertheless, he was determined to go through with his undertaking, and do his utmost to relieve the sufferings of the miserable tribes. We shall see him in the course of this narrative surrounded by a thousand difficulties and dangers, over which he triumphed with a force of will, an energy, and a genius of enterprise and resource, almost unmatched. The spirit in which he pursued his perilous task may be gathered from his own words, uttered at a later period: " I will do it, for I value my life as naught, and should only leave much weariness for perfect peace."

It had been Gordon's wish to proceed by ordinary steamer down the Red Sea to Suakim, but Nubar Pasha, who in many ways had tried his patience, declared that the Governor of Upper Egypt must go in state. So a number of servants were engaged, and, leaving his staff to follow, the new Governor, with an equerry of the Viceroy, departed on his way. A special train was in readiness to take him to Suez, but the engine broke down, and he had to continue the journey by ordinary train. This delighted him greatly. "They had begun in glory," he said, "and ended in shame." He reached Suakim on February 25th. On his arrival he was put in quarantine for the night, probably because the Governor was not ready to receive him. There were some 220 troops on board, destined to serve him as an escort across the desert to Berber. It was a fortnight's march; but the length was rather welcome, as Gordon, strong in his Chinese experience, felt that it would enable his soldiers, who were the merest ragamuffins, to know him better.

His staff consisted of Romulus Gessi, an able and daring Italian, whom he had known as an interpreter in the Crimea; Mr. Kemp, engineer; the two Linants; Mr. Russell, son of Dr. W. H. Russell; Mr. Anson; Mr. Long, an American; and Abou Saoud, an ex-slaver whom Gordon, in the teeth of all sorts of opposition, had determined on converting to honesty and usefulness. They were thus divided:—Gessi and Anson, presently to take charge of Khartoum, were sent to the Bahr Gazelle to make friends with the natives, and observe what they could of the workings of the slave-trade; Kemp and Russell were despatched to the foot of certain falls, fifteen miles north of Gondokoro, to discover how far the river was navigable towards the Albert Nyanza, and eventually to launch a steamer on the lake; Linant was deputed to make excursions among the tribes; Colonel Long to take charge of Gondokoro; while Abou Saoud, known up country as the "Sultan," was to help his captain to a knowledge of the enemy's movements. Gordon, I may note, had found this fellow a prisoner at Cairo. The Khedive knew not how to deal with him, when Gordon, seeing the use to which his knowledge of the country could be turned, offered to take him on his staff. The Khedive and Nubar Pasha refused to sanction the scheme. They knew that in employing one who had already shown himself to be a treacherous desperado, the Governor would be risking his life. Nevertheless, at his request, an interview was arranged; and as he still persisted in his determination, the slave-hunter was set at liberty and sent with him into the Soudan.

The party left Berber by boat on March 9th, and after three days' sail arrived at Khartoum, a place well situated, but of flat-roofed mud houses. The Governor-General, in full uniform, came out to meet Gordon, and he landed to salutes of artillery and the strains of a brass band. He was greeted with excellent news; the "sudd," a grassy growth on the river, had been cleared away by the soldiers, so that the journey from Khartoum to Gondokoro, which had taken Sir Samuel Baker upwards of fourteen months, was reduced to no more than three weeks.

He remained at Khartoum eight days. During this time he busied himself, notwithstanding the excessive heat and dryness of the air, to which he was not yet habituated, in holding a review, in visiting the hospital and the schools, and in issuing this decree :—

"By reason of the authority of the Governor of the Provinces of the Equatorial Lakes, with which His Highness the Khedive has invested me, and the irregularities which until now have been committed, it is henceforth decreed :

"1. That the traffic in ivory is the monopoly of the Government.

"2. No person may enter these Provinces without a 'teskere' from the Governor - General of Soudan, such 'teskere' being available only after it shall have received the *visa* of the competent authority at Gondokoro or elsewhere.

"3. No person may recruit or organise armed bands within these Provinces.

"4. The importation of firearms and gunpowder is prohibited.

"5. Whosoever shall disobey this decree will be punished with all the rigour of the military laws.

"GORDON."

On the 22nd of March he sailed for Gondokoro. Great crocodiles basked on the Nilotic mud; flocks of migratory birds wheeled through the burning air. Here were storks, and pelicans, and tiny egrets; while huge river-horses splashed and blew, and troops of monkeys, their tails "stuck up straight over their backs like swords," came down to drink of the sacred stream. The banks were thickly wooded with gum and tamarisk. Some of the inhabitants wore gourds for hats; others wore nothing at all, not even gourds, and fled affrighted at a pointing telescope. As the staff had not yet come up, Gordon had to look after nearly everything himself. Nevertheless, his spirits were good, and his remarks on his strange surroundings are often full of humour. One moonlight night, for instance, as he was thinking of home behind and the difficulties ahead, there came a loud laughing from a large bush on the bank. "I felt put out," he writes; "but the irony came only from birds, that laughed at us from the bushes for some time in a very rude way. They were a species of stork, and seemed in capital spirits, and highly amused at anybody thinking of going up to Gondokoro with the hope of doing anything." Six days up the river he met a steamer from Gondokoro, in which, being a faster one, he continued his journey. No one had the slightest idea that he was coming ; and he foresaw a surprise both general and unwelcome.

They entered Saubat River on the 2nd of April. Lingering here to cut wood for the steamer's fires, they surprised a tribe of Dinkas—a black, pastoral people, who worship wizards. The chief was with great difficulty induced to come on board with four of his tribe. He was in full dress, says Gordon—a necklace. His form of salutation was first to softly lick the back of the white man's hands ; then to hold his face to his own and make as if he were spitting. He proved himself a glutton and a tyrant by devouring his neighbour's portion of the general meal. After this he and his liege-men sang a hymn of praise and thanks to Gordon. They then proceeded to crawl to kiss his feet, but this luxury was not allowed them. They were enriched with a splendid present of beads, and went off rejoicing.

Resuming her way, the steamer cleared the Bahr Gazelle in twelve hours ; for though the river is very narrow there, and the banks are marshy, the "sudd," as I have said, had been cleared, and the passage was easy. Gordon did not find the look of the place so bad as might have been expected, considering the many that have died there. What troubled him most was the mosquitoes. He found them worse than any he had ever endured : in China, at Batoum, or on the Danube itself.

On April 4th they reached the Bahr Gazelle, where it joins the Gondokoro River, and forms a small lake rimmed with morasses. As they steamed on they met swarms of natives, many of whom had rubbed their faces with wood-ash, and made unto themselves complexions the colour of slate-pencil. These, the Governor-General found, were badly fed and in much suffering. "What a mystery, is it not?" he writes, "why they are created ! —a life of fear and misery night and day ! One does not wonder at their not fearing death. No one can conceive the utter misery of these lands—heat and mosquitoes day and night all the year round. But I like the work, for I believe I can do a great deal to ameliorate the lot of the people."

At Bohr, a slavers' hold, the inhabitants were anything but

civil; they had heard of the Khartoum decree. At the mission at Sainte-Croix, on the other hand, the people came out with songs and dances as the steamer went by. She cast anchor off Gondokoro on the 16th of April, twenty-four days after leaving Khartoum. The townsmen were amazed by Gordon's advent, for they had not even heard of his nomination. He found his seat of government scarce less dangerous than wretched. Half a mile from its walls, owing to the ill-treatment to which the natives had been subjected, the Governor-General himself would have gone in peril of his life. Still, though the state of the people was as bad as it could well be, he was confident that he could relieve their sufferings and bring about a better state of things for them. The toughest part of his task, he felt, would be to win their confidence.

In this spirit we find him constantly travelling between point and point, making friends with his subjects as he goes. To some he gives grain; others he employs in planting maize—an occupation they had hitherto feared to follow, as always when they sowed a patch of ground, their little harvest was taken from them; till it came to pass that these poor negroes flocked about him in great numbers. They mostly had a grievance; sometimes they wanted him to buy their children, whom they were too poor to feed themselves. Important in the achievement of this admirable result was his prompt and resolute action with their tyrants, the slavers. These blackguards, he found, were often in collusion with the Government. They stole the cattle and kidnapped their owners, and they shared the double booty with officials of a liberal turn of mind. Thus, in these early days, through the curiosity of his interpreter, who got possession of some letters from a gang of man-hunters to the Governor of Fashoda, he discovered that 2000 stolen cows and a number of kidnapped negroes were on their way from these gentry to their estimable correspondent. He confiscated all the cattle, as he could not return them to their owners, who were too far off. The slaves he either sent home or bought himself. They, poor creatures, were only too glad to be with him; they showed it by coming up and trying to touch his hands, and even the hem of his garment; and he did not hesitate to go among them alone. One of the slaves recaptured on this occasion was a Dinka chief, and him he turned to good account. The chief slavers he took and cast into prison. Afterwards he discovered useful qualities in them, and took them into his employ; dealing with them, in fact, as he had dealt with the Chinese rebels, whom he first conquered and then enlisted.

In the middle of May he went down to Berber to fetch his baggage, which had been left behind. An interesting account of what happened to him on the journey is given by one of his staff : "Colonel Gordon turned up last Saturday, having run down from Khartoum in three days; but he very nearly came to grief on the way at one of the cataracts. There were two fellows at the wheel, and one wanted to go to the left and the other to the right of the reef, and between them were making straight on it, when Gordon rushed to the helm and just made a shave of it; but as it was, they carried away a lot of paddles, and had rather a smash. *When he arrived, he put us all to rights at Berber, and was very kind and considerate.* He soon put the very troublesome gentleman who was ordering us about in his proper place, and was surprised to find him with us at all."

At this time, and for a period of nearly two months, Gordon was at Saubat River. The country was utterly forlorn and desolate; the slavers had passed that way, and scarcely a soul was to be seen for miles. But for his passionate interest in humanity, the solitude must have proved overpowering. The land lay so remote from even Cairene civilisation, that the Arab troops were deported there for punishment, as the Russians to Siberia. Nevertheless, Gordon retained his health and spirits. He was never idle; and when his public duties were done, he amused himself by inventing traps for the huge rats which shared his cabin.

He had no reason to regret his investment in captured slaves. They were strong, hardy rascals, and they worked well for him, especially in transferring the station to the other side of the river, to a drier site and better water. There he awaited the slave convoy, and a drove of asses (180 strong) from Khartoum. Meanwhile he interested himself in the natives who sought his aid, and dealt, as he knew how, with a captured cargo of slaves. He forgot no ministration, however trivial; he left no duty, however small, undone. "She had her tobacco up to the last," he writes of a poor old woman, whom he fed up for weeks, but who died at last. "What a change from her misery! I suppose she filled her place in life as well as Queen Elizabeth." To him she was as much as his "kings" at Gravesend—as anyone in need of solace or aid.

Towards the end of August he left this miserable place for

Gondokoro, where much trouble awaited him. As he expected, he found his staff in discontent, and intrigue at height among his officials. He arrived on the 4th of September; and with Raouf Bey, commander of the troops at Gondokoro, a man hostile to him, and Abou Saoud, his lieutenant, he went to receive the salaams of the functionaries, officers, and soldiers. Through the influence of Abou Saoud, all seemed quiet among the tribes; the chiefs had submitted, and were peaceably disposed. But Raouf Bey was jealous of Abou Saoud; he was angry, too, because Gessi and Anson had been sent to Bahr Gazelle, with three large boats and twenty Arab soldiers, to reconnoitre for stations and make friends with the tribes. With all his opportunities, as Gordon knew, he had done absolutely nothing; so of Raouf he had resolved to be rid, and to start him for Cairo with letters to the Khedive. Another heavy trouble was that his staff was down with ague and fever to a man, so that, worn to a shadow himself, he had to play sick-nurse day and night. Linant, Campbell, and Russell were very ill (the latter in Gordon's own tent); and Gessi, before his departure for Bahr Gazelle, had only recently recovered from fever. Even his servants were helpless. Add to this that he had all the money arrangements and officers' accounts on his hands, and the picture will be complete. Linant died the day he left Gondokoro.

Gordon's next move was to Rageef; to build a new station on higher and healthier ground. There he found that Abou Saoud had been taking elephant tusks from the chiefs, and deceiving him in other ways. It was the beginning of the end for the ex-slaver. He made himself so objectionable by bullying the people, and coming into the Governor's cabin and usurping the Governor's functions, that there was nothing for it but there and then to get rid of him. Gordon dictated the following letter, and sent Abou down to Gondokoro:—

"Abou, when I took you up at Cairo, there was not an Arab or a foreigner who would have thought of employing you; but I trusted to your protestation, and did so. When I got to Gondo- koro, you were behaving properly, and I congratulated myself on your appointment to the high post I gave you. Soon, however, I came little by little to repent my action, and to find out my fair treatment was thrown away. You tried to deceive me about ——, about ——, and about ——; you misstated ——; you told me falsely about ——, etc., etc. To come to more personal

matters, you strangely forgot our relative positions; you have
forced your way into my private apartments at all times, have
disputed my orders in my presence, and treated all my other
officers with arrogance, showing me that you are an ambitious,
grasping man, and unworthy of the authority I gave you.   If you
do this under my eyes, and at the beginning of your work, what
will you do when away from me ?   Now hear my decision.   Your
appointment is cancelled, and you will return to Gondokoro and
wait my orders.   Remember, though I remove you from your
office, you are still a Government officer, subject to its laws, which
I shall not hesitate to put in force against you if I find you
intriguing."

"I then went on to say," writes Gordon, "that his scheme to
cause the troops to revolt had never alarmed me, and that I felt
confident that they would see their interest lay with me and not
with him ; so it ended with my saying that I would be merciful to
him, and let him go away on leave, not to return."

It was fortunate that Gordon was thus summary, for there is
no doubt that he would have been in peril of his life.   Abou
Saoud had tried to get up a mutiny among his own soldiers, a set
of cannibals from the Niam-Niam, in order to force Gordon to let
him go to Duffli with the steamer, which was in parts, and had to
be pieced together at that place.   The black soldiers said they
would not go without him ; so Gordon, who had some time before
proclaimed as a motto for all the word "Hurryat," or "Liberty,"
said, "Do not go at all, then ; but you will not make me send
Abou Saoud with you ; that would infringe my Hurryat."   He
then added that, as they were in receipt of Government pay,
he expected that they would obey him.   This seems to have
frightened them ; so they came and begged him to let them go
with the steamer.

So little help had he from some of his subordinates, that the
Commandant at Gondokoro sent up to him, with a mountain
howitzer, old ammunition tubes instead of new ones ; they had
been recently used for a salute.   This humorous proceeding imperilled Gordon's life.   It left him defenceless, and with only ten
men, in a place where no Arab would have stayed without a
hundred.

The climate at Rageef was much better than at Gondokoro,
and the country had better features.   Gordon set to work to
instruct the people in the use of money.   This was not easy, as

the custom was for the chiefs to farm their men, and take payment in beads or calico. Gordon's first aim was to stop the system, and to this end he showed the people that they might earn for themselves. First, he gave a man so many beads for his work; next, he gave him half a piastre, or one penny, and offered to sell him beads for that amount. The men soon caught the idea, and Gordon fixed certain prices for certain things, and put together little lots for sale; in fact, as he himself says, he made a regular shop, much to the discontent of all the old hands, who were dead against "these new-fangled ideas." He found that many of the negroes did not work well on daily wages, so he introduced the system of task-work. He gave himself up to the amusement of the soldiers, and delighted them with a magic lantern and a magnesium-wire light, and by firing a gun 150 yards off with a magnetic exploder.

Meantime, three weeks having gone by since Abou Saoud's dismissal, Gessi and Kemp asked Gordon to reinstate him. Gordon forgave his ex-lieutenant. "One wants some forgiveness one's self," he said, "and it is not a dear article." He wrote to Abou, saying that if he liked he could join Kemp at Duffli, and take Rageef on his way. On the night of his arrival at Rageef, Abou asked for his old post. Gordon gave him what he asked, and talked about his journey to Duffli; whereupon Abou said he could not go without 100 soldiers. As there were not so many on hand, he had to stay where he was. He hated the new system of buying for money; and later on, while some ivory was selling, he was seen in earnest conversation with a certain chief. After this not a negro came near the place, though crowds had been there regularly before his arrival. Presently Gessi wrote that someone was with Gordon whom the blacks did not like, and that they would not come over while he was there. Gordon was wroth that no name was given, but he at once concluded that Abou was the man. The mystery was soon cleared up. Gordon soon found that the chief referred to, who had hitherto shown himself friendly, had been intriguing with another for a canoe to be used in an attack on the station. Gordon opined that probably Abou had egged him on—had told him the Pasha was coming to take his cows; or that the sight alone of the ex-slaver had aroused his fears. In any case, a conspiracy was undoubtedly afoot when Gordon came back to Rageef. He had been to Gondokoro to arrange for Abou's departure, when he met the hostile chief on the road, and was invited into his hut. As it was dark, he

declined to go. Next day the chief visited him with a great bulk
of armed men, and after some apparently friendly intercourse
withdrew. Soon after he and his following returned, and surrounded the tent. Gordon, who had watched their movements,
got down his guns; he then told the would-be rebel to walk off,
and the would-be rebel at once obeyed. He was bent on mischief;
but the lonely hero was too much for him.

Abou was by no means the only traitor in the camp. It was
not long ere Gordon learned that the passage of a convoy of
slaves on their way to Fashoda had been connived at by his
Mudir. This piece of ill news was soon followed by another.
Kemp, the engineer, came in from Duffli, at the head of the
cataract, 134 miles from Rageef, where he had been trying to
build and launch the steamer, thence to work down to the Albert
Nyanza. Some tribesmen there had come to blows with the slave
soldiers and then robbed them, so that he had to come back,
leaving the greater part of the steamer behind. But in other
directions the prospect was more cheering. Long returned from
a visit to Mtesa, King of Uganda, to report a good reception
from that suspicious monarch. The discovery of a water-passage
between Urundogani and Foweira was another important event,
and is commented on by Gordon in one of his letters as matter for
great congratulation.

During these months, November and December, there was a
great deal of illness among the members of the staff. In fact, the
majority were down with fever, and had to leave one after the
other, their leader being almost alone in resisting the climate,
though he was fast making himself ill by nursing and waiting on
the others. At length things got so bad that he had to give
orders that all illness should be kept away from him, and that the
staff should not come near him except on duty. Sickness, however, so increased—probably owing to a heat unusual even in
these horrible regions—that at last only one of the original staff
was left, eight having gone from the place. Then Gordon made
up his mind to move the station twelve miles off, to Lardo, which
stood higher above the marshes. This involved a great deal of
work; but in four days he got clear of Gondokoro, and before the
end of the year was settled in his new quarters.

"Gordon has certainly done wonders since his stay in this
country," says one of his staff. "When he arrived, only ten
months ago, he found 700 soldiers in Gondokoro, who did not

dare to go a hundred yards from that place, except when armed
and in small bands, on account of the Baris, who were exasperated
at the way Baker had treated them.   With these 700 men Gordon
has garrisoned eight stations, namely, at Saubat, at Ratachambe
Bohr, Lardo, Rageef, Fatiko, Duffli, and Makraka, the frontier of
the Niam-Niam country.   Baker's expedition cost the Egyptian
Government £1,170,247, while Gordon has already sent up
sufficient money to Cairo to pay for all the expenses of his
expedition, including not only the sums required for last year, but
the amount estimated for the actual one as well."

CHAPTER XI

CHIEF among Gordon's projects for 1875 was the junction of the stations of Gondokoro and Foweira by a chain of fortified posts a day's journey apart. The stations were a six months' march from each other; the journey could only be undertaken by a body of 100 men. After the change, travelling was much more rapid; and a company of 10 was large and strong enough for safety. Gordon also proposed to concentrate himself in the south, and open a route to Mombaz Bay, 250 miles north of Zanzibar; and should Victoria Lake turn out as large as it was reported, he looked to making it much easier of access. These plans he had laid before the Khedive, and had asked him to send a steamer with 150 men to Mombaz Bay, there to establish a station, and so push towards Mtesa's country. All these reforms were important, for in the then state of affairs the whole north of his province was worthless marsh and desert, and the navigation to Khartoum was extremely difficult, the Arab mariners being quite unskilled, while firewood was growing scarce. It was part of the Khedive's purpose to hoist the Egyptian flag on the Albert Nyanza. To do this, Gordon chose the western bank of the river, and worked his way along to Duffli, which lies some 800 miles due south of Khartoum towards Lake Victoria; with the stream on his left, he could only be attacked from the right.

Meantime he had received news from Foweira, 100 miles farther south of Duffli, that Kaba Rega, King of Unyoro, in league with the old slavers now ostensibly in the Khedive's service, was planning an attack thereon. The officers of the station had expelled the slave-hunters from their service. Some fifty came down to Gordon, and were ordered on to Khartoum, with ninety other bandits from the Fatiko province. He had recaptured fifty-two slaves, and he describes the lamentations of

the kidnappers as terrible. He now determined to drive Kaba
Rega out of his kingdom, and give it to Rionga, who, in 1872,
had been Sir Samuel Baker's Vakeel.

But before these plans could be even set in train, he had to
deal with a troublesome chief named Bedden. To Bedden, in the
autumn of the previous year, he had sent an envoy with presents.
Bedden replied that the next ambassador would be killed. Next,
Bedden, who ruled a district very near the station at Rageef,
attacked a friendly chief in the neighbourhood. Gordon, though
averse from the step, felt that the only means of bringing about
his submission would be to make a raid, and drive off his cattle.
He therefore sent sixty men east of the river, while he himself,
with one officer and ten men, sailed up the western bank to the
islands where the cattle-pens were. It was moonlight when the
raiders landed; and as they marched along the shore to Bedden's
camp, which was fifteen miles off, they fell in with some mighty
hippopotami. Gordon, as they stood with their vast hides
glistening in the moonlight, playfully waved his handkerchief at
them, but they answered the friendly greeting by "plumping into
the river with a great splash."

The boat then struck a shoal, and Gordon, fearing for the
men in her, sent her back. While he was giving these orders,
nine of his party went on without him. He, with the two men
left and an interpreter, soon found himself within earshot of the
cattle-pens. They were, he writes, in a very bad military
position, inasmuch as they were open to attack from the front
and the left alike. On starting, the two detachments had had
orders to close in on their commander. There was, however, not
much faith to be placed in them. The Soudanese, indeed, were
in such a state of panic, that they mistook some rocks on the
rising ground for villages. The plight was a bad one; but there
was no help for it, and Gordon lay down and slept, till he was
roused by the dawn and the sound of a drum from the kraals.
He thus describes the end of the affair :—

"The cattle at night are enclosed in *seribas* or kraals, with
one entrance. The warriors sleep inside. The mode of attack is
to put a few men near the entrance, with orders to fire three
shots at dawn, before the cattle are let out; for if once out, you
can scarcely catch one of them. On hearing the shots the
warriors escape, beating the war-drum if they have time. They
never defend the *seribas* ; and it is always the best policy to let

them go harmless, as the cows are the great object. As the red glow of a hot day increased, we heard, on the far-away hill opposite to us, to the east, the three signal-shots; and then our island *seriba* sounded its *nozan* or drum. It was a mild one, and was not taken up by other drums, as I expected; then silence ensued. As day advanced, we saw the supposed villages of the soldiers were rocks, and not a native was to be seen. Soon afterwards some appeared, but they seemed puzzled by the three signals, and went off. Before long, our allies—the friendly sheikh's people—came up; and some of their little warriors swam across to the island, but reported that the Bedden warriors were in the midst of the cows, and shot arrows at them when they approached. However, these soon went off, and we got the cows. We rewarded, with what was not our own, the 'friendlies,' and came back. The other party on the east coolly passed down the other side with herds of cattle, and never paid any attention to us. The party on the west were never seen by us. It appears that they reached the scene of their operations at midnight, and sent a guide on to explore. This guide met a woman going for water; he tried to catch her; she cried out and gave the alarm, so the natives let out the cows. However, including our herd of 600 head of cattle, we got altogether 2600 head; so that without any effusion of blood on either side, or burning of villages, we punished Bedden severely."

Next day Gordon made a similar expedition against a chief named Lococo. He, however, had had warning from a neighbouring tribe, into whose territory he drove his herds; some 500 cows were taken all the same. About a fortnight later the Governor was out riding, when he suddenly came upon Bedden, and found him old and blind. Seeing some natives seated under a tree, he asked them if they were Bedden's people; whereupon they pointed to an old man among them, and said "Bedden." Gordon went up to him, gave him his whistle and some tobacco and told him that if his tribe behaved well, nothing would be taken from them. Two days after, the old chief returned the visit, when Gordon returned him twenty of his cows; a piece of generosity which had an excellent effect on the tribes.

For some time Gordon moved from one station to another, shooting hippopotami, cleaning guns, mending watches and musical-boxes. He was waiting for the Nile to fall, that he might get his steamers up from Khartoum, and find out whether there was any means of passing the rapids at Duffli. First of all, however, he had to march some thirty miles to southward, with forty Soudanese, fifty Makraka recruits, and a gang of porters. He got as far as Kerri, and, returning to Rageef, found that the Nile was navigable between. While encamped at Kerri, a thunderstorm gave his ragamuffins an opportunity of pillaging some houses under pretence of taking shelter. Gordon would not allow them to enter the villages, and got them camped under some trees. Suddenly, in the midst of the storm, shots were fired, and the cry arose that they were attacked. A reconnaissance showed no enemy of any kind. Nevertheless, the men insisted they had been attacked, and fell to sacking the houses, while some actually fired on the natives on the opposite bank, to give their abominable stratagem an appearance of truth. Of such was his material for the regeneration of the Soudan.

From Rageef he went north again to Lardo, and then, with 100 soldiers to form a station, back to Kerri. He had to get three nuggars (strong boats used on the Nile) to withstand the charges of the hippopotami. To put these nuggars through the violent eddies was both difficult and dangerous. Sixty or eighty went hauling at the boat; and if the strain was slackened for an instant the boat capsized. No sooner had Gordon settled things, to some extent, at Kerri, than he was off again to Lardo, to upset the do-nothing Governor, and transport him to Khartoum (which he called his Botany Bay). Here, while waiting for his steamers (stuck fast at Khartoum for some five months through mismanagement), he made up for the ex-Governor's loss of time by himself attending to every detail of the administration. His extraordinary energy received a new impulse from the inactivity of his Arabs. All day long they stood and stared at their strange Governor—the "Little Khedive," as they called him—watching his every movement as if it were something miraculous; noting, in an ecstasy of amazement, how he would come down from his divan, and put his kingship behind him, while he cleaned his guns or contrived a rocket-machine out of an old pump.

At last the nuggars were started up the river, and a tremendous business it was to get the lazy Arabs to work. They went "as if they were at a funeral;" they hid in the grass whenever they could get a chance of shirking. Sometimes a rope would break, and a nuggar go off on a six-knot current; sometimes the waters would rush from both sides of the rocks, and tear the mast right out. Then there were the difficulties with shy and unknown tribes to be encountered; there was the encumbrance of over 100 women and children, who accompanied the soldiers, to be dealt with; there was the army of wizards beating the water and shrieking incantations to speed the white men on. In this last amusement, Gordon, taking the lead, would "pray the nuggars up," he says; as he used to pray up the men of the Ever-Victorious Army when they wavered in the breaches. It was a picture unmatched in its contrasts of torpor and energy, of Eastern and Western faith.

All this time it was impossible to judge what real progress they had made, or to fix their wherabouts, though sometimes they got over eight or ten miles a day. The tribes, besides being exceedingly timid, knew nothing of distance, and could not count. When asked how far off was this place or that, they invariably pointed to some point in the sky, to show that when the sun was there the traveller would arrive. Sometimes they were inclined to show fight; but the burning of a single hut or the discharge of a rifle brought them to their senses. It was, however, impossible to get any sort of help from them, either by persuasion or by force. And one day, in the middle of August, the need of help was desperate. One of the nuggars broke loose, and floated down into the middle of the rapids. Another boat had to be sent in pursuit, and, in Gordon's absence, it got entangled in the rocks. This delayed the party a whole day. They got off at last, however, and arrived, without further accident, at Laboré. Here they waited for ropes for their farther journey, and for the arrival of 250 soldiers from Lardo, together with some natives from Makadé. The tribes were wroth to see them encamped, but Gordon put things right by shooting a hippopotamus and giving them the carcase. They came about him in a most friendly spirit, whereupon he showed one of them how to fire his rifle; I need scarcely say that he held it while his pupil drew the trigger. But though the tribes fraternised with him, they soon attacked another station a mile from his own. Feeling that, with so many women and children about, it would not do to be thus molested, he kept a sharp look-out, and did not allow the negroes within a thousand yards of his hut. At night, to guard against an assault, he put up posts with telegraph wires between them, at a good height, so as to stop a rush. Meanwhile, the wizards were seen cursing their enemy, and waving him off the face of the earth. Gordon now and then threw a bullet into them, and spied the movements of their spies, who slunk about the camp, suddenly disappearing in the long grass or maize.

Very soon, Linant, a brother of the Linant who died at Gondokoro, came in with a party from Makadé. Gordon's opinion of
his Arab soldiers was now to be confirmed, under extremely
painful and trying circumstances. He had passed thirty men
over the river to the east bank, as he believed they would find
his steamer in the east channel. The moment they landed, the
natives came down on them, as they lay in the grass before the
station. Gordon at once crossed over. The moment they saw
him coming they made a rush at his men, but were repulsed.
He then attempted a parley, but they would none of it. They
knew him for the chief, and they made an attempt to surround
him. He let them come quite near, and then drove them back
with bullets. In the attack they showed great courage, crawling,
in the teeth of a heavy fire, close up to him on their bellies—
an attitude which made it most difficult to hit them. At this
pass Linant proposed to cross to the east bank, and burn their
houses; and Gordon, fearing that unless he took reprisals they
would attack the steamer, agreed. At 8 o'clock, on the 25th
August, he sent off thirty-six soldiers, two officers, and three
irregulars. About mid-day he heard firing, and then saw Linant,
in a red shirt he had given him, on a hill. The party remained
in view for about two hours, when they disappeared. Later in
the afternoon Gordon saw some thirty or forty blacks running
down to the river. He concluded that they had gone to see the
steamer; and, as they ran, he dropped a few bullets among them.
Ten minutes later he saw one of his own detachment on the
opposite bank without his musket, and he at once sent a boat to
bring him across. The fellow declared that the natives had
disarmed him, and had killed the whole party besides. Gordon
had only thirty men at his station, and it was not possible to
communicate with the steamer, where there were ninety more.
But he was determined to act, though his thirty men showed
signs of panic. As the station was not fortified, he thought it
best to move down to the other; but this was not easy to do.
The wives and children of the soldiers had first to be disposed
of; then there were many mishaps with the boats, one of which,
filling with water, stopped the passage of the others, and delayed
the party till dawn. Happily, they were not molested by the
tribesmen; these, with one exception, held resolutely aloof from
the proceedings. The exception was a wizard. With singular
indiscretion, this sage elected to survey the retreat from the top
of a rock. Here he grinned and cheered and vaticinated while

Gordon was giving his orders. The Governor took up his rifle. "I don't think that's a healthy spot from which to deliver an address," he said; and the wizard prophesied no more.

At last the other station was reached. Only one soldier was found on the field; and a boat was sent to bring him into safety.

It turned out, eventually, that four of Linant's men had escaped, but that Linant himself had been the victim of Gordon's red shirt. It had maddened the natives, who had come at him with a rush, and speared him where he stood. The whole affair, as far as can be gathered, seems to have been the result of a want, not of ammunition (every man had thirty rounds in his pouch, and there were two boxes of cartridges besides), but of discipline among Gordon's wretched soldiers. The party got scattered, and the natives came suddenly upon Linant. The trumpeter was one of the first to fall, and it was impossible to call the men together again. Gordon's grief at the loss of his friend was very great, the more so as he had lent him the fatal shirt. When Linant proposed the attack, he assured his chief that he was used to the work, and that he had defeated thousands of the tribesmen on his way back from King Mtesa's territory.

At the end of August the Governor of Fatiko arrived with more soldiers, and Gordon now had nearly 500 men. He therefore at once set to work to punish the natives by means of razzias. His first essay resulted in the capture of 200 cows and 1500 sheep. The chief's daughter, too, was seized; and Gordon sent her father a message that if he would submit he could have her again. The excitement caused by these raids was terrific. The tribes gathered on the hills and indulged in the wildest war-dances, while, night and day, the magicians were hard at work imploring curses and producing incantations. Poles were set up with the heads of Linant's party at top. The bodies had been buried for fear of ghosts, but the heads were kept as trophies.

By the middle of September these many difficulties were lightened by the arrival from Fatiko of Nuehr Agha, a capital officer. At last the steamer was got off, and the expedition set out for Laboré. There were many halts, however, occasioned by the Arabs' incapacity to carry out orders, or indeed to do in any way as they were told. They arrived on the 24th, established their station on a hill, and found the natives friendly. Gordon spent much of his time in exploring the country, about which he could gain not the slightest information from any of his followers.

One raid—only one—he had to make on a troublesome tribe between Moogie and Laboré. He was in even better health than usual, owing to the helpful presence of Nuehr Agha, and he was able, without breaking down, to walk twenty miles in the burning sun.

At last they came to Duffli. They camped between two high ranges of mountains, but only to find that the idea of taking up the steamer or the nuggars was hopeless. The Fola Falls were impassable for two miles. It was a great disappointment; but Gordon consoled himself by reflecting that up to this point the river had been proved navigable at certain seasons for steamers, and all the year round for small boats, and that much good would come of the line of posts which connected this southern portion of the province with the north, since it would now be difficult for the tribes to continue their hostilities. Besides this, it was easy to find the way and to know of everybody's whereabouts; to say nothing of the comfort of a plentiful supply of wood and of water along the line.

The halt at Duffli lasted a little over a fortnight. The tribes were a quiet race, living in kraals and out of sight, so that it was an event to see a human being. The silence and monotony of the place affected Gordon's spirits. Nor were they improved by news from certain of his stations. From Laboré [he heard that his interpreter, without whose aid he had managed all this time, was dead; that one of his commanders had allowed a man to go alone between two posts, and that the man had been murdered on the way; that at one place the sentries slept all night, and that an attack by the tribes was meditated on another. In the midst of this, he was seized with ague, and had to shift his quarters. He crossed the river and settled at Fashelie, a place nine miles from Duffli, on higher ground, and surrounded for hundreds of miles by yellow grass which stood six feet high. Hither, with the aid of fifty camels, it was his intention to move all his belongings along the Asua River, which at Duffli joins the Nile. Ere he did so, however, he had to rout out and send to Khartoum a gang of Dongola slave-dealers, who had settled at Fashelie and were making raids on the tribes.

It was all-important, before proceeding further south, to thoroughly subdue the tribes round Moogie, since, if the country was left in its then disturbed state, the communication between the posts from north to south would be constantly subject to interruption. At this place Gordon found an irritating letter, full

of complaints, from the Khedive. He at once wrote three telegrams, telling the Khedive that he should be at Cairo in April, and
that his successor had better be sent up without delay. Before these
telegrams were despatched, however, he received from the Khedive
a letter in a very different strain. It stated that His Highness
had placed Admiral McKillop under his command, and had sent
him with three men-of-war and 600 men to Juba, on which place
he proposed that he should march. Gordon, feeling that it would
be unfair to the Khedive to resign at such a pass, unpacked his
baggage and determined to continue his work, much to the astonishment of his followers, who did not know what this packing
and unpacking might mean. All the same, he resolved not to
fall in with the Khedive's plans, and made up his mind not to
march on Juba with the wretched troops at his command.

Scarce two months back he had lost his interpreter; now
there befell a new calamity. His servant fell sick of fever, and
died in a few hours. Gordon sorrowed much, though he had but
little time for sorrow. His hands were full; he was at the heart
of his work; and in a raid on some offending tribes he drove off
over 1500 head of cattle. This achievement, and a visit to
Laboré, for the parts of the steamer, brought the busy year to a
close. Successful so far, he was resolved on one thing more, and
that was not to explore the Albert Nyanza. He had told the
Khedive in 1874 that he would not do it; and though the feat
was generally expected of him by the Geographical Society and
the world at large, he was contented to have prepared the way
for another. What he wanted to do was to push on to Lake
Victoria Nyanza, and fulfil his promise to the Khedive of hoisting
the Egyptian flag upon its waters. The steamer which was to
enable him to do this was to follow him on his journey south,
Gessi having been left at Duffli to put it together and launch it,
with the lifeboat.

The year (1876) opened with a disappointment. On his way
from Fashelie to Fatiko, a distance of nearly fifty miles south-
wards, Gordon was overtaken by a courier, who came to inform
him that an influential chief under arrest had been allowed to
escape by the guard. The circumstance was the more annoying,
as the prisoner might have been of great service in bringing about
an understanding with his tribe. At Fatiko Gordon stayed but a
week. He then pushed on to Foweira, a hundred miles nearer
Lake Victoria Nyanza. The dreary drag through jungle grass
and thorns tore his clothes to tatters. His object was to swoop

down upon Kaba Rega, at Mrooli, put Rionga in his place, and establish a post. Rionga, a fine-looking fellow with prominent eyes, arrived at Foweira three days after him, and they left together. The journey to Mrooli was no better than the one just completed. Kaba Rega had taken to his heels, and transferred himself, magic stool and all, to Masindi, and Rionga was made king in his stead. Rionga, however, was in mortal dread of Kaba Rega, who was only a few miles off; and Gordon saw that it would be necessary to set up Anfina, another Unyoro magnate, at Masindi; since, if Kaba Rega were unmolested, he would have to station 150 men at Mrooli to keep him in check, while, with garrisons at Masindi and Mrooli, there was nothing to be feared. "I do so cordially dislike these wretched troops," he writes.

"They started off this morning to capture some cattle, and will soon be back, and there will be fine accounts of their bravery. Whoever has Masindi and Mrooli, to him or them the natives turn, so that, Kaba Rega being a refugee, the capture of Masindi renders him harmless. I have to go to all these places myself, for these slaves would never go. With troops one is not sure of, and in whom you have no confidence, I can imagine no position more trying. In all cases commanders have some reliable men. There is a moral conviction which it is necessary for soldiers to have, namely, that they will conquer; let this be wanting, and they are worthless. The Khedive has taken not the least notice of my complaints of them, but urges me on still further. What is it to him what tenfold additional trouble I have to take in consequence?"

Anfina was set up at Masindi accordingly. This made him Rionga's superior, and Rionga was furious. Gordon, when these matters were settled, went back to Fatiko, and joined Gessi at Duffli in February. A month later, after much trouble, his preparations were complete, and Gessi started with the two boats for Magungo and the Lakes. While his faithful lieutenant was hoisting the Egyptian flag, and being driven by a storm into the thick of Kaba Rega's troops, Gordon proceeded with his survey and with the administration of the various stations, going as far south again as Lardo, and back once more to Kerri. On his arrival here on April the 12th, he wrote home :—

"I have definitely, I hope, settled the stations along the line from Duffli to Lardo. Lardo and Duffli are termini; Rageef, Bedden, Moogie, and Iyoo " (a new station he had just made) " are postal stations; and Laboré and Kerri are main stations, and possess passages across the river, and enable raids to be made on the east bank, where a vast extent of country exists. Through this country used to pass the old land road south."

Of course these journeys were not without adventures, and of one of these I give an account in Gordon's own words :—

" You may remember that last year I had here a great deal of trouble to pass a rope across the river. I got one over—or rather the boatmen did—easily this time. However, on the other side the rope caught on a rowlock of the boat, and the current bore down with such force that it was difficult to release it. One of the men was hammering the rowlock while I lifted on the rope ; the rowlock slewed, and off went the rope. Before I could let go, it dragged me into the river; but I soon rose and caught the rudder, and was all right. A Reis (captain) jumped in after me, and his chemise got swept over his head, so, when he bobbed up near me, he was like the veiled prophet of Khorassan. I caught him by his veil, and we got out all safely. Yesterday, as we were hauling at the rope (I being seated under or near a tree to which we had it attached), a whip-snake was shaken down, and tried to obtain cover between me and the ground. However, I got clear of it."

At this time he was much alone, and his letters are long and interesting. He began to get anxious about Gessi; but that valiant Italian returned towards the end of April, after sailing round the Victoria Nyanza in nine days. He found it 140 miles long and 50 wide. The natives were hostile, and refused to parley till Gessi went away, for they took him by his colour for a fiend. But at Unyoro, Kaba Rega's chiefs had sent in their submission, and all was quiet. There was little to do at this time, as they were still waiting the completion of the steamer; and with nothing else to think of, it amused them not a little when the wizard of the tribe near Kerri announced that he should not allow them a single drop of rain, unless the Government gave him cows—" Which it has not done," says Gordon ; " and it is very odd that all around we have had rain, except near the station."

Gessi, during this period of inaction, made himself ill by smoking and lounging all day long. But Gordon made up his mind to give the three weeks he would have to wait for the steamer to exploring an "unknown branch" of the Nile. Away he went to Lardo. Here, during a storm, he was roused in the night by loud cries and shots close to the house. "I guessed what it was," he says, "and rushed out. Three elephants had chosen to try to land at the place cut in the bank to enable the servants to get water from the river. The sentry, however, saw them, fired at them, and made them give up their intention. You see, if they landed and got frightened, they would break down my house in a moment, and do a deal of damage. This is a favourite landing-place for them."

A fortnight later, homeward-bound for Kerri, he writes :—

"During a heavy thunderstorm to-day, while putting the side of my tent straight, I received, at the moment of a flash of lightning, a couple of severe shocks similar to what a strong electric machine would give. What an escape ! The verdict on people killed by lightning was in olden times 'killed by the visitation of God.' The heathens considered death by lightning was a special mark of distinction."

On his return he learned at Laboré that Gessi's presence was necessary at Khartoum ; and not long after he was able to say of him, "Gessi is now a great man at Khartoum ; he is my Vakeel-in-Chief, and has a lot of work." On the other hand, we learn from him that "Kaba Rega is now nearly deserted by all his adherents, and I hope soon to hear that this young man, repenting the evil of his ways, has made his submission." Gordon expected to be able to concentrate in all 250 troops at Unyoro, which, in those parts, would make him a mighty power.

At this time he was in very much better health, and the worries of office do not seem to have troubled him as they had. His letters abound in speculations on the subject of the Lakes ; and, despite his resolve not to explore, the exploring spirit was strong in him. He had been reading what Dr. Schweinfurth says of Lake Albert : "that it may belong to the Nile basin, though this is not certain, inasmuch as with seventy miles between Lake Albert and Foweira, it would be presumptuous, without the ocular proof, to derive the river from the lake." So, on the 20th of July, he left Duffli for Magungo, with the steamer and two lifeboats.

The steamer was not more than fifty feet long, and had but a couple of screws. The only way to the cabins was through the engine-room, down a break-neck ladder; but Gordon built a house on deck, and used the cabin as a storeroom. He took beads with him for the native chiefs. Writing from a place about half-way between Duffli and Magungo, he describes the river as varying in width from two to five miles, with no visible current, with a fringe of papyrus ten or twelve yards deep, and innumerable eyots of papyrus besides. He thought the rainy season was over, but in the night there was a tremendous shower; and as he had neglected to trench his tent, which he nearly always made it a rule to do, he was flooded out. He found Baker's maps wonderfully correct; and from these he had hoped to find a spot which would command a general view of the lake. But though he tried he failed. Of the tribes he remarked: " It is odd that the totally naked tribes seem to be in one circular place, between Duffli and Fashoda, and that then you have a ring of partially naked, and then the clothed tribes. Adam knew he was naked, but these naked tribes have no notion of it whatever; this is some great mystery. Up here they are all clothed."

He heard that Kaba Rega with six chiefs, but few soldiers, was about fifty-eight miles south of Masindi; the ex-King had forty muskets with him, but no powder, and appeared to have territory on the other side of the lake. A little later, about 300 of a tribe faithful to Kaba Rega, came down on a marauding expedition to Gordon's camp; but they were soon repelled. Early in August the party was three miles west of Murchison Falls, marching, some fifteen or twenty miles a day, now through pouring rain, then under a burning sun, through jungle and along ravines, and mapping the river as they went. They were often exposed to the attacks of the natives, who would suddenly appear and fling spears at them. " I do not carry arms, as I ought to do," says Gordon, " for my whole attention is devoted to defending the nape of my neck from mosquitoes." Having penetrated the country as far south as Nyamyango, he returned by river to Mrooli. It was a journey more dangerous even than the one by land; for in the many narrow channels through which they steered the natives stood in ambush among the papyri, and speared the boats as they passed.

On the way from Mrooli to Masindi, Gordon discovered that the troops he had left in charge at the latter place were at Keroto, a day's journey on the other side of it. The consequence was that the tribes came down on him, and he was in no slight peril of defeat. His troops made no attempt to meet him. Between September 26, when he arrived, and October 6, when he departed, he visited in turn Magungo, Murchison Falls, and Chibero, with a view to forming a line of posts from the Victoria Nile, or Somerset River, to the lake. Then, having arranged with his force for an assault on Kaba Rega—who was severely handled, but who eventually went back to his own country—he returned to Khartoum, and thence by Esneh to Alexandria, his health and spirits as good as ever.

CHAPTER XII

No sooner was Gordon in London, and it was known that he had not decided to resume his campaign in Upper Egypt, than people began to proclaim his fitness for the Governorship of Bulgaria. The *Times*, appreciative and admiring as always, published a vigorous account of the work he had been doing for the Khedive. "Surely," urged the writer, "his genius for government and command might be profitably utilised nearer home. If the jealousies of the Powers would permit him to be made Governor of Bulgaria, he would soon make that province as peaceful as an English county." This led to the publication of a number of letters. All were in favour of the idea ; some brought forward again some one or other of the young captain's many achievements to prove how apt for such a post he was. Gordon felt, however, that he could do nothing without first consulting with the Khedive. At the same time he was resolved not to go to Central Africa unless he went with greater powers. His relations with the Governor-General of the Soudan, Ismail Pasha Yacoob, had made it impossible for him to deal successfully with the slave question outside his own province ; and he had made up his mind that unless the Khedive threw in the Soudan, he would not return to his work. In this determination he left for Cairo early in the February of 1877. His visit was a complete and splendid triumph. Ismail Yacoob was removed, and Gordon was appointed Governor-General of the Soudan, with Darfour and the provinces of the Equator—a district 1640 miles long and close on 700 wide. He was to have three deputies, one for the Soudan, one for Darfour, and one for the Red Sea littoral and Eastern Soudan ; and it was formally declared that the objects of his governance were the improvement of the means of communication, and the absolute suppression of slavery. He was furthermore deputed to look into the Abyssinian affairs, and empowered to enter into negotiations with King John with a view to the settlement of matters in dispute between Abyssinia and Egypt.

The new enterprise was infinitely greater and more difficult than the old. Gordon was keenly alive to the tremendous responsibilities he had assumed. With all his strength of will, with all his trust in the guardianship of an unseen Power, we must not marvel if, alone in the great desert, with the results of ages of evil and wrong, the mystic and the man of action sometimes gave way in him, and he uttered a cry of despair. We must not forget to look back at what he had already suffered and done, and to remember how he longed for quiet. We must bear in mind that he was doing heroic work for the hero's true wages—the love of Christ and the good of his fellow-men. We must consider him as one who labours not for himself, but as the hand of the providence of God, and in the faith that his mission is of God's own setting. For all that, it is small wonder that out of the darkness which encompassed him on every side he sometimes cried out for rest—even the rest of death. The wonder is that in the teeth of perils so dire, and work so hard, and sufferings so manifold, he was allowed to pursue his mighty purpose and be with us still.

He left Cairo for the eastern borders of his government in the middle of February. He intended first to deal with Abyssinia. His last words on writing from the capital were these: "I am so glad to get away, for I am very weary. I go up alone, with an infinite Almighty God to direct and guide me; and am glad to so trust Him as to fear nothing, and, indeed, to feel sure of success."

Fully to understand the purpose of the mission to Abyssinia, it will be necessary to look at what had been going on there since King Theodore's death, in 1868, at the hands of Napier and the British. When Theodore was retreating to Magdala, a chieftain named Kasa offered Napier his services. They were accepted; and when our army evacuated the country he was rewarded by a gift of arms and ammunition. Thus furnished, Kasa at once swooped down on certain provinces, annexed them to his own dominion, and set up as a potentate under the style and title of Johannis, King of Abyssinia. At first his conquest made him nothing but enemies. Before long Theodore's heir took arms against him; but Johannis routed him, made him prisoner, and put him to the torture. This exploit strengthened his position, and in no great while he had succeeded in laying hands on the whole country, with the exception of Shoa and Bogos, and in achieving such an anarchy as made commerce impossible. Meanwhile Egypt had turned her attention to these parts, and in 1874 she annexed Bogos. This move, with her neighbourhood on the coast, to the west and to the south, caused her to be regarded with suspicion and alarm. The ill-feeling grew; and Walad el Michael, the hereditary Prince of Bogos, who had been imprisoned by Johannis, was released on the understanding that he should join in a crusade against her. In the war that ensued, the Egyptians began by holding the Abyssinian forces too cheap, and were severely beaten. Later on, the Abyssinians carried the war into the enemy's country, and were beaten in their turn. Meanwhile, Walad el Michael had quarrelled with Johannis (who after his first victory had robbed him of his spoils), and deserted to the enemy. After repulsing the Abyssinians, Egypt asked a truce; and while this was in operation, Walad returned to Bogos with 7000 men. There he set to work to make new mischief between the two countries. Johannis, finding that no decision as to terms of peace could be come to, and fearing the increased power of his enemy, the kinglet of Bogos, sent an envoy to Cairo offering to give up Hamacem. But the envoy was first of all detained, and afterwards, when he was released, was mobbed and pelted in the streets. Finally, he was packed off to Abyssinia, without a word of any kind. It was in the face of this insult—which was bitterly resented by Johannis — that Gordon went to Magdala as the Khedive's ambassador. His instructions were of the vaguest; his powers of the most imperfect. To orders in Arabic, which were practically useless, Mr. Vivian, the English Consul-General, had induced the Khedive to add the rider: "Il y a sur la frontière d'Abyssinie des disputes; je vous charge de les arranger."

Before the middle of March Gordon reached Massawa,[1] and pushed across the desert to Keren, the capital of Bogos, over which there had been so much fighting and bad blood. He journeyed on the back of that "cushion-footed camel" which was destined to bear him over such vast tracts of country, and through scenes the most romantic. Once afoot and on the march, his great weariness fell from him, and the cheerful humour, the valiant simplicity, the frank and happy faith of old times, came back to cheer his way, and aid him in his noble enterprise.

[1] The vessel which took Gordon to Massawa was the steamship *Latif*, which on her return voyage was burnt at sea, about sixty miles from Suez.

Some miles from Keren he was met by 200 cavalry and infantry; and henceforth, whether marching or halting, he was carefully guarded by six or eight sentries, while eight or ten cavaliers stood at his stirrup and helped him off his camel. "I can say truly," he remarks, "no man has ever been so forced into a high position as I have. How many I know to whom the incense would be the breath of their nostrils! To me it is irksome beyond measure. Eight or ten men to help me off my camel! as if I were an invalid. If I walk, everyone gets off and walks; so, furious, I get on again."

Outside the capital on the 20th of March, the Bogos army was paraded to receive him; a band of musicians danced and played before and about him; while three mounted kettle-drummers rode on in front. He had not been three days at Keren before Walad el Michael came in with 200 infantry and 60 horsemen. Gordon pitched tents for them, and took Walad into his own house. He ordered the missionaries to translate him a paper he had written, which explained that Egypt, deferring to the wishes of Europe, had determined not to carry on the war, and that he, her representative, proposed to ask a government of Johannis for Walad, or else to give him a government in his own territory. Walad went away, saying that he would think it over. Next morning the French priests came in with the news that he wanted a great deal more; whereupon Gordon sent for him, and told him plainly that he could only give him the government of two or three semi-hostile tribes. Then the chief gave in, and accepted the offer. He was urged by the priests to ask for more guns; but that request was peremptorily refused. The fact is, the situation was critical. Gordon, who had no force at his back, feared a *coup de main* on Walad's part.

"There were two courses open to me with respect to this Abyssinian question," he wrote; "the one, to stay at Massawa, and negotiate peace with Johannis and to ignore Walad el Michael, and if afterwards Walad el Michael turned rusty, to arrange with Johannis to come in and catch him. This certainly would have been easiest for me. Johannis would have been delighted, and we would be rid of Walad; but it would first of all be very poor encouragement to any future *secessions*, and would debase Egyptian repute. The process of turning in the polecat (Johannis) to work out the weasel (Walad el Michael), would play havoc with the farmyard (the country) in which the operation was carried on, and it might be that the polecat Johannis, having caught the weasel Walad, might choose to turn on the hens (which we are), and, killing us, stay in the farmyard. For, to tell the truth, we, the hens, in the days of our prosperity, stole the farmyard, this country, from the polecats, when they were fighting among themselves, and before they knew we were hens. The other course open to me was to give Walad el Michael a government separated from Johannis, which I have done, and I think that was the best course; it was, no doubt, the most honest course, and though in consequence we are like a fat nut between the nut-crackers, it will, I hope, turn out well."

Meantime Menelek, King of Shoa, Johannis's enemy in the south, had descended on Gondar and taken it. Johannis had gone with Aloula, a good general, to meet him; and it was probable that Ras Bariou, the King's uncle, who had his forces near Massawa, might rebel in his nephew's absence. Gordon cordially wished that something could be done with Walad el Michael, for he threatened to march on Hamacem, and complicate matters between the peacemaker and the King. Had he chosen to arm the people in Bogos, they would soon have disposed of Walad and his hordes; but they would have disposed of Gordon and his followers also. Through all these complications, however, there shone this gleam of hope for him: that Johannis, being sore beset, would get frightened, and sign the treaties he had brought in his pocket. It was a relief to him when Aloula sent a messenger to say that, if the Khedive approved, he would attack Walad, and refrain from ravaging the country. In this way he threatened one ruffian with another, and so was able to keep them on their best behaviour.

But he was unable to await the development of events in these regions. He was wanted at Khartoum, for the slavers were out, and were giving a great deal of trouble. He started at once, and, taking the several stations on his way, he did at each his utmost to relieve the people's wants, and give justice as he went. The fact that he listened to everybody was noised abroad. It spread like wildfire, and there was such a rush of petitioners that he had to institute a box—a kind of post-office—for the memorials hurled in upon him. Nor did the toils of his march begin and end with these achievements in charity. There was the daily ride of thirty and forty miles; there were the chiefs, the pashas,

11

the priests to receive; there were endless letters to write and innumerable details of practical kingship to attend to—all without help of any sort. Now and then he complained of fatigue; now and then he regretted his destiny. "Sometimes I wish I had never gone into this sort of Bedouin life," he says, "either in China or here. Is it my fault or my failing that I never have a respectable assistant with me to bear part of my labours? The men who would suit me are all more or less burdened with their families, etc.; those who are not so loaded are for money or for great acts which do not accord with my views."

At a station on the route to Kassala, a number of his camel-drivers were set upon and killed by the Barias, a wild tribe from the region between Khartoum and the marches of Abyssinia. Of course he himself escaped; but such was the uncertainty of life in these parts, that in a letter home he wrote as follows:—

"I have written to say that if anything happens to me the Khedive is to be defended from all blame, and the accident is not to be put down to the suppression of slavery. I have to contend with many vested interests, with fanaticism, with the abolition of hundreds of Arnauts, Turks, etc., now acting as Bashi-Bazouks, with inefficient governors, with wild independent tribes of Bedouins, and with a large semi-independent province lately under Zebehr, the Black Pasha, at Bahr Gazelle."

At last he arrived at Khartoum, and the ceremony of installation took place on the 5th of May. The firman and an address were read by the Cadi, and a royal salute was fired. Gordon was expected to make a speech, but all he said was, "With the help of God, I will hold the balance level." This delighted the people more than if he had talked for an hour. In an account of his installation by an eye-witness, it is stated that "the Pasha afterwards directed gratuities to be distributed among the deserving poor"; and that in three days he gave away upwards of £1000 of his own money.

To his disgust he had to live in a palace as large as Marl-borough House. Some two hundred servants and orderlies were in attendance; they added to his discomfort by obliging him to live according to the niceties of an inflexible code of etiquette. He was sternly forbidden to rise to receive a guest, or to offer a chair; if he rose, everyone else did the same; he "was guarded like an ingot of gold." This formality was detestable to him;

but he made a good deal of fun of it ; and more than once, while certain solemnities were proceeding, he would delight the great chiefs, his visitors, by remarking in English (of which they knew nothing), "Now, old bird, it is time for you to go."

His elevation had awakened a great deal of ill-feeling among the officials, and especially among the relations of Ismail Yacoob. Indeed, it is told of the ex-Governor's sister that, on hearing of Gordon's appointment, she expressed her opinion of the transaction by breaking some hundred and thirty of the palace windows, and by cutting all the divans to pieces. The second in command, too, Halid Pasha, was hostile from the first, and even tried to get the upper hand. Need it be said that he failed miserably ? He began with impudence and swagger, but he soon submitted and promised amendment. Ten days after, he broke out again. His insubordination was telegraphed to Cairo, and he was instantly cashiered and sent about his business.

On his ride from Massawa to Khartoum, the "Little Khedive" had relieved the wants of so many of his people, and had effected so much good, notwithstanding his abolition of the whip (a mighty influence under his predecessor), that, as soon as he arrived in his capital, great crowds of petitioners besieged him in his palace in the hope of getting a hearing. It was impossible to see them all ; so, as on the march, a box was instituted, and every case was carefully noted and considered. Before, it had been impossible to approach the Governor-General except by bribing his underlings. As much as £600 was commonly paid down for appointments not worth more than £200 a year. Gordon soon knew all this, and a great deal besides ; but he felt the uselessness of attempting the reform of a system which had grown into a usage. He therefore punished no one for these rascalities ; he took the money, and put it in the Khedive's treasury.

A very serious problem had presented itself at Khartoum. During his long rides from place to place, between Keren and the seat of government, he had pondered deeply on the suppression of slavery in the vast regions he ruled. He had looked back on the consequences of the abolition of Colonial slavery in years gone by, and in his rapid way had touched the heart of the matter at once. In the one case it was a matter affecting the Colonies only ; in the other, it was a question of home interests affecting all sorts and conditions of men. Still, he took a cheerful view of the difficulties of his task. He went so far, indeed, as to hope that he had solved the problem, and laid the details of his scheme before Her Majesty's Consul-General, Mr. Vivian.

The work he had begun and was bent on finishing was fraught with peculiar perils. It demanded a tact, an energy, and a force of will almost superhuman. He had to deal not only with worthless and often mutinous governors of provinces, but with wild and desperate tribesmen as well; he had to disband 6000 Bashi-Bazouks, who were used as frontier guards, but who winked at slave-hunting and robbed the tribes on their own account; he had to subdue and bring to order and rule the vast province of the Bahr Gazelle, but now beneath the sway of the great slaver Zebehr. It was a stupendous task: to give peace to a country quick with war; to suppress slavery among a people to whom the trade in human flesh was life and honour and fortune; to make an army out of perhaps the worst material ever seen; to grow a flourishing trade and a fair revenue in the wildest anarchy in the world. The immensity of the undertaking; the infinity of details involved in a single step towards the end; the countless odds to be faced; the many pests—the deadly climate, the horrible vermin, the ghastly itch, the nightly and daily alternation of overpowering heat and bitter cold—to be endured and overcome; the environment of bestial savagery and ruthless fanaticism—all these combine to make the achievement unique in human history. As it seems to me, the two words placed at the head of this chapter so far symbolise the whole position. Like the adventurer in Browning's magnificent allegory, my hero was face to face with a vast and mighty wrong; he had everything against him, and he was utterly alone; but he stood for God and the right, and he would not blench. There stood the Tower of Evil—the grim ruined land, the awful presences, the hopeless task, the anarchy of wickedness and despair and wrath. He knew, he felt, he recognised it all; and yet—

> "And yet
> Dauntless the stag-horn to my lips I set,
> And blew : *Childe Roland to the Dark Tower came.*"

He had got through a great mass of work at Khartoum, as we have seen. One of his reforms was a public boon. Many of the houses lay far inland, and the labour of supplying them with water from the river was immense. Gordon came; and thenceforth the river-water could be pumped up into the town, and this at but a moderate cost. In the course of this reform he had some trouble with the Catholic missionaries; they persisted in giving asylum to runaway slaves, and when he remonstrated with them they behaved with surpassing arrogance. Finding that they would not listen to him and reason, he at once wrote off to the Pope, requesting him to restrain his servants from interfering in the Khedive's administration. Then he told the missionaries what he had done, and though they were wroth in the extreme, they offended no more.

His presence was all-important at Khartoum; but at Darfour it was more important still. The country was in revolt, and the Khedive's garrisons at Fascher, Dara, and Kolkol were besieged by the rebels in their several barracks. A rescue had been sent to Fascher in March; but no news of it had yet arrived. Gordon therefore determined to march at once to its relief. About the middle of May he set off on camel-back for what turned out to be a five months' ride. On the road to Obeid, the capital of Kordofan, in company with the Governor-General's ordinary retinue of 200 cavaliers, he wrote home thus: " I am quite comfortable on the camel, and am happier when on the march than in towns with all the ceremonies. The route here is over a plain and bushes quite uninteresting." His camel was an exceedingly fine one, and astonished the escort by the pace at which it carried him along. Gordon knew that it does not do to curb your camel, so he let it go as it would. Not far from Obeid this system almost proved fatal to an urchin who got in his way. " I nearly acted as Juggernaut to a little black naked boy to-day," he says; " my camel had shaken the nose-ring out of its nose, and ran off with me. I could not stop it, and of course the little black ran right under the camel, who, however, did not tread on him, though it was a miracle he escaped being killed. Nothing is so perverse as a camel; when it runs away it will go anywhere."

On the frontier of Darfour he hoped to make friends of the rebel tribes between Fogia and Fascher, and to march on the latter city with a body-guard of subdued and converted enemies. Such superb self-confidence was habitual to him. It was an outcome of that profound religiousness which was an integral part of his character and his life. The Cross's true soldier, a mystic and a leader of men, he fought and conquered much as Columbus voyaged and as Cromwell ruled. "Praying for the people ahead of me whom I am about to visit," he says, " gives me much strength; and it is wonderful *how something seems already to have passed between us* when I meet a chief (for whom

I have prayed) for the first time. On this I base my hopes of a triumphant march to Fascher. I have really no troops with me, but I have the Shekinah, and I do like trusting to Him and not to men. Remember, unless He gave me the confidence and encouraged me to trust Him, I could not have it; and so I consider that I have the earnest of success in this confidence."

And so, in an aureole of faith, he pushed across the desert. One day his camel bore him far in advance of his train. He had put on his marshal's uniform, and, leaving his men miles behind, he rode into the station of Fogia, an Arab chief his only following; the Governor was dumbfoundered by his approach. Hardly had he arrived ere there came in a telegram from Cairo asking him for £32,000! It is not surprising that he should have written home in such terms as these: " I have certainly got into a slough with the Soudan; but, looking at my Banker, my Commandant-in-Chief, and my Administrator, it will be wonderful if I do not get out of it. If I had not got this Almighty Power to back me in His infinite wisdom, I do not know how I could even think of what is to be done."

He could not march at once upon Fascher; he could get no farther than Oomchanga, five or six days off. Here he had to await the arrival of the two or three hundred ragamuffins he called his army; here he halted for a whole fortnight. With his ever-active mind, and the consciousness of the worlds of work awaiting him elsewhere, this forced inaction proved almost insupportable. He had suffered too keenly in the past to derive any comfort from retrospection; but he could always—and he always did—find the consolation his soul so much desired. "It is lamentable work," he writes, "and over and over again, in the fearful heat, I wish I was in the other world. When I look back on the hours and hours of waiting for this and that, during China and later campaigns, and here, I really think few men have had such worries in this way. But I am wrong in it; the lot is cast evenly to us all. We are servants; sometimes our Master gives us work, and at others He does not, and our feelings in both circumstances should be the same. All I can say is, that this inaction, with so much to do elsewhere, is very trying indeed to my body. It is such a country, so worthless, and I see nothing to be gained by its occupation."

His feelings took a more cheerful turn as soon as the Darfourians, who had been horribly maltreated by the Bashi-Bazouks, came flocking in to lay their troubles before him, and to ask his pardon. Great must have been their wonder when the Governor-General told them that it was rather for him to ask pardon of them. Again, it was a joy to him to find that his trust in a bloodless victory had not been vain. He made peace with all the tribesmen round him, and as far as half-way to Fascher. At last, however, his "nondescripts," as he called the Egyptian military, came in; and on June 30th, with 500 men, he left Oomchanga for Toashia. There he meant to pick up another 350, and, vacating that station, to move on to Dara, increase his force by the 1200 there in garrison, and march on to Fascher with an army 2000 strong. By the way he proposed to still further relieve and help his new subjects, by breaking up the robbers' dens that honeycombed the country, and making examples of the gentry who harboured in them. At Shaka—"the cave of Adullam, all robbers and murderers"—was housed the horde of Zebehr Pasha, the great slave-dealer, under the command of his son Suleiman. He could put 11,000 men into the field—"a huge army for these parts"; and Gordon, conscious of the incapacity of his "nondescripts," had been planning his subjugation without the firing of a shot. "I feel no excitement about my operations," he says; "I hope they will go well, and that there will be no fighting." Fighting there was, this hope notwithstanding; but his armed victories were as nothing to the victories of his genius and his soul.

When Gordon reached Toashia, he found his 350 in a state of semi-starvation. He was told that they had received no pay for three years; and his thoughts must have travelled back to China, and the legion of rowdies and the empty chest with which he had broken the empire of the Heavenly King. As we follow his career, it seems as though it were his destiny to do great deeds with nothing. The cane with which he won his early victories had been from first to last a symbol of his means. Such a miserable set were this garrison of Toashia, that he determined not to take them with him, but to send them to Kordofan to be disbanded. This he did in the hope of making friends with a certain chief (whose brother he had released), and of getting men from him. It had been arranged that the potentate in question should join him at Toashia, and go on with him to Dara. But Toashia was admirably unhealthy, and he had no choice but to begin his march at once, and trust to picking up his ally on the route. He had with him no more than 500 men (350 of them in little better case than the scarecrows he was disbanding), all armed with flint-locks or worse, and with but a single field-piece among them. At the rendezvous no chief was visible, and the wretched army was threatened by thousands of "determined blacks," who knew that the Governor-General was with it. "I prayed heartily for an issue," he says, "*but it gave me a pain in the heart like that I had when surrounded at Masindi.* I do not fear death, but I fear, from want of faith, the result of my death, for the whole country would have risen. It is, indeed, most painful to be in such a position ; it takes a year's work out of me." And again, in another strain, he says, "You do not know how unpalatable these positions are to my pride. If I had my way, I would have ridden through with 100 horsemen and not feared ; it is the grander state one has to go on. With *that* gun, which nothing would induce my black secretary to abandon, I made him give up 200 rounds."

Matters were made worse by the fact that the contingent from Dara marched by a different route, and so missed the main body. Fortunately no attack was made, for, had the tribesmen chosen to fall upon Gordon and his miserable following, there can be no doubt that they would have been slaughtered to a man. Gordon himself was completely at their mercy. "When I had got through my dangers," he says, "I saw some deer, and took my rifle. Of course he" (the bearer) "had thrown it down and broken the stock. Thus, had I been attacked, I should have been defenceless."

CHAPTER XIII

THE ROBBERS' DEN

WHEN the Governor-General, on the 12th of July, rode into Dara, the people were astonished to see him. "They had been six months without news from without," he says; "it was like the relief of Lucknow." Haroun, the pretender to the throne of Darfour, had been stirring up revolt and threatening the garrison; many of the tribes were hostile; and Suleiman, the son of Zebehr, with 6000 armed slaves at his back, finding that Gordon would not side with him, was plotting his murder. Many were the suggestions as to the course he should pursue. One, which emanated from his black secretary, showed how Suleiman should be lured to Dara, taken prisoner, and stabbed or shot to death if he resisted. Gordon felt this inspiration to be a trifle too Asiatic. Of the others he took no heed. What he did was to despatch an expedition, numbering 8000 natives and 1500 troops, under his lieutenant Hassan, against the self-crowned Sultan, and to set a price upon his head.

The position was exceedingly delicate; the more so as there were other matters of as pressing import as this of Haroun which demanded all his energy and skill.

He was ringed about with perils. On the one hand was Haroun; on the other were the hostile tribes, who had taken the field against his men; in front of him was Suleiman, the most desperate foeman of all. His proposed solution of the problem is almost startling : he would strike first at Suleiman, and quell him, not with arms, but with friendship and trust. "The happy thought struck me," he says, "of making Zebehr's son Governor of Dara, thus cutting him off from intrigue with Shaka. I separate him from the cave of Adullam, and prevent his making any more slave-raids. He will find occupation for his armed slaves in keeping the tribes in order around him." The plan was

160

so beset with difficulties as to be impracticable, and another soon took its place. This, however, was in the same direction; Suleiman was to be subdued, not by the sword, but by the spirit. Before Gordon could set about its execution, however, he had to confer with one of Zebehr's chiefs, a man named El Nour, whom he knew to be faithful to the Government, and who could bring him tidings of what was going on in the robbers' dens. Then, to move to the relief of Fascher, with Dara undefended, and Haroun at large, was out of the question; for that rebel might at any moment swoop down on Dara. Gordon's new plan, therefore, was to appoint El Nour his Governor. From this eminence the Arab might corrupt the ruffians in Shaka, weaken the famous slaver's position, and defend his charge from Haroun's attacks, while his new commander marched to the relief of Fascher.

Unfortunately, El Nour was out raiding, in company with two other chiefs, Awad and Edrees, both faithful to the Government, but all three suspected and watched by Suleiman, so that they could only write to Gordon by stealth, and lie in wait for an opportunity to visit him in person. Their loyalty was Gordon's own work. When at Massawa, he speculated on the chance that they might be on bad terms with Zebehr, and got them promoted to be Lieutenant-Colonels. "Zebehr's son," he says, "accuses them of being in correspondence with me; at any rate, the yeast has worked among them." The slave-dealer was right to be suspicious; for Gordon knew a good deal of what was going on. He knew, for instance, that Suleiman was constantly in receipt of letters from Zebehr, all containing the mysterious sentence, "Take care of Abdoul Razoul." He knew that Suleiman had a great quantity of ivory, which, being Government monopoly, he was determined to have. He knew, too, that the slavers used to say that "he wanted to get the hippopotamus with its skin"; but what this meant he had not thought it worth while to discover.

Presently he learned from El Nour and Edrees, both of whom had ransomed themselves from Shaka for £600 apiece, that it was impossible for Suleiman to leave his den till the rains were over—that is, for three months. Meantime, the chief of the Razagats, a powerful tribe, pillaged and maltreated by the slavers, had fled, with 600 riders, to Dara, and was ready to side with Gordon in a raid upon Shaka. This was a gain in one sense, but a loss in another, for so naked and ruinous was the countryside that Gordon had barely food enough for his own men. And worse was behind. Not only did the whole tribe threaten to take shelter in the fort; many others, hearing of their resolves, began to move towards Dara with the same intent. The Razagats alone were able to put over 7000 horsemen in the field,—they move with extraordinary swiftness, for they carry no baggage and ride without stirrups,—and it was a matter of surprise to Gordon that, with such an army, they did not oppress their oppressors.

Another event which made Gordon feel the utter helplessness of his position happened about this time. An expedition for the recapture of slaves brought in some 210 of them. They were starving, and when they looked up at him their faces were wistful for food. He had little to give them, though. They had been thirty-six hours unfed, and the sight of their misery brought tears to his eyes. He sent them some corn. "What could I do?" he says; "I could only address the Arabs with me, and tell them that if they took Mussulmans as slaves they did it against the command of the Koran; and I took sand and washed my hands, in order that they might see I put on them the responsibility of the decision." He was fast finding his suspicions confirmed, and that, difficult as it was to crush the slavers, to deal with the slaves was more difficult still.

At last the troops returned whom he had sent out against the tribes, and with their return came the means of action. He had projected an attack on Suleiman's advanced guard (400 in number), with the intention of cutting it off from Shaka. But he found, to his disgust, that in the expedition his soldiers had done nothing themselves, but had allowed their allies, the friendly tribe, to do all the fighting for them; the fact being, as he learned later on, that their commander had taken a heavy bribe from the opposing chief. There had been great delay; no ground had been won; and the Leopard tribes were out, and were threatening Toashia. He therefore abandoned the attack on Suleiman for the relief of his own stronghold. With his " nondescripts " and a contingent of Masharins, a friendly tribe, he marched straight for the camp of the Leopards. They were caught in a terrific storm, and had to come to halt for the night in a waving deluge of rain, which, says Gordon, took some 50 per cent. of strength out of them. "I put on my coat," he writes, " put up my umbrella, and wished for dawn. It was not pleasant, but I had my blanket, and rolled myself up in it, and slept well." The next day they marched to the field of battle. The Masharins were so eager for the fray, that, without waiting for the " nondescripts," they fell upon the

Leopards and routed them with great slaughter. Of course the
"nondescripts" had lagged on the march. When they came up,
the whole army encamped at the Leopards' headquarters (where
they had, as prisoner, the chief's brother), and a council of war
was held; in the middle of it, the Leopards, in two divisions, each
350 strong, came boldly up and prepared to fall on. The
Masharins went out to meet them; but in their teeth, and under
a steady fire of musketry, they moved up valiantly to Gordon's
very camp. Here, however, after a severe struggle, they were
beaten back with loss, not of course by the Government troops,
who took shelter behind the stockades, but by the bold Masharins,
whose chief, Ahmed Neurva, was mortally wounded. Gordon's
disgust at the conduct of his troops on this occasion knew no
bounds. "No one can conceive what my officers and troops are!"
he says. "I will say no more than that for my own personal
safety I must get 200 men as a bodyguard. I do not think one
of the enemy was killed at the assault of the station. Not one
ought to have escaped. I was *sickened* to see twenty brave men
in alliance with me ride out to meet the Leopard tribe unsupported by my men, who crowded into the stockade! It was
terribly painful. The only thing which restrained me from
riding out to the attack was the sheep-like state in which my
people would have been had I been killed. What also would
have become of the province?"

After a two days' campaign, the Leopards were cut off from
three of their watering-places. Only one being left them, and
that in constant danger, they began crowding in with their submission; for, without the means of satisfying their thirst, they
had nothing to look forward to but death from drouth or in battle
with the tribes into whose territory they might venture in search
of water. The heat was terrific; the plight of the penitent
Leopards, "with throats unslaked, with black lips baked," was
piteous in the extreme. Gordon took pity on their misery,
received their homage (sworn on the Koran), and let them go
down and drink. Then, the tribesmen having begun to take the law
into their own hands, the Governor-General had to give way to
the justiciar. One man had speared one of another tribe through
the arm; another had shot his comrade dead. Gordon settled the
first difficulty by giving the wounded man £6; the second, by
sentencing the assassin to be shot.

"My soul revolts at these horrors, of which I used to think

nothing," says Gordon. " All these troubles come in quarrels for plunder—some miserable grain or an earthenware pot. . . . I have just disposed of the man who shot the other, who, I am sorry to say, died. I called the chiefs of the tribe to whom the dead man belonged, and the prisoner; and I asked the chiefs whether they would prefer me to shoot the murderer, or to give him to them to serve as an assistant to the family of the dead man. The latter course they acceded to, I am glad to say. The murderer was the slave (I have let out the word) of one of the soldiers before ; so I have only changed his master. You should have seen the fright of everyone around me—even the chiefs of the tribe of the murdered man—as I took the rifle and cocked it, with the pretence of shooting the poor black, ivory-teethed murderer ! I need not say I felt quite sure that the tribe would not wish it. In all natures, however savage, there is good ; but, nevertheless, everyone around me thought I would shoot him if they did not intercede. I said, ' Shall I shoot him now, and leave him a stinking carcase ? or will you take him, and make him work for the family he has bereaved ?'

"It is a question of cows, nothing else, with my allies ; and one of the greatest trouble is the division of spoil. Like David at Ziklag with his men, and Mahomet with his men at Mecca, and us with our men in India. Every general wishes there was no plunder ; it is a source of weakness. If my expedition is successful, we shall be bothered with thousands of cows and sheep, and thus open to attack. In China, I never could move for days after a victory. I have received a very strong letter from the Khedive, pressing me to put an immediate stop to the slave-raids ; and also one from Cherif Pasha, both very kind, but strong in words,—that I am not to hesitate at any act that I think fit to put a stop to it. I have asked the Khedive to publish them. This determines me more and more to destroy the nest at Shaka. I hear some of Zebehr's people are coming up to join me ; if so, I shall try and disarm them. What a complex question this is ! I wish it was unravelled ; for the tension on me now for six months has been great, and I have not finished the half of my troubles. There are besides this and Shaka, Galabat, Abyssinia, and Aboubekker, Pasha of Zeila, who is semi-independent. You will easily see that to attempt a wholesale clearance of all these obstacles by orders, without means of carrying them out, would be foolish. The retail clearance is the only one possible to succeed, and the retail business requires me to see to it; for, owing to the Government being an absolute one, it is difficult to find people to carry out an obnoxious order, for the fear that the Government may not support them."

The Leopards were soon in trouble again. They stole a number of slaves from Gordon's allies; and, on the 12th August, an expeditionary force was sent out against them. A thousand cows were lifted, and a large number of the enemy was disarmed. But the injured parties demanded the stolen slaves from Gordon's people, and some curious scenes were the result of affairs. Gordon, finding it necessary to follow up the force, started next day for Duggam. Owing to the badness of the water, he was obliged to move on to Kario. Here he learned that Haroun was backing the rebels, had sent forty horsemen to reinforce them at Gebel Heres, and, on his own account, was ravaging the country to the north. Joining the force, he found the usual amount of work awaiting him. His subordinates, indeed, were perfectly incompetent. Thus he had ordered the major commanding to look after the sick; but he had himself, on the way to Fascher, to find transport for such as could not follow on foot. "This sort of thing," he says, "wears me; for it is really not my duty to see to such details. In fact, I may say it is not my duty to be commanding an expedition like this; but there is no help for it." Again, on the 15th August, he writes: "All the morning I had nothing but slave-questions to settle; some of the most troublesome kind. I wish that the Anti-Slavery Society were here, so that I could put it on them to decide. I had nearly a row to-day about it with the soldiers, and only hope things will go no worse."

And, while he was bewailing his army, the army, on their part, were plotting for his life. After a thirty miles' ride through bog and sand, he entered Fascher, with 150 men, to the extreme surprise of its beleaguered inhabitants. Near the place where his camp was pitched, a muezzin was in the habit of calling to prayers. The Arab lieutenant-colonel, and some of the men, in the hope of rousing the people, ordered him to desist from his task, inasmuch as he disturbed the Governor-General. By a fortunate chance, Gordon's secretary missed the sound; and, making inquiries, discovered the culprit. "I gave the crier £2," says Gordon; "and I bundled off my friend the lieutenant-colonel into banishment at Katarif, where he will have time to meditate. I never hesitate a moment in coming down on such fellows. The man now cries with double energy, even as I write this."

We are now approaching a crisis in affairs which Gordon (who had read his *Midshipman Easy*) called "a triangular duel," though he might with better reason have called it a quadrilateral. It needed all his energy and all his indomitable will to keep him master of the situation. On the one hand, as I have said, his presence in the field against Haroun was urgent; on the other, many of the tribes were hostile and threatening; while, worse than all, Suleiman with his 6000 robbers had sat down before Dara, and was ravaging the country round, and even menacing the city itself. This was the position. Let us see how Gordon dealt with it, and faced the tremendous odds in his disfavour.

Of these three enemies the least important was probably the would-be Sultan. Could Gordon have met, as he longed to do, the pretender in the field, the result, as he felt, was not doubtful, notwithstanding the utter want of discipline among the "nondescripts." But this in the then state of affairs was impossible. To make matters worse for him, his lieutenant, Hassan, with 5000 muskets, still lingered on the road, afraid to march to the attack without his chief.

Then for the tribes. Many were hostile, and those in other districts were doing their best to confederate with and to come to the aid of those he had recently subdued. His energy, therefore, was constantly being frittered away on expeditions against the new enemy, the capture of prisoners, and the lifting of cows. The amount of work this petty warfare involved was enough to prevent him from entertaining the idea of assaults on either Haroun or Suleiman. To add to the confusion, his secretary fell ill, and all the tiresome details of business had, of necessity, to pass through his own hands; while interviews were asked of him —and obtained—on pretexts the most trivial, and for interests the most wretched and sporadic imaginable. "For the very smallest thing men come direct to me," he writes, "and force their way in, let me be as engaged as possible. There is no chain of responsibility, everyone thinks he has a perfect right to come to me, and also thinks himself aggrieved if I do not give him an immediate hearing. Besides this, in giving or taking a paper to you they take two or three minutes. You never saw such a dilatory set! The consequence is that papers are snatched out of their hands, and also thrown at them. All very undignified; but I cannot help it. If you send for a man he takes a nice funeral pace to come to you. You see him afar off long before he arrives, and sometimes I am so undignified as to rush to meet him. All this is not good, for my post is a very high one; but I cannot help it, and I do not care. I have the power if I have not the glory, and, at any rate, I get through a mint of work."

The third enemy—the strongest and most desperate of all—was Suleiman. This daring scoundrel was harrying and pillaging the tribes all round, while they, on their part, were crying out for help. Suleiman all the time was tendering his services to Gordon against Haroun, but the offer was rightly interpreted into a pretext for opportunities of professional work. What was really going on in the robbers' den Gordon in no way suspected. Two years later, it turned out that Suleiman's desperadoes were plotting to catch and kill him. It would have been an easy matter enough, as he had no sentries.

When Zebehr was in the fulness of his power, he gathered his chiefs together under a tree on the road between Obeid and Shaka. Here he made them swear to obey him. Later on, when he went to Cairo to spend £100,000 in bribing the Khedive's ministers, and was held a prisoner, he met Gordon, and solicited his aid. Of course the request was refused. He sent at once this message to Darfour: "Obey the orders given under the tree;" which was another way of saying, "To arms, and to the road!" On Gordon's arrival at Khartoum, as we have seen, these orders were obeyed, and whole provinces became one anarchy. Nor was this all. When Gordon lay at Fascher, Zebehr's lieutenants met and swore upon the Koran to attack the Government, while El Nour, the slaver, with whom he had dealt in secret, had fallen away from his allegiance, and was numbered with the enemy: it was "Childe Roland to the Dark Tower came," and with a vengeance.

And there were matters which, if of less import, were none the less wearing and trying. They taxed his patience to the utmost, and his temper too; and we find him now in the highest spirits, now longing with all his heart for the blessing of death. He began to fear, for instance, that the delays of Hassan and his 5000 in the campaign against Haroun were of a piece with that other abortive affair against the tribes; and, having these suspicions, he felt it to be his first duty to deal with Haroun. Hardly, however, was he ready to take the field, ere it turned out that Haroun had retired. So much energy had been wasted; so much energy was gone. He had to face in another direction, and begin his work of preparation and enterprise and combination all anew.

His movements at this juncture were so rapid and so many, that it is impossible to give more than a mere sketch of them. They were confined for the most part to the immediate neighbourhood of Kario and Fufar; to clearing the road at one point; to despatching expeditions against hostile tribes at another; to searching for grain, of which there was a great scarcity; to capturing spies; and to vainly essaying to control the Bashi-Bazouks, whom he had learned to hate as cordially as he loved the oppressed blacks, for whom he would have given his life. In the midst of these vain efforts and vexations of spirit he is tormented by scorpions; or he is beset by storms so furious, that his tent is torn down in the dead of night, and he is left shelterless and drenched to the skin. "I do not suppose you could find a more useless set of servants than I have," he says; "the Maltese, on occasions like this, is completely paralysed, and sits down, leaving everything to its fate—a regular tumble-down sort of fellow. I have been in a towering rage with him. They were cowering under their blown-down tent, not making an effort to put things straight. It is one comfort to be utterly uncomfortable, for it cannot be worse, and *may* be better."

At this point the measure of his troubles seems full. But this was by no means the case. News came in which made all other troubles trivial. It roused his spirit to its highest, and led to such a victory as could never have been won by arms alone. Suleiman, with his frightful 6000, was on the eve of attacking the Government at Dara. Gordon lost not a moment. Ignoring alike his "nondescripts" and his allies, he mounted his camel, and rode to Dara unarmed and virtually alone. Of this tremendous ride, one of the most striking achievements in his career, I cannot do better than let him tell the story himself. This he did in a letter (dated September 2nd) to his sister; like all he wrote, it is the more remarkable in that it was never intended for publication:—

"I got to Dara about 4 P.M., long before my escort, having ridden eighty-five miles in a day and a half. About seven miles from Dara I got into a swarm of flies, and they annoyed me and my camel so much, that we jolted along as fast as we could. Upwards of 300 were on the camel's head, and I was covered with them. I suppose that the queen fly was among them. If I had no escort of men, I had a large escort of these flies. I came on my people like a thunderbolt. As soon as they had recovered,

12

the salute was fired. My poor escort! where is it? Imagine to yourself a single, dirty, red-faced man on a camel, ornamented with flies, arriving in the divan all of a sudden. The people were paralysed, and could not believe their eyes. No dinner after my long ride, but a quiet night, forgetting my miseries. At dawn I got up, and, putting on the golden armour the Khedive gave me, went out to see my troops, and then mounted my horse, and, with an escort of *my* robbers of Bashi-Bazouks, rode out to the camp of the other robbers three miles off. I was met by the son of Zebehr —a nice-looking lad of twenty-two years—and rode through the robber-bands. There were about 3000 of them—men and boys. I rode to the tent in the camp; the whole body of chiefs were dumbfoundered at my coming among them. After a glass of water, I went back, telling the son of Zebehr to come with his family to my divan. They all came, and, sitting there in a circle, I gave them in choice Arabic my ideas: That they meditated revolt; that I knew it, and that they should now have my ultimatum, viz. that I would disarm them and break them up. They listened in silence, and then went off to consider what I had said. They have just now sent in a letter stating their submission, and I thank God for it. They have pillaged the country all round, and I cannot help it. I feel very sorry for the poor people, for they were my allies at Wadar, and through their absence with me, their possessions were exposed to the attacks of these scoundrels. What misery! But the Higher than the highest regardeth it, and can help them. I cannot. The sort of stupefied way in which they heard me go to the point about their doings, the pantomime of signs, the bad Arabic, etc., was quite absurd. Fancy, the son of Zebehr only three days ago took his pistol and fired three shots close to my cavass, because the poor fellow, who was ill, did not get up when he came to him. . . . You should have seen his face, when I told him all this, when he protested his fidelity. However, I said it was all forgiven. Maduppa Bey has come here, and says, when the son of Zebehr got home, he lay down and said not a word, and that the Arabs say *I have poisoned* him! with coffee."

After delivering himself of his feelings to Suleiman and his horde, Gordon resolved to make a clean sweep of the den at Shaka. With this view he sent a body of men to take possession. Meantime, there was division in the slavers' camp, one party being still in favour of war, the other in favour of peace. Suleiman, the "Cub," as Gordon called him, was in a towering passion at his own surrender. He was unable to hide his feelings from the Governor-General; and it was evident that, had it been in his power to persuade the chiefs to revolt against the Government, he would have gladly done so. They, however, kept sending in their submissions with great punctuality, thus rendering resistance less and less possible, till at last he himself was obliged to obey Gordon's order to proceed to Shaka. Before his departure he requested the Governor-General to give him robes in accordance with custom, and as a sign that the Governor-General was satisfied. To this Gordon replied: "I have no robes; you have not filled me with over-much confidence in your fidelity, and you have been very rude to me, while I have shown you every attention, and have gone out of my way to be civil to you—a mere boy—have done my best for you, and tried to protect you." At this the young slaver was furious; and Gordon and his "garrison of sheep soldiers" were for a time in the greatest peril, for, had the slavers, who were brave men, all trained to war, unanimously agreed on an attack, they could at any moment have put the Governor-General and his handful to the sword. The crisis, however, like so many others in Gordon's career, was to end in victory. Suleiman left quietly for Shaka. From that place he despatched a letter in which he declared himself Gordon's son, and asked for a government. In reply, he was informed that until he either went to Cairo to salute the Khedive, or gave some other proof of fidelity, the Governor-General would never give him a place, even if the refusal cost him his life. After imparting this message to the chiefs who brought the letter, Gordon turned to one of them and asked him if he was a father. The man said "Yes." Whereupon Gordon said, "Then do you not think a good flogging would do the 'Cub' good?" And the chief agreed that it would.

This manner of dealing with the slavers was certainly most efficacious. It is, however, abundantly apparent from Gordon's letters that he felt deeply for Suleiman. More than once he expresses a great pity for him, and a hope that the rebel will forgive him his hard treatment. That harshness was necessary (Bonaparte would have decimated the horde, and plumed himself upon his leniency) there cannot be a doubt. Only a few days later Gordon writes: "Suleiman no longer hopes to conquer, but wants to get away from my proximity. He may try to go up to the other stations inland, but I do not expect it will last long;

a retreating commander is rarely in a good temper, and he will soon disgust his people." While all this worry was going on, it came to Gordon's knowledge that his secretary, in whom he had placed the greatest confidence, had taken £3000 backsheesh. He was at once sent to Khartoum, there to be tried; though Gordon was afraid he would be very severely punished. He was succeeded by Berzati Bey, a young Mussulman of high attainments, of whom Gordon afterwards said : " He had the invaluable quality of telling me when he disagreed with me."

Early in September the Governor-General was making his way, over a bad road and through a dense and thorny forest, to Shaka. He had not proceeded far when he received a letter from Suleiman inviting him to take up his abode in his house. Gordon accepted the invitation at once. As he neared the robbers' den, Suleiman and his chiefs came out to meet him, and gave him a cordial welcome. The slaver was on his best behaviour. He treated Gordon with the greatest reverence; but he renewed his request for a government, and fawned at his sovereign's feet on every opportunity. The Governor-General, however, was not to be thus cajoled. He reminded Suleiman that he had not yet earned his promotion; but he gave him his own gun, and taught him its use.

He only stayed two days in the robbers' den. Perhaps this was as well, for he was without sentries, and it turned out later that the slave-dealers had been plotting to make him prisoner. Why they did not must remain a wonder. The only explanation is that, as at Dara, he amazed and awed them by his utter indifference to danger. He left in the middle of September for Obeid, lest the humidity of Shaka should affect his servant's health; and he had a strong suspicion that a caravan of slaves was accompanying him—a suspicion soon verified by his discovery of some eighty men, women, and children in chains. He remonstrated with the slave-merchant; he was told that they were wives and offspring. They were too far from their homes to send back, and had Gordon released them they would have starved to death; so, at the risk of a probable scandal through the missionaries, he let the caravan alone, insisting only that the chains should be removed. Between Obeid and Shaka the camel-rides seem to have been specially fatiguing, but the journey was not without its diversions.

" To-day," he writes, " I had meant to leave my caravan and

ride past to Obeid; but, as I went along, I heard reports of there being a lot of brigands on the road, who were robbing everyone who passed. We came on a flock of cows belonging to these brigands, and I halted. The caravan came up to me, and I seized twenty-four of the Arabs who owned the cows, and who were said to be the robbers. I then determined not to hurry on; so I went quietly with six men to a watering-place near, while the caravan went by another road to the same watering-place. On my road we met two fugitives, who stated that their caravan, coming from Obeid to Shaka, had that moment been attacked near us. We pushed on, and the plunderers bolted; but we rescued five charged donkeys and captured the chief of the robbers, with some twenty others. I judged the question of the chief, and have had him hanged (at least ordered it, having tossed up), and then of course, when the man was begged off, I let him off. I declare it is necessary to make an example, but my heart shrinks from the killing of these poor brutes, who may have heard Zebehr's son was at war with me, and who thought they were doing me a service and themselves also in plundering those going and coming from the son of Zebehr. Of all painful decisions these are the worst, and I do not know where to turn in them. If there were courts of justice it would not be so bad; but there is none to speak of, and all would take a bias from my point of view. It was one of the slave-dealers' people who begged this man off! I like these slave-dealers; they are a brave lot, and, putting aside their propensity to take slaves, are much finer people than those of Lower Egypt. They are far more enterprising."

In the same letter he goes on to talk of an albino negress whom he had found at Shaka, and whom he had intended to send to the Khedive. For some reason unexplained, he seems, however, to have altered his mind; for he says, "I shall give her to the convent at Obeid. I know of a male albino negro in Darfour; I shall try and marry the two. I shall make the convent people report on the result—whether it is white or black. She is not lovely, and looks very sickly, but is not so."

Here is another specimen of his less serious experiences. "Yesterday," he writes, "a black soldier came to me with a black girl he said belonged to him; but an Arab said he had bought her for £4. I disposed of the Arab owner by giving him £4, and said to the girl, 'You belong to me—will you stay with me, or go with the black soldier?' 'No,' said she; 'I will go with the black soldier.' So off she went. This is all the marriage which takes place. I did not want the girl, as you may imagine."

All the rest of the journey, he picked up slaves along the route. Many lay dying in the sun; some he bought, the others he sent down to a watering-place. The sight of their misery made him wretched. His letters teem with descriptions of their sufferings, and with proofs of his passionate desire to crush out the horrible traffic of which they were the staple. He knew that, except at the frontier, it was useless to attempt the work. Slavery was the custom of the country, and there was no one to enforce his decrees against it. The ruin of Shaka, however, was a great stride towards the end desired; and, on his arrival at Obeid on October 3rd, and at Khartoum in the middle of the month, the effects of his daring and splendid achievement were perceptible among the people in more ways than one.

Indeed, his action with Suleiman and the robber den, with the extraordinary speed of his movements, had made him famous through all the length and breadth of the land. The people were amazed by his daring, his firmness, his irresistible energy. To tell a lazy functionary that if he did not get on with his work the Governor-General would be after him, was better than the whip itself. Everywhere the cry, "The Pasha is coming," became a signal for action. At such a pace did he traverse the continent he ruled, that his camels, which, under another rider, could have gone for ten days, gave in at the sixth. More than once, when the sun was at its fiercest, they dropped dead beneath him. When this happened, he took a new mount and rode on.

CHAPTER XIV

THE mass of work awaiting him at Khartoum, he got through in a week. Much of the time was taken up by petitions and petitioners; some by the trial and sentence of a murderer. "I cannot go out," he says, "without having people howling after me with petitions that I will let their sons out of prison, or such like things; and they follow me wherever I go, yelling all the time. I will not let them be beaten away, as is usually the case; but I take no notice, for how can I release every prisoner?" "Were it not," he continues, "for the very great comfort I have in communion, and the knowledge that He is Governor-General, I could not get on at all."

His work despatched, he left Khartoum for Hellal, on a visit to Walad el Michael. The sail to Berber was the first real rest he had had since his first appearance in these lands, early in 1874. Thus he writes of the voyage—with the only touch I have noted in him of anything that could possibly be mistaken for vanity :—

"The quiet of to-day on board the steamer going down the Nile is quite delightful; a month later last year, I was coming down to you from the Lakes. What a deal has happened since then —with you, and me, and in Europe! I feel a great contentment. A star, when it makes its highest point, is said to have culminated; and I feel I have culminated — *i.e.*, I wish for no higher or other post than the one I have; and I know I cannot be removed unless it is God's will, so I rest on a rock, and can be content. Many would wish a culminating point with less wear and tear. But that very wear and tear makes me cling more to the place; and I thank God. He has made me succeed, not in any very glorious way, but in a substantial and lasting manner. *I entirely take*

*that prophecy of Isaiah as my own, and work to it as far as
I can."* [1]

At Berber (October 24th), his first act was to make his clerk
clear the ante-chamber of the eight or ten guards who, under the
pretence of doing him honour, were keeping him under strict surveillance. Here he had again to endure three nights of illumina-
tions and ceremonies. Of course he came in, too, for the usual
accumulation of letters and telegrams from the various stations.
It was everybody's theory of subjectship, that, though there were
governors on the spot, no one could help him but the Governor-
General in person. In this way was he rewarded for the taking
of Shaka.

On his way—as far as the river—to Dongola, his next
resting-place, he was unlucky in his camels. They had been
ill-fed, and they were weak and easily worn out; but the quiet,
and the dry, dewless nights of the desert, after the storm and
stress and the damp airs of Darfour, were soothing to his spirit,
though he suffered tortures in the body from the " courash "—a
horrible eczema, which he describes as like the biting of a
thousand mosquitoes. At Merowe, which is said to be the
southernmost point reached by ancient Egyptian civilisation, he
was met by a shower of complaints, such a monster as a governor
not having been seen in the neighbourhood for years. He stayed
but three hours ; but the people followed him out, and yelled
their griefs at him for miles. Dongola was only twelve miles off;
but a heavy gale obliged him to lay-to all day. The telegrams he
received meanwhile were infinitely discomforting. On the one
hand, Walad el Michael was threatening the fort at Senheit, and
he had no troops ; and, on the other, the Khedive was urging him
to return to Cairo.

At Dongola, where he stayed till November 9th, he went
into the question of the cost of a railway contract. Then, as he
was pushing on to Cairo, telegrams overtook him bringing the
news of an Abyssinian invasion, and that " Sennaar and Fazolie
were threatened by Ras Arya (one of Johannis's generals)." He
could hardly believe it possible. If it were true, there were few
troops to resist the attack; and, with not a soul at Khartoum on

---

[1] "And it shall be for a sign and for a witness unto the Lord of hosts in
the land of Egypt: for they shall cry unto the Lord because of the oppressors,
and He shall send them a saviour, and a great one, and he shall deliver
them."

whom to depend, the risk of going on to Cairo was too great to be faced. He rode back to Dongola, and went on thence to Khartoum over the Bahouda desert, a five and a half days' ride. The way was long, cold, and tiring; and he reached Khartoum to find that the invasion was no invasion at all. It turned out later to be merely a food-raid of the Abyssinian marchmen, which had been heavily repulsed.

He remained at headquarters for three days. Then, having got through certain business, he mounted his camel and started once more on a visit to Walad el Michael, who was threatening to be troublesome. In Gordon's opinion, the best thing to be done at this time would have been for King Johannis to pardon Walad, and translate him and his gang to the province of Hamacem, which was his by inheritance; but to this it was more than doubtful that Johannis would agree. Walad was a standing danger to the Khedive's Government; he might attack it any day, or, by his raids on Abyssinian territory, he might set up a complication with Johannis. He was also a great expense; and this, in the bad state of the finances, was a consideration of some importance. It would have been easy to dispose of him by giving him up to Johannis; but this would have dishonoured the Government, and so was out of the question.

On the way to Senheit, where Walad was quartered, Gordon met with no particular adventures. He had the usual trouble with his suite, but to this he was inured. His Arabs resented the swiftness of his march, and did everything in their power to hinder and delay. This, though, was of little avail, for he knew the country, and went on at his own speed, whether they would or no. Weary with his long journey, and wishing himself rather dead than alive, he would seek rest and shelter, not in the towns, but in the villages hard by; but the despicable scoundrels almost invariably went on to the towns themselves, and camped outside the gates, for the express purpose of proclaiming their master's approach, and of bringing down upon him the avalanche of petitions and complaints with which they knew he would be greeted. To baffle these tricks, he used to rise at dawn, well knowing that the sentries, being Arabs, would be fast asleep, ride alone to a station two or three hours off, and there seek the rest of which he stood in such sore need. He had passed through Abou Haraz, Katarif, and Kassala, when, near the last of these places, he received a visit from the Holy Man, Shereef Seid Hacim, whom once before he had met on his way to Khartoum, and who, as a descendant

of Mahomet, had been greatly scandalised by his sitting in
European fashion on his sacred divan. This time Seid unbent a
little from his holiness, accepted £20, and begged of Gordon to
take the turban and become a Mussulman. Many others had
made the same request.

On his arrival at Walad's camp—to reach it, by the bye, he
had to scale two mountains—he found the people a little odd in
their manner. There were 7000 of them, he tells us, all armed
with muskets. They were drawn up to receive him; and, as on
his previous visit, he was met by Walad's son and a number of
priests. He at once demanded an interview with Walad, but the
son replied that his father was ill. This the people of Senheit
declared a lie. Gordon and his party were then lodged in some
wretched huts, within a narrow pass outside the town, shut in by
a fence ten feet high. At this the faces of his servants and his
ten soldiers fell miserably; and he himself could not suppress a
suspicion that he was "in the lion's den." "I spoke to the
interpreter," he writes, "and told him that if Michael wanted to
make me prisoner he could do so; but that he would suffer in
the end. It was a want of faith on my part to say this.
However, he and Michael's son were so profuse in their apologies,
that I feel sure that, as yet, I am not a prisoner. I excused
myself to them for my remark, by saying that if the news arrived
at Senheit that I was boxed up, it would be taken for granted
that I was a prisoner, and it would be telegraphed to His Highness
at Cairo."

Next day he had an interview with Walad. He advised the
invalid to ask Johannis's pardon. The invalid replied that this
was impossible, and took the opportunity to beg more territory,
suggesting that if Gordon would only wink and look away, he
would go up and take the Abyssinian town Adowa. This, of
course, was not to be thought of; and Gordon, disgusted with
him and the Abyssinians generally, went on to Massawa. There
he awaited the reply to a letter he had written to Ras Bariou, the
Frontier-General. In this he had warned Johannis that he
would be responsible for Walad no longer, and suggested that
the brigand should be seized and sent to Cairo; while his troops
should be given a free pardon, and the chance of getting clear
away, inasmuch as, if they were attacked, with Abyssinia shut to
them, they would fight desperately.

No answer came. Johannis was campaigning against Menelek,
King of Shoa; but, small as the country is, nobody knew where.

Gordon waited on for some little time. Then, hearing nothing, he started for Khartoum, by Suakim and Berber. He was, however, stopped on the road by a second telegram from the Khedive, bidding him to Cairo, to take part in the financial inquiry then being organised. The idea was distasteful in the extreme. He fancied that his rough, nomadic life as Governor-General of the Soudan had unfitted him for the dinner-parties and entertainments of civilisation. During his year of office he had ridden over 4000 miles of desert, without a bandage across the chest and round the waist. The consequence of this omission he sets forth in one of his letters. " I have shaken," he says, " my heart or my lungs out of their places ; and I have the same feeling in my chest as you have when you have a crick in the neck. . . . I say sincerely that, though I prefer to be here sooner than anywhere, I would sooner be dead than live this life."

But there was no help for it. The Khedive had spoken, and to hear was to obey. Steaming and sailing down stream, he reached Cairo in the first week in March. The Khedive had telegraphed him an invitation to dinner at 8 o'clock; but the train was late, and on reaching the palace Gordon found that his host had waited an hour and a half for him, and that he insisted on his joining the party, begrimed with travel as he was. He was received with every mark of distinction. After the first greeting, the Khedive asked him to act as President of the Finance Inquiry ; he was placed at His Highness's right hand ; after dinner he was lodged in the Kasrel Kousa, a palace of the Viceroy which was set apart for royal visitors to Egypt. The splendour of the place and the attentions of courtiers and servants appear to have bored him terribly. " My people are all dazed," he says ; "and so am I, and wish for my camel." To an English friend who called on him, he said, " I feel like a fly in this big place." Great things were expected of him ; but the Khedive, in inviting him to become President of the Finance Inquiry, does not seem to have taken into account the fact that he was the last man to mould his views to those of other men. As on his previous sojourn at Cairo, he felt that he was being "used"; and this, with his outspokenness, led to a rupture. He was confident, had the Khedive backed him more vigorously, of being able to settle the whole question out of hand.

His failure as a financial adviser, the loss of time his visit had entailed, the anarchy he ruled, the dismal and dreadful lookout ahead of him, had all tended to depress him deeply ; and as he left the capital to return to the duties he had quitted so unwillingly, he could not suppress the desire within him that his final rest were near. He had chosen a new route, for his goal was Harrar, where he intended to turn out Raouf Pasha, who had been guilty of cruelty to the people. In the letters he wrote on his way through Suez, Aden, Berberah, and Zeila, if he refers at all to the Cairo episode, it is with visible reluctance; and the only memories which are touched with pleasure are those of a few of the many people he had met: M. de Lesseps, for instance, of whom he speaks with great kindness, and the Khedive's sons, whose manners impressed him very favourably indeed.

His short sojourn at Suez, Aden, and Berberah is marked by no incident of note. The air was full of the rumours of war, and he thought it by no means unlikely that he would be obliged to join his regiment. "The pith is out of me for the moment," he says; "I go with only a half heart, for I would wish to be at Gallipoli. I know it was wrong in one way, but I cannot help it. It would be a great trouble for the Khedive, I know; but if God took me away He would not have any trouble in finding another worm to fill the place. You may imagine my feelings in going down to Aden to-morrow just at the crisis; it is truly *déchirant.*" At Aden, Mr. Julian Baker (nephew of Sir Samuel Baker), who was on board the Admiral's flag-ship the *Undaunted,* called on him, and they made the voyage together to Zeila. Before going on to Massawa, Gordon quitted Zeila for Harrar, where Raouf Pasha was behaving like a "regular tyrant." Gordon, it will be remembered, had deposed this fellow, and sent him down to Cairo from Gondokoro in 1874. The eight days' journey inland to Harrar he made on horseback. On his way he met £2000 worth of coffee, which Raouf was packing off on his private account to Aden, intending to buy merchandise with the proceeds, and sell it at exorbitant prices to the soldiers at Harrar. Gordon confiscated the coffee off-hand; and before he reached Harrar he received a letter from Raouf acknowledging his order of dismissal. He rode into Harrar on April 28th, and was met by the sight of several dying cows which had been slaughtered in his honour; the scene made him miserable, inured as he was to the spectacle of suffering by his apprenticeship in China and the Soudan. Raouf, who looked downcast and penitent enough, left the place next day. "I cannot help feeling sorry for him," says Gordon. "God grant I have not been unjust, but seeing the people, as they were, so fearfully cowed by him, made me feel that the sorrow of one man ought not to be weighed against the sorrows of many men."

Gordon did not stay long at Harrar; he returned to Zeila, and reached that place at dawn on the 9th of May, "after a terrible march of eight days." Fagged as he was, he pushed on straight for Massawa. There, on the 12th of May, he met with an enthusiastic reception. But he was anxious to get back to Khartoum and his arrears of work; and on the 3rd of June we find him near Berber, having done the distance between Suakim and that place in nine days. At Atbara River the steamer met him for Khartoum. The heat was greater than even he had ever experienced; and he was in no humour for trifling with his subordinates. His first trouble at headquarters was the refusal of Osman Pasha, his second in command in the Soudan, to go to Darfour. He pleaded illness, but Gordon knew this to be false. The truth was that Osman, in the Second Class of the Medjidie, which the Governor-General had asked for him at Cairo, had achieved his ideal, and wanted no more. Finding him in this lofty humour, and suspecting him of a tendency to treason, Gordon packed him off to the capital there and then, to be dealt with by the authorities. This, however, was a trifle in comparison with the rest. Everything was in arrears: there were mountains of papers to go through, crowds of people to see, swamps of peculation and wrong to be traversed; and all the while the Governor-General saw no chance of making ends meet, and entertained no hope of permanent good. The people were delighted to have him again among them, for they knew there would be no delays. But the state and ceremony by which he was surrounded was sore upon him, perhaps as sore as the thought of his unrequited labour.

His news from Abyssinia was that Walad had evacuated Egyptian territory, and had gone towards Adowa with an eye to business. Gordon's letters to King Johannis and Ras Bariou, discrediting his deeds, but stipulating that his life should be spared, had fallen, as he had foreseen they would, into the rebel's hands; and he was rather pleased than otherwise that Walad knew the Governor-General to entertain no personal wish to do him harm.

Soon, however—in July 1878—the news came in that Suleiman had revolted, and had laid hands on the Bahr Gazelle. It was a critical time; for, while the Governor-General had been keeping the slavers in check, breaking their communications with the northern provinces and blockading them in the south, they had gathered head under Suleiman and overrun the Gazelle. Gordon

acted with his wonted swiftness and assurance. He despatched
Romulus Gessi with an expeditionary force to the south, and, seizing the persons of such of Suleiman's family as were within his
reach, imprisoned them and confiscated their goods.

After a march for reinforcements into the Equatorial Province,
Gessi returned down the river and landed his troops at Rabat-
chambé. It was not until August 26th, however, that he pushed
on through a flooded country to Rumbek, a station on the Bahr-
el-Kohl. Beyond him, to westward, the waters of all the
tributaries of the Bahr Gazelle were out, and incessant rains
delayed his advance until far on into November. In this inaction
Gessi learned that Suleiman had proclaimed himself Lord of the
Province, and had surprised the Khedive's garrison at Dem Idris,
seized the stores, and massacred the troops. This success decided
the neutral Arab tribes, and Suleiman was strongly reinforced
from them. It was even rumoured that with 6000 men he contemplated an attack on Rumbek. Gessi had but 300 regular
troops, two guns, and 700 ill-equipped and ill-drilled irregulars.
He entrenched himself, and sent to Gordon for aid ; but, owing to
the blockade of the river by the "sudd," his letters took five
months to reach Khartoum. In the meanwhile he got no help
from the officials, whether civil or military, and his soldiers began
to desert. Desertion he checked by a right use of the lash and
a certain number of executions, and on November 17th he left his
camp and started on his famous march. Pressing on through a
land of streams, crossing three rivers on rafts, he reached the
Dyoor, on whose farther bank he first sighted the enemy. The
current was too strong and the water too deep for rafts ; but in
the boats of a friendly chief he got his men across. Thence he
marched to the village of Wau, on the river of that name, and
interned his numerous camp-following of women and children in
a stockade. On the 11th a friendly Arab reinforced him with
700 armed men, and he pushed on to Dem Idris, which he occupied
and strengthened with stockades against the coming Suleiman.

His advance was not so tardy and chequered that it found
Suleiman ready. It was not till the 27th that the son of Zebehr
set out ; but on the following morning he fell in force upon Gessi's
entrenchments. Four times did he assault ; and four times was he
driven back with desperate slaughter. Broken, but not beaten, he
retired to some neighbouring heights, a thousand dead and five stan-
dards the poorer for his advance. Gessi, however, was too weak to
attempt the offensive. He wanted ammunition, too, and he wrote

to Gordon for a further supply. Strongly reinforced, and encouraged by the enemy's silence, Suleiman, on January 12th, 1879, led up his men to a fresh and even fiercer assault, and was twice hurled back as before. Gessi was now so pressed for want of ammunition that he had to gather and recast the bullets Suleiman had fired into his camp. Next morning the fight was won. Suleiman had prepared for one supreme effort, and for seven hours the event was of doubtful issue. At last, however, the slavers were completely routed. Suleiman was dragged off the field by his own men; while Gessi, leaving his entrenchments, hunted his broken host into the surrounding forests. For a fortnight Gessi lay in peace; but on the night of the 28th the enemy once more came up. One of Suleiman's shells set fire to a hut, and a high wind fanning the flames, Gessi was driven out into the open. Here, after a three hours' fight, he flung off his enemy, and then retired behind his lines to wait for ammunition.

While Gessi was thus keeping Suleiman at bay, Gordon was at work in Khartoum. He was greatly annoyed by the cold support he received from Cairo, and greatly concerned for Gessi. The finances of the Soudan were a source of continual trouble, and he was even threatened with the unwelcome presence of Zebehr, who had promised Nubar a revenue of £25,000. Gordon knew well that this could only be effected by shipping slaves down the river; and that if Zebehr were once permitted to return to his country, there was an end both to Gessi's expedition and his own royal programme. Slavery would again become the chief traffic, and the old anarchy would prevail once more. He met Nubar's suggestion with a positive and stern refusal, for he was determined to crush Suleiman as speedily as possible. He received no less than three orders to return to Cairo; but he answered decisively that the condition of affairs was critical, and that if he returned he would resign. Soon came the good news of Nubar's dismissal, of the disappearance of one of his most active enemies. Presently his anxiety about Gessi became so great, that he telegraphed repeatedly to the Khedive for permission to visit Kordofan and Darfour; and in the middle of March he was able to leave Khartoum for Shaka. His object was to dislodge the slavers from their hold, and to break it up and leave it in ruins. He had no fear for his communications with Gessi; for every mile he made would bring them nearer together. Meanwhile, Gessi had resumed his operations. He had received fresh munitions on the 11th of March, and he determined at once to attack the enemy behind his barricades. During the engagement, a Congreve rocket set fire to the slavers' camp. The flames spread to the stockades, and the rebels were forced into a sortie. They were driven back on their defences, and they fled in disorder, leaving their fortified camp a fire-stricken ruin. The want of ammunition again kept Gessi from following up his victory. His requests for help to the Governor of Shaka and other officials were wholly disregarded ; and fever breaking out in Dem Idris, his situation grew desperate.

Gordon all this while was pressing on to Shaka. The climate was bitter and changeful. Over vast tracts of sand the grasses and scrubby vegetation were withered. The heat was intense by day, and the cold intense by night. But he did good work on the road : arresting caravans of slave-dealers, releasing the slaves, and punishing the ruffians who held them. A message from Gessi, crying out for powder and shot, reached him near Edowa ; and he pushed on at top speed towards Shaka, from whence he intended to forward help to Gessi, not feeling justified in risking his communications by proceeding beyond that point. On the 27th of March he crossed the frontier of Kordofan, and entered Darfour. The weather was most trying. " I have never," he writes, " in China or elsewhere, felt such heat." During his long night-rides, he was actively engaged in solving the difficult question of the slave-trade. In the course of his calculations, a novel idea occurred to him. Seeing that all slaves must pass through Darfour from the south-west on the road to the Soudan and Nubia, he determined to frame a decree that should strike the traffic at its heart. It was to consist of two regulations only : " (1) All persons residing in Darfour must have a *permis de séjour* ; (2) All persons travelling to and from Darfour must have passports for themselves and suite." " Thus," he adds, " no person can reside in Darfour without an ostensible mode of livelihood ; and no one can go to or from Darfour without Government permission for himself and his followers." Imprisonment and confiscation of property were the penalties for infringing these regulations. But the shifting, conflicting, dubious policy of the Government on the question of legality of slavery hampered him sorely. Against the Khedive's personal orders to punish slave-dealing with death, he had to weigh the Khedive's firman declaring slave-dealing only punishable with imprisonment of from five months' to five years' duration, and Nubar's positive decision (recently telegraphed to him) that " the purchase and sale of slaves in Egypt is legal." Thus he was often prevented from summarily shooting the slavers whom he captured, and was forced to be content with sending them to prison, chained with fetters off their own slaves. On this march to Shaka he released many hundreds of slaves, all in the most wretched plight, and all of the most abject condition. He says, "We must have caught 2000 in less than nine months; and I expect we did not catch one-fifth of the caravans," though of these, between June 1878 to this date (March 1879), he had captured no less than sixty-three. "At Edowa," he writes, "a party of seven-slave-dealers, with twenty-three slaves, were captured and brought to me, together with two camels. Nothing could exceed the misery of these poor wretches. Some were children of not more than three years old; they had come across that torrid zone from Shaka, a journey from which I on my camel shrink." And again of a subsequent capture: "When I had just begun this letter, another caravan, with two slave-dealers and seventeen slaves, was brought in; and I hear others are on the way. Some of the poor women were quite nude. Both these caravans came from Shaka, where I mean to make a clean sweep of the slave-dealers." Just before arriving at Shaka, a post from Gessi reached him with intelligence of his successes; and a few days later, on April the 10th, came a further message from him to the effect that he was reinforced, and needed no more troops.

This news enabled Gordon, on his arrival at Shaka, to lay by his anxieties, and proceed with his work. In the meanwhile, Gessi, having received supplies from the Bahr Gazelle, had again resolved on the offensive. All April through, he had been unremittingly active in chasing, and breaking, and punishing innumerable gangs of robbers; and in the beginning of May he set out from Dem Idris, and marched against Suleiman, who had taken refuge in Dem Suleiman, a town named in his own honour. His assault was so brilliantly planned, and so splendidly done, that Suleiman himself nearly fell into his hands. Taking possession of his capture, he learned that Suleiman had merely moved farther west, and was in the company of Rabi, one of the most formidable of the rebel slavers. He instantly started in pursuit. Through a ruined country, hideous at every mile with traces of the enemy, he pressed on. He had 600 men with him, and he was victorious; and he went on Gordon's work, at Gordon's own pace.

On the 10th of May he fell upon the village where Suleiman, it was said, lay hiding; but one sick woman was its only occupant. Past ruin after ruin, in tropical rain, and through a country harried to the very quick, he led his hungry men. In a

village but newly forsaken they found some food. Beyond was
a dense forest. Gessi sent out scouts, and got intelligence of a
great clump of camp-fires. Thinking that here was a slave-
caravan, with the rebels themselves in force in advance of it, he
divided his troops, and made a detour so as to avoid the main
body, and strike the advance-guard. Missing their way, a column
of his army came into sudden conflict with some of the slavers,
under a notorious chief, Abu Shnep, and put them to rout.
Meanwhile the firing had alarmed the rebel vanguard, and they
set fire to the village and abandoned their position. Once again
Gessi was foiled; for he found the place deserted by all save a
little child, who told him that Suleiman had passed the night in
that very place. Avoiding the highway, he pushed forward at
top speed; and next night his camp was visited by seven men,
who mistook his fires for Rabi's. Completing their blunder, they
informed him, through a messenger, that they had come on from
the army of Sultan Idris, who was coming up behind as fast as
he might; and they begged him to delay his advance that the
two forces might effect a junction. Gessi (as Rabi) made answer
that he would wait for Idris on the road. But while one of the
seven was taking this reply to his fellows, the six were pressed to
spend the night in the camp, where they were seized and made
prisoners.

This singular occurrence was both momentous and fortunate.
Gessi at once resolved to attack and finish Rabi before his ally
could come up. He set off at extreme speed. At daybreak he
fell upon Rabi in his camp, and utterly defeated him, securing
his flag and all his stores, and only missing the chief himself
through the swiftness of his horse. While the engagement was
in progress, Idris and his men were on the march. The situation
demanded strategy; and Gessi supplied the demand out of hand.
He encamped away from the scene of Rabi's disaster, cleared the
field of battle of all tell-tale signs, and ran up Rabi's standard
beside his empty tent. He then despatched half a dozen of his
men to meet Idris. These men, falling in with the Sultan as by
accident, reported themselves as of Rabi's army, and out hunting.
Idris bade them return and announce his approach. Gessi
immediately drew his men out round a glade in the forest, and
awaited the issue in ambush in the long grass. A sudden storm
came on at the moment of the enemy's arrival, and he hurried in
disorder to the shelter of the camp. A deadly fire was poured
on him by Gessi's men, and the fury of the wind and the rain

completed his demoralisation. Idris himself and a few attendants alone escaped. His wealth fell into the hands of Gessi's followers. This brilliant victory broke up the league of slavers for a while ; and Gessi, after an absence of nine days, marched back to Dem Suleiman with his spoils. Here he rested for some weeks, contenting himself with exploring the surrounding country, and keeping in check the many marauding bands by which the province was harassed.

While Gessi was engaging Suleiman and breaking the power of the slavers, Gordon was active in Shaka. The slavery question was ever before him. He had to consider not merely how best to stop the traffic, but how to revive the exhausted revenue, which would suffer still farther from its abolition ; and also, how to obtain recruits for an army consisting of 25,000 bought or captured slaves. Beside the consideration of these intricate questions, he was indefatigable in hurrying his officials, particularly in respect of the execution of sentences on the slave-dealers. This work of supervision obliged him to make frequent and sudden movements ; and his rapid rides occasioned delinquents much dismay. It was just previous to starting to Kalaka on one of these expeditions, that he heard from Gessi of his advance on Suleiman. His own position in Shaka was anything but secure. This he felt, for he writes : "I hope soon to leave for Dara, for I am not exactly safe here. If Zebehr's son knew how few men I have, and could break away from Gessi, he might pay me a visit." But he found that he had allies on the road, though they could not be always relied on. The various tribes of Arabs, who were scouring the country in bands, were beginning to foresee the issue of events. The news of Gessi's exploits and Gordon's frightening activity and rapidity of movement forced them into action, and on every hand they fell on the scattered parties of slavers. Many captures were made by these dubious friends, who brought them in to Gordon *en route* to Kalaka, where they had caught and imprisoned a number of dealers. Their slaves were wandering about the country in thousands, and were being "snapped up," as Gordon says, "by the native Arabs in all directions, as if they were sheep." He reckoned there must have been a thousand in Kalaka alone. Yet it was impossible to send them back to their own countries, owing to the lack of food and water and the means of transport. From Kalaka he journeyed to Dara, leaving 100 soldiers behind him. Through a monotonous sandy plain, with a scanty vegetation of scrub, he passed from Dara to Fascher

and Kobeyt in the extreme north of Darfour. At Kobeyt he
learned that the route to Kalabieh and Kolkol in the west was
beset by brigands, and this in spite of the garrison at the latter
place. This made him push on to Kolkol; and on the 25th of
May he was attacked by about 150 men, and, as he puts it, "had
a bad time" with them for four or five hours. Towards evening
they were driven off, and Gordon's party encamped nine miles
from Kolkol, thoroughly exhausted. He found Kolkol, the
ultimate post of the Egyptian Government, in a miserable state.
"Nothing," he says, "could describe the misery of these utterly
useless lands, they have been made perfect deserts by the
Government."

From this desolate spot he despatched to Khartoum, by way
of Dara, a forlorn band of Arabs—soldiers, officers, women, and
children—all utterly broken and useless. His chief concern now
was for Gessi. He had received, on his return from Kolkol to
Fascher, a despatch from the Italian on the 5th of June, informing
him of the capture of Dem Suleiman; and he believed that
Suleiman was completely crushed. He started for Khartoum by
way of Oomchanga and Toashia. On the road he learned that
the robber chiefs had broken out of Shaka, and he feared a
renewal of troubles. Haroun was still afield with 300 men, and
he wished to prevent a junction of the forces; so rapidly and
unexpectedly did he advance on Toashia, that he surprised a troop
of 100 slavers and despoiled them of 300 slaves. His plan was
to watch the wells, until the caravans, unable to hold out, were
fain to surrender at discretion. The number of skulls along the
road was terrible. He had great piles of them put up as monu-
ments of the horrible cruelty of the slavers. He calculated the
loss of life in Darfour during 1875–79 at 16,000 Egyptians and
50,000 natives, exclusive of the loss among the slaves, which he
put down at from 80,000 to 100,000. He remarks at this time,
"I feel revived when I make these captures. From Oomchanga
to Toashia, during say a week, we must have caught from 500 to
600. I suppose we may consider that nearly that number must
have been passing every week for the last year and a half or two
years along this road."

On the 25th of June, Gessi arrived. Gordon found him
looking much older. Before leaving for Khartoum, he made
arrangements with his lieutenant for the future government of
the Bahr Gazelle, presented him with £2000, and created him
a Pasha, with the Second Class of the Osmanlie. Leaving his

chief to make his way to Khartoum, the new Pasha returned to his old quarters. Although the rebellion was not crushed even yet, Suleiman being still at liberty, the end was not long in coming. Early in July, Gessi learned of a deserter that the son of Zebehr was not far off, and was attempting a coalition with Haroun. Suleiman, the terrible Pasha at his heels, fled, with nearly 900 men, towards the Gebel Marah, a difficult and little-known country; Rabi, with 700 men, retreating in another direction. Gessi had but 290 soldiers with him, but they were well armed, and flushed with victories. By an admirable forced march he overtook the enemy in the village of Gara. Surprising them in their sleep, and concealing his numbers, he persuaded them to capitulate. They laid down their arms in ignorance of his real strength, and great was Suleiman's mortification on learning to what a little force he had succumbed. By Gordon's orders, the chiefs (including Suleiman and Abdulgassin) were afterwards shot. Rabi alone seems to have escaped. Gordon had made a hero of Gessi, and here was his reward.

Thus fell the power of Zebehr in the person of his son Suleiman, and with it the whole fabric of his ambition. Gordon's prophecy was realised to the full. Zebehr himself was tried in Cairo for rebellion against the Viceroy, found guilty, and condemned to death. But, as the Governor-General had anticipated, "nothing was done to him." He was suffered to live in Cairo, with a pension of £100 a month from the Khedive. This impolitic leniency did much to weaken the moral force of these splendid and ruinous attacks on the slave-trade in the Soudan.

CHAPTER XV

THE news of Gessi's final success reached Gordon at Toashia. Satisfied that the stern lessons he had himself been teaching the slave-traders were so much inspiration for the oppressed tribes, he set off on the 29th June 1879 for Fogia. Gessi, he knew, could do more than hold his own in the south; and he felt that the slave-trade had at length been dealt a powerful blow. If ineradicable, as he himself believed, it was so from causes existent at head-quarters—causes over which he could exercise no control. At Fogia he heard of Ismail's deposition, and received orders to proclaim Tewfik Khedive throughout the Soudan. Beyond acknowledging the official intelligence to Cherif Pasha, the new Khedive's minister, he did no more than telegraph the order to the several governments. He then went on to Khartoum. About this time he received from his old colleague, Li-Hung-Chang, an interesting letter, dated Tientsin, March 22nd, 1879, in reply to his communication to the Chinese generalissimo of the 27th October 1878. At the end of July he left Khartoum, and reached Cairo on August 23rd; and one week later he left that city for Massawa on a mission to the King of Abyssinia.

He had not heard of Ismail's abdication with equanimity. He respected the late Khedive's character and abilities, however much he reprehended the morality of his statecraft. With characteristic generosity he writes: "It grieves me what sufferings my poor Khedive Ismail has had to go through." His instructions for the conduct of his mission to King Johannis, written in French, were couched in terms the most guarded; they were, at the same time, extremely polite to himself personally. At Cairo he had shown his annoyance at the new turn in affairs by refusing a special train, and declaring he would go to the hotel in preference to the palace prepared for him. He did not carry out the latter resolve, feeling he "should not be justified in such a snub." He was admitted to more than one audience of Tewfik, who expressed his entire confidence in him. In these conversations it was at first evident that the new Khedive was somewhat nervous as to whether the Governor-General was not too intimate with King Johannis. "In fact," says Gordon, "the general report in Cairo was that I was going in for being Sultan! But it would not suit our family." The Khedive, I should note, had to deal not merely with King Johannis, but with our old acquaintance, Walad el Michael, who was threatened with attack by the Abyssinian Aloula. This greatly complicated the situation, and it behoved the Khedive to act with great circumspection. Before leaving Cairo, Gordon paid off some old scores, and did much work in the hearty and determined style we know. "I wrote," he says, "to the Consuls-General of France and England, and told them they had interfered to get sweet things, and now they must interfere to avoid bitter things. I attacked in an official letter the Italian Consul-General, for it is an Italian who has put Johannis up to this" (*i.e.* to the claim on Egyptian territory in Bogos, etc.), "and I expect I made him ashamed;" and so forth. He took with him as secretary, Berzati Bey, of whom he has recorded a high estimate. "He was my most intimate friend for three years; and though we often had tiffs, I always had a great respect for his opinion. He is about twenty-nine years of age, yet perfectly self-possessed and dignified; and I can say that, in all our perils, I never saw him afraid. A few men like Berzati Bey would regenerate Egypt; but they are rare. Scoffers call him the 'black imp.'" All this while the Abyssinians were actually in possession of the Bogos district. On September 11th Gordon started *en grande tenue* for Gura, where Aloula was encamped. On the way he heard that Walad and his officers were prisoners there, by order of Johannis. He suffered much from prickly heat. The roads were terrible and the climate intolerable, yet he meditated his policy all the march through. "I determined," he says, "to get rid, either *with* or *without* Johannis's help, of Walad el Michael and his men, and then to come to terms with Johannis. Now Johannis will not give me his help for nothing, when we persist in keeping what we have stolen from him" (*i.e.* Bogos, etc.); "I do not mean physical help but moral help—*i.e.*, that he should offer a pardon —that is, an asylum to which Walad el Michael's men can go when they leave Bogos. Otherwise they will fight with desperation against us." He reached Gura on the 10th, at half-past three in the afternoon, overcome with fatigue. Aloula was encamped on the top of an almost inaccessible hill, and Gordon's mule was so broken down that he had to climb to the great man's tent. The audience was not satisfactory. In a long shed, made of branches, Aloula was seated on a couch, and swathed like a mummy in white garments, even to his mouth. "Nearly everyone had his robe to his mouth, as if something poisonous had arrived. The figure at the end never moved, and I got quite distressed, for he was so muffled up that I felt inclined to feel his pulse. He must be ill, I thought." The apparent invalid was in excellent health; and Gordon saw, when he showed his face, "a good-looking young man of about thirty or thirty-five." After a little while "the poisonous effect had also gone off to some degree, for the others also removed their mufflers." Aloula received the Khedive's ambassador with a good deal of the ludicrous self-importance and assumption of wisdom of Johannis himself. He put the Khedive's letter aside unread, and behaved quite slightingly throughout the audience. He condescended to inform Gordon that he might smoke if he chose, in spite of the King's decree that smokers caught in the act should lose hand and foot. He proposed that the Envoy should camp at the bottom of the hill, and climb to the top whenever he wanted an interview. This Gordon positively declined to do; so a hut was found for him near the General's shed. The result of these interviews was that Gordon agreed to see Johannis himself, and Aloula undertook not to attack Egypt in his absence.

On the 19th Gordon left Gura for Debra Tabor, near Gondar. He went by horrible roads, over the steepest mountains, through the country of Rasselas, but without a sight of the Happy Valley; and so towards the Abyssinian capital—"crawling over the world's crust." Near Adowa, on the 27th, he passed the Amba, the mountain prison where Walad el Michael was interned. Of this he says, "When you get close to it you have to be hauled up in a basket. There was a tent pitched on the top, in which—to-day being the first of the Abyssinian year, as the King's interpreter told me—there was feasting." After a fatiguing march by execrable bridle-paths, the river Tacazzi was reached on October 12th. Here he heard from the officer of Aloula, who travelled with him, that a robber chief with 300 men was meditating attack, and was reported to have said, when he heard that

Gordon's luggage and presents for the King were not with him, that he would "take the Pasha and the black imp, and get the boxes afterwards." He also heard of another robber on the road between Galabat and Debra Tabor, with several guns; as he himself had only six black soldiers, this was not reassuring. On October 27th, however, without further adventure he arrived at Debra Tabor, convinced that Aloula had sent him through a network of byways to impress him with the difficulties of the country in case the Khedive should declare war.

He was received at the court of Johannis with a salute of guns. With the King at Debra Tabor were Ras Arya, his father; the Itagé, or high-priest; the Greek Consul from Suez; an Italian named Bianchi; and two Italians named Neretti. The night of his arrival Gordon was visited by fifteen black soldiers, who had been captured at Gondet in November 1875, and nine Arabs, whom Aloula had made prisoners at Ailat in January 1877; these men all begged him to intercede with Johannis for their release. Next day he had his audience. Johannis began with a tedious recital of his grievances against Egypt, and asked Gordon what was the nature of his mission. He was referred to the Khedive's letter, which it appeared had not even been translated. He then put forward a number of outrageous claims: the "retrocession of Metemneh, Changallas, and Bogos, cession of Zeila and Amphilla (ports), an Abouna, and a sum of money from one to two million pounds." As alternatives, he suggested that he should take Bogos, Massawa, and the Abouna; adding: "I could claim Dongola, Berber, Nubia, and Sennaar, but will not do so. Also, I want a certain territory near Harrar." "Here," Gordon remarks, "his Majesty seemed a little out in his geography, so he added that he would waive that claim for the moment." These demands were thought too monstrous, even considered as a price for peace; and Gordon told his Majesty, in his private capacity, that he did not think the Khedive would accept them, and urged him to put into writing what he considered his just dues. Johannis shuffled, and suggested a new discussion at some neighbouring baths which he proposed to visit. Gordon acquiesced, and presented him, through Berzati Bey, with presents worth £200. Nothing occurred till November 6th. In the interim Gordon discovered that the King was backed in his obstinacy by the intrigues of the Greek Consul and others. On the 6th Johannis returned from the baths without the written claims. But to these Gordon determined to fix him. He told his Majesty that he had positive orders not to cede Bogos, or any territory, but that he would use his private influence to obtain for him an Abouna, the free import of arms, and letters for himself at Massawa and Bogos. At length, on the 8th, he was assured he should receive the written demands in the form of a letter to the Khedive. He had an audience that day, however, and found the King in a sulky and resentful humour. Johannis bade him go back, and added that he would forward a letter to the Khedive by an envoy of his own. Gordon then asked for the release of the Egyptian soldiers. This enraged the King, who told him to go.

An hour after, he went. Just as he was starting, the interpreter brought him the letter and $1000. The money he returned, but at his first halt on the road he opened the letter, in his capacity as Envoy, suspecting a trick, and found it only twelve lines long. He saw that, making allowance for the usual salutation and valediction, it could not possibly contain the specific statement required. Translated, he found it ran in these insulting terms: "I have received the letters you sent me by *that man*. I will not make a secret peace with you. If you want peace, ask the Sultans of Europe." He wrote to the Greek Consul, demanding an explanation, and was answered, "that the King said he had written as he saw fit, and, if he judged right, would write other letters to the Khedive." Gordon calmly pursued his road to Galabat, intending to reach Khartoum by way of Katarif, instead of following the mountainous route he had travelled from Massawa. Before him, a revolted chief named Gadassi occupied the country, and to him he applied for an escort of 200 men. Waiting a reply, he encamped at Char Amba, the Gate of Abyssinia, fronting a gorge in the mountains that commanded a prospect of the Soudanese plains. At five in the afternoon he was suddenly arrested by 120 of Johannis's men, under three of Ras Arya's officers, and the little party was marched back to the village of the King's uncle. Gordon, on the way, destroyed his journal, that it might not fall into the hands of Johannis. Ras Arya was a cunning, self-seeking fellow, with an eye to bribes. He had once despatched a false embassy to Gordon at Katarif, and he now entertained him with hearty abuse of Johannis. He even suggested that the Khedive should take the country, as everyone was disgusted with the King. Gordon gave him £70 to ensure the safe passage of his telegrams to Galabat. On the 17th, the party, still guarded, passed on to Gondar, and reached

Ras-Garamudhiri. Here the escort left them, and for a while
they were free. Over snowy mountains, and suffering considerably
from the want of shelter (for he had no tents), Gordon pushed
forward to the frontier, not without an expenditure of £1400 in
gold for bribes in the shape of tolls and safe-conduct. At Kya-
Khor, a village on the frontier, he was again arrested, and
subjected to a great deal of bullying and extortion. At last, on
December 8th, he reached Massawa, and there he was lucky
enough to find the *Seagull*, an English gunboat.

Thus ended this fatiguing and fruitless mission. The Khedive
had shown himself indifferent to his Envoy's safety and the honour
of his own name. He had taken no notice of Gordon's application for troops and a steamer, which, on his arrest by Johannis,
he had desired should be sent to Massawa. Considerable apprehension was felt as to his safety. Had it not been for the
timely despatch of the *Seagull*, affairs might have taken an
awkward turn.

There is nothing surprising in Johannis's wish to make Gordon
a prisoner; rather is it a wonder that it did not take effect in
the court itself. The uncompromising candour with which the
Envoy unburdened his mind to this King of kings would have
cost most envoys their lives. Gordon had told him that "the
King would be better if he would not try and be God"; and
"that six feet of earth would hold the one as it would the other."
Another and not smaller source of irritation was that the King's
people—especially the beggars—crowded round Gordon's tent,
deserting his Majesty; and that the strange Ambassador went
about unguarded and on foot. The following amusing account of
an interview between this extraordinary pair was given not long
after the Governor-General's return :—

"When Gordon Pasha was lately taken prisoner by the
Abyssinians, he completely checkmated King John. The King
received his prisoner sitting on his throne, or whatever piece of
furniture did duty for that exalted seat, a chair being placed for
the prisoner considerably lower than the seat on which the King
sat. The first thing the Pasha did was to seize this chair, place
it alongside that of his Majesty, and sit down on it ; the next, to
inform him that he met him as an equal, and would only treat
him as such. This somewhat disconcerted his sable Majesty, but
on recovering himself he said, 'Do you know, Gordon Pasha,
that I could kill you on the spot if I liked?' 'I am perfectly

well aware of it, your Majesty,' said the Pasha. 'Do so at once if it is your royal pleasure. I am ready.' This disconcerted the King still more, and he exclaimed, 'What! ready to be killed!' 'Certainly,' replied the Pasha; 'I am always ready to die; and so far from fearing your putting me to death, you would confer a favour on me by so doing, for you would be doing for me that which I am precluded by my religious scruples from doing for myself—you would relieve me from all the troubles and misfortunes which the future may have in store for me.' This completely staggered King John, who gasped out in despair, 'Then my power has no terrors for you?' 'None whatever,' was the Pasha's laconic reply. His Majesty, it is needless to add, instantly collapsed."

Gordon returned to Egypt at the end of the year. He had sent in his resignation to the Khedive on his way; and universal was the regret at his determination to quit the country in which he had wrought so much good. Much as the ex-Khedive had been blamed for his misrule, it was unanimously acknowledged that he had done an act of eminent wisdom in appointing Gordon to the Governor-Generalship of the Soudan; and few could resist the temptation of comparing his appreciation of the great Proconsul with Tewfik's. Against the latter there was a general feeling of resentment, even of indignation; this notwithstanding the tenour of the Viceroy's letter to his Governor-General on his arrival at Alexandria: "I am glad to see you again among us, and have pleasure in once more acknowledging the loyalty with which you have always served the Government," writes the Khedive. "I should have liked to retain your services, but in view of your persistent tender of resignation am obliged to accept it. I regret, my dear Pasha, losing your co-operation, and in parting with you must express my sincere thanks to you, assuring you that my remembrance of you and your services to the country will outlive your retirement."

The fact is that what took the world by surprise at the time had been decided on months before. Gordon, before going to Abyssinia, had been urged by certain ministers, notably Riaz, Cherif, and Nubar, to make certain reforms in his government, of which he did not approve; and he thereupon announced his intention to quit the Soudan. It was only as a personal favour to the Khedive that he carried letters to King Johannis at all. This he had done at the peril of his life. On his return to Egypt the interfering ministers began their interfering once more.   There were stormy interviews between Gordon and Nubar and Riaz. They grumbled angrily at his proposed cession of Zeila to the Abyssinians, and they resented the fact that the proposal had reached the papers.   That it had done so was entirely their own fault; for the suggestion had been telegraphed to them in cipher. These unpleasant conferences, with what had gone before, led to his final resignation.   "I am neither a Napoleon nor a Colbert," was his reply to someone who spoke to him in praise of his beneficence in the Soudan; "I do not profess either to have been a great ruler or a great financier; but I can say this—I have cut off the slave-dealers in their strongholds, and I made the people love me."   What Gordon had done was to justify Ismail's description of him eight months before.   "They say I do not trust Englishmen," said the old Khedive.   "Do I mistrust Gordon Pasha?   That is an honest man; an administrator, not a diplomatist."

Apart from the difficulties of serving the new Khedive, Gordon longed for rest.   The first year of his rule as Governor of the Tribes—during which he had done his own work and other men's — the long marches, the terrible climate, the perpetual anxieties—all had told upon him.   Since then he had had three years of desperate labour, and ridden some 8500 miles.   Who can wonder that he resented the impertinences of the Pashas, whose interference was not for the good of his government or his people, but solely for their own.

But it was not for him to stay on and complain.   To one of the worst of these Pashas he sent a telegram, which ran: "Mene Mene Tekel Upharsin."   Then he sailed for England, bearing with him the memory of the enthusiastic crowd of friends who bade him farewell at Cairo.   His name sends a thrill of love and admiration through the Soudan even yet.   A hand so strong and so beneficent had never before been laid on the people of that unhappy land.

CHAPTER XVI

ONLY a few weeks' rest fell to him on his return. These were spent for the most part in London and at Southampton. His treatment at the hands of Egypt, and his subsequent resignation, made a great stir. The general feeling was one of regret rather than surprise. Everybody knew of his magnificent campaign against the slave-trade, unaided and alone; and that, unless support were given him, he must sooner or later abandon the task. The manner in which his services had been contemned by the Government which had been so eager to secure them, was looked on as a disgrace; and it was felt as a certainty that the traffic he had broken and ruined would be revived ere long.

The English press could not say enough in his praise; and, with reference to the vast province over which he had ruled, it was for a time the fashion to call him "The Uncrowned King." The same attempt as before, but if anything a more strenuous one, was made by the fashionable world to lionise him. And many amusing stories might be told of the way in which he avoided those who sought him out; as well as of the strategy he employed to elude the many invitations sent in.

Early in May, when the London world was discussing the resignation of one Viceroy of India, and the accession of another, people were amazed at the announcement that Lord Ripon had asked Gordon to be his Private Secretary, and that Gordon had said "yes." Many at first refused to believe; and when it was telegraphed to India, it created a sensation not unmixed with alarm. One correspondent wrote that "with the arrival of Colonel Gordon we shall have an end of favouritism, and all cliqueism will disappear from the face of official society." The journals themselves were not so sanguine. "Official society without cliques and favouritism is to us unimaginable," says one. "If Colonel Gordon were Viceroy, he could not entirely eradicate these deep-seated diseases. But if our correspondent means—as we suppose he does — that no cliqueism nor favouritism, nor any meanness nor charlatanism, will receive any toleration from Colonel Gordon, but will meet with stern suppression, so far as he may have power to deal with it, then we agree with him. There is not in the world a man of gentler, kindlier nature than Colonel Gordon; we know of no man more terrible to shams and charlatans. His mere presence in Indian society will be a kind of shock which will send a shiver through all its vanities, and may indeed in time create a sort of revolution."

There is little doubt that many thought the appointment an absurdity. The expression of such an opinion was checked by a belief in the existence of occult reasons for inducing so illustrious a soldier to fill so unimportant a post. The Central Asian Question had been recently revived; the effects of the Afghan War were being hotly discussed; and the Government was credited with an ulterior aim—that of entrusting to one man the solution of a problem which had already baffled hundreds, and will baffle hundreds more.[1]

[1] Mr. Charles Marvin, in his *Merv, the Queen of the World,* speaking of the importance of establishing a barrier between Russia and India, showed his appreciation of such a choice in the following terms :—

"To select the border-line between the English and Russian Empires in Asia, there should be no appointment of committees or commissions; the task should be given to a single man. In the multitude of counsel there may be wisdom, but rarely, if ever, decision. It is with public affairs as with private : one man will always carry out a scheme more quickly, more cheaply, and more satisfactorily than a committee of a dozen. You have the advantage of aggregate wisdom in confiding a task to a committee ; you have the drawback of their aggregate foolishness. Even if you are lucky in securing a choice selection of sages, experience warns you beforehand that the more their originality the greater will be the conflict of opinion, which can only end in a compromise—a term signifying feebleness of decision.

"No ; we should choose a good man for the solution of the Anglo-Russian Frontier Question; we should allow him to choose his own advisers; we should give him abundance of time to form his own opinions on the subject. He should have unlimited funds to conduct explorations and to appoint assistant explorers. He should visit in succession Russia and Persia, to realise correctly the genius of those countries. He should have absolute freedom in the preparation of his plan, and the plan when complete should be made the basis of a definite and final settlement of the Central Asian Question.

"I may be asked to point out the Atlas who can bear this enormous responsibility upon his shoulders. We have not to go far to seek him. His name is well known. He is not the offspring of a clique ; he is not the creature of a fraction. He has fought well, he has ruled well. His Christian piety is a proverb among those who know him ; his scorn of pelf and prefer-

So it came to pass that he who had been a Sultan suddenly became a Secretary, though it was said at the time that there was not a post from Constantinople eastward which would have been too much for him. As for Gordon himself, he accepted the appointment in the spirit in which he would accept any station in life, high or humble, provided that out of it good might come. And the world took it for granted that he went as something more than as a mere Secretary.

Towards the end of May, the Viceroy left London for his seat of government, and loud were the cheers for him and his Secretary as the train moved out of the station at Charing Cross. The journey was watched with eager interest by the public, and the correspondents kept them well informed by telegram of what happened at the several stages. The surprise at the appointment was great, but a greater was in store. Hardly had we heard of the Viceroy's arrival in Bombay, when we heard of Gordon's resignation. The Anglo-Indian journalists were right who said there was something whimsical in turning Gordon Pasha into a small official; the anomaly had proved impossible. With perfect frankness and simplicity, and in a spirit of self-accusation which everybody could but applaud, Gordon gave his reasons for the unexpected step he had taken. He wrote: "Men, at times, owing to the mysteries of Providence, form judgments which they afterwards repent of. This is my case in accepting the appointment Lord Ripon honoured me in offering me. I repented of my act as soon as I had accepted the appointment, and I deeply regret that I had not the moral courage to say so at that time. Nothing could have exceeded the kindness and consideration with which Lord Ripon has treated me. I have never met anyone with whom I could have felt greater sympathy in the arduous task he has undertaken."

The words were a puzzle to many; not a few believed the announcement to be a hoax. The way in which it was received by the press is somewhat amusing. To a large number it proved at once that Gordon could never have fulfilled his duties: "He would be more at home in the Soudan where he was a King, or

ment is so remarkable that he almost stands alone—he hardly belongs to a place-hunting, money-grubbing generation. He possesses the entire confidence of all parties ; he enjoys the admiration and love of the nation. Russia knows nothing to his detriment, and he has recently earned her respect by his disinterested exertions on her behalf in the distant East. I have no need to utter his name. It springs spontaneously to the reader's lips—Chinese Gordon."

in China where he was a General, than in the Private Secretary's
room in Government House." To some he was mad, or at best
a "little eccentric"; others were aggrieved at his suppression of
his motives. When this last complaint reached his ears, he said
at once that, in such a position, with a turbulent spirit like his,
he would be likely to do more harm than good, and would only
too probably hamper the Viceroy, and involve him in difficulties.

He had resigned on June 3rd. He was planning a journey
to Zanzibar to help the Sultan, Syed Burghash, in a campaign
against the slave-dealers, when he was suddenly summoned to
Peking. His old colleague, Li-Hung-Chang, had sent him a
message through Mr. Hart, Chinese Commissioner of Customs.
The despatch had been sent to Mr. Campbell, Mr. Hart's agent
in London, who, seeing the news of the resignation, at once
forwarded it to India. Thus ran the telegram: "I am directed
to invite you to China. Please come and see for yourself.
This opportunity for doing really useful work on a large
scale ought not to be lost. Work, position, conditions, can all
be arranged with yourself here to your satisfaction. Do take
six months' leave and come." The "Uncrowned King" replied :
"Inform Hart, Gordon will leave for Shanghai first opportunity.
As for conditions, Gordon indifferent." Government was at once
applied to for the requisite leave ; but as his purpose in going and
the position he was to hold on his arrival could not be explained,
permission was withheld. Upon this he referred the Government
to Mr. Campbell, sent in his papers to the War Office, and sailed
on the 12th June for Hong - Kong. As everyone knows, war
was imminent between Russia and China, and great excitement
prevailed at St. Petersburg when his departure got wind. A
report was current that he had gone to China to organise
another Ever-Victorious Army. "It is all the work of Lord
Beaconsfield," said the excited *Golos*; and it hoped that Mr.
Gladstone and Lord Granville would blast the adventure with
public displeasure. Gordon, with his wonted foresight, had
anticipated the misconstruction to which his visit was open, and
had told his purpose before leaving India. "My fixed desire,"
he said, "is to persuade the Chinese not to go to war with Russia,
both in their own interests and those of the world, and especially
those of England. To me it appears that the question in dispute
cannot be of such vital importance that an arrangement could not
be come to by concessions on both sides. Whether I succeed in
being heard or not, is not in my hands. I protest, however,

14

against being regarded as one who wishes for war in any country, still less in China. In the event of war breaking out, I could not answer how I should act for the present; but I shall ardently desire a speedy peace. Inclined as I am, with only a small degree of admiration for military exploits, I esteem it a far greater honour to promote peace than to gain any paltry honours in a wretched war."

He arrived at Hong-Kong on the 2nd July, and at once received an invitation to stay at Government House from Sir John and Lady Hennesey. At Canton he paid a visit to the Viceroy, and saw many of his old friends in the City of Rams. When they asked him of his personal attitude towards China, he said that if his opinion were sought at Peking, he should give the "quinine and mixture," but not ask them to take it. He wished his visit to be clearly understood as unofficial, as indeed it was: he was taking a holiday, and had come to see his old friend Li. When the interviewers inquired his views as to the formation of an Anglo-Chinese force in case of war, he said: "I should strongly advise the Chinese to use their own forces; they do not want to teach the men to right-wheel and left-dress, and to show up a good line as soldiers are expected to do, because fighting is done more now by skirmishing." He earnestly recommended the Chinese, too, not to go to work with "cut flowers"; meaning that it was useless to take a lot of trained men, put them in the field, and as soon as the season is over let them all disperse again. It was the same at Tientsin and Peking—to all he spoke with equal frankness.

Since the days when they two had fought together against the Tai-pings, Li had proved himself a great soldier and administrator—had, in fact, justified Gordon's opinion that he was the ablest man in China. He had filled the highest positions in the councils of the Empire: he had been Junior Guardian of the Heir-Apparent, and Governor-General of Nanking; he had received the hereditary title of the Third Degree, the Double-Eyed Peacock's Feather, and the Yellow Jacket; now he was Senior Guardian to the Heir-Apparent, and Senior Grand Secretary and Viceroy of Chihli. The growth of his power had been so rapid that more than once he had been suspected of designs upon the Dragon Throne, and more than once he had been severely rebuked from the Throne itself. These suspicions were due to his belief in the Barbarian and his methods: to an unfaltering faith in the value of foreign principles and progress, of foreign policy, and of foreign arms. It was natural that so powerful a satrap should have a rival. Li had his in the person of Tso, a soldier-statesman like himself, who had seen service against the Tai-pings—he, indeed, who led the Franco-Chinese in 1864, while Gordon was winning his supreme victories. These two great intelligences figured as the heads of two powerful parties; Tso was in favour of war, Li was in favour of peace. Never, perhaps, were the positions of the two more clearly defined than when Gordon, on his old colleague's invitation, appeared upon the scene. It was thought that the tussle between the war party, led by Prince Chun and Tso, and the peace party, led by Prince Kung and Li, was not unlikely to have a tragic end. For a time it seemed as though the war party would get the upper hand; its adherents even began to speculate as to what would be the fate of Li and the Prince. Li was sending urgent messages to the Taotais, bearing the significant "fire-mark," with a view to ascertaining what support, in the event of civil war, he might command, when the Captain of the Ever-Victorious Army came to Peking. When Li-Hung-Chang saw his old friend, he fell on his neck and kissed him. Seventeen years before, he had brought peace to China; he brought it once more. He conferred with Li—with all the great satraps of the Empire; and he turned the scale.

When Li and the others asked his advice, he gave it in a memorandum, the wise and relentless outspokenness of which had the effect of bringing about the peace he was so anxious to maintain. Here it is: a State paper of the highest importance, in any case; and perhaps, after the campaign of the Ever-Victorious Army, the true beginning of the regeneration of China:—

"China possesses a long-used military organisation, a regular military discipline. Leave it intact. It is suited to her people.

"China in her numbers has the advantage over other Powers. Her people are inured to hardships. Arm with breech-loaders, accustom to the use and care of breech-loaders, and no more is needed for her infantry. Breech-loaders ought to be bought on some system, and the same general system applicable to the whole nation. It is not advisable to mauufacture them; though means of repair should be established at certain centres.

"Breech-loading ammunition should be manufactured at different centres. Breech-loaders of various patterns should not be bought, though no objection could be offered to a different breech-loader in, say, four provinces from that used in another group of four provinces. Any breech-loaders which will carry well up to 1000 yards would be sufficient. It is not advisable to spend money on the superior breech-loaders carrying farther. Ten breech-loaders, carrying up to 1000 yards, could be bought for the same money as five breech-loaders of a superior class, carrying to 1500 yards. For the Chinese it would cost more time to teach the use of the longer-range rifle than it is worth; and then, probably, if called to use it, in confusion the scholar would forget his lesson. This is known to be the case; therefore buy ordinary breech-loading rifles of 1000 yards range, of simple construction, of solid form. Do not go into purchasing a very light, delicately made rifle. A Chinese soldier does not mind one or two pounds more weight, for he carries no knapsack or kit. China's power is in her numbers, in the quick moving of her troops, in the little baggage they require, in their few wants. It is known that men armed with sword and spear can overcome the best regular troops, if armed with the best breech-loading rifles and well instructed in every way, if the country is at all difficult, and if the men with the spears and swords outnumber their foe ten to one. If this is the case when men are armed with spears and swords, it will be much truer when the same are armed with ordinary breech-loaders.

"China should never engage in pitched battles. Her strength is in quick movements, in cutting off the trains of baggage, and in night attacks not pushed home; in a continuous worrying of her enemies. Rockets should be used instead of cannon. No artillery should be moved with the troops. It delays and impedes them. Infantry fire is the most fatal fire; guns make a noise far out of proportion to their value in war. If guns are taken into the field, troops cannot march faster than those guns. The degree of speed at which the guns can be carried along, dictates the speed at which the troops can march. Therefore, very few guns, if any, ought to be taken; and those few should be smooth-bored, large-bore breech-loaders, consisting of four parts, to be screwed together when needed for use. Chinese accustomed to make forts of earth ought to continue this, and study the use of trenches for the attack of cities. China should never attack forts. She ought to wait and starve her foes out, and worry them night and day. China should have a few small-bored very long range wall-pieces, rifled and breech-loaders. They are light to carry, and if placed a long way off will be safe from attack. If the enemy comes out to take them, the Chinese can run away; and if the enemy takes one or two, it is no loss. Firing them in the enemy's camp, a long way off, would prevent the enemy sleeping; and if he does not sleep, then he gets ill and goes into hospital, and then needs other enemies to take care of him, and thus the enemies' numbers are reduced. When an enemy comes up and breaks the wall of the city, the Chinese soldiers ought not to stay and fight the enemy; but to go out and attack the trains of baggage in the rear, and worry him on the roads he came by. By keeping the Chinese troops lightly loaded with baggage, with no guns, they can move two to every one li the enemy marches. To-day the Chinese will be before him; to-morrow they will be behind him; the next day they will be on his left hand; and so on till the enemy gets tired and cross with such long walks, and his soldiers quarrel with their officers and get sick.

"The Chinese should make telegraphs in the country, as a rule, to keep the country quiet and free from false rumours; but with the Chinese soldiers in the field, they should use sun-signals, by the means of the heliograph. These are very easy, and can do no harm. For this purpose a small school should be established in each centre. Chinese ought not to try torpedoes, which are very difficult to manage. The most simple torpedoes are the best and the cheapest, and their utility is in having many of them. China can risk sowing them thickly; for if one of them does go astray and sink a Chinese junk, the people of the junk ought to be glad to die for their country. If torpedoes are only used at certain places, then the enemy knows that he has to look out when near these places; but when every place may have torpedoes, he can never feel safe; he is always anxious; he cannot sleep; he gets ill and dies. The fact of an enemy living in constant dread of being blown up is much more advantageous to China than if she blew up one of her enemies, for anxiety makes people ill and cross. Therefore China ought to have cheap simple torpedoes, which cannot get out of order, which are fired by a fuze, *not* by electricity, and plenty of them. She ought not to buy expensive complicated torpedoes.

"China should buy no more big guns to defend her sea-coast. They cost money. They are a great deal of trouble to keep in order, and the enemy's ships have too thick sides for any gun China can buy to penetrate them. China ought to defend her sea-coast by very heavy mortars. They cost very little; they are easy to use; they only want a thick parapet in front, and they are fired from a place the enemy cannot see; whereas the enemy can see the holes from which guns are fired. The enemy cannot get safe from a mortar-shot; it falls on the deck, and there it breaks everything. China can get 500 mortars for the same money she gets an 18-ton gun for. If China loses them, the loss is little. No enemy could get into a port which is defended by 15,000 large mortars and plenty of torpedoes, which must be very simple. Steam-launches, with torpedoes on a pole, furnish the best form of movable torpedo. For the Chinese fleet, small quick vessels, with very light draught of water, and not any great weight of armour, are best. If China buys big vessels they cost a great deal, and all her eggs are in one basket—namely, she loses all her money at once. For the money of one large vessel China would get twelve small vessels. China's strength is in the creeks, not in the open seas.

"Nothing recommended in this paper needs any change in Chinese customs. The Army is the same, and China needs no Europeans or foreigners to help her to carry out this programme. If China cannot carry out what is here recommended, then no one else can do so. Besides, the programme is a cheap one.

"With respect to the Fleet, it is impossible to consider that in the employment of foreigners China can ever be sure of them in case of war with the country they belong to; while, on the other hand, if China asks a foreign Power to lend her officers, then that foreign Power who lends them will interfere with her. The question is: (1) Is it better for China to get officers here and there, and run the risk of their officers not being trustworthy? or (2) Is it better for China to think what nation there is who would be likely to be good friends with China in good weather and in bad weather; and then for China to ask that nation to lend China the officers she wants for her Fleet? I think No. 2 is the best and safest for China.

"Remember, with this programme China wants no big officer from foreign Powers; I say big officer, because I am a big officer in China. If I stayed in China it would be bad for China, because it would vex the American, French, and German Governments, who would want to send their officers. Besides, I am not wanted. China can do what I recommend herself. If she cannot, I could do no good."

This manifesto excited a storm of comment both at home and abroad. The native journals, into which it was instantly translated, were almost unanimous in recommending their Government to lose no time in putting its precepts into practice, the more so as they emanated from the man who, in saving China in the field, had learned exactly how best she might save herself. Li needed no promptings ; he was too large-minded and vigorous a statesman to waste such precious counsels. They were followed to the letter.

CHAPTER XVII

HE returned to London in the winter of 1881, to find himself the object of more attention than ever before. The papers gave him a hearty welcome, and many were the speculations as to what he would do next. His own wish was to leave for Syria, and there take the rest he so much needed; but the plan, dear as it was to him, was soon abandoned. He visited Ireland, and gave his whole mind to her troubles. A friend to whom he addressed his views, published them. They were daring, they were new, they were thorough; but they were not such views as the majority could approve, and they met with some adverse criticism and a little ridicule. Gordon cared as much for the one as the other. He took a deep interest in the question of the evacuation of Candahar, and his opinions, though all could not agree with them, had doubtless no little influence in deciding the course that was pursued.

The fact is, he may be said to have avoided the repose he talked about so much; for, besides taking an active interest in all the questions of the hour, he paid a visit to the King of the Belgians to discuss an international expedition to the Congo which his Majesty wished him to lead. In short, a brief stay on the Lake of Lausanne was the only holiday he gave himself; for in May he had abandoned all idea of going to Syria, and was making preparations for a journey to Mauritius, whither he had been ordered as Commanding Royal Engineer. The announcement gave great satisfaction to many of his admirers; it was felt that, although the position was not a prominent one, it was, at any rate, one in which he would serve his own country, and be at the disposal of the authorities, should any necessity arise for calling upon him to undertake more important duties.

At this time the news of the death of his lieutenant, Romulus

Gessi, reached England. It was a blow to him, for he knew
that with the life of his fellow-worker ended all the good he had
achieved in the Soudan,—good which, in his master's absence,
Gessi had striven to perpetuate, and to the trials of which he had
succumbed. "He died on the evening of the 30th April, in the
French hospital at Suez, after protracted sufferings caused by the
terrible privations in the months of November and December
last, when he was shut in by an impassable barrier of weed in the
Bahr Gazelle River." That was his epitaph in the press. Gordon,
on his way to Mauritius, stopped at Suez, and visited the grave
of his follower. The period of his sojourn in Mauritius—
some ten months—was not eventful; it was, however, a happy
and a peaceful time. He became deeply interested in the
Seychelles; he made some curious researches concerning the
site of the Garden of Eden; he planned and suggested certain
excellent schemes for the defence of the Indian Ocean. On
March 6th he was made a Major-General; and on April 4th,
1882, he left Mauritius for the Cape. The Government had
asked his services, and he was free to give them.

Subsequent events have made the precise wording of the
telegrams which led to his departure important. The first, dated
February 23rd, 1882, from Sir Hercules Robinson to the Earl of
Kimberley, runs as follows:—

"Ministers request me to inquire whether Her Majesty's
Government would permit them to obtain the services of Colonel
Gordon, R.E., C.B. Ministers desire to invite Colonel Gordon to
come to this country for the purpose of consultation as to the best
measures to be adopted with reference to Basutoland, in the event
of Parliament sanctioning their proposals as to that territory, and
to engage his services, should he be prepared to renew the offer
made to their predecessors in April 1881, to assist in terminating
the war and administering Basutoland."

The second, from the Premier, Cape, to Colonel Gordon,
March 3rd, 1882, runs thus:—

"Position of matters in Basutoland grave, and of utmost
importance that Colony secure services of someone of proved
ability, firmness, and energy. Government therefore resolved
asking whether you are disposed to renew offer which they learn
you made, last April, to former Ministry. They do not expect
you to be bound by salary then stated. Should you agree to

place services at disposal this Government, it is very important you should at once visit the Colony, in order to learn facts bearing on situation. Could you do this at once, you would confer signal favour upon Colony, leaving your future action unpledged. To prepare the way, application was made to Lord Kimberley, with view to ascertain if Government had objection to your entering this Government's service. From reply received, I learn that War Office gives consent. It is impossible within limits telegram to enter fully into case, and, in communication with you, Government rely upon same devotion to duty which prompted former offer, to excuse this sudden request."

The offer to which these telegrams refer was made by Gordon to the Premier of the Cape Government, on April 7th, 1881, and it was this :—

"Chinese Gordon offers his services for two years at £700 a year to assist in terminating war and administering Basutoland."

Thus it was evident that the object with which Gordon was invited to place his services at the disposal of the Cape Government was twofold : he was " *to assist in terminating the war and in administrating Basutoland.*" I am disposed to lay some stress on this, because in the previous year the Deputy-Adjutant-General, R.E., War Office, London, had telegraphed to Gordon at Lausanne, that the Cape Government offered him the *command of the Colonial forces*, with a proposed salary of £1500 a year, which offer he had declined. Yet when he arrived at the Cape, after a miserable month's voyage in a sailing vessel, the only post offered him was that of *Commandant-General of the Colonial Forces.* Sir Hercules Robinson, Merriman, and the Premier all said that they wanted him to take charge of the Basuto question, but that they did not like to remove Orpen—in whom they had no confidence—as his removal would be unpopular. Thus, on May 18th, 1882, we find Gordon installed in the very appointment he had declined to accept two years before, and in no way officially concerned in the administration of Basutoland, which was probably his chief motive in accepting the invitation of the Colonial Government. It was altogether a bad beginning. Certainly it was strange behaviour on the part of the Government ; they had distinctly led Gordon to believe that they needed his services, not as Commander of their Forces, but solely as adviser and administrator. But as the post he took was stated to be merely temporary, he doubtless believed that the Government intended later on to employ him officially as at first proposed. On May 21st, then, he addressed a memorandum to the Ministers and the Governor. It stated that in his opinion the primary mistake was that, in transferring Basutoland from the Imperial Government to that of the Cape, the Basutos themselves had never been consulted; and it suggested that, to correct this mistake, the Basutos should be called together and encouraged to discuss the terms of their agreement with the Colonial Governor. It stated, moreover, that he, the author, did not believe that there were was any real antagonism between Letsea and Masupha; that Letsea only pretended to oppose Masupha and side with the Colony, and that all the while he was inspiriting his supposed enemy to so behave towards the Government as to keep them in perpetual hot water. No answer was returned to this memorandum.

On the 29th of May Gordon proceeded to King William's Town, and drew up the report on the Colonial Forces which the Premier had requested him to make. It was both able and exhaustive. Gordon suggested many changes, and showed that the Colony could save £7000 a year, and yet maintain an army 8000 strong, instead of 1600, as it then was. This, of course, meant economy in new directions; Gordon had begun with himself, and had accepted only two-thirds of the salary offered him, saying that the Colony could not afford to pay more. The report and his suggestions were laid before the Cape Parliament; but, like the memorandum which had preceded them, they were left unnoticed.

On the 4th of June the Premier requested the General to go up country and report on the trekking of the Boers into native territory, and on the condition of the native holdings in the Transkei. This Gordon at once proceeded to do. He sent in a third memorandum, to the effect that the natives were goaded into rebellion by the badness and inefficiency of the magistracy. Hereupon the Government asked him to suggest remedies, and to embody his suggestions in a series of regulations. He did so; and, as twice before, no notice whatever was taken of his work.

By this time he had been in the Colony some ten weeks only. During this short period, however, he had made himself master, not only of the condition of the forces under his command, but also to a very great extent of the facts and circumstances which were the source of all the native troubles. As will be seen from what I have already stated (of the accuracy of which I have complete evidence), Gordon, during these ten weeks, was used by the Government rather as an adviser than as a Commander-in-Chief—as an adviser who would presently become an administrator as well, in the event of his views being suited to those of the Ministers. Presumably they were not. His advice was not regarded; his recommendations fell on idle or indifferent ears.

This action on the part of the Government is noteworthy; it quite justified Gordon in the course he adopted a little later on, when the Ministry requested him to go to Basutoland. This was on the 18th of July; and he replied by a memorandum enclosing a copy of a proposed convention, by which the Basutos would have semi-independence under a Resident, and stating that it was impossible for the Government to revert to the condition of things that existed before the war. Of course he waited vainly for an answer. This time, however, he sent a private note to the Premier, saying that it was quite useless for him to go up to Basutoland unless the Government were prepared to acknowledge his presence and take account of his proposals. This, of course, was tantamount to saying: "You invite me to your Colony as adviser and administrator; when I come you give me a post I had already refused, employ me in an amateur way in the other two capacities, and take no notice of the results of my work. This being the case, please leave me to my official duties as Commander-in-Chief, and send me on no more bootless errands." The Premier seems to have understood, as, for some time, Gordon was left in peace. He heard nothing more from the Government about the journey into Basutoland, though he offered to resign his office of Commandant-General, and to be Resident with Masupha for two years at no more than £300 a year. He believed, he said, that in that time he could gain the old chief's confidence, and restore order to the country. No doubt he was right; but he was no longer his own master, and the heroic work of the Soudan was impossible in the superior civilisation of the Cape.

In August, however, the Secretary for Native Affairs came to King William's Town, and, after talking things over with Gordon, requested him to accompany him into Basutoland, whither he was going to see Mr. Orpen, the Ministerial representative. Gordon explained that, as he was adverse from Orpen's policy, and as the Government had taken no notice of the convention he had suggested, he could be of no possible use; in other words, he told Mr. Sauer, *vivâ voce*, what he had already told the Premier

by letter.   Sauer, however, said that "he was free of all engagements," and urged the General to come with him.   Gordon
reluctantly gave way.   In September he reached Basutoland, and
had a personal interview with Letsea—the chief, it will be
remembered, who was feigning friendliness to the Government,
and antagonism to the action taken by Masupha.   After this
interview, Gordon was more than ever convinced that no *modus
vivendi* could be arrived at except on such terms as those embodied
in his proposed convention; and when he went to Leribe with
Mr. Sauer, he presented that gentleman with a memorandum, in
which he laid down the utter futility of trying to settle matters
by getting one set of Basutos to coerce another.   This was Orpen's
policy, and it had at least the tacit consent of the existing
Government.   Mr. Sauer, having considered the memorandum,
asked the writer if he would go, *as a private individual*, to
Masupha, and see what he could do.   He made this request,
knowing the General's views, and knowing also that Gordon
would lead no force against the Basuto chief unless an improvement were made in the magistracy—that is, unless bad magistrates
were replaced by good ones, and bad legislation abolished
altogether.   In a word, he knew perfectly well that Gordon
sympathised with Masupha, as one more sinned against than
sinning.   All the same, he persuaded the General to undertake
this adventure, but gave him neither instructions nor credentials,
and left him to act as he might think fit.

Gordon went, and went unarmed.   How he ever got back,
has been matter of astonishment to not a few; for, while he was
negotiating with Masupha as a messenger of peace, Sauer, probably at Orpen's persuasion, got Letsea to send his son Lethrodi
to attack Masupha.   The Ministerial tactics consisted in allowing
their representatives to settle the Basuto difficulty by egging on
the chiefs to eat each other up.   Of this Masupha was well
aware; he had in his camp an emissary of peace, assuming a
certain influence with the Cape Government, or at all events sent
by a Cape Minister; while outside his camp he had a warlike
demonstration organised and set afoot by the same Government
and the same Minister.   Gordon's power of inspiring savages with
confidence in his complete uprightness was probably what saved
his life at this desperate pass, as at so many others in so many
lands.   Masupha, seeing his guest to be no less mortified and
astounded than himself, allowed him to depart as he had come.

He departed next day, and his first act on reaching Aliwal

North was to send this telegram (Sept. 26th, 1882) to the Under-Colonial Secretary at Cape Town : "As I am in a false position up here, and am likely to do more harm than good, I propose leaving for the Colony, and when I have finished some reports, I will come down to Cape Town, when I trust Government will accept my resignation." Four days after (September 30th) he received this reply : "The Honourable the Premier has no objection to your coming to Cape Town as proposed." Next day he sent another telegram to the Under-Colonial Secretary : he remembered that at Port Elizabeth he had agreed to serve the Government until Parliament met, and he felt bound to abide by his promise ; he therefore telegraphed that, if it was desired, he would keep to his agreement. But the Premier relieved him of his promise in a telegram dated October 5th : "The answer to your telegram, proposing to come to Cape Town, and expressing a wish that Government would accept your resignation, and to subsequent messages intimating that when you telegraphed it had escaped your memory that you had stated your willingness to remain till Parliament met : I have to state that I have no wish to hold you to your promise, and am now prepared to comply with the desire expressed, that your resignation should be accepted ; after the intimation that you would not fight the Basutos, and considering the tenor of your communication with Masupha, I regret to record my conviction that your continuance in the position you occupy would not be conducive to public interest."

Gordon replied that he was much obliged, and that it would be scarcely necessary for him to come to Cape Town. He added : "Did I do so, it would be on the understanding that I was free. Government were not ignorant of my antagonism to Mr. Orpen's policy, yet they wished me to go up with Mr. Sauer ; therefore the sequel was to be expected." To this the Premier replied that it was not necessary for the General to return to Cape Town, and that he did not doubt that the General's proposals to Masupha were good, considering the circumstances under which they were made, but that they were such as Government could not adopt, nor Parliament sanction.

And thus it came to pass that, a little more than five months after his arrival in South Africa, Gordon severed his connection with the only country which had proved unable to appreciate the value and use of the genius he placed at its disposal.

CHAPTER XVIII

AT last Gordon could be at rest; at last he could depart for Mount Carmel and be alone. Those in authority at the Cape had done thus much for him, if no more.

"My present idea," he wrote, in the thick of his toils of 1876, " is to lie in bed till eleven every day; in the afternoon to walk not farther than the docks; and not to undertake those terrible railway journeys, or to get exposed to the questionings of people and their inevitable dinners—in fact, to get into a dormant state, and stay there till I am obliged to work. *I want oysters for lunch.*" This is a humorous paraphrase of an ideal, hopeless then and for long years after unattainable. No such time of rest had come for him till now. He had been to India on a bootless errand. He had gone to China—the ancient Empire to which he had brought new life and light—and saved her from war— perhaps defeat. He had served in Mauritius. He had laboured at the Cape, and perilled his life for a crew of time-servers. Now, at last, he was his own master. He returned to London, and set out on a new pilgrimage to the East. He settled outside Jerusalem. There he lived on bread and fruits (tobacco he reserved for great occasions: Soochow and Dara, for instance), and gave the bulk of his pay to those who hungered and were in need. But after such a life of action, rest was impossible. How could it be otherwise for him who held such views of the life beyond as these? "The future world must be much more amusing, more enticing, more to be desired than this world— putting aside its absence of sorrow and sin. The future world has been somehow painted to our mind as a place of continuous praise; and, though we may not say it, yet one cannot help feeling that, if thus, it would prove monotonous. It cannot be thus. It must be a life of activity; for happiness is dependent on activity. Death is cessation of movement; life is all movement."

Still, there were no terrible railway journeys; there were no questionings—save those of stray interviewers; above all, there were no inevitable dinners; and he was happy. With an interest as keen as ever, he watched the world's affairs. But most of his time was devoted to research; and it was with an eagerness that was almost a passion that he pursued the survey of the Holy Sepulchre, the Tabernacle, and the walls of Jerusalem. Some of his theories were curious and surprising; they puzzled those who had made the exploration of Palestine their life-study; they perplex, they irritate, they confound, and they end by almost persuading. He took the holy sites in hand to prove them not the holy sites at all: greatly to the horror and scandal of clerical tourists. But he was no mere iconoclast; he worked as one seeing sermons in stones and good in everything—with the faith of a Christian but the eye and brain of an engineer. The Bible was his guide; and he "did not care for sites if he had a map." "In reality," he said, "no man, in writing on these sites, ought to draw on his imagination; he ought to keep to the simple facts, and not prophesy or fill up gaps." For his own part, he did no more than aim at proving the correctness of his ideas by elaborate diagrams and figures. But these were not his sole occupations. "I have gone in for the stars in these splendid nights," he said, "and know them pretty fairly."

There are many who cannot understand how Gordon, despite the obstacles in his way, consistently maintained his unlikeness to the majority of men. It was because his spirit had ever refused to mould itself to the world. His was the high humanity that said "the procuring and boiling of potatoes is as much to a poor woman as the re-organising of the army is to Cardwell"; his was the hope that said "ninety-nine men out of a hundred may be worthless, but we should go on and find the hundredth"; his was the tolerance that said, "the Mussulman worships God as well as I do, and is as acceptable, if sincere, as any Christian." It was because his hope in all things and his faith in God had never faltered, that his strength had never failed.

"No man ever had a harder task than I, unaided, have before me; but it sits as a feather on me," he said, in the midst of his great campaign in the Soudan. "As Solomon asked, I ask wisdom to govern this great people; and not only will He give it, but all else besides. And why? Because I value not the 'all

besides.' I am quite as averse to slavery, and even more so, than
most people. I show it by sacrificing myself in these lands,
which are no paradise. I have naught to gain in name or riches.
I do not care what man may say. I do what I think is pleasing
to my God; and, as far as man goes, I need nothing from anyone.
The Khedive never had directly gained any revenue from slaves.
I now hold this place here; and I, who am on the spot with
unlimited power, am able to judge how impotent he, at Cairo, is
to stop the slave-trade. I can do it with God's help, and I have
the conviction He has destined me to do it; for it was much
against my will I came here. What I have to do is so to settle
matters that I do not cause a revolution on my own death—not
that I value life. I have done with its comforts in coming here.
My work is great, but does not weigh me down. I go on as
straight as I can. I feel my own weakness, and look to Him who
is almighty; and I leave the issue without inordinate care to Him.
I expect to ride 5000 miles this year if I am spared. I am quite
alone, and like it. I have become what people call a great
fatalist, namely, I trust God will pull me through every difficulty.
The solitary grandeur of the desert makes one feel how vain is
the effort of man. This carries me through my troubles, and
enables me to look on death as a coming relief, when it is His
will. . . . It is only my firm conviction that I am only an
instrument put in use for a time that enables me to bear up; and
in my present state, during my long, hot, weary rides, I think my
thoughts better and clearer than I should with a companion."

It will be seen that his fatalism was not a belief in unchange-
able destiny, independent of a controlling Cause; but a deep faith
in a controlling Cause which guides the erring and props the
weak. Here are some of the maxims which he had made himself,
and by which his spiritual life was governed: "It is a delightful
thing to be a fatalist, not as that word is generally employed, but
to accept that, *when things happen* and *not* before, God has for
some wise reason so ordained them to happen—*all* things, not
only the great things, but all the circumstances of life; that is
what is meant to me by the words 'you are dead,' in St. Paul to
Colossians." Again: "We have nothing further to do when the
scroll of events is unrolled than to accept them as being for the
best. *Before* it is *unrolled* it is another matter; and you could
not say I sat still and let things happen with this belief. All I
can say is, that amidst troubles and worries no one can have peace
till he thus stays upon his God; it gives a man a superhuman

strength." And elsewhere: "If we could take all things as ordained and for the best, we should indeed be conquerors of the world. Nothing has ever happened to man so bad as he has anticipated it to be. If we would be quiet under our troubles, they would not be so painful to bear. I cannot separate the existence of a God from His preordination and direction of all things good and evil; the latter He permits, but still controls." And for a glimpse of his outlook on life as it was: "There would be no one so unwelcome to come and reside in the world as Christ while the world is in the state it now is. He would be dead against, say, nearly all of our pursuits, and be altogether *outré*. I gave you Watson on Contentment; it is this true exposition of how happiness is to be obtained—*i.e.*, submission to the will of God, whatever that will may be; he who can say he realises this, has overcome the world and its trials. Everything that happens to-day, good or evil, is settled and fixed, and it is no use fretting over it. The quiet peaceful life of our Lord was solely due to His submission to God's will. There will be times when a strain will come on one; and as the strain, so will your strength be." What to a spirit thus tempered were the kingdoms of this world?

CHAPTER XIX

" WE have nothing to do when the scroll of events is unrolled but to accept them as being for the best." These words—Gordon's own—may be taken as a fair text to the incidents which follow; while the part he played fitly illustrates how word and deed with him go hand in hand. In a paradise of peace and fancied obscurity in Palestine, he had dreamed of days he would devote to the London poor—of a renewal on a large scale of the happy times at Gravesend. But the world which he so ardently hoped would forget him had not forgot. While he was mapping out a missionary life at Whitechapel or Bethnal Green, a King and his ministers were busy planning an enterprise which they intended he should lead.

The King of the Belgians, some three years before, had conferred with Gordon concerning a scheme for the administration of certain territory on the Congo, and so perpetuating in these latitudes the memory of his dead son. The ex-Governor-General, fresh from the miseries of the Soudan, lent a willing ear to a cause which so nearly resembled the one he had reluctantly abandoned; and he agreed, should the assent of his Government and of the Powers be secured, to give his services in its aid. When, therefore, three years later, there were letters from the King reminding him of his promise, and asking him to take up the work now far enough advanced for his control, he at once put by his antiquarian studies, postponed his schemes for the London poor, and with characteristic promptitude left Jaffa by the first ship—a battered merchantman, which was nearly wrecked on the way. Once at Brussels, the final arrangements for the new undertaking were not long in being completed. The King, delighted to have secured so able and willing an envoy, lost not a moment in discussing his plans and in placing the fullest instructions in Gordon's hands. But the "scroll of events" was not yet unrolled; and the Envoy had after all to accept another mission and other masters as being for the best.

When he took leave of the Soudan, it had been unhesitatingly predicted that his good work would be rapidly undone: the slavers so effectually broken would regain their lost power; instead of order there would be anarchy, instead of peace there would be war. Never was prediction more credible or more true. Before a year had, passed the Soudanese were clamouring for his return; and, in another, rebellion and slavery had repossessed the land. The Egyptian Government, too much concerned with internal troubles, had, during the rising under Arabi, paid scarce any attention to the changed condition of the Soudan; they regarded the tumult as a mere outbreak of internecine warfare, easily compassed and as easily quelled. But before the Arabi riots were put down, or the ringleaders condemned, they began to perceive that they had blundered. They had to admit the existence of a Pretender, who, if not at once faced, might rapidly become more formidable than Arabi himself. This was Mahomed Achmet, better known as the Mahdi, a name given him by Raouf Pasha. Of his personality and the extent of his influence next to nothing at first was known; but it is clear, judging from the scattered accounts we have of him from those who had seen him, that he had studied the Prophet's part profoundly, and could put his studies to excellent purpose.

Colonel Stewart, when engaged in reporting on the Soudan for the English Government, collected information about the Mahdi's history, and discovered that he was a Dongolawi, or native of Dongola. His grandfather was called Fahil, and lived on the island of Naft Arti, which lies east of and opposite to Ordi, the native name for the capital of Dongola. His father was Abdallahi, by trade a carpenter. In 1852, Abdallahi left Naft Arti and went to Shendy, a town on the Nile south of Berber. At that time his family consisted of three sons and one daughter, whose names were Mahomed, Hamid, Mahomed Achmet (the Mahdi), and Nur-el-Sham (Light of Syria). At Shendy another son was born to him, and was called Abdullah.

One day Mahomed Achmet received a beating from his uncle, to whom he was apprenticed. Thereupon he ran away to Khartoum, and joined the free school or "Medressu" of a Faki who resided at Hoghali, a village east of and close to Khartoum. This school is attached to the tomb of Sheikh Hoghali, the patron saint of Khartoum, who was greatly revered by the inhabitants of that town and district. The Sheikh of the shrine, although he kept a free school and fed the poor, derived a handsome revenue from the gifts of the pious. He claimed to be a descendant of the original Hoghali, and through him of Mahomet. Here Mahomed remained for some time studying religion, but making little progress in the profane accomplishments of reading and writing. Presently he left Hoghali and went to Berber, where he joined another free school kept by one Sheikh Ghubush at a village of that name, and attached to a greatly venerated shrine. Here in six months he completed his religious education. Thence he went to Aradup (tamarind tree), a village south of Kana. In 1870 he became a disciple of another Faki—Sheikh Nur-el-Daim (Continuous Light). Nur-el-Daim subsequently ordained him a Sheikh or Faki, and he then took up his abode in the island of Abba, near Kana, on the White Nile. Here he began by making a cave, into which it was his practice to retire and to repeat for hours one of the names of the Deity, the effect of which practice he greatly heightened by an accompaniment of fasting, incense-burning, and prayers. By degrees the fame of his sanctity spread far and wide; and he grew rich, collected disciples, and married several wives, all of whom he was careful to select from among the daughters of influential sheikhs and other notables. To keep within the legalised number (four), he was in the habit of divorcing his surplus and re-espousing according to his fancy.

About the end of May 1881 he began to write to his brother Fakis, and announced himself the Mahdi foretold by Mahomet. He had (it appeared) a divine mission comprehending the reform of Islam and the establishment of a universal equality, a universal law, a universal religion, and a community of goods; and it also appeared that all who did not believe in him should be destroyed, were they Christian, Moslem, or Pagan. Among others, he wrote to Mahomed Saleh, a learned and influential Faki of Dongola, directing him to collect his dervishes and friends, and to join him at Abba. Mahomed Saleh, however, informed the Government of his proceedings, and added on his own account that the poor man must be mad. This information, with more collected from other quarters, alarmed Raouf Pasha, and the result was the expedition of August 3, 1881.

In person the Mahdi was tall and slim, with a black beard and a light brown complexion. Like most Dongolawis, he read and wrote with difficulty. He was local head of the Gheelan or

Kadrigé order of dervishes, a school founded by Abdul Kader-el-Ghulami, the saint whose tomb is at Bagdad.[1]

The Government's first step was to recall Abdul Kader, the general then in command. So far this officer's achievements had been poor enough ; he had led an army against the rebels without effect, and had allowed the Mahdi to advance within easy distance of Khartoum. Their next move was to appoint Alaidin Pasha in his place, with Colonel Hicks, a retired British officer who had done good service in India, as chief of the staff. The force consisted of 8 English officers, 6000 infantry, 1000 irregulars, 500 cavalry, and a small force of artillery. After reconnoitring the district round Khartoum, Hicks and his little army, on April 9, gave battle to the rebels, 5000 strong, defeated them, and left 500, with their leader, one of the Mahdi's captains, dead on the field. The False Prophet at once entrenched himself at Obeid, gathered together all the tribes at his command, and patiently awaited the event of a more decisive encounter. Meantime the two commanders of the Egyptian force were working ill together ; jealousy culminated in quarrel, and the result was that Alaidin Pasha was recalled, while Colonel Hicks was promoted to the Command-in-Chief of the army of the Soudan.

In September he moved to Duem, with the intention of advancing on Obeid. It was generally accounted a rash and ill-considered move, and one which, however daring in intention and fortunate in issue, was, under the circumstances, in the highest degree uncertain and improvident. Hicks knew next to nothing of the strength of the enemy, and seemed unaware of the intense heat of the waterless desert into which he had elected to plunge. Even Lord Dufferin, who in many respects spoke favourably of the scheme, admitted that the means of transport were deficient, and the troops not of the best. This view was fully justified by the event ; but the English Ministry raised no objection, and the expedition went on.

News came in of uprisings in the Eastern Soudan, and when it was ascertained that the Bedouins had overcome certain reinforcements sent into the district of Tokar, under the command of Mahmoud Pasha and Captain Moncrieff, the public anxiety was greatly increased. It transpired that the square had been broken and cut to pieces, and the English commander killed. The intention of the Government to reduce the British force in Egypt

[1] See Appendix 1.

had hardly been made known to the world when fresh and terrible tidings arrived: Hicks' army, 11,000 strong, had been lured into an ambuscade by the Mahdi and destroyed. According to a trustworthy chief in the Egyptian service, the expeditionary force was led, on November 1, by a treacherous guide into a defile, where the rebels lay in ambush. For three days they made a desperate stand, but the superior numbers of the enemy, the scorching heat, and, above all, the terrible thirst they suffered, disorganised them utterly. Out of the eleven thousand not eleven escaped to Egypt; they were massacred, or they surrendered themselves prisoners, or they joined the Mahdi. This statement, I may add, must be taken *cum grano salis*. It is difficult to believe, however numerous and however fierce the rebel army, that eleven thousand men were either killed or captured. Of trustworthy details concerning the three days' tragedy there are few or none; but it is estimated that the number of renegades—Egyptian "nondescripts," as Gordon called them—ragamuffins in no way adverse to the False Prophet—must have been very large. All that is really known is that Hicks was trapped into a position in which he could not use his guns, that the square was broken, and that the army vanished. The English officers fought bravely and well; Hicks, according to later authority, receiving his death-wound from a lance on the third day, when he had burned his last cartridge.[1]

This disaster left only two Englishmen in the Soudan: Mr. Frank Power, correspondent of the *Times* at Khartoum, and Colonel Coëtlogon, who had stayed behind in that city. Its import was very great: it meant another and a greater army to the False Prophet, and a lost kingdom to the Khedive. Governors hitherto loyal surrendered their provinces or towns; tribes hitherto friendly sent in their adherence to the Mahdi. The panic from the loyal centres worked its way into the councils of Ministers at Cairo; but it did not reach the bureaux of Downing Street. A general cry of "Clear out of the Soudan!" went up from the Ministerial camps, and in due time Sir Evelyn Baring was instructed to advise the Khedive to abandon that troublesome province, and establish a strengthened frontier at Suakim. Our interests in Egypt being thus threatened, the old orders to withdraw the army were countermanded; Rear-Admiral Sir W. Hewett, Commander-in-Chief in the Indian Ocean, was called upon to support Egyptian interests on the Red Sea; while the care of Egyptian interests on land was

[1] See Appendix 2.

handed over to Baker Pasha, one of the ablest and most distinguished of then living soldiers. Proceeding to Suakim with a native force, he took supreme military and civil command in the Soudan. His first operations were to consist of an attempt to break through a great army of rebels infesting the Red Sea littoral, and to rescue and withdraw the Egyptian garrisons in Sinkat and Tokar, both hard pressed by the enemy.

Such, together with the concentration of the Egyptian troops already in the disaffected province, were the means taken to check, and, if possible, beat back the armies of rebellion, which from their recent victories had gained a power and an authority that boded ill, not only to Khartoum, but to Cairo itself. By those best acquainted with the character of the enemy and the country he was contesting, they were held to be wholly inadequate. Egyptian linesmen, it was pointed out, would prove valueless in an encounter with swarms of fanatics fighting for freedom and careless of death ; it was felt that only English or Ottoman soldiers were equal to the situation. Yet the policy of abandonment prevailed. It was decided not to despatch British troops beyond the Egyptian border; and if the Mahdi were veritably an envoy of the Prophet, how, it was asked, should the Caliph, the Commander of the Faithful, give countenance and aid to the suppression of a Holy War? That it was accepted as a Holy War by thousands, is unquestionable ; and that a belief in its leader as inspired of Heaven was general, and for the most part enthusiastic, is no less certain. The sudden growth of the Mahdi's power had shown the oppressed the way to liberty, and the whole country, ripe for rebellion, had risen at his call.

Gordon had foreseen the difficulty for years. "In spite of the heavy blow that has been struck at revolt," he said, in 1877, "any great leader could still make himself master of the Soudan." It was not alone the slave-dealers who were to be feared, but the vast tribes, born to the arts of war, ever ready to act as allies, and holding in contempt the feeble and effeminate rule of the divan at Cairo. "Had it not been," he adds, "that Zebehr and his party were the most inveterate slave-hunters, and had committed the most fearful cruelties, it might have been better for the people of the Soudan had the revolt been successful. There is no doubt that, if the Governments of France and England do not pay more attention to the Soudan—if they do not establish at Khartoum a branch of the mixed tribunals and see that justice is done, the disruption of the Soudan from Cairo is only a question of time.

This disruption, however, will not end the troubles, for the Soudanese, through their allies—the Black Soldiers, I mean—will carry on their efforts in Cairo itself. Now, these Black Soldiers are the only troops in the Egyptian service that are worth anything." These forecasts, as we have seen, were only too accurate. A leader—and a great one—arose; the disruption was complete; the line of communication was cut between Khartoum and Suakim. Can it now be doubted that the Mahdi, the number of whose following was at one time estimated at three hundred thousand, availed himself of the aid of these very tribes, "who can put from two thousand to six thousand horse and camel men in the field"?

Meanwhile, there was absolute diversity of opinion, both in Downing Street and at Cairo, on the subject of offensive and defensive operations alike. An English note to the Khedive insisted upon the abandonment of the Soudan and the withdrawal to Wady Halfa of the Egyptian garrisons, and was yet couched in such terms as seemed to deprive his administrators of the power to devise a line of action suited to the policy. They had been told to withdraw at an early date, and to surrender territory which belonged not to Egypt but to Turkey. When the Ministry under Cherif Pasha were called upon to consider this note, they replied by sending in their immediate resignations. The Queen's Government, they said, had commanded them to abandon the Soudan; this step they had no right to take, inasmuch as the Soudan was not their own, but a possession of the Ottoman Porte entrusted to their care. And Cherif Pasha said: "We have thousands of men in the Soudan, and nothing should ever induce me to allow them to be abandoned to the miseries of the Mahdi rule. I am sure I am right. Time and posterity will judge in this matter between Mr. Gladstone and me."

The Ministry which succeeded was at first averse from abandonment, and only in favour of withdrawal; so, at least, said Nubar Pasha, who formed the new cabinet and played in it the threefold part of President of the Council, Minister of Justice, and Minister of Foreign Affairs. On being told that the other Ministers seemed wisely chosen with reference to the present crisis, he said: "Yes; but just now the word 'Minister' in Egypt is derived from the Latin word *minus*, and Ministers here are equal to an algebraical *minus* sign, meaning something less than nothing." And so, indeed, it seemed. Nubar's assent to withdraw the garrisons contributed nothing to a solution of the problem how the withdrawal was to be effected ; and every day bred new plans, each more impracticable than the others.

Between Dongola and Gondokoro there were 21,000 Egyptian troops, 81 guns, a whole population of civilians, with their wives and children, all loyal to the Government, and every day more seriously threatened by the rebel advance. Of the centres, peopled by these subjects, Khartoum was, of course, the most important ; and it will give some notion of the uncertain mind of the Egyptian authorities, when it is stated that at the very moment when every conceivable measure of evacuation was being proposed and discussed, a council was sitting—composed of Nubar Pasha, Sir Evelyn Baring, and Sir Evelyn Wood—for the devising of means for the retention of the Soudanese capital.

The cry for help that came from its 11,000 citizens, through Colonel Coëtlogon, had doubtless its effect. He had telegraphed from Khartoum as follows :—" I implore you, in view of the impossibility of relieving the garrison, to give orders for our retreat, as one third of the troops are disaffected, and cannot be depended upon, even for maintaining order in the town. The inhabitants and their neighbours are against them to a man. With twice their number we could not resist an attack. While regretting the necessity of advising his Highness to abandon territory, yet it is the only way of saving the army. Escape is now possible, but it will not be later." This was peremptory enough ; and it was natural that Ministers should debate the project of keeping Khartoum for the Khedive, even though arrangements were on foot by which Abdel Kader Pasha, Minister of War, should proceed by the Nile route to superintend the evacuation. This was one of the many contradictions of the time. Like all the others, it contributed to the general anxiety, and materially strengthened the cause of those who cried out for annexation and the return of Ismail.

Such was the state of affairs when, early in January, Gordon came once more to England to see his friends. He had returned to find that, in entering the service of King Leopold, he must quit that of the Queen ; and this after a career of administration and of war unequalled in contemporary history. It is true that his work had been for the most part done under a foreign flag ; but this seemed no reason why so eminent an officer should be summarily forced to retire from the shadow of his own. It was the story of the Active List over again. It did not prevent him from resigning his commission, but it did give rise to a controversy which brought his brilliant services again before the public. Indignation was general. The country awoke to the fact that in Gordon it had a far greater than Garibaldi, a hero of the noblest and rarest type. It could not look on with patience and see him expelled its service. It was quick to perceive that his advice should be sought as to the best means of solving the present problem. It was not less quick to feel that, with such work in hand to be faced and done, he, and he only, was the man to face and do it.

The suggestion came first from Sir Samuel Baker. On January 12 he had received a letter from Gordon, in which a hope was expressed that the author of *Ismailia* might himself be induced to undertake the duty which few were so well fitted to perform. The writer had jotted down a general view of the situation : of the Mahdi's prospects if he were left unmolested, and of the programme to be followed for the restoration of peace and order. "If the Sultan allows the Mahdi to be head of the Government," Gordon said, "he virtually abdicates all authority over the Hedjaz, Syria, Palestine ; therefore, if we prevent his action, or refuse propositions such as I have made, we virtually upset the Sultan in the countries I have named. I take it for granted, then, that you will go ; and I would recommend (1) permission to be got from the Sultan to engage 4000 of his reserve troops, both officers and men, which will be under your brother's command, and be volunteers, with a promise of remuneration at end of their services : (2) that some 2000 Beloochees, under the native officers, should be enlisted in India, who have been soldiers of Her Majesty, old sturdy warriors; for your cavalry, you can horse them in the Hedjaz, Palestine, and Syria : (3) that Her Majesty's Government will allow you to purchase from Her Majesty animals, paying a percentage on all purchases : (4) that Her Majesty's Government should allow military store officers to aid you, but not to go into the field."

But it was reserved to an enterprising journal to give the world a yet more important exposition of Gordon's views, and to suggest a certain means by which he might be employed. The recluse had not long set foot in England when he received a telegram from the editor of the *Pall Mall Gazette*, begging him to allow a reporter to visit him at Southampton and take note of his views on the situation. The reason given was that his expression of opinion would materially influence the prospects for good or evil of the heathens he had ruled. The request was refused, on the ground that the worth of the opinion asked was overrated ; but the editor, thinking differently, hurried off to Southampton. The result was an interview, during which Gordon freely expressed his ideas: on the difficulties and dangers of evacuation, and of the cause of the revolt, its chances of increase, and the means for its suppression. He laid special stress on the fact that it would cost more to retain a hold on Egypt proper if the Eastern Soudan were abandoned to the Mahdi or the Turk, than to retain a hold upon the Soudan itself by the aid of material already on the ground. That Darfour and Kordofan must be abandoned, he readily admitted ; but, considering the influence a conquering Mahomedan power established close to the frontier would exercise upon the destinies of Egypt, he held that the provinces lying to the east of the White Nile and to the north of Sennaar should be retained. He pointed out that, if the whole of the Eastern Soudan were surrendered to the Mahdi, the Arab tribes on both sides of the Red Sea would take fire and rise ; and that the Turks, in self-defence, would have to face a formidable danger, inasmuch as it was quite possible that the whole Eastern Question might be re-opened by the Mahdi. At the same time, he in no way accepted the False Prophet as a religious leader, but as a personification of popular discontent, engendered by a renewal of government under Turkish oppressors. The man, he said, was apparently a mere puppet put forward by Zebehr's father-in-law, the largest slave-owner in Obeid, and had assumed a religious title to give colour to his defence of the popular rights. Returning to the subject of evacuation, Gordon put the pertinent question : "What is going to be done with the garrisons in Khartoum, Darfour, Bahr Gazelle, and Gondokoro, whose only offence is their loyalty to their sovereign? As the army could not go to their relief, there was no remaining there with their lives; so that there were but two courses left—either absolute surrender to the Mahdi, or the defence, at all hazards, of Khartoum. The latter, in Gordon's opinion, was the only one to be followed. "There is no difficulty about it," he said. "The Mahdi's forces will fall to pieces of themselves; but if, in a moment of panic, orders are issued for the abandonment of the whole of the Eastern Soudan, a blow will be struck against the security of Egypt and the peace of the East, which may have fatal consequences."

He considered that the Eastern Soudan might be saved if a firm grip was taken of the helm in Egypt. The first step, and the best, was to set up Nubar Pasha, and to leave his hand free ;

he was the ablest of Egyptian Ministers, proof against foreign intrigue, and a perfect master of the situation. His policy could only be conjectured, but it was probable that he would appoint a Governor-General at Khartoum, and give him two millions sterling,—a large sum, but one " which had much better be spent now than wasted in a vain attempt to avert the consequences of an ill-timed surrender. Sir Samuel Baker, who possesses the essential energy requisite to the office, might be appointed Governor-General of the Soudan ; and he might take his brother as Commander-in-Chief." But before such a plan was set in operation, it should be made clear to the Soudanese that a permanent constitution was granted them—by which no Turk nor Circassian would ever be allowed to enter the provinces, to plunder the inhabitants in order to fill their own pockets—and that no immediate emancipation of slaves should be attempted. With regard to Darfour, Nubar would probably restore the family and the heir of the late Sultan ; the new ruler, if he were subsidised by the Government, and sent back with Sir Samuel Baker, would not have much difficulty in regaining possession of the kingdom, which had once been one of the best governed in Africa.

The *Pall Mall Gazette* accompanied the publication of these views with a strong recommendation that Gordon himself should be allowed to solve the difficulties with which the Gladstone Ministry had contrived to beset themselves.[1] This was the expression of a national desire. There were rumours, from Berlin and elsewhere, that the Government were re-considering their policy with the view to employing him ; but they made no sign, though the War Office went so far as to retain his name on the Active List. But this was not enough, and there was universal discontent that the aid of one who knew the Soudan better than any living European should not have been immediately invited. The King of the Belgians was no bar to such a scheme, for it was felt that, much as he desired to carry out his long-projected expedition to the Congo, he would freely release Gordon from his promise in face of such an emergency. Meantime, Baker Pasha declared the relief of Sinkat impossible ; and with fresh disaster on every hand, the sense of anxiety as to what would happen next grew more intense with every day.

But though rumour was busy, no word came from the Government, and Gordon left London for the Congo on January

[1] See Appendix 3.

16, 1884, *viâ* Belgium, to bid the King good-bye. He had not been twelve hours in Brussels when he was recalled by the Ministry. The measure had been kept so profound a secret, that when, on the 18th, he returned to London, none but the Cabinet were aware of the fact, and it was only after a prolonged interview with its members that his own relations had an opportunity of seeing him. This was only for a few minutes, for, on being asked at Downing Street whether he was willing to undertake a mission to Khartoum, he had expressed his readiness to go by that night's mail. So hurried was his departure, that much of his baggage had to be sent after him. On leaving for Brussels two days before, he had taken an early train, and thus avoided the ceremony of leave-taking on the railway platform—a ceremony he much disliked. On leaving for the Soudan, he was met at Charing Cross by the Duke of Cambridge, who had known him from a boy ; Lord Wolseley, his comrade of the Crimea ; Colonel Brocklehurst ; and Mr. Robert Gordon, his nephew, and Lord Hartington's secretary. The train was delayed a quarter of an hour to allow of a last word on the subject of his mission ; and then, amidst a hearty God-speed, the new Commissioner started for Khartoum, in company with Colonel Stewart, whom he had chosen for his Military Secretary.

CHAPTER XX

THE policy of the Government up to this point had been regarded as so pernicious in its effects, that the public refused, until more was known, to take any other view than that the sudden choice of so able a representative meant either a change in tactics or a desperate effort to obtain shelter from universal censure. The story of Gordon's resignation, his reinstatement on the Active List, his departure for the Congo, his return to London, and his start for the Soudan, seemed so ludicrous to those not behind the scenes, that most of us were ready to consider the appointment as the last card in a monstrous game of vacillation. So infatuated were the public with this idea, they believed that no action would have been taken but for their clamour, and that, even as it was, the Ministry were greatly to blame for not sooner asking and taking Gordon's advice.

Now, the facts were these. The English Government had acted with unnatural promptitude, and the Egyptian Government with all its habitual dilatoriness. Lord Granville, through Sir Evelyn Baring, had more than once put the question to Cairo whether a British officer would be of use, and had as often received for answer that he would not. More than this, a month before the appointment he had suggested Gordon himself; but the suggestion likewise was evaded. The Cairo pashas, as is their wont, had taken their own time to consider the measures necessary to meet the crisis, and it was not far short of six weeks after the first offer from Downing Street that they disclosed their views. The intimation came through the British Agent at Cairo, and it was to the effect that the services of a capable officer might be used after all. The telegram in which this surrender was conveyed was followed on the same day by one more private, and sent as a rider to the first, in which Sir Evelyn

Baring gave it as his own opinion that Gordon was the right man.

Nor was the action of the Ministry less consistent towards Gordon in the matter of the Congo than it was in the affair of the Soudan. Foreseeing that their suggestion for his employment might ultimately be reconsidered by the Khedive, they had retained him in the Queen's service, and were prepared, should he not have already left Europe, to use him at Khartoum. The proof of this is that, as soon as they were in a position to carry out this plan, they lost not an hour in placing him in charge of English honour and the destinies of the Soudan.

News soon came of Gordon's arrival in Egypt. He had announced it as his intention not to travel by way of Cairo, but to proceed *viâ* Suakim direct to Khartoum : his view being that it was better to go into the disaffected provinces as a peacemaker from England than as a ruler from Cairo, especially as a visit to that city would, in all probability, result in a firman of instruction from the Khedive. Through representations made to him, however, by Sir Evelyn Baring, on the importance of a few days' sojourn in the capital, and, what was still more authoritative, by reason of the fact that the Berber-Suakim route was blocked by the rebels, he abandoned his first plan. He was met at Port Said on January 24 by Sir Evelyn Wood. The two Generals had not seen each other since the days when they were subalterns in the Crimea ; but their mutual recognition was immediate. In the few hours they passed together, these two soldiers, whose careers have so much in common, soon filled up that gap of thirty years, and became the warmest friends. Sir Evelyn said afterwards that Gordon's only fault was that he was too good for his time, and should have lived centuries ago. He compared him to Bayard.

The enthusiasm at the Government's choice was perhaps even greater in Egypt than it had been in Europe, and this because its bearings were better and more fully understood. All classes, on his landing, were filled with confidence. The memory of the great work he had already achieved was revived. Many an Arab who had served under him told with bated breath the story of the Pasha's rule. "The Mahdi's hordes will melt away like dew," they said, "and the Pretender will be left like a small man standing alone, until he is forced to flee back to his island of Abbas." And these instances of faith were not confined to the populace. The Egyptian Ministry and the Khedive himself were equally reassured. The sole question which troubled the minds of those who could estimate the difficulties of the enterprise was whether, through delays incurred, he would not come upon the scene too late to effect his object. The two days spent in Cairo were, for the most part, devoted to conferences with Sir Evelyn Baring, the Egyptian Ministers, and the Khedive, who at once appointed him Governor-General of the Soudan. Sir Evelyn had urged the visit to Cairo in order to secure facilities which could not be obtained without an understanding with the Egyptian Government. The result was a commission from the Khedive, fully endorsed by the English Government, and which, together with the nature of Gordon's mission, it is important to elucidate and disclose.

It was distinctly understood, then, between Gordon and the English Government, that the object of his mission was to report on the military situation in the Soudan, and on the measures it might be deemed advisable to take for the security of the loyal garrisons, and the safety of the Europeans in Khartoum. He was further desired to consider and report upon the best mode of effecting the evacuation of the Soudan, to devise a scheme by which the safety and the good administration, by the Egyptian Government, of the ports on the sea-coast could best be secured, and to give special attention to the question of counteracting the stimulus which might possibly be given to the slave-trade by the insurrection and by the withdrawal of Egyptian authority.

On these instructions, Gordon, while on board the *Tanjore*, between Brindisi and Port Said, wrote a memorandum, in the course of which he confirmed his past understanding with the Cabinet and sketched a programme for the future. He laid it down as fully agreed between the Government and himself that they would not undertake to secure to the peoples of the Soudan a just future government, but that they did undertake to restore their independence, and to prevent the Egyptian Government from interfering with their affairs; and, further, that the object of his mission was to arrange for the evacuation—the manner to depend on circumstances—and the safe removal of Egyptian employés and troops. This, then, being what he was expected to do, he went on to suggest how it could best be done. He began by resolving that the country and its arsenals should be handed over to the heirs of the petty Sultans existing at the time of Mehemet Ali's conquest, the princes being left to recognise the Mahdi's rule or not as they pleased. To provide against a certain contingency, namely, that the Mahdi's force might attack the evacuating

16

columns, he took it for granted that not only resistance, but even retaliation would be allowed, provided always that such action insured the future safety of his march. It was his fixed intention to fulfil his mission as a peace-maker as far as he might; at the same time, he looked to the Government for support and consideration should the condition of affairs compel him to the use of arms. Such, in brief, was the tenor of this memorandum. To it Colonel Stewart added a statement of his views, which accorded, for the most part, with those of his chief.[1]

Meantime a very striking scene had been enacted at the British Agency at Cairo. Among the witnesses were Nubar Pasha, Sir Evelyn Wood, Giegler Pasha, Colonel Stewart, and Colonel Watson. But the personages of the drama were Zebehr —the Black Pasha—Sir Evelyn Baring, and Gordon himself. He had intimated to Sir Evelyn Baring his desire to meet the ex-slaver in the presence of others, and the British Agent had accordingly arranged the interview. Aware of the deep-rooted hatred entertained by Zebehr for the man who had signed his son's death-warrant, Sir Evelyn Baring took occasion, prior to the meeting, to discuss the manner in which the Black Pasha should be treated; for he saw danger in reviving the enmity of the one whose influence was so great in the province to which Gordon was going. The precaution was scarcely necessary. Not only did Gordon entertain a high opinion of Zebehr's energy and talent, he even believed that events might take such a shape as to make his reinstatement desirable.

An eye-witness of the scene was much impressed by the contrast presented by the two Pashas: the one, with his black, shining skin, his scowling face, his picturesque appearance; the other, with his fair complexion, his honest blue eyes, and simple dress. Their conversation is best given word for word. After the usual salutations, Gordon desired Zebehr to make any complaints against him which he might wish to make, and added that his statements would be written down.

ZEBEHR PASHA.—" I want to know why my property in the Soudan was confiscated ?"

GORDON.—" Because you wrote a letter to your son Suleiman, inciting him to revolt."

ZEBEHR.—" Produce the letter, and then I will speak."

GORDON.—" It was produced at the court-martial. The Khedive has the letter."

[1] See Appendix 4.

ZEBEHR.—"When you went as Governor-General to the Soudan, I solemnly entrusted my son Suleiman to you, and told you he was thenceforth your son. He was only 16 years of age."

GORDON.—"The question at present is about the letter. Do you deny its existence?"

ZEBEHR.—"I wrote to my son, but in the letter I did not incite him to rebel."

GORDON.—"Well, I say that you did incite him."

ZEBEHR.—"Then, if such a letter exists, what you did was right. Produce the letter."

GORDON.—"The court-martial condemned Suleiman to death; they had your letter before them."

ZEBEHR.—"Who was the President of that Court?"

GORDON.—"Hasan Pasha Hilmi."

ZEBEHR.—"And who was over him?"

GORDON.—"I was."

ZEBEHR.—"Produce the letter. Where is it? If such a letter existed, I ought to have been myself brought before a court-martial, and also condemned to death."

GORDON.—"That letter was given to the present Khedive, and was kept with the proceedings of the Court."

ZEBEHR.—"You are the subject of a great and just nation; there is no nation greater than England. I entrusted my son to you. Why did you not write and tell me, at the time, of the letter?"

GORDON.—"We do not write to tell a man of his sin when we have his letter before us. As for the letter, you had better ask the Khedive."

ZEBEHR.—"For your own honour you ought not to have given up the letter, but kept it privately yourself."

GORDON.—"But I gave it to the proper Court."

ZEBEHR.—"Your name is known everywhere. You have been writing against me in the papers and in your books. Produce the letter."

GORDON.—"Ask the Khedive, your master, for it. I had fifty copies of the trial printed, giving the whole history, and containing that letter."

ZEBEHR.—"Why did you print it?"

GORDON.—"Because I wanted to show the peoples of Soudan that I was fighting, not about the slave-trade, but against rebels, and to settle who was to govern the Soudan."

ZEBEHR.—" My son met you at Dara with 4000 men, and you refused his help."

GORDON.—" That is not the question."

ZEBEHR.—" But my property was seized eight months before you found that letter."

GORDON.—" Yes; but even before I found that letter, I had had enough evidence to prove that you had been inciting your son to rebel."

ZEBEHR.—" Produce that letter ! "

GORDON.—" Well, there ! That ends that business. Zebehr says that if the letter is found I am justified."

ZEBEHR.—" My son sent you nine emissaries from Dara; you shot them. He sent two more, and you shot them also."

GORDON.—" Then you have finished with the question of the letter. Now I will ask you if your son Suleiman did not kill the whole of the black garrison in the Bahr Gazelle ? "

ZEBEHR.—" My son came to you at Dara, and offered you 4000 men. He . . ."

GORDON.—" That does not matter. Answer my question. During my absence from the Soudan, while I was at Aden, never mind where, did not your son Suleiman kill 200 black troops ? "

ZEBEHR.—" When you were Governor-General I told my son to obey you . . ."

GORDON.—" Did your son kill those 200 Egyptian soldiers ? "

ZEBEHR.—" My son offered these troops, 4000 men, to you, and you refused, and you dismissed . . ."

GORDON.—" Did your son kill those 200 men ? That is the point."

ZEBEHR.—" It was not my fault. You recommended my son to the Khedive, who made him a Colonel, and after that . . ."

GORDON.—" Answer my question."

[Nubar Pasha repeats question to Zebehr.]

NUBAR PASHA.—" Zebehr says that his son was no longer under his influence, but under the orders of Gordon Pasha. While under his father, Suleiman did no such things, but while under Gordon Pasha he could not answer for him."

GORDON.—" I want an answer to my question." [Repeated.]

ZEBEHR.—" You recommended my son . . ."

NUBAR.—" Zebehr says he was not responsible for Suleiman, as the latter was then a Colonel under Gordon Pasha."

GORDON.—" Then I understand, Zebehr Pasha, that you do not deny that your son rebelled, or that, if he rebelled, he was liable to be put to death. I say your son did kill these 200 black troops in the Bahr Gazelle."

ZEBEHR.—"But what about my property having been confiscated?"

GORDON.—"I told you before that the letter is my justification for the confiscation. That ends the first question. If the letter is found, it will show that not only was all your property liable to be confiscated, but that you, too, were in danger of being put to death. On the other hand, if the Government will allow me, I say that, if the letter does not exist, and if your property has been unjustifiably confiscated, I shall then recommend the Egyptian Government to compensate you for your loss. I shall be the first to see that reparation is done to you."

ZEBEHR.—"I did not come to Cairo for money, but to see what was the will of the Government, and to enlist men. As to my son . . ."

GORDON.—"That is unnecessary. I treated your son with every consideration. I was not unkind to him; I did my best for him."

ZEBEHR.—"But you killed my son whom I entrusted to you. He was as your own son."

GORDON.—"Well, well, I killed my own son. There is an end of it."

ZEBEHR.—"And then you brought my wives and women and children in chains to Khartoum, a thing which, for my name in the Soudan, was most degrading."

GORDON.—"I differ from you. They were not in chains. I gave them every facility in the matter. But there! there is no use in Zebehr Pasha continually saying one thing and I another."

ZEBEHR.—"The greatness, the justice of England is known throughout the Soudan, but you did not treat me justly."

SIR E. BARING.—"General Gordon, have you any other questions to ask him except on these two points?"

GORDON.—"No."

SIR E. BARING.—"Then I wish to explain to Zebehr Pasha that I called this meeting at my house at General Gordon's request; that General Gordon had heard that Zebehr had certain complaints to make against him; and that, although it was not particularly my business to hear these complaints, at the same time, as General Gordon wished it, I was quite willing to be present at the discussion between General Gordon and Zebehr Pasha." [Zebehr here rose and kissed Sir E. Baring's hand.]

"At present, the conversation, which has been rather desultory, has ranged over two points. The first point was whether Zebehr's property was justly or unjustly taken away from him. In respect to this point, if I understand rightly, the whole difference of opinion between General Gordon and Zebehr lies as to the existence of a certain letter which, General Gordon alleges, was a letter from Zebehr to his son Suleiman inciting him to rebellion. Is that correct, General Gordon?"

GORDON.—"Quite correct."

SIR E. BARING.—"Zebehr denies the existence of that letter. General Gordon says that if that letter does not exist, and if, in fact, Zebehr Pasha was condemned upon evidence which, in default of the letter, would not have been conclusive, that he then thinks Zebehr should be compensated for his losses . . ."

ZEBEHR.—"Compensation cannot be given to me for the honour of my wife and family, that is lost for ever."

SIR E. BARING.—"Zebehr recognises, on the other hand, that if that letter does exist, then that all that was done to him was justly done."

ZEBEHR.—"If that can be proved, that I incited my son to rebellion in the letter, I do not want to live; put me to death with the sword."

SIR E. BARING.—"General Gordon, to whom did you give that letter?"

GORDON.—"To the present Khedive and to the court-martial."

SIR E. BARING.—"Then it must be in the Government archives."

GORDON.—"Yes; but, happily for me, I had it printed—in fact fifty copies—and there is a copy at Khartoum."

SIR E. BARING.—"But the original would be annexed to the proceedings of the Court. All we can do is to have a search made for it. Sir Evelyn Wood, will you see to that?"

SIR E. WOOD.—"Yes; and failing that, shall I get certificates from the people still alive who saw the letter?"

[A short discussion ensued, and it was decided, first, to try and find the letter, and then to consider what would have to be done.]

GORDON.—"It will, of course, be fully understood that the mere fact of the letter not being found in the archives will not satisfy me that it never existed."

SIR E. BARING.—"Of course I fully understand that. The second point refers to Zebehr's son. General Gordon put to

Zebehr a very direct question, namely, whether his son had been a party to the killing of 200 black Egyptian troops in the Bahr Gazelle. Zebehr's answer is that, whatever his son may have done, he, Zebehr, is not responsible for his actions; but he does not, as I understand it, specifically deny what General Gordon alleges—that his son killed these 200 men. Is that correct, Zebehr?"

ZEBEHR.—"I do not by any means deny it. I deny my responsibility for my son's conduct."

SIR E. BARING.—"Then Zebehr does not deny the action of his son, but only his own responsibility for his son's action. I do not think that we need discuss these two points any further."

A more truly Oriental method of defence than Zebehr's could hardly be found. Admission of the letter's existence was the one thing he eluded. Why this was so will presently be explained. That Gordon was unable to produce a copy was due to the simple fact that he was not in the habit of travelling with all his papers about him.

Before Gordon took leave of Cairo, his suggestion that a Sultan of Darfour should be created as a check to the Mahdi's rule, had been acted upon by the Khedive; and Ameer Abdel Shakoor, the heir, was summoned to the Ghiezeh Palace, and there, on condition that freedom of commerce was maintained, and the slave-trade suppressed within his borders, he received back the province which had been wrested from his father. This settled, he accompanied Gordon to the Soudan. They quitted the capital on January 26th, and went by rail as far as Assouan. There the General embarked for Wady Halfa, from which point he purposed to cross the desert for Abu Hamed, and thence to follow the Nile as far as Khartoum.

In every quarter, both at home and abroad, considerable doubt was felt as to whether he would ever reach the garrison, and doubt as to his means was soon intensified by anxiety as to his position. On February the 4th, Baker Pasha, with 3500 Egyptians and a number of English officers, was totally defeated in an attempt to rescue the garrisons of Tokar and Sinkat. The Egyptian soldiery, which he had been at some pains to drill, as well as Zebehr's black slaves, turned out a complete and despicable failure. Panic-stricken at the fierce onset of the enemy, led by Osman Digna, one of the Mahdi's lieutenants, they made no effort to keep the square; some fired in the air; others crouched for mercy, and were speared; the rest flung down their arms and fled. In the rout many English officers were killed, and the guns and ammunition captured. General Baker, in trying to rally the runaway herd, had a narrow escape, and was finally obliged to return to Suakim by transport. The quality of his material this one fact will be enough to show: out of the 3500 he had led to the relief, some 96 officers and 2200 men were killed.

The effects of this disaster were most serious. Osman Digna, flushed with triumph, and possessed of some three thousand rifles and their ammunition, was not slow to follow up his victory. His emissaries were soon scouring the country, rallying the tribesmen to the Mahdi; the wires between Massawa and Kassala, and between Berber and Khartoum were cut; and a forward movement on Suakim was daily expected. Meanwhile the condition of that port was bad enough to be almost hopeless. The flying Egyptians started a rumour that the defeat was a planned affair between Osman and the English officers, who had led them and their comrades to slaughter. The effect was sufficiently disturbing: some of the townsfolk showed signs of discontent, others declared for the Mahdi, and the streets were crowded with scowling men and women wailing their dead.

At home there were not a few who firmly believed that England was to blame, though not in the sense reported by the heroes of Tokar. As for the foreign press, it exhausted its vocabulary of abuse in strictures on the Ministry. But all this was because no one would take the pains to realise what the Ministry had undertaken to do and what they had not. What they had agreed upon was the defence of the Red Sea littoral; and on this, through Admiral Hewett, they were at work, in what they considered the best way. The presence of English officers in the Tokar affair misled the public and the press; the fact being overlooked that these gentlemen did not represent their own country, but Egypt, in whose service they fought. But it was Gordon's chance of reaching Khartoum that caused the greater part of the concern. That he would be waylaid and murdered was held for certain; and the wildest rumours were afloat of the dangers he must encounter, and of the dangers he had aready overcome. The alarm was increased by the publication of certain facts which were turned to sensational account by a section of the press. The young Sultan of Darfour, it appeared, had proved a troublesome drunkard; and it was told that Gordon had taken with his baggage no less a sum than forty thousand pounds.[1] To the heated imagination of the public these circumstances became of appalling significance. Scenes in which the Envoy was the victim not only of rebel tribesmen, but of traitors in his own suite, were readily conjured up. When, therefore, his capture by the Arabs was reported, there were plenty of prophets ready to declare him dead. The news of the fall of Sinkat, and of the slaughter of Tewfik's garrison, in an attempt to cut through the beleaguering rebels, completed the excitement. A wave of indignation at the desertion of these loyal and gallant men swept over Europe, and from all classes and from all communities there went up a cry of shame.

When the news arrived, the parliamentary session was not a week old. The leaders of the Opposition moved a vote of censure in both Houses for their vacillating and inconsistent policy in the Soudan. Lord Salisbury, with the Peers of his party, carried the resolution by a majority of one hundred; while, in the Lower House, Sir Stafford Northcote, after a stormy sitting, was defeated by the Government, though there were signs of defection among their supporters. The reason given by the Government for not sending relief to the garrison at Sinkat was, that such action might endanger the safety of those others which Gordon had gone out to rescue. But though this was stated in debate, it was instantly belied by circumstances. Scarcely was the debate over than steps were taken for the immediate relief of Tokar, as hard pressed as Sinkat had been, and of as much, and no more importance. To General Graham, then stationed at Cairo, was entrusted the task of its relief; but before his force of four thousand had landed at Trinkitat, the greater part of the garrison had surrendered and gone over to the rebels. The fall of Kassala, moreover, was every moment expected, and the district round about Massawa was threatened with general insurrection: so that nothing was left but to engage the enemy and hurl him back from Suakim.

The Arab leader was that Osman Digna who had beaten Baker. With nothing imposing in his presence, he was (and is) a curious mixture of merchant, politician, and fanatic. Some six years before, he had suffered heavy losses as a slave-dealer, through two of his cargoes being captured by a British cruiser on the voyage to Jeddah. In the course of his marketings in Obeid he had met the Mahdi, who, discerning his ability, and aware of his wide connections in the Eastern Soudan, chose him for one of his

[1] In reality he took but £2000 with him beyond Assouan.

lieutenants. In this, as events had proved, the impostor had shown his judgment. But circumstances had changed ; and now, instead of meeting a pack of worthless Egyptians, Osman had to face a disciplined English force. In a desperate fight at Teb, on February 29, he was worsted, and driven back into the interior with great loss. But he was not subdued. Proclaiming a Holy War, he rallied the tribesmen to his standard, entrenched himself at Tamanieb, and in a very few days was ready for action once more. Hereupon the English generals and admirals at Suakim issued a proclamation to the disaffected, recommending those who had grievances to send delegates to Khartoum to meet Gordon, who was known to be a good and just man ; and warning them that if they did not disperse and return to their homes, the English army would forthwith march on their camp, and treat its occupants as rebels. Osman countered with a manifesto, calling upon God to witness that He had sent the Mahdi to take away their property, and exhorting them to choose between Mahomedanism and the sword. General Graham at once marched his force upon Osman's camp. A battle was fought at Tamasi on March 13 ; and, supported by Admiral Hewett, General Graham completely routed the enemy, and put him to flight. These victories were regarded as a deathblow to the Mahdi in the Eastern Soudan. But, on the other hand, it was deemed highly important not to withdraw the conquering force, as such a step would inevitably cause a repetition of the old troubles.

And, meanwhile, where was Gordon ? While politicians were wrangling over the terms of his mission, while the churches and chapels of every sect were offering up prayers for his safety, he was speeding through the desert. Telegram after telegram warned him of danger, but he took no notice, and his news of himself was as meagre as his own faith in his safety was complete. To a troublesome chief on the way he said : "Meet me at Khartoum. If you want peace, I am for peace ; if you want war, I am ready." To the terror-stricken garrison of Khartoum he telegraphed : "You are men, not women. Be not afraid ; I am coming."

CHAPTER XXI

THE ENVOY OF PEACE

GORDON reached Assouan on January 30th, and soon had the situation at his fingers' ends. The Mahdi, it seemed, had with him still the deserters from Hicks' army; together with some half-dozen Arab tribes who could put from six to eight thousand horsemen in the field, and several influential chiefs all deeply interested in the slave-trade. But the tribes, who were Kordofanese, were averse from quitting their homes; and Khartoum, the Equatorial Provinces, and the Bahr Gazelle were really in much less danger than had at first appeared. Gordon at once addressed a letter to the Mahdi, bidding him at once send down the Europeans at Obeid to Khartoum.

The revolt between Khartoum and Sennaar was clearly the work of the Mahdi's agents. The revolt of the Hadendoa tribe, however, was due to a very different cause. When the Egyptian troops were despatched from Suakim to Berber, two Egyptian officials—Reschid Pasha and Ibrahim Bey—agreed to pay the Hadendoas seven dollars per transport camel for the march. Instead, they only gave them one dollar per camel, no doubt considering the other six their own. By this villainous breach of contract, the Hadendoas, who actually conveyed no less than ten thousand troops across the desert, were put to heavy losses. They were not slow to take the field, and their defection was the real cause of Baker's defeat. Osman, who had played but a small part until they joined him, suddenly became a power; and the history of their grievance is enough to account for the merciless onslaught.

Examples of Egyptian misrule were visible on every hand. The employés of the Soudan railway at Assouan were three months in arrears of pay. They were not merely upholding Mahomet and his Prophet: they were avenging their live stock;

and Gordon immediately telegraphed to Sir Evelyn Baring to send them their money. At Korosko, where he arrived on February 2nd, they told him the Sub-Governor and General of Brigade at Khartoum, through idlenesss and negligence, had allowed the revolt between that town and Sennaar to gain ground until communication was impossible. Gordon received these last tidings in silence; but he resolved within himself that, once at his journey's end, the cause of such a state of things should instantly be removed. Meantime, he appointed Colonel Stewart Sub-Governor-General of the Soudan, and expressed his confidence in Ibrahim Bey, whose abilities he knew, by making him Director of War and Marine. Having sent down the women and children, he telegraphed to Nubar Pasha for a kind-hearted man to meet them. This done, he plunged into the wilderness, and was lost to the world.

Every moment was precious, and between him and Abu Hamed there were two hundred and fifty miles of desert. Of his many rides, this was the most urgent and desperate, and, once on his camel's back, he sped through the dreary gorges of the At Moor at his old unrivalled pace : past the sand-strewn rocks that glitter in the sun, past doom-palm and mimosa, past the solitary encampments of the fierce Ababdehs, past carcases of man and beast that lay dry and scorching on the track ; till, in a space of time incredibly brief, he emerged at Abu Hamed. There, from all parts, were messengers to welcome him as Governor-General. From this terminus of the desert he wrote an important memorandum, suggesting that Her Majesty's Government should retain the suzerainty of Soudan ;[1] and then he took boat for Berber, before whose white houses, mud huts, and lively gardens, he arrived on February 11th.

He was received with enthusiasm, and the town was illuminated during his stay. The English Government had requested him, on public grounds, to run no risks. In reply, he was able to say that, with all the chief men to support him, he had no forebodings. His main desire, and this he put into effect at once, was to impress upon the people that his advent among them was the end of all corruption and tyranny. He told them the Soudan would soon be their own to govern for themselves ; that their old privileges would be renewed ; and that it would be his care to show them the way to peace and prosperity. That he was believed was shown by no less than four hundred candidates

[1] See Appendix 4A.

coming forward for appointments. And the people soon saw that
it was true; for on the same day they were given to know that
all arrears to their old masters for the last year, and one half of
those due to their new one for the next, had been struck off the
books. To fitly carry out these and other reforms in his absence,
and to provide for the defence of the district, he created a
council of twelve notables, and placed over them, as President
and Governor of the Province, Hussein Pasha Khalifa, a man
whom he had reason to esteem. These measures were embodied
in a proclamation, which was posted all over the town; and when
Gordon took leave of Berber on February 14th, he was in a
position to telegraph to the Ministry that they need have no
anxiety, for the people, great and small, were heartily glad to be
free of a union which had only wrought them sorrow. In three
days, then, as far as Berber was concerned, the recognition of his
assumption of supreme power was complete.

But his desire that no concern should be felt for his safety, if
understood by the Government, was unheeded by the public.
Some held the route from Berber to Khartoum more dangerous
than the desert itself; and letters to the papers described the
treacherous tribes that, ambushed in the long grass upon the
river's bank, would be waiting to hurl their spears upon the
Envoy. How different was the real picture! The people flocked
to the river's edge to acclaim him their deliverer; he went among
them, and conferred with their chiefs; to some he gave, and
others whom he could turn to account he took with him on his
way. At Shendy—the junction of the great caravan roads
between Darfour, Sennaar, and Suakim—the enthusiasm was
magnificent as it had been elsewhere; the people crowded to
bless him as the bearer of justice and of peace. His thoughts at
this moment must have reverted to the story of Ismail Pasha, son
of Mehemet Ali, who, at this very place, met with a reception,
the memory of which has never been effaced. He had arrived
from Cairo, not to help the inhabitants, but to exact certain dues
from their chief, the Tiger of Shendy. Ismail, while ordering
him to bring fodder for the troops, struck him with his pipe upon
the head, thus inflicting the greatest insult an Egyptian can
confer. The Tiger received the blow with a series of salaams;
and before nightfall Ismail and his men were supplied with stacks
of dried grass, ranged by order of the chief in a ring around the
camp. But before morning they awoke to find themselves en-
circled by tongues of flame and clouds of smoke, and faced by the

Tiger and his followers, who, with poised lances, bade them choose between two deaths.

A proclamation from Gordon, addressed to the people of Khartoum, preceded his arrival. He told them that, knowing of the general regret caused by the severe measures of the Government for the suppression of the slave traffic, and the seizure and punishment of all concerned, according to convention and decree, he had resolved that none should interfere with their property, and that henceforth whoever had slaves should enjoy full right to their service, and full control over them. When the terms of this document reached Europe, a storm of indignation was raised against both the law and the giver. Its terms were greeted as an insult to the honour of England, and as a violation of all the traditions of philanthropy. Few paused to consider who was the author of the concession, few to consider what that concession meant; almost all were as ready with their blame as but a short while before they had been prodigal of their praise. The implacable enemy of slavery was now its friend, and in the name of England had declared his change of front. What would the world say to this, and what could England say to the man who, however exceptional his character and career, had thus misrepresented her? Perhaps this proclamation, in Europe the motive of so much silliness and ill-feeling, did more than anything else towards enabling Gordon to win Khartoum. From the moment it reached the town the attitude of the inhabitants changed; sullen apathy was converted into joyful expectation, and thousands who had been ready to welcome the Mahdi became eager to show homage to Gordon. It was altogether a brilliant diplomatic conception, the work of a man who thoroughly understood the character of the people whom he addressed. It restored to those people rights of which they had been robbed, and which they were now in a position to regain for themselves whenever they would. Yet in the simple gift of what was already theirs lay the opportunity of avoiding much bloodshed and misery — an opportunity which Gordon's insight into national characteristics enabled him to understand, and his rapidity of action enabled him to grasp. By the treaty of 1877, the Soudanese were permitted to hold their slaves until the year 1889; and this treaty was made when Egypt had no notion of relinquishing her possession of the country. Yet it was known to be useless, as its conditions could never have been carried out. The avowed object of Gordon's mission to the Soudan was to remove the Egyptians, and to hand it back to its own children, an operation which in itself involved the permission to hold slaves for ever. Had Gordon said, "I come to concede you the Soudan, which is, when I leave, to be governed as you wish, but after 1889 you must not hold slaves," the Soudanese and the whole of Europe would have thought him mad; but as he said, "I come to concede to you the Soudan, which is, when I leave, to be governed as you wish, so that you will have the right to hold slaves as long as you like," it was only the Soudanese who were able to see the sense and value of the concession, and to call its author mad was a privilege reserved for certain European philanthropists.

CHAPTER XXII

A CHANGE OF FRONT

On February 18th Gordon entered his capital. The people, as he passed through the city, crowded in hundreds about him, and, kissing his hands, saluted him the saviour of Kordofan. His first address encouraged the hope that he would now be the saviour of Khartoum. "I come without soldiers, but with God on my side," he said, "to redress the evils of this land. I will not fight with any weapons but justice. There shall be no more Bashi-Bazouks." His promise had scarcely been bruited abroad among the people ere he had given them earnest of his sincerity. Summoning the officials, he held a levee at the Muderieh, to which he invited the rich and the poor alike. To all who had complaints he gave a hearing. This over, he ordered all the Government books to be collected, and heaped up outside the palace and burned, together with all the kourbashes, whips, and implements of torture. He visited the hospital and the arsenal, and, passing to the jail, flung open its doors. The condition of the prisoners was terrible. Two hundred men, women, and children, of all ages, were lying about in chains; some were innocent, some guilty; but most of these last had served a term of punishment far in excess of the law's demands. A rapid inspection and a careful inquiry were followed by an order to strike off all chains, and set the wretched creatures free. In several cases it appeared that there was no record of any charge, and the jailers could not even say what they had been imprisoned for. One woman had been lying there for fifteen years for a crime committed in childhood. Many were only prisoners of war; and others, immured for months, had been merely charged, but neither convicted nor even tried.

Hussein Pasha Cheri, ex-Vice-Governor of Khartoum, who left for Cairo the day before Gordon's arrival, was responsible for the maintenance and condition of this monument of injustice; and for innumerable iniquities besides. He had recently flogged the brother of one influential citizen to death; he had threatened to flog a young boy to death in order to obtain from him certain evidence; and he had bastinadoed an old sheikh until the tendons of his feet were laid bare. This poor creature was carried into Gordon's presence; and, after the interview, a telegram was sent to Cairo, in which Gordon desired £50 to be stopped from Hussein's pay for the benefit of the man he had so disgracefully mutilated. At nightfall he ordered a bonfire to be made of the prison; and within an hour it was in flames. Far into the night, men, women, and children were dancing round the blaze, laughing and clapping their hands.

On the day of his arrival Gordon heard of the intention to relieve Tokar, and he telegraphed to Sir Evelyn Baring that the British Admiral should make it known to rebel chiefs that if they had wrongs, and took them personally, or sent them by any representative, to Khartoum, the British Envoy there was invested with full powers of redress. The British Admiral, however, said he could not ask the chiefs to leave their people and go off to meet Gordon at Khartoum at a time when English troops were about to be sent against them.

Next day he established boxes into which the people could drop petitions and complaints, and the proclamation of freedom was posted on every wall. These petition-boxes, which were similar to those he had established in 1877, were examined daily, and if any official were found guilty of not allowing the petitioner the full benefits of the proclamation, he was immediately punished.

Gordon's next move was to free two more gates and to proclaim a free market; hitherto only one gate had been open, and the minor authorities were in the habit of demanding backsheesh from all who used it. Notice was also given here, as at Berber, that half the taxes would be remitted and all arrears of taxation would be wiped off. At first sight it would seem that to talk of taxation at all, in the same breath with concession of the country, must be a contradiction; but it should be remembered that the country could not be handed back in a day, and that for the moment Gordon was its administrator, and responsible for its government. Thus he did everything to conciliate the people, and to make them willing and anxious to co-operate with him in his endeavour to restore their land to a peaceful condition, so that

17

he might conduct the evacuation with the least possible risk, and also train them up in the way in which they could afterwards arrange their own government on a just basis.

In a few days an order was given that all Soudanese were to remain in Khartoum, and the white troops were to proceed to Omdurman, on the other side of the White Nile, thence to be sent down the river in detachments, with their families and such Europeans as wished to go. A negro, who had served under Bazaine, and received the Legion of Honour for service in the Mexican campaign, was made Commandant of the Troops in Khartoum, and the appointment was entirely popular. Everything for the time was *couleur de rose* ; the people were happy and content with the prospect before them, and Gordon was doubtless right when he told Colonel Coëtlogon that Khartoum had been in imminent danger, not from an external enemy, but from its own inhabitants, who, bullied by the effete Government of Hussein, took sides with the rulers in El Obeid. He said, moreover, to that officer when he bade him good-bye, " Rest assured you leave this place as safe as Kensington Park." No wonder, then, that Mr. Power, the *Times* correspondent, telegraphed home how Gordon was doing wonders in Khartoum.

So far we have seen how, from the moment he set foot in the Soudan, he was welcomed as a saviour, and how he strengthened his position by repeated acts of kindness and mercy. It is now necessary to see how the welcome he received, and the condition in which he found those who received him, induced him to suggest that Her Majesty's Government should modify the hard and fast line of policy they had adopted, and employed him to carry out. He saw that the Khartoumese were longing for a ruler who must needs be strong but would yet be just, and there was no such ruler to be found amongst them. He saw that, unless a man were forthcoming whom they knew and could follow, in giving them back their territory, he was only forcing them to join the Mahdi. He had hoped that the petty kings would have been strong enough to defend themselves ; he now saw they were nothing of the kind, and that as the emissaries of the Mahdi advanced, they would enlist the service of each petty king and his dependents, or eat him and his people up. Khartoum was safe as long as he was there to govern ; but when he left, there would be anarchy unless a strong ruler reigned in his stead. With these reflections, he wrote a memorandum to Sir Evelyn Baring, and requested him to advise H.M. Government upon it.

The time was coming, he said, when the Egyptian element in the Soudan would be removed, and we should be face to face with the task of administering the country, and he would have to withdraw; and that his doing so without providing a suitable successor would be the signal for general anarchy, which would be a misfortune and an inhuman action. As a remedy, he suggested that H.M. Government should give a commission to his successor, with the same moral support as was given to the Ameer in Afghanistan. Zebehr, the man he suggested, was, perhaps, his only enemy, and he urged the appointment because the Black Pasha was still a power in the Soudan, liked by the people, and capable of controlling them. Having detailed the terms which should accompany the nomination, he recommended that Zebehr should be made a K.C.M.G., and showed how his ten years' exile, the recent events, and his association with Europeans must have affected his character. Colonel Stewart endorsed this new line of policy, and urged that it would greatly facilitate the evacuation of the country; but he was not sure that Zebehr Pasha was the right man. Sir Evelyn Baring approved of the policy and of Zebehr, but would not countenance any meeting between Zebehr and Gordon in the Soudan.[1] H.M. Government returned a decisive reply. They notified that there existed the gravest objection to the appointment, by their authority, of a successor to General Gordon; and that, as far as they could see, no necessity appeared to have arisen for going beyond the suggestions contained in Gordon's memorandum of the 22nd ult. They added that public opinion would not tolerate the appointment of Zebehr Pasha.

On February the 23rd Gordon received the news of the fall of Tokar, and he at once telegraphed H.M. Government to remain quiet, as he saw no advantage to be gained by any action. He suggested that events should be allowed to work themselves out, and considered that the fall of Tokar would in no way affect the state of affairs at Khartoum. The Government intended to act, if possible, upon Gordon's suggestion; but Admiral Hewett showed the importance of an advance, saying that a decisive victory was necessary to establish order in the neighbourhood of Suakim. The Government then sent another telegram, saying that General Graham should, if possible, before attacking, summon the chiefs to disband their forces and attend Gordon at Khartoum for the settlement of the Soudan. This General Graham

[1] See Appendix 5.

did; but no reply was returned, and El Teb was fought and won.

Hitherto we have seen the effects of Gordon's peace policy upon all the people with whom he came into contact; we must now consider the state of affairs among those whom he had been unable to reach, but to whom his proclamation had been sent. The strength of the rebellion was at El Obeid. The Sennaar garrison was hemmed in by raiding tribes only, and the greater part of the country between Suakim and Kassala was either in open revolt, or was watching the tide of events before deciding with whom it should throw in its fortunes. Many tribes round Khartoum, Shendy, Berber, and Dongola were disaffected and troublesome, and therefore a source of danger to the towns in their neighbourhood. Numbers of these had not yet sent in their sub-mission, though Gordon had given them plenty of time; and unless they did, they might seriously interfere with the process of evacuation. Considering, on February 27th, that they had had notice enough, Gordon, hearing that a gang of rebels were on their way from Sennaar to Khartoum, determined on a demonstration. Before doing so, however, he issued a new proclamation, the text of which has given rise to much unnecessary comment.[1] Its substance was to the effect that, having since his arrival constantly assured the people of justice and good treatment, and advised them to desist from rebellion, which leads to wars and bloodshed, he was now resolved to use severe measures with those who had not followed his advice. British troops were on their way to Khartoum, and whoever persisted in bad conduct would be treated as he deserved. The statement that British troops were on their way to Khartoum is, of course, inexplicable. It was probably due to the fact that Gordon had heard that British troops were advancing along the Suakim-Berber route. Information as to what was taking place on this road was difficult to obtain, and uncertain when received, as the Hadendoa rebellion had blocked it up.

Colonel Stewart was despatched up the White Nile to explain the original proclamation. He found the country quiet on both banks for some fifteen or twenty miles, but beyond that limit the left bank was dangerous. At the first disaffected village he reached, he succeeded in interviewing some of the villagers. They appeared glad to see him, especially when they heard his mission was one of peace. Having expounded the proclamation,

[1] See Appendix 6.

he halted for the night, expecting to see the sheikhs in the morning. Instead of meeting them, however, he found the village occupied by about five hundred men. The rebels were partly armed with rifles, and some firing took place. Stewart then steamed an hour farther up the river, until he came to another village, occupied by a large body of infantry and many horsemen. It appeared that only a few days previously the sheikh had received a commission from the Mahdi, appointing him Governor of the district, and at the same time ordering him not to cross the river for the present, but merely to collect all the men, horses, arms, and provisions he could. No shot was fired, though the rebels followed the steamer a considerable distance as Stewart returned towards the friendly villages. There he had a satisfactory interview with the sheikhs, who told him that, in the event of a forward movement by the rebels—which was daily expected—unless they were protected by the Government, they would have to join them in self-defence, as they had no available means of defence. This was exactly what Gordon himself foresaw, when he found that it was useless to restore the country to the petty kings unless a stronger than the Mahdi—a cord for the faggot—were first placed over them. Gordon now prepared an elaborate memorandum,[1] showing the impossibility, in case of evacuation, of providing any defence for the towns, unless a Governor were first appointed with sufficient funds to raise and equip a native army. The only other scheme he could suggest was that of setting up a Governor and a Meglis in each large town, to be responsible for government and administration of taxes in their own district. This would demand an expenditure on the part of the Egyptian Government for some time of about £70,000 a year, and even then would not prevent the probability of anarchy. If, however, an outbreak did eventually occur, there would be no fear of massacre, as the troops would all be natives. The main question at issue, therefore, was whether Egypt could or would find the annual subsidy. Before H.M. Government received this memorandum, Gordon was informed that they would not personally authorise the appointment of a successor, and that Zebehr was out of the question; he also received a telegram from Sir Evelyn Baring, asking, among other things, whether he could suggest anyone besides Zebehr. His reply, dated February 26th, was in the negative. The Mahdi's agents, he said, were active in all directions; and though there was no fear at present that the prophet would leave El Obeid, it was

[1] See Appendix 7.

certain that he would occupy Khartoum the moment the evacuation was over. Gordon saw the possibility of evacuation, but none of establishing a govèrnment unless the Soudanese were given a ruler stronger than the Mahdi, or unless the Mahdi were "smashed up." Unpopular as the impostor was, the people would have to join him in self-defence, as there would be no one else for them to look to ; and the moment he obtained possession of Khartoum, he would become a serious menace to Egypt proper. Gordon ended by strongly urging the Government to change their policy, and to break down the power of the Mahdi as soon as possible ; and, as a first step towards this result, he recommended that two hundred Indian troops be sent to Wady Halfa, and an officer detached to Dongola, under pretence that quarters were required for the troops.

In commenting upon this telegram, Sir Evelyn Baring showed how, with the altered condition of affairs, the Government had now to decide upon one of two courses [1] : either the Soudan must be evacuated and abandoned entirely without any effort on our part to establish a settled government; or a strong endeavour must be made to replace the former Egyptian administration by another. Gordon had urged the latter course as the right one from every point of view — political, military, financial, and humane ; and Sir Evelyn Baring entirely agreed with him. The alteration in Gordon's programme was, after all, more apparent than real, as his memorandum of the 22nd of January was only a preliminary sketch of the line to be pursued, and referred specifically to the difficulties of providing rulers for Khartoum, Dongola, and other places where there were no old families to recall. With these difficulties he was now face to face ; and to surmount them he held that he must either bring down Zebehr, or smash up the Mahdi. H.M. Government now seriously reconsidered the arguments already advanced in favour of appointing Zebehr Governor-General of the Soudan ; [2] and they asked for enlightenment on three several points. The first was the possibility that Zebehr might join the Mahdi, for Gordon believed, and had said, that Elyas, Zebehr's father-in-law, was one of the chief's of the revolt, and probably Zebehr's own agent. The second was the consideration whether he would use his influence in furthering the development of the slave-trade ; and the third involved the question of his blood - feud with Gordon, which might imperil the Governor - General's life. These difficulties

[1] See Appendix 8.   [2] See Appendix 9.

Gordon and Baring endeavoured to explain away;[1] the Government remained unsatisfied. They were prepared to agree, they said, to any other Mohammedan assistance, and to supply any reasonable sum of money which General Gordon might consider necessary to carry out his mission. They were, moreover, prepared to extend his appointment for any reasonable length of time, if such extension would overcome the difficulty arising from the uncertainty felt by the inhabitants of the Soudan with regard to their government. But they were not prepared to send Zebehr to Khartoum, nor could they despatch troops to Berber, inasmuch as, in the opinion of the military authorities, such a measure was almost impracticable during the hot season. In fact, they declined to accept the immediate alternative placed before them by Sir Evelyn Baring: evacuation with abandonment, or evacuation with pre-arranged government. They wanted a third course, and they had their desire ere long.

Meanwhile, let us see what was taking place in and around Khartoum. Halfiyeh, a small town some miles north of Khartoum, containing about 800 faithful men, to whom Gordon had given arms, was surrounded by 4000 of the enemy, and the line of communication by steamer was cut. An attempt to run the blockade was frustrated, and three men on board the boat were wounded by the rebel fire. Gordon therefore determined to attack the besiegers on three sides: from Khartoum, from the beleaguered garrison, and with armed steamers from the river. Before this could be done the rebels paraded before Khartoum, and fired on the palace; they then pitched their tents by the water-side, and during the night surprised a party of 300 men, who, through the negligence of the black troops, were left unprotected, and killed 100 of them. Next day the situation was worse; for some Châggiahs, blockaded in Halfiyeh, escaped and went over to the rebels, who were now 6000 strong. It seemed as though the only thing to be done was to remain in Khartoum and act on the defensive, but Gordon determined to try and relieve the beleaguered garrison. He armed the townsmen, and started on his expedition with 1200 men and three steamers, armoured with boiler-plates, and carrying mountain-guns, with wooden mantlets. The troops were stowed below, and in large iron barges, so as to be protected from the rebels, who were now entrenched on the banks, and had command of the river. In a day or two the siege was raised, with a loss of only two men. The 500 soldiers of the

[1] See Appendix 10.

Halfiyeh garrison were rescued, and a great store of camels and horses, arms and ammunition, was captured. Amid great rejoicing —indeed, according to Mr. Power, the greatest rejoicings known at Khartoum for many years—the expedition returned; but it was only to learn that the whole country around Shendy was in the hands of the rebels, and Berber itself threatened. This victory was followed by a serious reverse. The rebels were still gathering on the banks, still firing on the palace, and still harassing Khartoum; so Gordon organised another sortie, in which the Egyptian troops and Bashi-Bazouks, commanded by their own officers, took part. Gordon and Mr. Power were eye-witnesses from the palace. The latter gentleman's account of the affair we have, and a complete and graphic work it is. The rebel lines, two miles long, and about eight miles distant, and running parallel to the Blue Nile, stretched from Halfiyeh to a group of wooded sand-hills. The troops, about two thousand strong, marched at an early hour. The Bashi-Bazouks and Egyptian regulars were in a long line facing the enemy, and also parallel to the Blue Nile. On the left flank was a small square of Soudanese regulars with one field-gun. On the right front flank was a handful of mounted troops. As the men advanced, the rebels began to file away to the right, and disappear behind the sand-hills. This supposed retreat commenced at 9.40; and at 10.30 there was not a man in sight. The enemy's rear was covered by about sixty Arabs, mounted on horses and camels. The Egyptian advance was steady enough, and the artillery fired two shells at the retiring rebels. As Gordon's horsemen entered the woods at the foot of the sand-hills, the five chiefs in command, who had been riding a little ahead, charged back upon their own ranks and broke them. At that moment the rebel cavalry shot out at full gallop from behind the sand-hills on the right, when the Egyptians broke up in confusion, and started at full speed for Khartoum. "The sixty horsemen," says Mr. Power, "who were only armed with lances and swords, dashed about, cutting down the flying men. One Arab lancer killed seven Egyptians in as many minutes. He then jumped off his horse to secure a rifle and ammunition, when a mounted Bashi-Bazouk officer cut him down. The rebel infantry now appeared, and rushed about in all directions, hacking at the men disabled by the cavalry charge. This slaughter continued for nearly two miles, the Egyptians not stopping to fire a shot. Then the Arabs halted, and an officer rallied some of the troops, and they commenced a dropping but harmless fire at the enemy. This continued till mid-day, some of the men dropping from stray bullets fired by the Arabs. The rebels then drew off to their old position, carrying a lot of rifles and cartridges, and one mountain piece. The irregulars, instead of returning into camp, coolly adjourned to a neighbouring friendly village opposite the palace. When they had completely looted this and killed some of the inhabitants, they strolled into camp."

The rout was hideous and disgraceful. Men of the Egyptian regulars and Bashi-Bazouks were crying out that they had been betrayed by their two generals. These gentlemen, indeed, were among the five horsemen who had started the panic by riding down their own men and breaking their own lines. Moreover, there was evidence to show that one of them had ridden up to a gun, and slashed through the brain of the sergeant in charge as he was about to lay his piece, while his comrade in treason had cut down two artillerymen. Seven hours after the battle, no doctors had seen the wounded; they were lying among the tents, each with three or four wounds—all from the sword or spear; there were only about twenty of them, for the Arabs gave no quarter. Colonel Stewart got them on board a steamer, and transferred them to the hospital. The plain was dotted with slain. All the bodies brought into the camp were wounded in the back, for such was the panic, that until the Arabs ceased from slaying, none turned to fire a shot or fix a bayonet. The Egyptian loss was about two hundred killed, and the enemy's loss not more than four.

Gordon did not consider that this defeat, disgraceful as it was, would affect the situation at Khartoum, for the townspeople remained as staunch as before. One Arab came forward at once and offered to lend him a thousand guineas without interest; and another equipped, armed, and paid two hundred blacks for his service. Everywhere loyalty to Gordon was loudly proclaimed, and everywhere the conduct of the troops was as loudly condemned. Later on the disaster was explained. Surviving Soudanese declared that the two Pashas in command charged back into their own square; the soldiers, recognising them, opened their ranks to let them through; and into the gap thus made the rebel cavalry followed. The treachery, doubtless pre-arranged, was complete in its success, but retribution was close at hand. When the battle was over, these two traitors, Said and Hassan, came into Gordon's tent, and the General offered them drink. They refused; Gordon's secretary, divining the reason, drank first, and the

Pashas, who had suspected poison, followed suit. During the remainder of that day they lay hidden in their homes, for the soldiers were crying aloud for vengeance, and would have murdered them at once had they appeared in the streets. The next day they were tried by court-martial, and found guilty of communication with the enemy, and of having treacherously murdered their own men. In the house of Hassan a great store of rifles and ammunition was discovered ; and it was proved that both he and his colleague had stolen the two months' pay given to the troops on account of six months' arrears. They had also taken into the field with them seventy rounds of cannon ammunition, instead of eight, the usual number, so that the rebels' guns might be well supplied for future attacks on Khartoum. The trial was long and patient, but the verdict was apparent from the beginning. Hassan and Said were found guilty, and on the same evening, amid expressions of universal delight, they were shot by the men they had betrayed. The scenes at Khartoum were, during this time, full of interest and excitement. Every day the palace was shelled or pock-marked with rifle bullets ; but the General, though he spent the greater part of the time in his verandah, was untouched. Many fell about him, some at his feet, but the old charm was still his.

One day there was a strange scene. Three armed dervishes arrived from the Mahdi and demanded audience. It was immediately granted. Their mission was to return the robes of honour which Gordon had sent to their Prophet, and to announce his refusal of the Sultanate of Kordofan. They handed Gordon a dervish's dress and a letter, calling upon him to become a Mussulman at once, and to embrace the cause of Mahomed Achmet, the Mahdi. From this moment it was recognised that Gordon had, as usual, been right. The policy of conciliation was a failure ; the Mahdi was daily gaining ground and increasing the number of his emissaries ; and evacuation was only possible by force of arms. Gordon, with his usual promptitude, accepted the situation, and ordered all Egyptian soldiers already on their way through the desert from Abu Hamed to Korosko to return to Khartoum without delay.

CHAPTER XXIII

AT this date H.M. Government received telegrams from Gordon which represented a reply to their question of March 11th. The question was, it will be recollected, whether an extension of his appointment as Governor-General would or would not enable him to overcome the difficulties with which he had now to deal. I have to say "which represented the reply," because the telegram containing the actual question was sent on March 11th, and Gordon received no telegram between March 20th and April 8th, excepting a supplementary message to the effect that neither Zebehr nor troops could be allowed him. Yet the question was answered as though it had been foreseen. Gordon telegraphed that in the present state of affairs it was impossible to withdraw the Cairene employés from Khartoum without permitting the town to fall into the hands of the Mahdi's emissaries, and losing therewith all hope of saving the garrisons of Kassala, Sennaar, Berber, Dongola, and the Bahr Gazelle; that there was now no probability that the Soudanese would rally round him, or accept his proclamation; and that the retreat to Berber might be out of his power in a few more days, and even if attempted at once might fail. He added, in another telegram, that if the immediate evacuation of Khartoum were determined upon, irrespective of outlying towns, he would endeavour to send all the Cairene employés and white troops with Colonel Stewart to Berber, and then request H.M. Government to accept the resignation of his commission. Thereafter he purposed to conduct all steamers and stores up to the Equatorial and Bahr Gazelle Provinces, and take possession of those provinces for the King of the Belgians, who had given him written authority to annex them.

In a later telegram he intimated that, through the weakness

of the Government, many had joined the rebels, and that before long Khartoum would be blockaded. Zebehr's usefulness was also declared to be greatly diminished by reason of the fact that a great number of the would-be loyal had been forced to join the enemy, and it was noted that speed was of the utmost importance should the Government decide under these circumstances to send an expedition to Berber. It is scarcely worth while, for the present, to refer to any more telegrams sent by the Government ; as far as Gordon was concerned, they were waste paper, for he never received them. All he knew between March 10th and April 8th was that he was to have neither Zebehr nor troops, and must do the best he could without them ; but before receiving the telegram of two lines which conveyed this intelligence, he expressed his thanks to H.M. Government, to Sir Evelyn Baring, to the Khedive, and the Egyptian Ministers, for their support, and acknowledged that he had received every assistance he could have expected. In this there is no touch of satire ; only a few days before Gordon had said that, as he had been inconsistent about Zebehr, he should bear the blame if Zebehr were sent, and put up with the inconvenience if he were not. The aforesaid telegram, ironic as it reads, was only the expression of a simple and unselfish desire to assume all responsibility. The scroll of events was partly unrolled, and Gordon was accepting them as for the best.

From this point onward, Gordon's difficulties, albeit apparently increased, were in reality diminished, from the circumstance that he had no one to rely upon but himself and a few followers. The Egyptian Government was a cipher, and H.M. Government an unknown quantity ; he was, by force of circumstances, free to act as he thought fit, and in that freedom lay his opportunity of success. The rebels were hemming him in, and absorbing those who would have remained loyal if they could. There were traitors in his own camp, and there were faint hearts and doubters as well. Was the ship sinking, or could the captain stop the leak and keep her afloat ? There had been a sail in sight, and she had seen his signals of distress, but had not altered her course. She had only signalled back, " Take to your boats and come to us ; we cannot afford to send a boat to you." But the captain would not desert his ship ; his cargo, a cargo of honour in all things and justice to all men, was too precious to be surrendered. Anxiously he searched the horizon for another sail, but he searched it in vain. Then he called his crew on deck,

and bade them help themselves. He made them haul down the
useless signal of distress, showed them how to patch the hole,
encouraged them to work with will, and said the time for taking
to the boats was not yet come. Clouds were gathering over-
head, the sea was rising, and waves were breaking in. The sail
was disappearing in a mist, and night was near ; but while there
was light he meant to hope and work, and when it was dark to
trust in God. There was no thought for himself, for all his
thoughts belonged to others ; no sign of fear, for fear he had
never known. He only lived to do his duty, and his duty was
to save his cargo and his crew.

The Mahdi's prospects had greatly improved. There were no
rebels about Sennaar, but between Sennaar and Khartoum they
had hemmed in Saleh Bey. The main strength of the rebellion
was still at El Obeid, the headquarters in Kordofan ; but Kassala,
Khartoum, Shendy, and Berber were surrounded, and Dongola
was threatened. The Suakim-Berber and Suakim-Kassala routes
were blocked by the Hadendoas, now in open revolt and likely
within a short time to be joined by their neighbours the Bishareens.
Wherever the Mahdi's emissaries had travelled they had recruited
their ranks, first from the disaffected and then from the would-be
loyal. It was the knowledge of this which made Gordon openly
express his sorrow at having to fight againt men who would have
been his allies if he could have given them any support ; but it
was now entirely a question of self-defence, and those who might
have been friends had to be dealt with as old and bitter foes. It
was still Gordon's opinion that the revolt was essentially trumpery,
and might be put down by 500 determined men. But such men
were not to be found in Khartoum, nor anywhere in the Soudan.
His appeal for Turkish troops, 3000 infantry and 1000 cavalry,
had been fruitless. Political considerations interfered ; H.M.
Government refused their sanction ; it was impossible for the
Egyptian Government to organise an irregular Turkish force in
time to be of use at all. Everything had to be accomplished from
within, for nothing was to be expected from without ; and when
a month had passed, and no word came from home, it seemed as
though all interest in the Soudan had ceased. It was then that
Gordon expressed his bitter indignation, and his determination to
act alone and accept the sole responsibility. He declared he
would never abandon a garrison who had not abandoned him,
without making every effort for their release, whether such efforts
were diplomatically correct or not. He had borrowed money

from the people and called upon them to sell their grain at a low price, and whatever now their lot was also to be his. He would hold on as long as possible, and suppress the rebellion if he could. If he could not, he would retire to the Equator with all who would follow him, and leave to H.M. Government "the indelible disgrace of abandoning the garrisons of Sennaar, Kassala, Berber, and Dongola." He concluded with another solemn warning, that smashing the Mahdi was an absolute necessity if peace were to be retained in Egypt; and that it was an operation which would soon be attended with the greatest difficulties.

He had scarcely made known his intentions to H.M. Government when they received urgent and piteous appeals from Hussein Khalifa at Berber.[1] "The Government having abandoned us," he said, "we can only trust in God." The rebels were advancing, and there was a panic in the town. All who could were leaving. The Mahdi had nominated another Governor, who had raised the northern portion of the province. The villages rose at his approach, and there were only sixty cases of ammunition in Berber. But all appeal was in vain. H.M. Government replied that no immediate assistance could be given, as there was no force at hand to give it; an expedition to Berber would take sixteen weeks, and help was wanted in sixteen hours. And they folded their hands, and waited "for something to turn up."

News from those in Khartoum could come to us, though nothing came from us to them. When the Mahdi's dervishes reached the city, the number of its inhabitants was already reduced by 3000 souls, whom Gordon had enabled to leave for Korosko. When Gordon declined the dress and the order to become a Believer, the dervishes waxed insolent, and refused not only to disarm in the presence of the Governor-General, but grasped their hilts with a gesture of defiance. Without concerning himself with this breach of etiquette, Gordon quietly sat down and dictated his reply to the Mahdi, addressing him as "Sheikh," and signifying thereby that his appointment as Sultan of Kordofan was cancelled. This reply was given to his emissaries, who were then taken to the gates.

His next care now was to see for how long the town was provisioned; he found that it would be possible to stand a five months' siege. He then began to carefully arrange his plan of defence, which also included a plan of attack, and in which he repeated the tactics he had used in China. Emissaries were sent

[1] See Appendix 11.

out on every hand, to offer freedom to all slaves who would abandon their masters and come into Khartoum; but only a few accepted the terms, for they knew they would have to fight if they were once inside the city gates, whereas while they remained without there was a chance to cut and run. Daily rations were issued to the poor, and a paper currency was established, which enabled Gordon to pay off the arrears due to such soldiers as had not deserted, and by this means to keep them faithful. The ammunition was removed to the mission station on the river, so that it might be safe in the event of an artillery attack on the fortifications; and around the walls, with crowsfeet, broken glass, wire entanglements, *chevaux de frise*, and so forth, three lines of land torpedoes or percussion mines were arranged. The health of the town was good, and the Nile was rising: the latter an all-important fact for Gordon, who was dependent upon the river for the success of his offensive operations.

But he did not wait upon the river to retrieve the disaster which had befallen his troops among the sand-hills. Within a week he sent a steamer up the Blue Nile, with a Krupp gun on a barge; good practice was made; the rebels on the bank were shelled, and 40 of them were killed. The next day was marked by a mutiny among the Bashi-Bazouks, when 250 of them were disarmed. Then another successful attack was directed against the rebel camp, while a sortie was made from Khartoum, during which the enemy were beaten back with heavy loss. Two days afterwards they were badly defeated again: 16 horses were captured, and 40 of their men were killed and 8 wounded. As the Nile rose the Governor-General's swoops became more frequent and more rapid. He armoured all his steamers with bullet-proof plates made of soft wood and iron; and he cuirassed all his barges in the same way, and built up on each of them a castle twenty feet in height, which gave a double line of fire. These improvised monitors did excellent service in clearing the banks by day; but the rebels were always strong enough to return at night, and would usually keep up a fire against the palace until daybreak. More than once they attempted an assault, but the torpedoes created such havoc among them that they failed to reach the city walls. During all this time—March and April — H.M. Government had something like definite information as to the state of affairs. Then followed a long interval of darkness, preceded by the fall of Berber, the link between Khartoum and the world. Hussein Khalifa having been authorised by H.M. Government to do as he liked, elected to retire northwards, and telegraphed to Mr. Egerton that for the future money could not guarantee the delivery of any message to Khartoum, whose inhabitants were now at the mercy of the enemy. In the interval, four divisions of Shageeyah Bedouins, together with 500 soldiers, had joined the rebels; and the capital was thus isolated and made helpless.

From May to the end of September was a time of silence, broken now and then by conflicting rumours, to the effect that Gordon and Stewart had been killed or taken prisoners, and that Khartoum was the headquarters of the Mahdi. The evidence upon which these rumours were circulated could never bear investigation; and Europe kept on hoping, almost without hope, wearily and anxiously awaiting the issue of H.M. Government's policy. The opening scenes [of this policy had been criticised as farcical, but the close suggested tragedy. With September came the last of the five months allotted to the garrison of Khartoum, and as the month drew nearer to its end the tension became more painful. There was little sense of relief when it was known that H.M. Government had arranged an expedition to assist their Envoy. There were a few to whom it seemed highly probable that Gordon would avenge himself by relieving the expedition; but to most men it seemed as if H.M. Government had pushed the principle of procrastination too far. A starving garrison, beleaguered by fanatical and savage hordes,—that was the picture which forced itself upon the world; and the central figures were two devoted Englishmen, doomed to death by the country they had done their best to serve.

The morning of the 29th September will long be remembered in England, for on that morning the *Times* relieved the aching hearts of a multitude. Great news from Mr. Power at Khartoum had arrived the previous evening. I give the diary of events, beginning with the first of May and ending with the last day in July. It shows the work accomplished by Gordon, Stewart, and Power, the three Englishmen in Khartoum :—

" *May* 1*st*.—The officer commanding Engineers having put down a mine of 78lb. of powder, trod on it, and with six soldiers was blown to pieces.

" *May* 3*rd*.—A man reported an English army at Berber.

" *May* 6*th*.—Heavy attack from the Arabs at the Blue Nile end of the works; great loss of life from mines we had placed at Buri.

"*May* 7*th.*—Great attack from a village opposite; nine mines were exploded there, and we afterwards heard that they killed 115 rebels. The Arabs kept up a fire all day. Colonel Stewart, with two splendidly directed shots from a Krupp 20-pounder at the palace, drove them out of their principal position. During the night the Arabs loopholed the walls, but on the 9th we drove them out. They had held the place for three days.

"*May* 25*th.*—Colonel Stewart, while working a mitrailleuse at the palace, was wounded by the rebel fire, but he is now quite well.

"*May* 26*th.*—During an expedition up the White Nile, Saati Bey put a shell into an Arab magazine. There was a great explosion, 60 shells going off.

"During May and June steamer expeditions were made daily under Saati Bey. Our loss was slight, and much cattle were captured.

"*June* 25*th.*—Mr. Cuzzi, English Consul at Berber, who is with the rebels, came to our lines, and told us of the fall of Berber. Mr. Cuzzi has been sent to Kordofan.

"*June* 30*th.*—Saati Bey captured 40 ardebs of corn from the rebels, and killed 200 of them.

"*July* 10*th.* — Saati Bey having burnt Kalaka and three villages, attacked Gatarneb, but, with three of his officers, was killed. Colonel Stewart had a narrow escape. Saati's loss is serious.

"*July* 29*th.*—We beat the rebels out of Buri, on the Blue Nile, killing numbers of them and capturing munitions and 80 rifles. The steamers advanced to El Efan, clearing 13 rebel forts and breaking two cannon. Since the siege began our loss has been under 700 killed.

"*July* 31*st.*—This is the end of the fifth month of the siege. Yesterday I sent you *viâ* Kassala a despatch giving the situation here and the chief incidents of the siege since March 23rd. I wrote you several times each week up to April 23rd, when all hopes of men getting through to Berber had ceased. For the last five months the siege has been very close, the Arab bullets from all sides being able to fall into the palace.

"Since March 17th no day has passed without firing, yet our losses in all at the very outside are not 700 killed. We have had a good many wounded, but as a rule the wounds are slight. Since the siege General Gordon has caused biscuit and corn to be distributed to the poor, and up to this time there has been no

18

case of anyone seriously wanting food. Everything has gone up about 3000 per cent. in price, and meat is, when you can get it, 8s. or 9s. an ober. The classes who cannot accept relief suffer most.

"Since the despatch which arrived the day before yesterday, all hope of relief by our Government is at an end, so, when our provisions, which we have at a stretch for two months, are eaten, we must fall, nor is there any chance, with the soldiers we have, and the great crowd of women, children, etc., of our being able to cut our way through the Arabs. We have not steamers for all, and it is only from the steamers we can meet the rebels.

"One Arab horseman is enough to put 200 of the bulk of our men to flight. The day Saati Bey was killed eight men with spears charged 200 of our men armed with Remingtons., The soldiers fled at once, leaving Saati and his Vakeel to be killed. A black officer cut down three of the Arabs, and the other five chased our men. A horseman coming up rode through the flying mass, cutting down seven. Colonel Stewart, who was unarmed, got off by a fluke, the Arabs not having seen him. With such men as these we can do nothing. The negroes are the only men we can depend upon.

"The attack made by the Soudani troops under Mehemet Ali Pasha, on the 28th of this month, was most successful; the Arab loss must have been very heavy. As General Gordon has forbidden the soldiers to bring in the heads of rebels they kill, it is now hard to know the exact number. We captured that day 16 shells and cartouches for mountain gun, a quantity of rifle ammunition, 78 Remingtons, a number of elephant and other rifles, nearly 200 lances, 60 swords, and some horses. Our loss was four killed and some slightly wounded. This action has cleared away the rebels, who day and night have been firing into our lines at Buri, on the Blue Nile.

"The following day (29th inst.) a flotilla of five armoured steamers and four armoured barges, with castles on them, went up to Gareff, on the Blue Nile. I went with them. On the way up we cleared 13 small forts, but at Gareff found two large strong forts —earthworks riveted with trunks of palm trees. There were two cannons in one. For eight hours we engaged these forts, and with the Krupp 20-pounder disabled their two cannons. The Arab fire was terrific, but, owing to the bullet-proof armour on all the vessels, our loss was only three killed and 12 or 13 wounded. Towards the evening we drove the rebels, who were in great numbers, out of the forts.

"In three days General Gordon will send two steamers towards Sennaar. It is hoped they will retake the steamer *Mehemet Ali*, which the rebels took from Saleh Bey. General Gordon is quite well, and Colonel Stewart has quite recovered from his wound. I am quite well and happy."

A thrill of pride and great joy was felt by every Englishman who read this record of the noblest of real romances. Then followed a thrill of pain: the words—"*So, when our provisions, which we have at a stretch for two months, are eaten, we must fall,*" stood out in heartrending relief, and recalled the half-forgotten fact that these lines, read on September 29th, were written on July 31st. August had passed away, and September had but one day left; what were the Englishmen in Khartoum doing now?

CHAPTER XXIV

DURING an interval of suspense, it is worth considering the subject of Zebehr Rahama, the Black Pasha. Among the arguments against his appointment was one which the Government were most anxious to employ, and this was the fact of his complicity in the revolt of the slave-dealers of 1879. But there were serious obstacles in the way, the most serious the absence of documentary evidence. This became especially the case when, in the thick of the controversy as to the wisdom of his reinstatement, the Black Pasha came forward and gratuitously denied his complicity. Moreover, his denial was so emphatic, and was backed by so circumstantial a statement, that for the moment the position was embarrassing. This was not because the Government believed his story, but because public feeling on the matter ran high, and to put an end to the question once and for all they desired to show the Opposition that the employment of a rebel was not, in their view, the way to curb rebellion.[1] On general principles they were no doubt right; but in this particular case, which was one of opportunism, they were wrong. Zebehr's innocence or guilt in the past had nothing to do with it. Had Gordon heard his story he would unhesitatingly have declared it a lie. But this would have in no way altered his opinion as to Zebehr's fitness for the Kingship of the Soudan. No man knew better the measure of Zebehr's iniquities than the slayer of Suleiman. What the Government therefore had to do was not to prove this or that, nor to be satisfied or dissatisfied with antecedents; but to resolve whether so bold a policy as their Envoy's did or did not suit them. As we know, they decided that it did not; and the question of wisdom or unwisdom need not here be discussed. As, however, much doubt has been raised by the controversy with

[1] See Appendix 12.

regard to Zebehr's innocence or guilt, it is but right to set at rest a matter which engaged so much of the public attention. This I can do by the production of documentary evidence such as not even Zebehr can gainsay.

Let us first take Zebehr's own account of himself; for by this means we shall be in a better position to estimate the worth of what follows. It should be mentioned that, when it was published, Gordon had just requested the Egyptian Government to remit Zebehr five thousand pounds, declaring a recent confiscation of his property in the Soudan to be unjust, and requesting them to restore his goods forthwith. These facts aroused in Zebehr admiration for the man he called his enemy; but they did not awaken in him the faintest sense of truth. Like all Orientals, he was a natural liar. As a preface to his story, he remarks that he had rendered greater services to Egypt than any living man, and in return had been as badly used as a subject could be. For his country's treatment of him he cared nothing; but Gordon's accusations "cut his heart out." He then went straight to the subject of his son's connection with the rebellion, and explained the treatment he received at the hands of Gordon's lieutenants. The explanation is daring; it is characteristic of the man who but a few months before accused Gordon of Suleiman's murder, and dared him to justify it by the production of evidence which he himself had supplied. He said that, on the occasion of Gordon's first visit to Cairo, he had himself gone to him protesting his innocence, and offering to go up with him into the Soudan and prove to him the falseness of the accusations. This Gordon had refused, but had told him to write to Suleiman and command him to submit. This Zebehr declared he did, telling his son that Gordon went up as the Khedive's representative and as his own; that he was to treat him as his master and lord; if he wished, to serve him as a slave, and to obey his lightest word. To Gordon he gave a letter to the same purport, and, accompanying him to the station, commended his son of sixteen years to his protection, to watch over as his own. After that he had no fear. The two men met, and Suleiman was treated with the greatest kindness, receiving a rank and the appointment to the Governorship of the Bahr Gazelle. In acknowledgment of these favours, he sent presents to his patron, including a hundred and eighty tons of ivory. Soon after this, one Edrees, a servant of the house of Zebehr, deserted to Gordon, and told him that Suleiman was a traitor, working against the Government. Gordon listened and believed. Suleiman was disgraced, and Edrees was promoted to his place. When Zebehr's son heard this, he sent nine Ulemas to assure the Governor-General of his respect and loyalty. But it was in vain. Gordon took the envoys and shot them to a man. And when Suleiman sent two more he shot these also.

At this point Zebehr naïvely remarked that he could not understand such treatment of ambassadors. He then went on to tell how Suleiman resolved to go himself to the Governor-General, and started with twelve hundred followers for Dara, where he believed his Second Father to be. Six miles from the place, he learned that Gordon was at Khartoum. He turned to follow, and was met by a hundred and fifty soldiers under Gessi, who, without parley, summoned him to surrender. He protested that he should not be treated as an enemy. Gessi replied that he was Gordon's representative, and that Suleiman would best show his loyalty by coming with him. Suleiman said that if Gessi would give him his solemn word that the charges against him should be properly sifted, he would at once surrender and abide by the sentence. This, added Zebehr, was the greater proof of his loyalty, as he and his men so far outnumbered Gessi that, had he wished, he could easily have taken that captain prisoner. But Gessi gave his word; and Suleiman ordered his escort to lay down their arms. For six or seven days Gessi and he were friends, eating at the same table and living in each other's company. On the tenth day, however, Gessi called to him Suleiman and others of his family. They heard and obeyed, and found him seated under a great tree. In five minutes he had shot them all.

"I do not believe Gordon ever gave him the order to do such an act," says the gifted narrator in conclusion, "for Gordon is a strangely merciful man. He cannot speak our language, and so is often apt to get wrong impressions; but I do not think he would have shot my son without hearing him. However, that is a thing of the past. I have forgiven him, as we all hope to be forgiven. Gessi died at Suez afterwards, and God will judge between him and me at the Last Day. I do not know how the idea has got abroad that I am a slave-dealer. Of course, there was slavery in my country, and has always been; but I never sold a human being. My people serve me gladly for the love they bear me. Let anyone go into my country and ask if Zebehr ever unjustly oppressed or killed a man, woman, or child. God is my witness, and I swear to you most solemnly, that the charge against me is false. And is England afraid of a broken man like me?

Can she not order me to put down slavery, and am I not forced to obey her commands? Am I a fool, if England sent me up, to go against her behests? I am a soldier and under authority, and the orders given me, by God's permission, I will carry out to the last letter, as I have always done. And as for the pacification of the country, so confident am I of my people's love, that I will go up alone among them, returning joyfully to my dear home, and I shall be received everywhere with the kisses of peace."

This pleasing romance is Zebehr's version of his son's experience and fate, as related to a friend of the present writer, and repeated at large by their amiable author. There is nothing extraordinary in the statements, considering their origin; like the conversation before Sir Evelyn Baring, they are only another example of Oriental plausibility and cunning. They deceived many, they converted some; but they failed to affect one jot the vital question of the hour—their author's reinstatement in the Soudan. It is only the habit of falsehood that can at all account for such effrontery. Zebehr's praise of Gordon, the forgiveness of his enemy, are inspirations conceived in the fervour of lying. Zebehr knew that he lied; he knew that in Gordon's hands was a refutation that would scatter these falsehoods to the wind. But Gordon is not the man to refute in self-defence. Only when the welfare of others is at stake does he come forward and brand the slanderer. Happily, an occasion arose in this connection which obliged him to unmask his Zebehr; and this he did in a Memoir of Zebehr, written by himself, that the people of the Soudan might know their ruler and his works. The document was never published, but the present occasion seems a fitting time for its production. The composition was as follows:—

Zebehr and his followers, he begins, aware of the difficulties occasioned to the Egyptian Government by the war with Russia, with Abyssinia, and with the outlying province of Darfour, took advantage of the position, and strove to make themselves masters of the Soudan, representing the Government as possessed of other strength than that derived from the possession of artillery. All this was proved by their correspondence, and particularly by letters from Zebehr to his son and to his wife. "If anyone imagine," the Memoir goes on to say, "that these events are to be ascribed to the prohibition by the Governments of Turkey and Egypt of the slave-trade, the answer is that there is little foundation for such a belief, considering the injurious effects which the existence of the slave-trade occasioned to the generality of the people. But even if the prohibition had any part in promoting the rebellion, it is beyond doubt that the practice of kidnapping the families and children of negroes and of the inhabitants of the Bahr Gazelle, and selling them into slavery, must be contrary to the will of God, and that no blessing can attend a country in which such deeds take place. It cannot be said, moreover, that any necessity existed for treating as enemies, attacking and enslaving a people who remained peacefully in their countries, engaged in procuring for themselves their means of sustenance. The existence of such a state of things would necessarily lead to the ruin of the whole of the Soudan. I am not influenced by any desire to injure Zebehr Pasha, but my object is simply to impart correct knowledge of the unhappy events that occurred, and which it has pleased God to bring to a termination."

After a brief account of Zebehr's origin, the Memoir deals with his part in the conquest of Darfour. About the middle of the year 1285, when Dafir Pasha was charged with the Governorship of the Soudan, there came to him a native of Darfour called Hafi Mahomed Bellali. He stated that the Bahr Gazelle and Hassalmahas (*i.e.* the "country of the copper mines"?) were thickly inhabited, that most of the people were Moslems, and were possessed of considerable wealth. He professed a complete knowledge of the country as well as of the people, and declared that they did not acknowledge the authority of the Prince of Darfour. He also expressed a wish to conquer the country and subject it to the authority of the Khedivial Government; to conciliate the goodwill of the people; and to utilise its resources, especially its mineral wealth, for the benefit of Egypt. From inquiries addressed to the Sultan of Darfour, it seemed that the Hassalmahas belonged to him; and that Bellali, who was one of his subjects, or slaves, had escaped the country. This and other information to a like effect being obtained by the Government, they were indisposed to adopt the course he recommended. Bellali, however, was appointed Governor of the Bahr Gazelle, and Mafrat el Mohar besides, and was provided with a sufficiency of soldiers, both regulars and Bashi-Bazouks, transports, money, and military stores.

At that time, Zebehr, anxious that Bellali's demands should not be agreed to, and foreseeing that the presence of the Government in these districts would affect his position and destroy his trade, came up to Khartoum. The steps he took to prevent an expedition failed, and he went with it. After its arrival,

Kerchak Ali Agha, Commander of the Bashi-Bazouks, died; Zebehr then showed his hand. He attacked the force, killed Bellali and many of his men, and took possession of the arms and stores.

He gave out that Bellali was the aggressor, and that his project was to take off the troops, and go filibustering in Darfour; and Dafir Pasha sent a person named Razi Ali Agha to investigate the matter. But Razi returned without any information, and meanwhile Dafir Pasha was recalled. The Governorship of the province was divided, and Ahmed Pasha Mumtaz arrived in the year 1288 as Governor of the Southern Soudan. He did nothing with the Bahr Gazelle, and its affairs remained in abeyance until he was in his turn replaced by Ismail Pasha Ayoub. The new Governor took up the question with vigour, and Zebehr became alarmed. To divert the attention of the Government, he organised an expedition against the Razigat and Mu'alish Arabs of Shaka, subject to Darfour. He conquered their country, and wrote to Ismail Ayoub that he had acted on behalf of the Government, and had made the conquest at his own expense and with his own men; but he took care to conceal the fact that he had done it with Bellali's arms and stores. In this way he not only obtained his pardon, but the rank of Kain-maker, and the despatch of reinforcements to Shaka. The Sultan of Darfour sent out an army and defeated him; and he, without authority from the Government, and under pretence of acts of aggression committed by his new opponent, began raiding in the outlying districts of Darfour. This gained him the rank of Colonel, and a second reinforcement of regular troops. With these and his own men he then invaded Darfour itself. The Sultan was killed, the country subjugated; and Zebehr once more boasted that he had accomplished the work with his own private means and by the aid of his own followers.

It is said that he took possession of all the Sultan's valuables and treasures, and kept his officers and soldiers in ignorance of the fact. Still, Ismail Ayoub made him a Pasha, and gave him the Governorship of Darfour. The Governor-General, however, soon saw that he was not to be trusted in this place, and made him Governor of Shaka and the Bahr Gazelle instead. Zebehr, furious at this check, got permission to lay a complaint before the Khedive. In this he was a little too clever. An investigation was held at Cairo, the result of which was unfavourable to the petitioner—so unfavourable, indeed, that, from fear of evil consequences upon his return to the Soudan, he was detained in the capital, where he has ever since remained.

At this time Gordon was appointed Governor-General of the Soudan and of the shores of the Red Sea. On his arrival at Khartoum, he sent orders to Suleiman, the son of Zebehr, then agent for his father at Shaka, to reinforce him in Darfour. Suleiman refused: he imagined that order could not be restored without him and his troops, and consequently his father would be allowed to return. But herein he was grossly deceived, for Gordon put down the revolt unaided, and Zebehr remained at Cairo. Then Suleiman determined, in conjunction with the Bazankars, his father's brethren and kinsmen, to march on Dara, attack and kill the garrison, and conquer the remainder of Darfour. He had upwards of 4000 men and two guns. Gordon, who was then three days' journey from Dara, hastened to the scene of action. He sent for Suleiman and his followers, charged them with disobedience, and acquainted them with his knowledge of their designs. Eventually he deprived Suleiman of his appointment as Deputy-Governor of Shaka; whereupon the young man's officers and soldiers abandoned him, and were given appointments and employment in Darfour. Taking into account the fact that Suleiman had been aided by these men in his disobedience, and influenced by other reasons of the moment, Gordon pardoned him in the name of the Khedive. He further appointed him to the Deputy-Governorship of the Bahr Gazelle, received of him the oath of allegiance, informed him that all the ivory, his property, would be delivered up to him, deducting only the legal Government dues. He accordingly quitted Shaka, but no sooner had he taken possession of his new district than he began plundering and murdering, and inciting the inhabitants against the Government. Gordon at once summoned him to Khartoum, but he had lapsed into open rebellion, and Gessi was sent out to bring him to book. At this point in the Memoir, details are given of the revolt and of the twelve bloody battles in which it was put down; and thereafter the writer goes on to tell of the proofs he had collected of Suleiman's treason.

"It is a notorious fact," he says, "known to all the inhabitants of the Soudan, that Zebehr Pasha ordered his son to rise in arms against the Government. And it is well known, in particular, that before starting from Shaka on his journey to Cairo, Zebehr Pasha assembled the chiefs of his troops and his kinsmen beneath a tree on the road, and made them take oath that, in the event of his not returning, they would combine together in rebellion and armed resistance to the Government, and that they would obey his son in whatever he commanded them. Among the proofs (against Zebehr) is a letter found at the Dim after his son's escape thence." This letter was found in one of Suleiman's trunks. It is written to him by the hand of his father, whose seal it bears, and is of the date 11 : Janad al Awal, 1295. It orders him to drive away by force Idris Bey Abtar, who had been appointed Mudir of the Bahr Gazelle, and after that to follow the instructions he had given him, taking possession of the district of Shaka and driving away its Governor, Said Bey.

Another letter from his cousin Ramli, informed the son of Zebehr that his father had sent him 1000 oker of gunpowder, which, the writer said, he held at Suleiman's disposal, and respecting which he requested instructions. Many other letters from their kinsmen and friends proved agreement to rebel. Among them was one from a kinsman, in an assumed tone of learning and piety ; it informed the son of Zebehr that he had three times tried his fortune, and each trial had shown him victorious ; it predicted success to his undertaking. In addition to this, several employés testified to having been present under the tree. These letters were read before the Council at Khartoum, composed of military officers and chief members of the Government. With other evidence, they clearly proved that Zebehr and his son were traitors. For that crime, for their having levied war against the Government, and for the slaughter of its officers and soldiers at the Bahr Gazelle, they were condemned to death ; and those persons who were proved to have taken part with them were sentenced to banishment.

The son of Zebehr, in making his escape with what remained of his followers and troops, determined to join the traitor Haroun, the self-styled Sultan of Darfour,[1] who was then engaged in rebellious opposition to the Government in the district of Mount Marah. They set out on the road leading to that place, and they had reached Dar Kaza, the country of the Toashia Arabs, when the news of their movements reached Gordon. He was then in the district of Toashia, waiting for Gessi Pasha. On Gessi's arrival, and on receiving confirmation of Suleiman's presence in the country of the Toashias, he ordered his valiant lieutenant to reinforce his 600 men from the Bahr Gazelle, with three com-

[1] Haroun was one of the most formidable enemies with whom General Gordon had to deal when he went up to Darfour in 1877.

panies of Soudani troops, to be taken from the Mudirieh of Dara ; to set out in pursuit of the rebel ; and to destroy Suleiman and his followers before they could enter Darfour and unite themselves with Haroun. Gessi accordingly proceeded to Dara, and on the 4th July he marched thence to Al Kalkaleh with 300 men. He had previously requisitioned 600 men at Shaka, where he had left them with orders to join him on the march. They were slow to come, and Gessi heard meanwhile that the son of Zebehr, who was only three days' journey from Kalkaleh, was likely to receive reinforcements. He accordingly started with his three hundred. The son of Zebehr remained at Toashia, exchanging provisions with the Arabs for slaves. At Gessi's approach he prepared for flight. But a dispute broke out between him and his followers : Râbih Agha (who wished to seek refuge in Darbanda near Barku, and whose opinions were opposed by Soliman-Râbih Agha) fled with 700 men by one road, and the rebel Abu'l Kâsim escaped with 400 men by another. Those who remained were Mûsa, the son of Al Haff ; Al Arbab, son of Diab ; Yakub, Hasan Sakîl, and Ibrahim, the brothers of Sa 'id Bey Hason ; Suleiman, son of Rahmah ; Bu Bekr, son of Mansur ; Birigi Ahmad, son of Idris ; and Abd el Kâdir, son of the Imar. Along with these, Suleiman had 600 Bazankars, and 300 slave-dealers (*jallabs*). They set off with Gessi at their heels for Mount Marah ; and, on the evening of the 16th July 1879, their pursuer came up with them, unperceived. The troops halted for the night, and at daybreak they surprised the sleeping camp. All the men I have named were captured. Many of the Bazankars and *jallabs* (slave-dealers) escaped. Of those that remained, some were sent, after investigation, to their homes, whilst such *jallabs* who were found guilty were sent to Dara. Suleiman and his principals, the heroes of my list, were put to death. It is said that none of them I have named showed any fear of death, excepting the son of Zebehr alone, who did not conceal his feelings, as is the custom of the people of the Soudan. It is also said that the rebels imagined Gessi's force to be at least 3000 strong, and that when they were undeceived they deeply lamented their folly and their fate.

" As to the rebel known under the name of Abu'l Kâsim, who fled as before mentioned, according to intelligence received, he also was arrested, and has most probably been put to death. And no rebels remained in these regions of whom anything is to be feared, since the destruction of the force described above, and since its desertion by Rabih."

"Such," says Gordon, "is the retribution to him who is ungrateful for the favours he has received from God, and for the benefits conferred by those in authority over him. And we pray unto God (be He magnified and exalted!) that He may ever grant victory to the Khedivial Government, and that He may extinguish and exterminate all its enemies by the hands of its servants filled with determination in the execution of their duty. And, verily, He is the possessor of infinite power over all things!"

The next paper is the report of Yusuf Pasha Hasan, giving an account of his operations for the suppression of the insurrection in the Bahr Gazelle country. It begins with an introduction in the usual strain. Most of it has been borrowed by the compiler of the Governor-General's narrative. Yusuf Pasha then proceeds to say that he was appointed to re-establish order in the provinces of the Bahr Gazelle, by "His Excellency the exalted Governor-General of the Soudan, Gordon Pasha, whom God hath made an ornament to the age and to the kingdom, who by his uprightness hath stopped the flowing of tears, and by his impetuous bravery hath destroyed the paths of the wicked." He arrived at the "Dim" of Idris Abtar Bey, the seat of the Government of the province, on the 23 Zul Kadah, 1295. The rebel Suleiman advanced against the expedition "with his numerous army," and there occurred twelve "battles," which the good Pasha gives us in detail.

Then follows Hasan Pasha's account of the twelve "battles," which has been incorporated, word for word, in the Governor-General's narrative. After relating the final flight of Suleiman, Hasan Pasha says that he sent 2000 men in pursuit, with the instructions transmitted to him by his Excellency the Governor, and ordered them not to return without having fulfilled their object. "And down to the present time," he adds, "I have no news of them." His report is dated 9 Cha'bar, 1296.

The next paper contains the official report of the proceedings of the Maylis (Court of Inquiry in Court-martial). It begins by stating that the papers framed by the written orders of the Governor-General directed to the Commander-in-Chief, dated 1st Sha'ban, 1296, show that Zebehr Pasha, before his departure from Shaka, assembled the chiefs of the Bazankars, his kinsmen and servants, and his son Suleiman, beneath a tree at the encampment of Sheikh Ahmad, or Dudan or Ruran, Dudaf, inspector (nazir) of the Arabs of Al Mu'alich, and made them swear on the Kur-an that, if he did not return from Cairo, they would combine together to refuse obedience to the Government, and strictly obey the orders of his son Suleiman. These facts are proved by the depositions of certain persons, who witnessed the proceedings : namely, Masri Effendi, Abd al Kādir, Deputy-Governor of Shaka, Ahmad el Kidr, Ma'awin Al Kalkelah, and Muhommad Ayha, or Ban Bareb Al Naka (?) Ma'awin of the Mudirieh. And inasmuch as Said Bey al Huseyn, formerly Governor of Shaka, was present at the meeting, and is now at Khartoum, he was brought before the Magylis and examined, and he confirmed the truth of the preceding statement.

A letter was also read from Zebehr to his son Suleiman, inciting him to rebel, and to levy war against the Government ; urging him to expel by force of arms Idris Bey Abtar, Governor of the Bahr Gazelle ; and desiring him also to send the means of combining with Awad Bey for the sake of his assistance in seizing the country, seeing that he is one of its old inhabitants, and is well acquainted with all its affairs, and with the language of the people. The letter goes on to say that, whereas the agents whom Zebehr had left in charge of his Zaribehs, had left their employment, and had taken service under the Government, he therefore desired his son to receive (or *take*) possession of the Zaribehs and their contents, and to receive (or *take*) possession of Shaka from Said al Huseyn ; and that, if the Government should remove Suleiman from his post, a person it approved of would be appointed.

Also a letter was read from Ramli, son of Suleiman, to Suleiman, son of Zebehr, acknowledging the receipt of 1000 okes of gunpowder from the Black Pasha, asking for instructions, and stating that it was meanwhile hidden underground.

Also a telegram from Zebehr at Cairo, to Awad (at Khartoum), inquiring after his son Suleiman, his loyalty to the Government, and respecting the state of the crops.

Also a telegram from Awad to Zebehr Pasha, referring in comforting terms to Ramli Suleiman and to the favourable condition of the Nile, and adding that there was no news from Suleiman respecting the crops.

The " Mayli " investigated the acts of open rebellion committed by Suleiman, in plundering Government stores, levying war against the force under the command of Yusuf Pasha, Hasar and Gessi Pasha, and slaying the Government soldiers. Idin Bey being brought before the Council and interrogated, deposed that 240 regular soldiers had been killed, including 1 captain, 4

lieutenants, and 27 cadets; that Awad, as Said Agha, the
Ma'awin, was killed; that 25 Remington rifles, 30 converted
French rifles, and two guns, with their ammunition waggons, had
been looted by the rebels, in addition to the aforesaid seizure of
the ammunition confided to Awad as Lezzid Agha. Also that
24 irregular soldiers had been killed, with 330 Arab *jallabs*
(merchants), and 12 men of his own people.

The Court judged that Zebehr Pasha had been found guilty
of rebellion, that he had encouraged and urged his son to resist
the authority of the Government, with a view to taking possession
of the country; and that he had supplied him with gunpowder
for that purpose; by which act he had rendered himself liable to
the penalty of death, and to the confiscation of his estate. As to
Suleiman, the son of Zebehr, the Court (after recapitulating his
offences) pronounced him to be beyond the reach of pardon, and
sentenced him and his confederates to death and to the forfeiture
of all their possessions.

And seeing that Elyas Pasha and Mahomed Bey Hadgi
Ahmad, who were related by marriage to Zebehr Pasha, had
aided and abetted him and his son in their rebellion, and in the
plunder of Government stores—as was proved by documents and
by letters from Zebehr appointing Mahomed Bey Hadgi Ahmad
his agent, and by telegrams despatched to him—the Court
approved of their banishment to the districts of Harar and Zeyla,
after the property in their possession belonging to the Government and to Zebehr Pasha should have been recovered from
them. And that all persons who should be found guilty of
aiding Zebehr and his son in the rebellion should suffer the same
penalty.

All this in conformity with the fifth and sixth sections of the
1st division of the Hamayuni Code, and articles 357, 362, and
379 of the Civil Code, etc. etc. Dated 3 Sha'ban, 1296.

The next paper contains copies of documents, namely : 1st.—
Copy of a letter from Ramli, son of Suleiman, to Suleiman, son of
Zebehr Pasha, dated 4 : Muharram, 1294. The writer addresses
his correspondent in the regular official style in use in Govern-
ment departments in Egypt, as "Mudir (Governor) of the Bahr
El Ghazal and Rûl," and gives him the title of *Bey*.

After the usual compliments, he begins by telling him that he
need be under no uneasiness about his father; that, with God's
leave, the latter will soon come; that no one, either Turk or
native, stands so high in the favour of the Viceroy, by reason of

the assistance he has given in the war with Russia ; that he (Zebehr) had written to Khartoum, desiring one of the best houses to be prepared, for that he knew he would soon return. " And then, be cautious : and again, be cautious. Do not believe the words of enemies." He goes on to say that Zebehr has sent a number of stores of considerable value, among them 1000 okes of gunpowder and lead, and many weapons of war ; that these have arrived at the White Nile ; that the people were much alarmed, and when they heard of Suleiman's departure for the " Dems," they wished to sell the powder ; that Ramé had prevented them from doing so, and had caused the powder and lead to be buried ; that he awaited Suleiman's instructions ; that he had, moreover, a small quantity of powder at Khartoum, and that if Suleiman required it he should let him know.

The letter ends with the following P.S. :—" We know from both high and low that your kingdom depends entirely upon Abu 'l Kasim. Persons of low degree have come to us, and have informed us that they have escaped from him. The ruin of your dominion is (or will be) caused by Abu 'l Kasim. It ought not to be so, and this is the hope we entertain for you,"— meaning, it is presumed, that the writer hopes Suleiman will be able to overcome the danger of which he is hereby warned.

2nd.—A long letter from Zebehr to his son Suleiman, dated 11 : Jamar Awal, 1295. This is the document of which a résumé is given on a preceding page. It is written in a rambling and disconnected style, and the writer often repeats himself. It will suffice to make the following additions to the abstracts already given :—

Zebehr addresses his son in the Muslim manner, in terms of strong affection, and styles him his appointed heir and successor. He gives him much good advice, religious and moral, and desires him to be just and upright towards those over whom he has authority. He again and again inculcates obedience to the Government, adding in one place, " with extreme caution for your own safety (or interests)." He denounces Idris Abtar for his ingratitude and intrigues, and requests his son to expel him the country,—him and all his kin. Idris, he says, is wicked, and God loveth not the wicked, neither doth the Khedivial Government love any but them who practise justice among its subjects. Idris and his people are full of envy and jealousy.

He desires his son to guard and preserve the country, and to protect the subjects of the Government ; to prohibit all proceedings in their prejudice, the plundering of their goods or the kidnapping of their children, seeing that they have now become Moslems, and must be held in honour as subjects of the Khedivial Government.

As to himself, he says he is trusted with great honours by the Khedive, who is assured of his fidelity and loyalty. He goes on to say : " Do not leave my slaves in the possession of the treacherous (Government) servants, least of all those who are with Said Bey. Receive (or take) them from him, and if it be expedient, receive (or take) Shaka and make over its administration to the Government, for Said, without doubt, will ruin it, as he ruins all places." He then mentions Awad's daughter ; exhorts him to be particular in treating her with kindness, and to show her greater favour than to any other of his women ; to regard Awad as his father, and to remember that without his assistance he cannot gain possession of the country : reminding him that when they parted he urged him to gain Awad's confidence, to refer all things to him, and to consider him as his father. " But you have disobeyed us, and your dominion has been ruined owing to the absence of Awad ; but next to the Faith, God has instituted forgiveness, and from report of what you have done I have pardoned, and so likewise has Awad. But find means to bring him and yourself together."

Next he desires his son to send him thirty bundles of ostrich feathers (best quality) along with the money that is to be remitted—not later than 1 : Shawal—elephants' tusks, as specified ; and other goods, including arms for purposes of defence deposited on the Seribas. Seeing that the agents who were in charge of these things have left their posts and taken service under the Government, the whole of the goods in question are to be taken over in accordance with the monitories existing in the books. He ends his letter thus : " What I have said is sufficient. He who is present perceives though the absent cannot see. It is for you to act."

3rd.—Copies of telegram from Zebehr to Awad, and from Awad to Zebehr : the former dated 11th March, '79 (European date), the latter without date.

4th.—Deposition of Masci Awad Abd al Kadir, Deputy-Governor of Shaka (and others), describing the meeting held by Zebehr under a tree, which, they say, was attended by thirty-three persons.

5th.—Copy of a letter from Zebehr to Mahommed Bey Haggi

19

Ahmad, dated 9 Safer, 1293, written after the Black Pasha had started for Cairo, empowering Mahommed Bey to name certain sums of money, and to give receipts for them, and requesting him to forward the money to headquarters.

The next and last paper is the deposition made by Sa'ad esh Shami, corporal of Artillery.

He says that the party to which he belonged was attacked by Suleiman, the son of Zebehr, at the head of 9000 Bazinkars, at the Dem of Idris Abtar. Suleiman was accompanied by the chiefs under his command (whose names he gives). "We numbered 600 rifles, and we had two guns." Severe fighting ensued, whereupon the Dongolawis and negroes fled, leaving the artillerymen to bear the burden of the fight. They defended themselves with their two guns until their ammunition was exhausted. Then Suleiman and his troops bore down upon them, killed some, and made prisoners of the others. After sending out a detachment, who captured the ammunition in charge of Idris Abtar, Suleiman ordered the prisoners before him, and compelled them, under pain of death, to promise they would fight for him. When the Government troops arrived, under the command of Gessi and Yusef Bey ash Shalali, Suleiman went forth and attacked them, and was defeated. He fortified himself (as previously described), and fighting went on for some months. The artillerymen pretended to fight, but took care that their guns should do no harm, and did not open (unscrew?) the shells. At length Suleiman evacuated his position with what remained of his forces. He carried off the guns; and the artillerymen, bound with ropes, were dragged after them. They reached Suleiman's great Dem, and fortified themselves therein. The Government troops soon afterwards arrived, and likewise entrenched themselves. Two days before any actual fighting commenced, the corporal succeeded in making his escape by night. He had an iron chain fastened to his neck. He wandered for nineteen days in the forest, and at length reached the settlement of the Toashia (Arabs). One of these, a man named Al Ghazala, relieved him of his chain, mounted him, and bore him company to Dara. The narrator makes no mention of the story of the deliberate and open sacrifice of a boy.

After such a revelation as this, it is not easy to see how such a man as Zebehr could have been entrusted by a cabinet of amateurs and doctrinaires with the task of establishing and maintaining order in the Soudan. From Gordon's point of view, however, the plan was not only possible, but eminently appropriate and judicious. As he was the last to condone any of the acts with which Zebehr stood charged, he was the last to admit his unfitness on their account. The proposal that Zebehr should be his successor was one of those daring strokes of policy which made his tactics unlike those of other men. They were generated by the difficulties of his position, and scarce ever had he found them fail. It must not be imagined that his most startling devices were conceived rashly or rashly carried out; they were invariably the result of deep but rapid reasoning, and of an unerring knowledge of both the peoples and the countries he was summoned to succour and to guide. He has been called a leader of men. He was more; he was a leader of events.

A great deal of his success consisted in the fact that he was always a generous and straightforward foe. As the Master whom he served first struck down his enemy Saul, and then converted him into His faithful servant Paul, so Gordon struck down his enemies, and used them as allies after changing them into friends. In this way he was wont to achieve prodigious results, though there were instances of failure now and then. In this spirit he would willingly have shaken hands with Zebehr, the notorious ravager and ruiner of countries. He had destroyed his power as a slave-hunter, and the power of those who helped him: he now urged that the employment of such power as he still possessed should be directed into a new channel. His theory was, that where courage, energy, and a talent for organisation and administration showed themselves in raids and devastating wars, they should now have a chance of shining in use, in the work of restoring peace and plenty to a ruined land. The result of this endeavour might have been a failure, it is true, but even then the condition of things could hardly have been made worse; on the other hand, the result might have been a success, and the addition of one triumph more to the Christian practice of making your foe your friend. The argument was this: Zebehr had treated others ill, but he had himself been ill-treated in return. If he could now be used for good, the past should be buried in the present. In a position from which he could see happiness where he only saw misery, and hear blessings where he had heard only cursings, he might realise how necessary it was that the old unholy power should have been crushed. An honest man in the East is rarely understood, but he is always respected, and, what is more, often appreciated. An idiot, though rarely an object of appreciation, is also an object of reverence, for reverence is given in the East to all that is mysterious, and the ways of an honest man are as hard to comprehend as the vagaries of a fool. Zebehr would never make an honest Governor-General of the Soudan, in the Western acceptation of the word. He would never tell the truth, for the truth was not in him; and he would always take bribes, and extort them if they were not offered. Lies and bribes are national attributes, and a native Governor-General who did without them would be regarded as a fool. But Zebehr, notwithstanding all this, might have proved an abler and more useful ruler of the Soudan than, with one exception, the Soudan had known, for he knew the people whom he would have been called upon to govern, and by them he was known and feared. They required to be governed courageously, and Zebehr had courage; they also required to be governed by kindness, and Zebehr could be made kind. The question was really one of expediency; and virtue in this case must be bought with pounds, shillings, and pence, if it could not be obtained by less ignoble means.

No one was so capable of deciding who should govern the Soudan as Gordon; and he, with all his knowledge of the past, and all his grasp of the future, decided that Zebehr would be the nearest possible approach to the right man in the right place. It is not for us to criticise his judgment or pick holes in the reasoning by which he was established in his mind. It commended itself neither to H.M. Government nor to H.M. Opposition; and we know the result.

CHAPTER XXV

ENGLAND'S POLICY

THE policy of H.M. Government in connection with Gordon, Zebehr, and the despatch of troops, had every possible epithet of abuse heaped upon it from the English and the foreign press, and from the English and foreign public. Sometimes a redundancy of epithets was applied, and then the term " vacillating " was almost inevitable. Why such a word should be used is not quite evident, for, as a matter of fact, the policy of H.M. Government in Egypt had been unfortunately only too consistent.

When Turkey declined to interfere with the Arabi scandal, England stepped in to protect her own interests, and expressed her intention of retaining her foothold in the country, and assisting in its government as long as she considered it necessary to do so for her own sake. She entered upon no engagement to protect Egypt's dependencies or the Sultan's possessions, unless such protection involved a duty she owed to her own subjects and her own commercial interests. When the revolt in the Soudan assumed heroic proportions, and there was a popular clamour that England should repress it, her reply was a simple repetition of her avowed policy. " We have nothing to do," she said, " with the Soudan, which at present does not concern us. If it ever does—that is, if the revolt extends to Egypt proper, where we have interests—we shall be prepared to deal with it (for we do not now intend to reduce the strength of our standing army in the country); but until it does, the owners of the Soudan must settle their difficulty in their own way, and rely wholly on their own resources." Whether this policy was good or bad is too complicated a question to be discussed here, but it was at least consistent and definite, the exact antithesis of what it has been called. On this theory our efforts for the relief of Sinkat and Tokar were simple acts of kindness, not admissions of responsibility: the Egyptians failed, and we lent them a helping hand. Our defence of Suakim was arranged on a different basis, for there we had commercial and political interests at stake. We raised no objection to the plan of making application to the Porte for troops, and stipulated that the Porte should pay all the cost and make use of Suakim as a base; and there were sufficient political reasons for these two conditions. When it became evident that Egypt was unable to reconquer the Soudan, we suggested she had better let it be, and content herself with trying to manage her own affairs; and this was not advice, but a simple recognition of the fact that it was Hobson's choice for her—that or nothing. The Khedive accepted the position, but his ministry resigned, and their reasons for doing so were more Irish than Oriental: they declared, through their President, Cherif Pasha, that they would rather resign their posts than surrender what had already been taken from them.

As matters became more serious, it was evident that in abandoning the Soudan the Egyptian Government would have to abandon such garrisons as were still loyal. In this dilemma we offered them assistance: we were prepared to relieve the garrisons, but there our action would cease; we would have nothing to do with any attempt to reconquer the country, nor would we assist in any endeavour to reconstitute its government which involved our support, whether moral or real. All this was consistent with our declared policy of helping the Government of Egypt and her people in so far as concerned what we believed to be our interests. The loyal garrisons in the Soudan appealed to their Government for relief, and their Government could not give it, and we answered the appeal in the cause of humanity. Of course it was advanced that in the cause of humanity we should have undertaken the reconquest of the Soudan and the establishment of a just and active government; but, said the Gladstone Ministry, it might as reasonably be advanced that we should expend our men and money in quelling any other rebellion—that we should constitute ourselves, in fact, the police of the human race. If our national philanthropy were allowed to run riot in this way, we should soon ourselves be entirely dependent on the philanthropy of other nations.

Having decided to attempt the evacuation of the loyal garrisons, the next point was the best way in which it could be done, and this was no easy problem. Many minds attempted its solution, but their schemes involved either the retention of part of the

Soudan or the subjection of the Mahdi and the constitution of a
government from without. To one and all H.M. Ministers returned
the same answer: " Our object is to relieve the loyal garrisons
only, and not to settle the future of the Soudan. We will
undertake so much, at any reasonable risk, but we will do no
more." Gordon, who at first was strongly in favour of the retention of the Soudan, east of the White Nile and north of Sennaar,
at last undertook to attempt the evacuation of the country on
these principles, but it was understood that H.M. Government
should give him their support and consideration should he be
unable to fulfil all their expectations.   What he said was tantamount to this, " I will do what you want if I can.   But it may
be impossible : I may find that I cannot relieve these garrisons
without destroying the power of the Mahdi first; and if so, I
must look to you to enable me to do it." To this the Government
agreed with enthusiasm. He had all their confidence, and all
their capacity of help was his likewise. And he went upon his
errand on this definite and particular understanding, namely,
that his only objects were the safe evacuation of Egyptian troops
and employés, and the restoration of their independence to the
Soudanese apart from any outside government.

An important consideration, associated with, but not dependent upon, Gordon's instructions, was the stimulus which
might be given to the slave-trade by the withdrawal of the
Egyptian authority from the interior. H.M. Government therefore
directed their Envoy to pay special attention to steps which
might be useful in counteracting this stimulus. Up to this time
the policy was accepted by the Khedive, Nubar Pasha, and Sir
Evelyn Baring as the best one possible; and Gordon himself
declared that " to secure a good government to the Soudanese was
impracticable at any cost." " Her Majesty's Government would,
therefore, after evacuating the Egyptian garrisons, etc., leave the
people as God placed them, not forced to fight among themselves,
and no longer oppressed by men coming from lands so remote
as Circassia, Kurdistan, and Anatolia." It has therefore to be
admitted that at starting he accepted the morality of his mission,
and believed his task at its inception fully practicable.

This is a conscientious, unbiased review of the action of H.M.
Government from the end of the Arabi rebellion to the departure
of Gordon for the Soudan, and is the first period of the so-called
vacillating policy of England. The second period extends from
Gordon's arrival in Egypt to the time when Khartoum was

entirely cut off from the rest of the Soudan, and therefore from all possible communication with Egypt and England.

Now, when Gordon drew up his Memorandum on board the s.s. *Tanjore*, he laid out a scheme of action which appeared to him feasible, but by no means certain of success, and Lieutenant-Colonel Stewart, in endorsing the greater part of it, wisely said that, as it was impossible for H.M. Government to foresee all the contingencies which might arise during the process of evacuation, the more judicious course would be to rely on General Gordon's discretion, and on his knowledge of the country and the people. Mr. Gladstone admitted this at once ; the Government, he said, were resolved to do nothing which should interfere with the plan of pacification—the only one which promised a solution of the Soudan difficulty ; and it was the duty of the Government to beware of interfering with their servant's plans. These, it should be remembered, involved the possibility of "Soudanese Conservatives of property fighting against the Soudanese Communists who might desire to rob them." While he was journeying to Khartoum, Gordon asked the Government, in a telegram dated Abu Hamed, February 8th, 1884, to change the firman with which he was provided into one recognising moral control and suzerainty, and gave his reasons very clearly for the suggestion. The Government, however, did not agree to any change of the firman. Before he reached Khartoum, they telegraphed to ask whether it would assist him in the policy of withdrawal to send a British force to Suakim, to operate, if necessary, in its vicinity ; and his reply to this was that he would care more for *rumour* of intention to send forces than for anything else ; he considered that rumour of English intervention would have great effect. Later on he sent another telegram, stating that the question of " getting out the garrison and families was so interlaced with the preservation of the well-to-do people of the country as to be *for the present* inseparable, and that, therefore, any precipitate action separating these interests would throw all well-disposed people into the ranks of the enemy." The natural reply on the part of the Government to this was, that Gordon would of course take his own time. It may be thought that this telegram of Gordon's sounded the first note of alarm ; but it should be read with two which preceded it—one dated from Abu Hamed on February 8th, the other from Berber on February 11th. The first said : "I beg you not to have the slightest anxiety about the Soudan. I trust security will be secured in a month." The second ran thus : "I understand your desire to be the pacification of the country without bloodshed, and the formation of a native Government. I will fulfil your orders, and feel sure I am not presumptuous in assuring you I have every hope of success."

The first radical change of programme was suggested in a telegram dated Khartoum, February 18th. Having alluded to the time when whites, fellaheen troops, civilian employés, soldiers' widows and orphans—in short, the Egyptian contingent in the Soudan—would be removed, Gordon went on to say that H.M. Government would then be face to face with the question of administration, and that, unless he had a successor, there would be anarchy throughout the country, which, though all the Egyptian element was withdrawn, would be "a misfortune and inhuman." He therefore suggested that Zebehr should be appointed his successor, created a K.C.M.G., and promised the moral support of H.M. Government. This telegram burst upon the Government like a shell; it involved a complete change of policy, and therewithal the necessity of admitting themselves, not centres of prophetic inspiration, but average human beings. Of course, too, it appealed irresistibly to their habit of procrastination, and was read as a suggestion for the future, not as a requirement for the present. The answer was decisive. The Government said that the gravest objections existed to the appointment by their authority of a successor to General Gordon, and that no necessity appeared to have arisen of going beyond the suggestions contained in Gordon's memorandum of the 22nd ult., and making any special provision for the government of the country.

On February 27th two satisfactory telegrams from the Soudan arrived at Cairo. The first, from Mr. Power, stated that the Mahdi had no standing army; that the town of Khartoum was peaceful and its market full; and that Gordon was working wonders. The second, from Gordon, announced that Sennaar had reported itself quite safe, but that there was a gang of rebels on the road between that city and Khartoum. But on the same day there came in the proclamation which Gordon had issued to the inhabitants of the Soudan; it was mysterious and somewhat perplexing. It set forth that, having in vain advised the people to abstain from rebellion, Gordon had been compelled to resort to severe measures; so that British troops were on their way, and would reach Khartoum in a few days, when whosoever persisted in wickedness would be treated as he deserved. Explanation of this is impossible. It may be that Gordon was working out his original notion of a phantasmagoria of British intervention; or, what is more likely, events at Suakim had given rise to serious rumours at Khartoum, and Gordon had been informed that a British force was really on its way to Berber. Be this as it may, it is evident that by this time he had recognised that his work was hardly to be done by him single-handed, and that the policy of evacuation, pure and simple, was not one that he, a Christian soldier, could countenance or maintain. Daily the breach was widening; daily the change of front was made more and more apparent.

In a telegram dated the 24th of February, Gordon said it was quite possible that in a short time the whole Soudan, comprising Dongola, Berber, Khartoum, Sennaar, and Kassala, would be quieted, and Bogos evacuated; and he then went on to discuss the future of the ill-fated country. To the telegram rejecting his ·scheme for the future, he replied that he knew his duty was to evacuate the garrison, and do the best he could for the establishment of a peaceful government; the first he hoped to accomplish, but the second was more difficult, and concerned Egypt more than himself. It practically amounted to "smashing up the Mahdi," and if the Government decided to do this, he recommended the despatch of two hundred Indian troops to Wady Halfa, and an officer to Dongola, under pretence of looking out for quarters for troops. He ended by repeating that evacuation was possible, but that the effect would be felt in Egypt; and that, for the protection of Egypt, H.M. Government would be forced to enter into a far more serious business than the immediate smashing up of the Mahdi. This was excellent advice, but it did not commend itself to H.M. Ministers. They still remained consistent, still adhered to their old programme. They wanted evacuation, and evacuation only. The country was to be given up to its own, to do as they would with it. They did not intend to smash the Mahdi in the Soudan, but they would be prepared to do so if he came into Egypt proper, and threatened existing British interests. And still the public and press cried out upon them, and swore their vacillating policy was making England ridiculous in the eyes of the whole world! They were right enough as to the effect, but wrong as to the cause. Our Ministers were ridiculous, not in their indecision, but their obstinacy.

On February 27th the whole condition of affairs was altered, and from this date H.M. Government were placed in a totally different position as regards facts. Gordon telegraphed: " To-day and daily go down all sick, widows, orphans, etc., and there remain 1400 fellaheen soldiers. Supposing I send down all these fellaheen soldiers, in a few days the town would send to the Mahdi its submission, and all the machinery of the Government would be caught. *The evacuation of the Soudan is impossible* until the Government asserts its authority, and I mean by evacuation the removal of all Egyptian employés who form the machinery of the Government, and not the departure of sick, etc., who may be considered to have gone from here. You will have to say if this partial evacuation fulfils your desires." In another telegram, dated March 8th, but received with the first, he firmly maintained the policy of eventual evacuation, but insisted that it was impossible to get the Cairene employés out of Khartoum unless the Government (having refused him Zebehr) sent British and Indian Moslem troops to Wady Halfa. He admitted the possibility of holding out in Khartoum and of forcing back the revolt, but declared that there was no chance of the position improving with time, that the money at his disposal must come to an end, and that anarchy would inevitably follow.

His next telegram, dated February 29th, threw no new light upon the situation, beyond the statement that, owing to Baker's defeat, Kassala had been attacked by the Hadendoas. Three days after this he telegraphed again, maintaining the policy of eventual evacuation, declaring the *immediate* withdrawal of the Egyptian employés to be impossible, urging fresh reasons for the appointment of Zebehr, and for the despatch of two hundred British troops to Wady Halfa. Next day he went still further, and wrote thus : " The combination of Zebehr and myself at Khartoum is *an absolute necessity for success.*" A telegram, dated March 4th, related that things were not serious, though they might become so if there were any delay in sending Zebehr. "My weakness," he added, significantly enough, "is that of being foreign, and Christian, and peaceful ; and it is only by sending Zebehr that prejudice can be removed." Colonel Stewart, on the same day, endorsed these views in the strongest terms ; it was *impossible*, he said, *to quit the country* without leaving some sort of established government ; and unless Zebehr was sent there *was little probability* of the policy of evacuation being carried out.

Now, in considering the action of H.M. Government, all these telegrams should be read together. They are weighty, but not very alarming, and to a certain extent they are contradictory. The new position was a revelation and a surprise to H.M.

Ministers. Previously they had only been recommended to send Zebehr or to send troops, that the country might have a just and settled government, and not because they were absolutely necessary for the evacuation of the garrisons. Under these circumstances, a pause for reflection and a desire for further information were natural enough; and our rulers can hardly be blamed for their indulgence therein. Had they been capable of a new departure, of recognising the logic of events and preferring expediency to consistency, had they, in a word, been statesmen, the difficulty had been overcome with ease, and Gordon still living.

Unhappily, they would neither see nor hear, neither listen nor invent. Lord Granville's reply was to this effect: That H.M. Government saw no reason to change their impressions about Zebehr, which were formed on various grounds, among others on Gordon's Memorandum written on board the *Tanjore*; that unless those impressions were removed, they could not take upon themselves the responsibility of sending him; and that they would like to know how it was possible to reconcile such an appointment with the prevention or discouragement of slave-hunting and the slave-trade, with the policy of complete evacuation, and with security to Egypt. They also desired a detailed account of the progress which had been made in evacuating the garrisons, and requested to know the length of time likely to elapse before the whole or greater part could be withdrawn. Gordon's reply was a masterpiece of statecraft. He proved that the despatch of Zebehr meant the extrication of the Cairene employés from Khartoum and the garrisons from Sennaar and Kassala; that no other means of achieving these things was possible; that as to slave-holding, even if we held the Soudan we could not interfere with it, the treaty of 1877 being impracticable; that as to slave-hunting, the evacuation of the Bahr Gazelle and Equatorial Provinces would entirely end it. He related what had been done, and explained the positions held by the rebels. He declared his efforts to divide the country among the native chiefs or kings to have failed: the chiefs would not collect; they knew they could not hold the country a day against the Mahdi's agents. He showed that Zebehr could do this: the Mahdi might be the Pope, but Zebehr would be the Sultan; and he admitted that Zebehr had probably stirred up the revolt in hopes he might be sent to quell it. "It is the irony of fate that he will get his wish if he is sent up." Now the whole slave question was really one which required no discussion nor consideration at all; if we determined to abandon the country we had to accept the inevitable consequences of our policy. That this fact is one that might well have commended itself to H.M. Government, corrupt with sentimentalism and high principle as they were, is possible, though far from probable. What is certain is that some pressure was put upon them from without, and that they decided to stick to their colours.

Scarcely were they in possession of Gordon's telegram when they received a petition, signed by the Chairman of the British and Foreign Anti-Slavery Society (Mr. Edmund Sturge), protesting in strong terms against Zebehr's employment. Now, if this petition had anything to do with deciding the Government not to send Zebehr—and, as appeared by the sequel, practically to sign their Envoy's death-warrant—it is a pity that the British and Foreign Anti-Slavery Society ever existed. Looking only at the immediate issues, it is extremely silly and improvident. Anarchy in the Soudan meant slave-hunting in the Soudan, whatever happened in the Bahr Gazelle and Equatorial Provinces; and the best authority in the world showed that anarchy could only be prevented by Zebehr. The Anti-Slavery Society therefore did their very best to stultify the proposed object of their existence. They prevailed, however, and at once. The reply returned by H.M. Government on March 11th was consistent even to puzzle-headedness. They did not consider their arguments against the employment of Zebehr satisfactorily answered. They were, however, prepared to agree to any other Mohammedan assistance, and to supply any reasonable sum Gordon considered necessary for the achievement of his mission. They were not prepared to send troops to Berber. Finally, they had no desire to force the hand of their Envoy prematurely, and, therefore, would extend his appointment for any reasonable period. This was, of course, a vote of want of confidence. It really signified, "You have already had to change your mind more than once; stay a little longer, and see if you may not change it again."

We now come to a series of telegrams, dated March 8th. These stated that the Mahdi had raised the tribes, who would try and cut the road to Berber, and who would also cut the telegraph and prevent supplies from reaching Khartoum; they also mentioned that Khartoum had provisions for six months. On March 9 another series of telegrams were sent, dated at different hours of the day, and these were most disturbing. Gordon announced that there was no possibility of the people rallying round him, or of paying any heed to his proclamation; that unless troops were sent to Berber, and Zebehr to the Soudan, it was not worth while holding on to Khartoum; that he could get the Khartoum garrison to Berber, but that such action would sacrifice all outlying places except Berber and Dongola; that once the Mahdi was in Khartoum, operations against him would be very arduous and would not save Sennaar and Kassala; *that it would be possible to retire all Cairene employés and white troops with Stewart from Berber to Dongola and thence to Wady Halfa*; but that if the evacuation of Khartoum was decided upon, he would ask H.M. Government to accept the resignation of his commission, when he would take all his steamers and stores up to the Equatorial and Bahr Gazelle Provinces, and consider those provinces under the King of the Belgians, from whom he had written authority to that effect. He requested a speedy reply, as in a few days even the retreat to Berber might be impossible.

Next day, March 10th, another telegram reported that the recent exodus,[1] including the invalids and widows, had failed to satisfy the wavering tribes between Khartoum and Berber; that, had he been able to give hopes of a future establishment, things might have been better; but that it was now evident no one would throw in his fortunes with a departing Government. At a later hour of the same day he says, "It is hardly worth while giving you all the rumours here. Through the weakness of the Government many have joined the rebels. All news confirms what I have already told you, namely, that before long we shall be blockaded. The utility of Zebehr is greatly diminished owing to our weakness, which has forced the loyal to join the enemy." On March the 11th came the announcement that the rebels were four hours distant on the Blue Nile, but that there was no panic; and on the same day Sir E. Baring received this startling communication: "Khartoum, March 11th, '84. I would like to express to you and H.M. Government my sincere thanks for the support you have both afforded me since I took up this mission, and to acknowledge that you have both given me every assistance I could have expected. It is not in our hands to command success. I say the same for the Khedive and the Egyptian Ministers." Of course the telegram sent by H.M. Government on March 11th had not yet been received. It is therefore to be feared that the irony of Gordon's message was only prophetic.

Between March the 10th and April the 9th Gordon received

[1] See Appendix 13.

only one of H.M. Government's many telegrams: that which told him not to expect any British advance from Suakim to Berber. They, on the other hand, received nearly all his telegrams between those dates, and it is with these that we now have to deal. Meanwhile it is worthy of special note that on March 24th a telegram from Hussein Pasha Khalifa at Berber reported that Khartoum was besieged by certain Arab tribes, and that others were arriving to assist in the investment.

A telegram from Gordon, dated March 17th, gave a detailed account of operations against the rebels in which the latter were victorious. Another showed how he had afterwards tried by court-martial and then shot the two traitor Pashas. He added that Khartoum was probably safe, and that as the Nile rose they would account for plenty of rebels, as there was no lack of ammunition. It was this message which enabled Sir Evelyn Baring to say that, as far as he could judge, Gordon was in no immediate danger—an expression of opinion which has somehow been greatly derided. The Envoy's next two telegrams, which had no date, were received on April the 9th. The one described an engagement and a rebel loss. The other said : " I wish I could convey to you my impressions of the truly trumpery nature of this revolt, which 500 determined men could put down. Be assured for the present, and for two months hence, we are as safe here as at Cairo. If you would get by good pay 3000 Turkish infantry, and 1000 Turkish cavalry, the affair, including crushing of the Mahdi, would be accomplished in four months."

About this time alarming news came in from Berber. The tribes south of Shendy had joined the revolt, and their fellows to the north were ready to march at any moment. The Bishareen Arabs were also in communication with the rebels, with a view to besieging Berber and cutting off communication with Korosko. Upon receipt of this information, the Government inquired from Sir E. Baring whether, under existing circumstances, a movement on Wady Halfa, such as had often been suggested by Gordon, would assist Berber. Sir E. Baring, after consulting with General Stephenson, replied that in the opinion of that officer the objections to such a movement were insuperable. The news from Berber grew worse ; and the Government, recognising that the danger to the town was imminent, again sent to know whether, after consultation with Nubar, Wood, and Stephenson, any steps, by negotiation or otherwise, could be taken to relieve it. The answer returned was, that nothing could be done except by sending an Anglo-Egyptian force to Berber, which would take eight weeks by one route and sixteen by another. H.M. Government therefore sent a message to Hussein Khalifa, at Berber, advising him that no immediate assistance could be given, as an expedition, even if one were undertaken, could not arrive at Berber in less than four months. At the same time several messengers were ordered to be despatched at intervals from Dongola and Berber to Gordon, desiring him to keep the Government informed of any prospective danger at Khartoum, and to prepare them for any such danger, by advices as to what force would be necessary to assure his removal—its amount, its character, the route it would take, and its time for operation. Expressions of gratitude were added for his gallant, self-sacrificing conduct, and for the good he had achieved.

Gordon's next message at once became historical. It was undated, but in all probability it was sent on April 8th. It ran thus : "As far as I can understand, the situation is this : you state your intention of not sending any relief up here or to Berber, and you refuse me Zebehr. I consider myself free to act according to circumstances. I shall hold on here as long as I can, and if I can suppress the rebellion I shall do so. If I cannot, I shall retire to the Equator, and leave you the indelible disgrace of abandoning the garrisons of Sennaar, Kassala, Berber, and Dongola, with the certainty that you will eventually be forced to smash up the Mahdi under great difficulties if you would retain peace in Egypt." The breach was complete. The great soldier declined to serve as an instrument of dishonour ; and his quondam employers accepted his reproof and the position with that complacency in the face of ignominy and disaster, which of all their titles to fame is perhaps the most valid and the least contested.

It is unnecessary to review the policy pursued by H.M. Government beyond this point, which marks the time when Gordon had to stand and to act alone. I have shown that throughout they have been heroically consistent; and that is enough. It has been remarked that with consistency of this sort the gods themselves war vainly. But the question of statesmanship is one that need not be debated here.

CHAPTER XXVI

ABANDONED

I DO not propose to tell the story of that expedition which was the immediate outcome of the policy of " Rescue and Retire." But it is worth while to review Lord Wolseley's instructions from the Ministry. As I need hardly remind my readers, they were the result of a consultation between Lord Northbrook, Lord Wolseley, and Sir Evelyn Baring. Apologists of the future will find it difficult either to excuse them or explain. It is laid down that the primary object of the expedition is the relief of Khartoum and the rescue of General Gordon and Colonel Stewart. It follows that the garrisons in Darfour, the Bahr el Gazelle, and Equatorial Africa are to be abandoned ; that the Sennaar contingent, however perilous its position, is to be left to its own devices ; and that Kassala, after negotiation from Suakim and Massawa, is to be abandoned to the clemency of the investing tribes. Lord Wolseley is to do his best to compass the safe retreat of the Egyptian troops in Khartoum, with such of the civil employés and their families as may desire to return to Cairo ; but though offensive operations are permitted for the extrication of Gordon and Stewart, the release of their aids and lieges is made dependent upon the success or failure of conciliatory measures. Lord Wolseley may fight for Gordon and Stewart ; for their soldiers, he is first of all to negotiate. Only when the diplomatist has failed, must the general come in. With a touch of Dodson and Fogg, he is to combine the aspirations of Wellington and Mr. Henry Richard. What he has in charge is not the honour of England, but her own pecuniary responsibilities and the quicksand of her rulers' " principles."

Nor is this the worst. This precious document breathes of illusion and inspired statesmanship throughout. H.M. Government will be glad to see a condition of order established at

Khartoum which, so far as all matters connected with the internal administration of the country are concerned, shall be wholly independent of Egypt, though the Egyptian Government are prepared to pay a reasonable subsidy to any chief, or number of chiefs, sufficiently powerful to maintain order along the Nile valley, from Wady Halfa to Khartoum, and sufficiently agreed among themselves to keep the peace, encourage trade with Egypt, and discourage by every possible means all expeditions for the capture of slaves. This is of course a metamorphosis of our old friend, the hard and fast line of policy, this time without the saving grace of evacuation; and this, as I need hardly remark, is the strong delusion against which Gordon had been steadily warning the Ministry from the day he set foot in Khartoum. Mark Twain's blue jay dropped innumerable acorns through a knot-hole in the roof of a log-house, under the impression that he was not dispersing his treasures in space, but making himself a hoard in a snug, peculiar crevice. Under a kindred impression, and with similar results, did H.M. Government proceed in Egypt. Almost from the beginning the cry of their Envoy at Khartoum had been this : "You can do nothing until you have 'smashed up' the Mahdi;" and now they were expending their strength in establishing the very power it was imperative upon them to destroy. The man they had sent out to withdraw the garrisons and evacuate the country had become the centre and rallying point of all the loyal souls about him; he was nevertheless to be rescued from this glorious position, and that by a force which was great and strong enough to achieve the succour of every Egyptian subject in the Soudan, but which was yet to cease from offensive operations on the instant of his rescue, and offer to the world the strange and perplexing spectacle of a British army refraining, unconcerned and idle, from any interference in the affairs of men in distress until that moment the comrades in duty and devotion of the most famous soldier in their own ranks. And then, this wonderful rescue accomplished, Lord Wolseley was to retire, and leave the Soudanese to the Mahdi and themselves.

H.M. Government were not anxious about the results. It was felt that something would turn up, which something would in no wise hamper the Chancellor of the Exchequer in the preparation of his next Budget, and in no wise traverse the famous policy of peace, retrenchment, and reform, on whose lines it was understood they were always trying to proceed ; and that was enough. They threw the puzzle into the air, and hoped to see its pieces come down in proper order, all accurately fitted together into an allegorical picture of economy, happiness, and universal suffrage. In this singular illusion H.M. Government persisted till the end; they had created it for themselves, and they had in it the pride of the author in his work. They were warned from Khartoum, and warned repeatedly; but, as is the wont of amateurs, they were contemptuous of professional opinion, and impatient of professional control. Their sympathies lay with the Mahdi (who was a religious man), and the "young nationality" as whose apostle he appeared. Gordon had nothing to back him but facts; and what are facts compared with principles and ideas? Moreover, their supporters thought him a little mad, and said so; and, after denying him publicly, and publicly repudiating their covenant with him, they had themselves advised him to desert his post and shift for himself, and he had been selfish enough to refuse. It was plain that in electing to rescue him at a cost of ten or twenty millions, they were doing as much as could be expected of them: that is to say, a great deal more than any but the best of all possible Governments in the best of all possible worlds would ever have consented to do.

A long silence was broken at last by a series of telegrams received at Massawa on the 25th of September, and at Cairo on the 5th October. Of these, three were dated April 27th, the two others the 30th and 31st of July; and though the intelligence conveyed in the earlier ones was superseded by Mr. Power's communication to the *Times* (already quoted *in extenso*), it is important to our history to reproduce in full—at least, as far as Ministerial "editing" will permit—whatever Gordon has to say.

"GENERAL GORDON TO SIR E. BARING.

"In rebel display to-day, the 21st April 1884, rebels fired two shots from their gun, from their camp. Thermometer, 92 degrees.

"*April 22nd.*—A lieutenant and two soldiers escaped from rebels; no news of import. We put down mines at village half-hour outside south lines. Spy reports Shendy is invested; if it is taken it is entirely due to you not sending up Zebehr Pasha. If it was justifiable to allow him to raise blacks and herd them down to the slaughter of Trinkitat, it would have been equally so to let him collect men for the Soudan. Steamer attacked rebels, drove them back with loss, and captured three camels, thirty goats. Nile began to rise to-day ; this is in advance of usual period. In rebel camp are rumours Abyssinian advance, which I trust, for honour of England, are not true, for what has Abyssinia to do with this question ? It is like a big boy getting a little boy to fight his battles.

"*April 23rd.*—Nile still rising. Thunderstorms in all directions at night. The rising of Nile will enable steamers to destroy irrigating machines along river banks, and thus prevent any cultivation. I will pardon peoples who give in allegiance ; if they do not, I will liberate their slaves. Thunderstorms over town and in every direction.

"*April 24th.*—Rain during night. Thermometer, 90 degrees. Report says that an expedition started with seventy of our captured soldiers, rockets, and guns, from Obeid, against Saleh Pasha ; that the regular soldiers feigned an attack against Saleh, and turned on the rebels, going over to Saleh, with guns, etc. This, if true, will effectually prevent Mahdi trying this again. On Greek Consul's recommendation, we have issued notes for payment of troops. Rebels made one of their distant attacks on Omdurman."

Still, despite his treatment by the Government, Gordon was full of hope; and some idea of his cheerfulness may be gathered from the following letters addressed by him to the officer commanding Royal Navy at Massawa :—

"KHARTOUM, *August* 24*th*, 1884.

"Received cipher despatch from you and Egerton, dated 27th April 1884. We have had a series of petty fights with Arabs from the 12th March to the 30th July, when we were able, thank God ! to drive them back and open road to Sennaar, and we are now relieved from the immediate pressure of Arabs. We are going to attack them to-morrow, and meditate a raid on Berber in order to let pass to Dongola a convoy which accompanies Colonel Stewart and French and English Consuls. We shall (*D.V.*) destroy Berber and return to our pirate nest here. Our steamers are blinded and bullet-proof, and do splendid work, for you see when you have steam on the men cannot run away and must go into action. I hope the *Euryalus* are all well, and hope you like Massowah in September. We are going to hold out here for ever, and are pretty evenly matched with Mahdi. He has cavalry and we have steamers. We are very cross with you all, for since 29th March we have had not one word from outer world. I have paid as much as £140 for a spy, and you gave that poor devil (so he says) 20 dollars to go from Massowah to Khartoum. However, I have given him £20. One of our steamers has 970 bullet marks on her; another 850 ditto. Our losses have been slight. We have provisions for five months, and hope to get in more. Stewart got wounded in arm, but is all right. The rôle of our country has not been very noble in Egypt or Soudan. I wish I had three or four of your gunners, for our practice is dismal. Kindest regards to all your officers.

" C. G. GORDON."

" KHARTOUM, August 26th, 1884.

"In continuation of letter of the 24th August 1884, in which I told you of our attack on Arabs which we meditated. We have (thank God!) succeeded taking Arab camp and killing Arab Commander-in-Chief (<i>R.I.P.</i>). I do not know our losses as yet. This victory clears our vicinity on three parts of circle. The Arab defeat may be put down to the defection of a part of their forces who came over to us at the moment of attack. The naval forces behaved splendidly, which will, of course, please my friends of Her Majesty's Navy. Remember me to Drury, Carter, Leslie, Target, Stopford, if still on board <i>Euryalus</i>.

"You would all delight to be here, and I wish you were, if it was possible.

"There is one bond of union between us and our troops: they know if the town is taken they will be sold as slaves, and we must deny our Lord if we would save our lives.

"I think we hate the latter more than they hate the former. <i>D.V.</i>, we will defeat them without any help from outside. Spies from Kordofan report advance of Mahdi with twenty-six guns towards Khartoum. I have always thought this is probable, and that the question will be solved here; but I trust he will not succeed, for we have made the place very strong; if he fails he is done for.

" C. G. GORDON."

"<i>April</i> 27th.—Usual Friday church parade. Not many rebels in south front. A party crept down into village opposite palace and fired volleys, but did no harm. Yesterday steamers went up White Nile, and captured 4 cows, 2 donkeys, 25 sheep, and 3 prisoners, killing 7. We are sending out negroes to entice the slaves of rebels to come to us on promise of freedom. The general opinion is, that all the slaves will desert by degrees, and that the rebels will leave this dangerous vicinity, not for fear of bullets, but for fear of losing their live chattels. We will take the slaves into Government service, giving them their freedom, clothes, and pay; they get nothing from rebels. It may be the beginning of end of slave-holding up here. If you cannot read this telegram make the clerk repeat it, and ask Floyer to order the original European telegrams to be sent down by post.

"*April* 26*th*.—Issued banknotes to amount of £2500, redeemable in six months. I heard from Kassala to-day, dated the 13th April; it is all right. Some English authority has threatened the Beni Amr tribe, north of Kassala, the Sheikh writes to me. This tribe has always been a good one; send a kind message to the Sheikh from me. One of our soldiers who formed part of expedition from Kordofan sent against Saleh Pasha with two guns and one rocket has escaped. He says that the expedition consists of 1000 men, 100 of whom are my soldiers of Soudan, who sent to say they will turn on the rebels when they fight. He says Slatin Bey still holds out, and that Mahdi is fighting in Kordofan with some tribes who have revolted. We are making decorations for defence of Khartoum—a crescent and star, with words from Koran and date, so we count on victory—officers, silver; men, copper. You will not be asked to pay for them.

"*April* 27*th*.—We are all well and strong.

"C. G. GORDON."

"GENERAL GORDON TO SIR E. BARING AND NUBAR PASHA.

"KHARTOUM, *July* 30*th*, 1884.

"Your telegram of the 5th May, 1884, received.

"Thanks for kind expressions. Nile now high, and we hope to open route to Sennaar in few days. We have had no serious losses. Stewart was slightly wounded in arm near palace; he is all right now. Be assured that these hostilities are far from being sought for, but we have no option, for retreat is impossible unless we abandon civil employés and their families, which the general feeling of troops is against. I have no advice to give; if we open Sennaar and clear Blue Nile we will be strong enough to retake Berber, that is if Dongola still holds out. As for Mahdi, he will not send succour here. Not one pound of the money you gave me got here; it was captured at Berber. We want £200,000 sent to Kassala. The expenses of these garrisons must be met.

Khartoum costs £500 per diem. If route gets open to Kassala I shall send Stewart there, with journal—that is, if he will consent to go. You may rely on this, that if there was any possible way of avoiding the wretched fighting I should adopt it, for the whole war is hateful to me. The people refuse to let me go out on expeditions, owing to the bother which would arise if anything happened, so I sit on tenter-hooks of anxiety. If I could make anyone chief here I would do it, but it is impossible, for all the good men were killed with Hicks. To show you that Arabs fire well, two of our steamers which are blinded received 970 and 860 hits in their hulls respectively. Since our defeat of the 16th March 1884, had only thirty killed, fifty or sixty wounded, which is very little. I should think we have fired half a million cartridges. The conduct of people and troops has been excellent. I was thinking of issuing proclamation liberating the slaves of those in arms, but have deferred doing so for fear of complication. I have great trust that God will bring us out triumphantly, and with no great loss on either side. We have queer stories as to fall of Berber. Arabs captured there all Stewart's hussar uniform, and my medals, etc. It may be bad taste to say it, but if we get out of this give Stewart a K.C.M.G., and spare me at all costs. You will thus save me the disagreeableness of having to refuse, but I hate these things. If we get out it is in answer to prayer, and not by our might, and it is a true pleasure to have been here, though painful enough at times. Stewart's journal is copious. I only hope it will get down to you when I send it. Land mines are the things for defence in future; we have covered the works with them, and they have deterred all attacks and done much execution.

"Since the 30th March 1884, date of your Cairo despatch, we have had no news from you. Seyd Mahomet Osman, of Kassala, ought to be the route for your despatches, and you ought to give him a present of £500, for he saved Kassala. We have made a decoration, with three degrees, silver gilt, silver, and pewter, with inscription, 'Siege of Khartoum,' with a grenade in centre. School children and women have also received one ; consequently I am very popular with the black ladies of Khartoum. We have issued paper notes to amount of £26,000, and borrowed £50,000 from merchants, which you will have to meet. I have sent in addition £8000 paper notes to Sennaar. What Kassala is doing for money I do not know ; of course we only get taxes paid in lead, so you are running up a good bill up here. The troops and people are full of heart; I cannot say the same for all the Europeans. The Arabs are in poor heart. I should say that about 2000 determined men alone keep them in the field. I expect it will end in a terrible famine throughout the land. Spy yesterday stated the 'Queen of England' had arrived at Korosko. Perhaps it is a steamer. The only reinforcements the Soudan has received since the 27th November 1883, date when Hicks' defeat was known at Cairo, is seven persons, including myself! and we have sent down over 600 soldiers and 2000 people. The people here and Arabs laugh over it. I shall not leave Khartoum until I can put someone in. If the Europeans like to go to the Equator, I will give them steamers, but I will not leave these people after all they have gone through. As for routes, I have told you that the one from Wady Halfa along right bank of Nile to Berber is the best, and, had not Berber fallen, would have been a picnic. The other route is from Senhit to Kassala, and to Abou Haraz on Blue Nile, which would be safe up to Kassala, but I fear it is too late. We must fight it out with our own means : if blessed by God, we shall succeed ; if not His will, so be it. The main thing is to send money to Kassala. Where is Wood? Kind regards to him and Generals Stephenson and Graham. Why write in cipher. It is useless, for Arabs have no interpreter. You say your feeling is to abandon Soudan; so be it, but before you do that you must take down Egyptian population, and this the Arabs do not see. According to all accounts, 5000 were massacred at Berber. All is for the best. I will conclude in saying we will defend ourselves to the last; that I will not leave Khartoum ; that I will try and persuade all Europeans to escape, and that I am still sanguine that, by some means not clear, God will give us an issue. What was result of your negotiations for opening road Suakim to Berber? The Arabs captured the money (you gave me) at Berber, but it is only the money which the Egyptian Pashas have ground out of the Soudan since their occupation.

"C. G. GORDON.

"*P.S.—July* 31*st*, 1884.—Reading over your telegram of the 5th May 1884, you ask me ' to state cause and intention in staying at Khartoum, knowing Government means to abandon Soudan,' and in answer I say, I stay at Khartoum because Arabs have shut us up, and will not let us out. I also add that even if the road was opened the people would not let me go unless I gave them some

government or took them with me, which I could not do. No one would leave more willingly than I would if it was possible.
"C. G. G."

"KHARTOUM, *July* 31*st*, 1884.

"We continue, thank God, to drive Arabs back up Blue Nile, and hope to open road to Sennaar in eight days or less, and to recapture small steamer lost by Saleh Bey. We then hope to send an expedition to surprise and recapture Berber. It is a *sine quâ non* that you send me Zebehr; otherwise my stay here is indefinite. And you should send £50,000 to Dongola, to be forwarded to Berber if we take it. River begins to fall in, say, four months. Before that time you must either let the Sultan take back the Soudan, or send Zebehr, with a subsidy yearly. *D. V.*, we will send down to Berber to take to it the Egyptian troops here, so that they will be on their way home; and I shall send Stewart. We hope (*D.V.*) to recapture the two steamers which were lost at Berber on its fall.

"The Equator and Bahr Gazelle provinces can be (*D.V.*) relieved later on, and their troops brought here. As to Darfour, it must be afterwards thought of, for we do not know if it still holds out. As for Kordofan, I hope and believe the Mahdi has his hands full. I would vacate Sennaar if it was possible, but I do not think it is, and also the moral effect of its evacuation would be fatal to our future success, while we have not food to feed the refugee people who would come here. You will see, if we open road to Sennaar from here, we cut the Arab movement in two by Blue Nile. I repeat, I have no wish to retain this country. My sole desire is to restore the prestige of the Government in order to get out garrisons, and to put some ephemeral government in position, in order to get away.
(Signed)   "C. G. GORDON."

These telegrams, as I have said, were handed in on the 5th October at Cairo, but nearly three weeks before two important messages from Gordon were received by the Privy Seal of the Khedive. They were in Arabic, and the only clue to their date was a reference to the fall of Berber, which showed that they had been written after May 20th. In the first Gordon states, as his reason for demanding reinforcements, that on his arrival at Khartoum he found it impossible to withdraw the soldiers and

employés, on account of the rising of the tribes and the sever-
ance of his communications. No heed, he adds, was paid to his
demands, and the result was the fall of Berber. He goes on to
put a most significant question : " Is it right," he asks, " that I
should have been sent to Khartoum with only seven followers
after the destruction of Hicks's army, and no attention paid to
me till communications were cut ? " The question is not personal.
Gordon does not mean to ask if this was right towards himself,
but if it was right towards the great cause in which he was
engaged, and for which he had jeopardised his life. A later
message, dated August 23rd, clearly shows what, in his opinion,
had resulted from the conduct thus challenged. It was now
necessary, he said, that English troops be sent to the Soudan,
and that Zebehr Pasha be appointed in his room, with an assistant, and a salary of £8000 a year; that not before the arrival of
an English army would the Egyptian troops be able to return
down the Nile; that if after this the Sultan wanted the Soudan
he could have it at the cost of 20,000 men; and that if no part
of this advice were taken, H.M. Government would be responsible
for his Egyptians' salaries and lives. The time when a handful
of British soldiers at Wady Halfa could have settled the Soudan,
was passed; the time when Zebehr's influence alone could have
been successfully pitted against the Mahdi's was passed likewise;
and now the solution of the problem meant the employment
either of Zebehr and an assistant with a backing of British
bayonets, or the permanent and sanctioned interference of the Turk.

Lord Wolseley was already on his way to Dongola when this
intelligence was conveyed to H.M. Government; and once again
were the pubic exercised in spirit as to the reason—the amazing
and impenetrable reason — why their rulers, not content with
questioning their Envoy, religiously insisted upon stopping their
ears to his replies. It was evident that Gordon's mission was a
failure, and it was as evident that it was so by no fault of
Gordon's. The paper plan of action drawn up in Downing Street
had been found impracticable at Khartoum. With certain altera-
tions, it might have worked; but these involved the immediate
expenditure of several thousands of pounds and a risk of future
political complications, and they were indignantly refused. The
inspired statesmanship by which this refusal was dictated was
ere long to cost the country many millions of pounds and the
world some thousands of lives, the noblest of these times among
them.

CHAPTER XXVII

In a despatch already quoted, Gordon announced his intention of
sending Stewart and Power to Berber "in order to open communications with Dongola, and in order to carry on the necessary
discussions in connection with the Soudan." This was confirmed
in the following message to Nubar Pasha, received later and dated
Aug. 23rd:—"To-day I have appointed the three steamers to
inspect the situation of Sennaar and to discover its news. On
their return here, I will detail a military force from Khartoum,
composed of 2000 men, and send it by steamers to Berber to
retake it from the hands of the rebels, with provisions for two
months only. We will send with this force his Excellency
Stewart Pasha, Sub-Governor, and all the Consuls here existing.
After the recapture of Berber, the troops and Consuls will remain
there, while his Excellency Stewart Pasha will proceed to Dongola
by a small boat especially dedicated (prepared?) for his voyage to
that direction, to parley on the Soudan question, and what the
situation of Berber will come to. These troops will leave for
Berber after fifteen days from this date."

Gordon's motive was twofold : he wanted to give his comrades
a chance of life and freedom on the one hand, and, on the other,
he purposed to collect such information as would stir the Government to some kind of action. But his prudence was unavailing ;
his magnanimity went unrewarded save with sorrow. The detachment marched on September 10th, 1884 ; and when the rebel
positions had been destroyed the main body returned to Khartoum,
while Stewart, Power, and about forty others, steamed down the
river for Dongola.

Early in October Major Kitchener sent home the news of
their fortune. The steamer had run aground, and the whole
party had been cut off. For a little while it was hoped that

Stewart had escaped with life, but by the end of the month all doubt was at an end. It was positively known that both he and Power had perished with the rest, and that H.M. Government might be credited with the authorship of a massacre the more. It was not on so large a scale as those at Sinkat and Tokar; but it included a couple of Englishmen, and that was enough to make it memorable. Stewart, like his chief, had gone out at a moment's notice, and like him he had fought as became an Englishman, against the odds for which, in their policy of impotence, H.M.'s Government were responsible. He had never seen his chief till the night of the 18th January, when they left London together on their desperate adventure; but the dream of his life had been to serve under Gordon's orders, and Gordon, when asked at Downing Street to choose his lieutenant, chose him upon the spot. He knew his man, and loved him; and that was enough. "Be sure," he said to a friend, on the platform at Charing Cross, "be sure that he will not go into any danger which I do not share; and I am sure that when I am in danger he will not be far behind." And it was, as I have said, in the hope of saving his valiant lieutenant from what by this time he had come to regard as the inevitable end, that Gordon sent him out of Khartoum. He despaired of life, and preferred to meet his fate alone.

It was through Lord Wolseley, then at Wady Halfa, that our worst anticipations were confirmed. He instituted an investigation; and towards the end of October he sent the following telegrams to Sir Evelyn Baring: — "Two messengers sent to inquire as to the fate of Colonel Stewart's party have returned. They report that the steamer was towing two boats containing M. Naoom, with his brother and family. As the enemy was found to be overtaking them, the convoy boats were cut adrift, and all on board of them were made prisoners. Shortly afterwards the steamer struck on a rock near Catadîch. There were at this time forty-five persons on board, four of whom were women. Colonel Stewart and two Consuls, one of whom was named Nicola, were among those on board. The whole party, except two natives, were killed by Sheikh Suleiman. This information was obtained from one of the two survivors by the messsenger. The man said that Colonel Stewart, whom he described as a tall man with a light beard, was certainly on board the steamer." It was not, however, till four months later that the full truth was known. Then Hussein, the stoker of Stewart's steamer, escaped from the enemy, and came into our camp. This

is the story he told :—The party had left Khartoum in September.
There were with them two other steamers. On board the *Abdai*
were Colonel Stewart, two Pashas, two European Consuls, Hassan
Bey, twelve Greeks, and some Egyptian soldiers, besides the crew.
When they reached Berber they shelled the forts there. After
this the other steamers went back. They came on down the
Nile. Nothing happened until they had passed Abu Hamed, but
on September 18th the steamer struck on a rock. They were
then passing through Wad Gamr's country. As they had passed
down they had seen the people running away into the hills on
both sides of the river. When it was found that the steamer
could not be got off the rock, the small boat, filled with useful
things, was sent to a little island near. Four trips were made.
Then Colonel Stewart himself spiked the guns and threw them
overboard, and also two boxes of ammunition. The people now
came down to the right bank in great numbers, shouting "Give
us peace and grain." Stewart's party answered, "Peace." Suleiman Wad Gamr himself was in a small house near the bank, and
he came out and called to Colonel Stewart to land without fear,
but said that the soldiers must be unarmed or the people would
be afraid of them. Colonel Stewart, after talking it over with
the others, then crossed in the boats, with the two English
Consuls and Hassan Bey, and entered the house of a blind man,
Fakir Etman, to arrange with Suleiman for the purchase of
camels to take the party down to Dongola. None of the four had
any arms, with the exception of Colonel Stewart, who carried a
small revolver in his pocket. While they were in the house the
rest began to land in the boat. After a little time these saw
Suleiman come out of the house, with a copper water-pot in his
hand. He made signs to the people, who were all gathered near
the house. They immediately divided into two parties, one
entering the house, the other rushing down towards those
gathered on the bank, shouting and waving their spears. Hussein
was with the party who had landed when they charged down,
and on seeing the move he and the rest threw themselves into
the river. The natives fired, killing some of the swimmers;
many others were drowned, and the rest speared as they came
near the bank. Hussein swam to the island, and hid there till
dark, when he was made prisoner with some others, and sent to
Berti. He heard that Colonel Stewart and the two Englishmen
were killed at once. Hassan Bey held the blind man before him,
so that they could not spear him. They spared his life, and he

afterwards escaped to Berber. Two artillerymen, two sailors, and three natives, were detained at Berber, where they were sent by Suleiman. All the money found on board and in the victims' pockets was divided among the men who did the murder. Everything else of value was placed in two boxes and sent under a guard to Berber. The bodies of Stewart, Power, and the others were thrown into the river.[1]

So now Gordon was alone, the only Englishman in the Equatorial citadel. Hunger and doubt were sore upon him and upon his people. But they still loved and believed in him, though, as he said, alluding to the long-delayed relief, " we appeared even as liars to the people of Khartoum." "While you are eating, drinking, and resting on good beds," he writes, " we, and those with us, both soldiers and servants, are watching by night and day, endeavouring to quell the movement of this false Mahdi." The old men and women had gone, and Gordon pulled down the empty quarters of the town, and walled in the rest. Meantime he had built himself a tower of observation, from the top of which he could command the whole country round. At dawn he slept; by day he went the rounds, looked to his defences, administered justice, cheered the spirit of his people, did such battle as he could with famine and discontent; and every night he mounted to the top of his tower, and there, alone with his duty and his God, a universal sentinel, he kept watch over his ramparts, and prayed for the help that never came. Of his thoughts and sufferings during these tremendous vigils who now shall tell?

Stewart's death had hardly been confirmed, when the most alarming rumours went afloat concerning the condition of Khartoum. They were French in origin and feeling—that is to say, they were at once unkindly and discreditable; but such was the public anxiety about Gordon that for a time they were fully believed. They indeed achieved such a point of verisimilitude that they deceived a number of the wisest. The best journals circulated a story about the Khedive having telegraphed to the Queen and Prince of Wales news of Gordon's capture by the Mahdi. In addition to this, a very circumstantial account of the fall of Khartoum came from Cairo, and, as a crowning sensation, it was averred that Gordon had exploded his mines, and blown himself and great numbers of the enemy into the air. One result of these reports was a touching tribute from his old friends

[1] See Appendix 14.

the Chinese.   On the announcement reaching Canton that General Gordon had been killed in the Soudan, the Viceroy paraded the garrison, who fired volleys as if over his grave, while the squadron in the river lowered their flags to half-mast, and fired minute guns.

To this time of doubt there succeeded a time of confidence and hope.   On the 14th November a messenger from Major Kitchener arrived at Dongola with a long letter from Gordon to Lord Wolseley, dated November 4th, and a set of cipher despatches for the Government.   Their contents were not disclosed, but the public were allowed to know that all was well at Khartoum, and that the hero hoped to hold out till the arrival of the expedition.   He had heard of Colonel Stewart's death, for which he expressed great grief; and the Mahdi was eight hours distant from Khartoum.   These statements the Mudir of Dongola was able to confirm.   He had received a message from Gordon promoting him and his fellow notables a step in rank, and exhorting him to fight to the last, as he himself intended to do. From the messenger himself the Mudir learned that the General had illuminated Khartoum in honour of Lord Wolseley and his men.   It was further reported that there was plenty of food, and that thirty boats had come in laden with grain from the Blue Nile on the day of the messenger's departure.   The price of corn, he said, was thirty shillings per ardeb, or forty-five shillings per quarter.   He added that Gordon was very powerful, and was believed in by every man in the city.   Soon after, another messenger stated that Gordon had even been joined by deserters from the Mahdi's camp; that he was making his own powder; that he had twelve steamers afloat and at work; and that the people were beginning to consider his rule preferable to that of the False Prophet's.

All this was significant of great activity on Gordon's part. Its import had not been lost on the Mahdi.   That leader, seeing that he must strike a decisive blow at once, or lose his ground for ever in the Soudan, marched up from Obeid with some thirty thousand men, took his stand at Omdurman, within a few miles of the beleaguered city, and summoned the Englishman to surrender. This was the answer: "If you are the real Mahdi, dry up the Nile and come over, and I'll surrender."   The challenge, it is said, was taken seriously, and the Mahdi bidding his followers walk across the Nile, three thousand perished in the attempt.   After this he at once began the attack.   But Gordon, with his twelve steamers and eight hundred devoted followers, after eight hours' hard fighting outside the walls, succeeded, by means of mines, in blowing up his forts, and drove him out of Omdurman, southward to a place called El Margat. There the defeated pretender went into hiding in a cave, and prophesied to the effect that there should be sixty days of rest, and that after these blood would flow like water.

Now, in Gordon's letter of November 4th[1] to Lord Wolseley, he said two things which (with others) H.M. Government thought fit to suppress. They were: that he had just enough provisions to last him forty days; and that he had sent certain of his steamers down the Nile towards Shendy to await the arrival of the expedition. These facts, hitherto not made known, are most important.

The progress of the expedition, up to this point, had by no means justified the calculations of those who planned it. From time to time the public had been treated to a number of ingenious prognostications of the date of its arrival. First it was said that our troops would be before the gates of Khartoum on January 14th; next it was the middle of February; and then the time stretched out to the middle of March. But signs of greater haste were soon apparent. Lord Wolseley offered a hundred pounds to the regiment covering the distance from Sarras to Debbeh most expeditiously, and with least damage to boats; and this was regarded as having extraordinary significance. He also despatched Sir Herbert Stewart on the immortal march to Gakdul. Stewart's force, composed principally of the Mounted Infantry and Camel Corps, and led by a troop of the 19th Hussars, acting as scouts—numbering about eleven hundred in all—set out from Korti on December 30th. Its destination was about one hundred miles from headquarters, and about eighty from the Nile at Shendy. The enterprise, difficult and desperate as it was, was achieved with perfect success. Stewart himself returned to Korti on January 5th, with a cheerful report as to supplies and position. He had established at Hambok a post to improve the water supply, and had left the Guards at Gakdul strongly fortified in an impregnable position. A strong convoy was now sent to the latter place, and General Stewart himself started with another for Metemneh. Altogether the prospect was hopeful enough; and to add to the general satisfaction, certain Arabs seized on the way had flung off the Mahdi's uniform and spat upon it, declaring that they would never have

[1] See Appendix 15.

joined the False Prophet had they known the English were
coming. All, indeed, were in dread of being shot or hanged. The
English army, they said, would meet with no resistance on the
way to Khartoum ; and General Gordon's steamers were waiting
on the Nile.

On the 17th January Sir Herbert Stewart engaged the enemy
on the road to Metemneh, and, after defeating some ten thousand
Arabs, collected from Berber, Metemneh, and Omdurman, pushed
forward to the Abu Klea Wells. His tactics were much the
same as those of General Graham at El Teb; and those of the
Mahdi's men—of attacking when thirst and fatigue had well-nigh
prostrated the force—were at all points similar to those adopted
against Hicks. Our losses were 65 non-commissioned officers and
men killed, and 85 wounded, with 9 officers killed—among them
Colonel Burnaby—and 9 wounded. Stewart at once pushed on
for Metemneh and the Nile. He left the Wells on the 18th
January to occupy Metemneh if possible, but, failing that, to
make for the Nile and entrench himself. After a night's march,
some five miles south of Metemneh, the column found itself in
presence of an enemy said to have been about eighteen thousand
strong. Stewart halted, and formed a zareba under a deadly fire.
He himself was mortally hurt in the groin, and Mr. Cameron, of
the *Standard*, and Mr. Herbert, of the *Morning Post*, were killed.
The zareba completed, the column advanced in square, and the
Arabs, profiting by Abu Klea, moved forward in echelon,
apparently with the purpose of charging. At thirty yards or so
they were brought to bay, so terrific was the fire from the square,
and so splendidly served was Norton's artillery. For two hours
the battle raged ; and then the Arabs, " mown down in heaps,"
gave way. Meantime Sir Charles Wilson had made a dash for
the Nile, where he found steamers and reinforcements from
Gordon, and the laconic message, " All right at Khartoum. Can
hold out for years."

Apparently a more fitting climax to that terrible day (the
20th) could not have been. With Sir Charles Wilson steaming
up to the gates of Khartoum in Gordon's own steamers, and the
city able to " hold out for years," nothing seemed wanting to make
the expedition a triumph. " Gordon and Wolseley have touched
hands," we said ; and the whole world (France excepted) looked
on and shouted with delight. In the joy at the good news, none
had stopped to consider the true meaning of the message, " All
right. Can hold out for years ;" for none was aware that nearly

two months before, Gordon had said he had just provisions enough for forty days, and that what he really meant was that he had come to his last biscuit. The message—which was written for the enemy—was dated December 29, and Sir Charles Wilson would reach Khartoum on January 28, just a month after its despatch.

The world knew nothing of all this, and rejoiced in the prospect of their hero's relief; but the anxiety of his immediate friends was intense. It was founded on their private knowledge, which, with Lord Wolseley's action, betrayed the fact that there was imminent and instant danger. A messenger who brought in a letter (written for the enemy, and dated Khartoum, December 14th), which said, "Khartoum all right," had a confidential despatch to the Commander-in-Chief whose tenor was as follows :—

"We are besieged on three sides, Omdurman, Halfaya, and Hoggi-Ali. Fighting goes on day and night. Enemy cannot take us except by starving us out. Do not scatter your troops. Enemy are numerous. Bring plenty of troops if you can. We still hold Omdurman on the left bank and the fort on the right bank.

"The Mahdi's people have thrown up earthworks within rifle-shot of Omdurman. The Mahdi lives out of gunshot.

"About four weeks ago the Mahdi's people attacked Omdurman and disabled one steamer. We disabled one of Mahdi's guns.

"Three days after, fighting was renewed on the south, and rebels were again driven back.

"Saleh Bey and Slaten Bey are chained in Mahdi's camp.

"Our troops in Khartoum are suffering from lack of provisions. Food we still have is little ; some grain and biscuit.

"We want you to come quickly. You should come by Metemneh or Berber. Make by these two roads. Do not leave Berber in your rear. Keep enemy in your front, and when you have taken Berber send me word from Berber.

"Do this without letting rumours of your approach spread abroad.

"In Khartoum there are no butter nor dates, and little meat. All food is very dear."

The public, carefully kept in ignorance of these necessities, and hopeful beyond their wont, were simply stupefied to hear, on Feb. 5, that Khartoum was in the hands of the Mahdi, and Gordon captured or dead. The news fell on them like a bolt from a clear sky. Sir Charles Wilson, detached to the relief of the beleaguered city after the battle of Metemneh, and journeying thither in one of Gordon's own steamers, for reasons not hitherto explained, delayed his start too long, and arrived on the scene of action two days too late. He found the streets of the fallen city crowded with rebels; the Government House, its flagstaff naked, was wrecked. Of Gordon there was nowhere any sign. He had to escape back down the Nile as best he could, under a heavy fire from both banks. "We could not land under such opposition," says Lieutenant Stewart-Wortley in his report to Lord Wolseley of these events, "so turned round and ran down stream. No flags flying from Government House in Khartoum, and the house appeared wrecked. Only one man killed and five wounded in steamers. On Jan. 31 the steamer on which were Sir C. Wilson and all his party was wrecked about four miles above enemy's position below bottom of Shabluka Cataract. The other steamer had been previously wrecked on Jan. 29. We reached Gubat in small boats at 2 P.M. the same day." Fall of Khartoum on Jan. 26 he reports to be without doubt; "but fate of Gordon uncertain, as reports are conflicting, but general opinion is he is killed, but no preponderance of evidence either way. Some say he is shut up in church at Khartoum, with some Greeks. Fall of Khartoum has determined Shukriyeh tribes to join the Mahdi, so east bank of Nile as well as left bank is now hostile to us. The fear of the English is great among the natives. General Earle's advance awaited with anxiety by them. Natives say Mahdi was very hard pressed for supplies at Omdurman. It is said by natives that he will have great difficulty in persuading his Emirs to attack us. Messenger from the Mahdi reached Sir C. Wilson when in steamer on Jan. 29, telling him Gordon had adopted Mahdi's uniform, and calling upon us to surrender; that he would not write again, but if we did not become Mohammedans he would wipe us off the face of the earth. It is said that Faragh Pasha treacherously made terms with Mahdi, and opened the gates of the city to Mahdi's troops."

The release of Sir Charles Wilson and his party seems to have exercised the official mind far more than the fall of Khartoum or the fate of Gordon; yet the position, perilous for a few hours, was scarcely comparable to that which the English Envoy had been constrained by his employers to take up and defend during the whole of the past year. While only Arabs could be spared to collect details about the fall of Khartoum, Englishmen hastened to Tuti Island to rescue the belated expedition. So that, while

the whole world waited breathless for news of Gordon, our correspondents had no voice save for the brilliant little feat of arms by
which Lord Charles Beresford delivered Gordon's would - be
deliverers.

The news was true: Gordon was dead. The Nemesis had
come at last. Napoleon gilded the dome of the Invalides to
divert the mind of France from the consideration of his flight
from Moscow; and Mr. Gladstone, hungering for peace and
security in office, his conscience sophisticated to the highest
capacity of self-delusion, had masked his desertion of Gordon in
a new Franchise Bill demonstration and a second Midlothian
campaign, and, deceived in these, had achieved a spectacular
expedition for the relief of an Envoy who had protested against
being relieved. "Your expedition," Gordon had said in the suppressed letter of November 4 to Lord Wolseley, "is for relief of
garrison which I failed to accomplish. I decline to agree that it
is for me personally." Now the bubble had burst, and the whole
object of the expedition had vanished into space. His choice of
the Nile route notwithstanding, no layman had in his mind to
blame Lord Wolseley, nor any of those entrusted with the task of
getting the expedition to its journey's end; but the Government
were not so fortunate. Their indifference was patent; the stupid
selfishness by which their schemes of policy and no policy had
been dictated was miserably apparent; and by all, save the dolts
and formalists who could see no wrong in anything that Mr.
Gladstone did, they were charged with the authorship of this
heavy calamity. Gordon had asked them nothing they had not
refused, had offered no suggestion they had not contumeliously
put by. He had stood to his post like a soldier and a gentleman;
and they had looked on from afar, counselling the shame of flight
while counsel was possible, and electioneering and talking nonsense
to the mob when the isolation of Khartoum was accomplished,
and their Envoy, having so far forgotten their transcendent merits
as to find fault with them, had become of greater account to the
country than themselves. It was common talk that to their great
leaders, rapt in that ecstasy of self-approval to which the Empire
is indebted for so much fine principle and bad statecraft, Gordon—
refusing alike to run away or get himself killed, and demonstrating
publicly that duty and honour are facts beyond the touch of
sophistry—was not merely an eyesore in the fair prospect of
Egyptian business, but a living impeachment, a personal and
peculiar reproach. It was suspected, and that not silently, that

their desertion had been wilful, their inability to make up their minds apparent rather than real. It was remarked that, with the news of the fall of Khartoum a few hours old, Mr. Gladstone felt light-hearted enough to spend the evening at a theatre of farce. It is not surprising that in no great while these suspicions became certainties; so that, when the Prime Minister, with rare good taste, enrolled himself a member of the Gordon Memorial Committee, a number of people protested vigorously, refused to subscribe unless his name were withdrawn, and even referred, with some bitterness, to the very different behaviour of Iscariot.

Meanwhile, the rumour of Gordon's death was but half-believed, the wish being father to the thought. Until it was confirmed there was nothing to be done. Were he alive, there was nothing left but to await the dictation of the Mahdi's terms, and what these terms would be had long ago been elucidated by a certain scout escaped from Obeid: "The Mahdi is going to Khartoum to take Gordon prisoner and exchange him for Arabi." To move before Gordon's fate was known would be to spoil what little chance there was of saving him. On the other hand, if he had taken refuge in the citadel, where he was known to have magazined his stores and ammunition, with his wonderful resource, there was yet a hope of his holding out; but even then, it would be impossible for Lord Wolseley to reach Khartoum under a month, or for General Earle to lend any aid from the Suakim side in less time. In this way speculation ran riot for many days; and though reports of assassination, each differing from the other, came in with every telegram from the seat of war, people could not bring themselves to believe that Gordon was dead.

CHAPTER XXVIII

THE confusion of events was almost equalled by the confusion of reports. From one quarter it was asserted Gordon had been murdered; from another, that he was alive and holding the Catholic Church with some Greeks and a band of faithful Soudanese. Some said he was killed fighting to the last; while others described how he was stabbed as he hurried into the street to encounter the invading forces. One writer set forth particulars of a desperate struggle and general massacre; another was positive there had been neither battle nor slaughter. This last account for a time was credited, as it received a sort of confirmation through the Mahdi himself, whose messenger to Sir Charles Wilson told him Gordon was in his master's hands and had assumed his master's uniform. The dates imagined were as perplexing and contradictory as the incidents. Moreover, one and all were based on probabilities, and on the various reports gathered from natives, so that for a time hope was uppermost, and few would believe the worst.

One thing was clear. Khartoum had fallen, and this through the treachery of Faragh Pasha, Commander of the Soudanese troops. Gordon had always mistrusted this rascal, though he was a creation of his own. Treason, indeed, had been proved against him on a former occasion, and he had been condemned to death. But Gordon, who, like Cæsar, always erred in the direction of mercy, had yielded to his false lieutenant's prayers and professions of loyalty, and had forgiven him. For a time the traitor's conduct appears to have been stainless; but it is inferred that, from fear of punishment on the arrival of the expedition, he made terms with the Mahdi and received the promise of a price for Khartoum. This portion of the story was presently confirmed; and on February 13th the world knew that Gordon was certainly dead. The black news was conveyed in a despatch from General Brackenbury. On the previous day, it ran, a private soldier found, in a donkey's saddle-bag on the battle-field of Kirbekan, a document which stated that Gordon had been killed. Then messengers arrived across the desert bringing news from Khartoum, and the Mudir of Dongola, who had steadily refused to believe in the fall of the city, was at length convinced. The account was given by a certain cavass, a native of Wady Halfa. After remaining a prisoner a few days, this man was released, and some of his money returned. With this he bought a camel, and made his way across the desert to Debbeh, where he arrived in twelve days. Faragh Pasha, he said, was a black slave liberated and made military commandant by General Gordon. He was suspected of treachery, and dared to receive letters from the Mahdi, which he told the General were of no importance. He opened the gates in the south wall to the Niami men (of the great slave tribe), who were besieging that side. "General Gordon, hearing the confusion in the town, went out armed with a sword and axe.[1] He was accompanied by Ibraheim Bey, the chief clerk, and twenty men. He went towards the house of the Austrian Consul. On his way he met a party of the Mahdi's men, who fired a volley. General Gordon was shot dead. The Arabs then rushed on with their spears, and killed the chief clerk and nine of the men ; the rest escaped."

Then came the following despatch from a correspondent at Abu Kru, dated February 12, and his account was but too soon confirmed by Lord Wolseley himself :—

"General Gordon's trusted messenger George, a well-known Khartoum Greek merchant, who for months past has been entrusted with all letters passing from or to the besieged, and who has been living on board one of the steamers sent here, states that nearly all the natives' stories agree that General Gordon—on hearing that he was betrayed—made a rush for the magazine in the Catholic mission. Finding that the enemy were actually in possession of that building by the treachery of Faragh, General Gordon returned to Government House, and was killed while trying to re-enter it. Some say that he was shot, others that he was stabbed. The Mahdi's people were admitted to Khartoum at ten o'clock on the night of January 26. George adds that the rebels massacred all the white people, men, women, and children,

---

[1] This, like the story of the revolver, repeated some weeks afterwards, is so uncharacteristic that I do not hesitate to reject it as impossible.

throwing the bodies into the Nile, many of which corpses he and others saw while with Sir Charles Wilson's party. The families of all the men on board General Gordon's steamers were also murdered. General Gordon clearly anticipated his fate, for he wrote a number of farewell letters during the month of January. These were sent off in a mail-bag on board the steamer, and given to George, who handed them over to Sir Charles Wilson on January 21. Among the letters were one for his sister, and others for his brother, for Captain Brocklehurst, Lord Wolseley, and Sir Charles Wilson. There were also six complete monthly diaries of the siege of Khartoum, narrating all the events that had taken place since Colonel Stewart left him. In his letter to Sir Charles Wilson, General Gordon wrote that he hoped, by God's will, the English would arrive in time to save him and others, but feared they would be too late ; that he knew he was being betrayed, but was powerless to prevent it. His information was that Khartoum was to be surrendered on January 19 to the Mahdi. He could get away if he wished to run ; but refused to go, and would remain to the last. As he would not permit himself to be taken prisoner, there was nothing left but death. Khasm-el-Mous, the commandant with the steamers here, who has proved so loyal throughout, states that even had the English got to Khartoum a month earlier, they would have been too late to save Gordon, for the two traitors had committed themselves, and would never have awaited our arrival, as they feared that General Gordon would punish them.[1] The people of Khartoum had despaired of ever seeing English soldiers, and tried to make the best terms they could. After the battle of Abu Klea the Mahdi no doubt promised much."

In this way died Charles George Gordon. In a lost battle, yet trailing such clouds of glory as scarce any of his race have been apparelled withal, did this rare and shining spirit return to his home. From that moment of the ride to Abu Hamed, he had been the most conspicuous figure of all Christendom ; and to the world at large the fact of his death was a shock of pain. His heroism had become a universal possession. It was felt that he belonged not to England, but to humanity. It was recognised that all this while he had been doing battle, not alone for Khartoum and his

---

[1] Khasm-el-Mous is an Arab, and native reports must be received with a certain suspicion. The Arabs are born liars. Mr. Gladstone himself, though he tried his hardest, and deeply as his sympathies were engaged, failed to make anything of this and similar reports.

"poor sheep" of the Soudan, but as Civilisation's knight-errant in her eternal conflict with the forces of Barbarism. And in China as in Spain, in Italy as in Russia, in Berlin as in London, in Brussels and Copenhagen as in New York and San Francisco, his loss was accepted as a local and peculiar calamity. There is no more eloquent and enlightened tribute to his memory than that we owe to the genius of Castelar; I am told that Count von Moltke mourned him almost as a son; even in France, with its mean ambitions and single-minded stupidity of devotion to the practice of realism and the theory of the "human document," there were men who proclaimed his worth. All over England there were funeral services in his honour; in many cities was ordained and observed a day of mourning. To the sense of national disaster there was superadded a sense of national humiliation. As was but just, we suffered most in his loss who were primarily and directly responsible for his desertion and death.

He died at two-and-fifty years old; in the fulness of genius and energy, in the plenitude of experience, at the very top of influence and authority; with such a capacity of work as has been possessed by no man since Napoleon, and with potentialities of active life and service unequalled in his generation, perhaps the foremost man of the world. In holding Khartoum with the pitiful means at his disposal against the splendid fanaticism which broke the English square at Tamai and Abu Klea, he had done an achievement which amazes the more, the more it is considered; but there is no doubt that, had he survived, it would have been paralleled, if it had not been surpassed, by his work for the enlightened monarch whose commission brought him westward from Jerusalem. It is an open secret that it was His Majesty's purpose to make him King of the Congo, and give his genius full play in the task of laying the foundations of civilisation in the vast country watered by that great and mysterious stream. Much as we know of him, and magnificent as are the results we saw him achieve, it is impossible to estimate the value of the services he might here have done. But we know that they could not but have been great; we know that Mr. Gladstone willed otherwise; we know that a great influence for good was removed from us, that the cause of humanity is the poorer by the loss of one of its noblest heroes. And that is enough. If it were possible to condone his desertion, the example he has bequeathed, the influence he exercises from beyond the grave, would make such condonation possible.

I have shown how up to a certain stage in Gordon's mission the Government had made his task doubly difficult by their refusal to carry out his recommendations; how, by an obstinate resolve not to declare their policy, and not to send Zebehr Pasha for the establishment of a government at Khartoum, they had stumbled upon the necessity of an expedition for the relief of garrisons which he would otherwise have withdrawn; and how, by reason of their obstinacy, their ruinous delays, and their unexampled desertion at the last, they had rendered themselves responsible for his death. This, it need hardly be noted, was not their opinion, nor the opinion of a portion of their henchmen. Votes of censure on the Ministry, for their conduct of affairs in the Soudan, were moved on the reassembling of Parliament. In the Commons the debate was feeble and spiritless, save for a few speeches—notably those of Mr. Gibson and Mr. Goschen. It presented little interest save to the student of parliamentary human nature—of the natural man that is, as modified by the operation of party politics. It was notorious that the Government had been guilty of one of those blunders which are more criminal than crime; it was suspected, as I have said, that their action had not been involuntary, nor its consequences wholly unconsidered or unweighed. On these two points the country was agreed; and on these two points the country was misrepresented by the House. The Premier, not content with sacrificing Gordon, dared to excuse, if not to praise himself; Sir William Harcourt, Sir Charles Dilke, and the Marquis of Hartington, went on to do likewise; and by a majority of fourteen the party re-affirmed its confidence in their capacity and its satisfaction with their practice of affairs. In the Upper House, the debate—save for a halting discourse by Lord Northbrook— was remarkable in a better sense. Here the accuser was the Marquis of Salisbury. His speech, one of the best in all his career, was of those that carry conviction. Lord Granville had nothing of value or of weight to advance in reply; and the vote was carried by a very large majority. But the position remained unchanged. Nothing had happened save that there was one great Englishman the less. The Government refused to go out; and Mr. Gladstone, who by his personal authority had kept back the expedition for upwards of two months, and who to many people was as plainly responsible for Gordon's death as Faragh himself—Mr. Gladstone saw fit to remain at the head of affairs, to go on playing at statesmanship, and paving with good intentions as much of hell as, after fifty years of active political life, he had still left unrepaired.

The issue was a grave and melancholy comment on the condition of both England and the English. It revealed a new stage of development in the national character; it verified the cruellest sayings of our cruellest foes. Had the Envoy stooped to play the Ministerial game, and taken his mission not seriously, but as an appeal to the British voter, he would have been covered with honours and loaded with rewards.

For, indeed, the facts of the case are all too plain enough. The Ministry were at their wits' end what to do; Gordon was hurried off to Khartoum to appease the populace and do duty as an electioneering agent. When his employers found that the man they had chosen was not of those who sell their souls for place and profit, but, yielding to the pressure of events, persisted in his work as one to whom God is of more account than Mr. Schnadhorst, their anger and resentment knew no bounds. This is no theory of mine. It is the simple truth—a fact which, when the secret history of these times is brought to light, will be made dreadfully clear. True it is that there were members of the Cabinet who stood up in council and urged the expediency of relief; but the Premier willed otherwise, and an expedition which had been advised as early as May was not sent out until October. Nor is this all. It remains to be told, after the debate on the Vote of Censure in the summer, when it was made known that the Government refused to act, how a lady intimately known to me collected subscriptions to the amount of no less than eighty thousand pounds for the equipment of a private expedition. In three several interviews with a certain Minister, she implored official sanction for her enterprise, and three times was she refused. Not only, therefore, did the Cabinet—or rather one section of the Cabinet—decline to save their Envoy's life themselves; they also declined to allow that work to be done by others. He had not followed their lead and deserted his post, and the loyal souls he had gathered about him. His morality was not their morality; his theory of right and justice and honour had nothing in common with theirs; and since he would have none of their devices, he must be left to his own. And left he was, till the nation grew impatient once more, and our rulers, with the ballot-boxes full in view, equipped a force for his relief. It was a farce, and they knew it; but it kept them in office: it was excellent argument to the constituencies to vote straight at the

coming elections, and it served its turn. Mr. Gladstone's faculty of self-delusion, as we have but too much reason to know, can only be qualified as exceptional. It is possible, therefore, that when, in the autumn of '84, he made his parade through Scotland for the exceeding good of his country, he knew not, or had forgotten, that he had betrayed his trust, and sacrificed her greatest son. It is certain that, months afterwards, he received the news of Gordon's death with the equanimity of one who has done his best to avert the inevitable, and that he attributed the misfortune not, of course, to himself, but to his victim's peculiar "temerity." On Gordon's part there were no such comfortable illusions. He died in utter scorn of the men who had betrayed him. "I will accept nothing from the Gladstone Government," he wrote in the late December of '84, "not even my expenses." It is almost the last word of his that it is given us to hear; and it will serve with history for the epitaph of Mr. Gladstone's reputation.

"Anyone whom God gives to be much in union with Him cannot even suffer a pang at death, for what is death to a believer?" Thus had Gordon written to his sister Augusta not long before the day of his passing. That he died in this belief, as he had lived in it, is the only comfortable circumstance in our bereavement.

"I am the Resurrection and the Life, saith the Lord; he that believeth in Me, though he were dead, yet shall he live: and whosoever liveth and believeth in Me shall never die."

APPENDIX

No. 1

ACCORDING to an Austrian missionary, Father Dichtl, Mahomed
Achmet was born at Dongola, about 1840, and was tall, and of
coppery red complexion. For a long time he worked with his
two brothers in the neighbourhood of Khartoum at building boats
for the Nile, but got tired of his trade and aspired to become a
fakir, which is about the same thing as a priest. To this end he
applied to the sheikh of an island close to Khartoum, and after a
few years' study succeeded in taking the order of fakir. He then
sought to become a sheikh, and was again successful. Thenceforth he had but one object in view, to assume the character of
prophet. He retired to the Island of Abba, near Kana, on the
White River, took up his abode in a dry cistern, and led the life
of a sheikh. Here for six years he remained among sheikhs,
with the exception of a weekly visit to the mosque. In course
of time his reputation for piety spread throughout the land; and
from a saint he became a saviour eloquently expounding his
mission to a crowd of Moslems at Kana. He told them that the
Archangel Gabriel had twice commanded him to unsheath the
sword of faith, in order to reform the bad Moslem and to found a
Mussulman Empire, which would be followed by universal peace.
He held his mission from the Prophet, and would achieve what
Mahomet had been unable to do. He therefore urged them to
follow him; he was the Mahdi, and would lead them to the kingdom founded by Allah for true belivers. Abdel Kader, the ex-
Governor-General of the Soudan, a man of high probity and
ability, endeavoured by theological argument to convince the
people that Mahomed Achmet was an impostor, but to little purpose. Not only the lower classes, but also the Government

officials and many officers secretly believed in the Mahdi's mission. Raouf Pasha, at the time he was Governor-General, sent an emissary to the False Prophet. Father Dichtl happened to be present when that emissary on his return gave the following account of his interview with the Mahdi :—" On arriving at Abba I found Mahomed Achmet surrounded by five hundred or six hundred followers, all of them naked, with iron chain belts round their waists and broad drawn swords. The Mahdi occupied a raised seat in their midst, and in his right hand he held the Prophet's staff. When I asked him what his object was he described his pretended mission. I answered that the Government and myself were as good Mussulmans as he. But this he denied, on the grounds that we allowed the Christians to have churches of their own, that we afforded them protection, and that the Government levied taxes. I advised him to abandon his plans and to surrender, adding that he could not resist a Government which disposed of soldiers, Remington rifles, guns, and steamers. To this he rejoined :—' If the soldiers fire upon me and my followers, their bullets will not hurt us ; and if you advance against us with steamers, they will sink with everything on board.' "

No. 2.

At a later date, when on his way to Khartoum, Gordon ascertained that the march lasted from the 10th Sept. to 3rd Nov., or some forty days. During this interval the troops only succeeded in getting over ground which he had ridden over in four days. Owing to the intense heat, the troops were probably greatly worn out. It would then seem that Hicks separated from Alaidin Pasha, but subsequently rejoined him and found him engaged with the enemy. In the confusion of the fight both parties would appear to have fired into each other. The Tribal cavalry then came down on them and crushed them.

No. 3.

FROM THE *Pall Mall Gazette*, JAN. 9TH, 1884.

" At present it is obviously out of the question to send an army to the relief of Colonel Coëtlogon. Baker Pasha's force seems inadequate even to relieve Sinkat. In common with the ex-Khedive, of whom he speaks with remarkable cordiality,

General Gordon deprecates the despatch of either Indian or English troops to the Soudan. But if we have not an Egyptian army to employ in the service, and if we must not send an English force, what are we to do? There is only one thing that we can do. We cannot send a regiment to Khartoum, but we can send a man who on more than one occasion has proved himself more valuable in similar circumstances than an entire army. Why not send Chinese Gordon with full powers to Khartoum, to assume absolute control of the territory, to treat with the Mahdi, to relieve the garrisons, and do what can be done to save what can be saved from the wreck in the Soudan? There is no necessity to speak of the pre-eminent qualifications which he possesses for the work. They are notorious, and are as undisputed as they are indisputable. His engagement on the Congo could surely be postponed. No one can deny the urgent need in the midst of that hideous welter of confusion for the presence of such a man, with a born genius for command, an unexampled capacity in organising 'ever-victorious armies,' and a perfect knowledge of the Soudan and its people. Why not send him out with *carte blanche* to do the best that can be done? He may not be able single-handed to reduce that raging chaos to order, but the attempt is worth making, and if it is to be made it will have to be made at once. For before many days General Gordon will have left for the Congo, and the supreme opportunity may have passed by." This view was generally supported in the press, irrespective of party, but for several days the Government made no sign.

No. 4.

MEMORANDUM BY GENERAL GORDON.

(*Received February 1st,* 1884.)

1. I understand that Her Majesty's Government have come to the irrevocable decision not to incur the very onerous duty of securing to the peoples of the Soudan a just future government. That, as a consequence, Her Majesty's Government have determined to restore to these peoples their independence, and will no longer suffer the Egyptian Government to interfere with their affairs.

2. For this purpose, Her Majesty's Government have decided to send me to the Soudan to arrange for the evacuation of these

countries, and the safe removal of the Egyptian employés and troops.

3. Keeping paragraph No. 1 in view, namely, that the evacuation of the Soudan is irrevocably decided on, it will depend on circumstances in what way this is to be accomplished.

My idea is that the restoration of the country should be made to the different petty Sultans who existed at the time of Mehemet Ali's conquest, and whose families still exist; that the Mahdi should be left altogether out of the calculation as regards the handing over the country; and that it should be optional with the Sultans to accept his supremacy or not. As these Sultans would probably not be likely to gain by accepting the Mahdi as their sovereign, it is probable that they will hold to their independent positions. Thus we should have two factors to deal with, namely, the petty Sultans asserting their several independence, and the Mahdi's party aiming at supremacy over them. To hand, therefore, over to the Mahdi the arsenals, etc., would, I consider, be a mistake. They should be handed over to the Sultans of the States in which they are placed.

The most difficult question is how and to whom to hand over the arsenals of Khartoum, Dongola, and Kassala, which towns have, so to say, no old standing families, Khartoum and Kassala having sprung up since Mehemet Ali's conquest. Probably it would be advisable to postpone any decision as to these towns till such time as the inhabitants have made known their opinion.

4. I have in paragraph 3 proposed the transfer of the lands to the local Sultans, and stated my opinion that these will not accept the supremacy of the Mahdi. If this is agreed to, and my supposition correct as to their action, there can be but little doubt that as far as he is able the Mahdi will endeavour to assert his rule over them, and will be opposed to any evacuation of the Government employés and troops. My opinion of the Mahdi's forces is, that the bulk of those who were with him at Obeid will refuse to cross the Nile, and that those who do so will not exceed 3000 or 4000 men, and also that these will be composed principally of black troops who have deserted, and who, if offered fair terms, would come over to the Government side. In such a case, namely, "Sultans accepting transfer of territory and refusing the supremacy of the Mahdi, and Mahdi's black troops coming over to the Government," resulting weakness of the Mahdi; what should be done should the Mahdi's adherents attack the evacuating columns? It cannot be supposed that these are to offer no

resistance, and if in resisting they should obtain a success it would be but reasonable to allow them to follow up the Mahdi to such a position as would ensure their future safe march. This is one of those difficult questions which our Government can hardly be expected to answer, but which may arise, and to which I would call attention. Paragraph 1 fixes irrevocably the decision of the Government, namely, to evacuate the territory, and, of course, as far as possible involves the avoidance of any fighting. I can, therefore, only say that, having in view paragraph 1, and seeing the difficulty of asking Her Majesty's Government to give a decision or direction as to what should be done in certain cases, that I will carry out the evacuation as far as possible according to their wish to the best of my ability, and with avoidance, as far as possible, of all fighting. I would, however, hope that Her Majesty's Government will give me their support and consideration should I be unable to fulfil all their expectations.

5. Though it is out of my province to give any opinion as to the action of Her Majesty's Government in leaving the Soudan, still I must say it would be an iniquity to reconquer these peoples and then hand them back to the Egyptians without guarantees of future good government. It is evident that this we cannot secure them without an inordinate expenditure of men and money. The Soudan is a useless possession, ever was so, and ever will be so. Larger than Germany, France, and Spain together, and mostly barren, it cannot be governed except by a Dictator, who may be good or bad. If bad, he will cause constant revolts. No one who has ever lived in the Soudan can escape the reflection, " What a useless possession is this land ! " Few men, also, can stand its fearful monotony and deadly climate.

6. Saïd Pasha, the Viceroy before Ismail, went up to the Soudan with Count F. de Lesseps. He was so discouraged and horrified at the misery of the people, that at Berber Count de Lesseps saw him throw his guns into the river, declaring that he would be no party to such oppression. It was only after the urgent solicitations of European Consuls and others that he reconsidered his decision. Therefore, I think Her Majesty's Government are fully justified in recommending the evacuation, inasmuch as the sacrifices necessary towards securing a good government would be far too onerous to admit of such an attempt being made. Indeed, one may say it is impracticable at any cost. Her Majesty's Government will now leave them as God has placed them ; they are not forced to fight among themselves,

22

and they will no longer be oppressed by men coming from lands so remote as Circassia, Kurdistan, and Anatolia.

7. I have requested Lieutenant-Colonel Stewart to write his views independent of mine on this subject. I append them to this Report.

(Signed)   C. G. Gordon, Major-General.

Steamship Tanjore, at sea, January 22nd, 1884.

———

Observations by Colonel Stewart.

1. I have carefully read over General Gordon's observations, and cordially agree with what he states.

2. I would, however, suggest that, as far as possible, all munitions of war be destroyed on evacuation.

3. I quite agree with General Gordon that the Soudan is an expensive and useless possession. No one who has visited it can escape the reflection : " What a useless possession is this land, and what a huge encumbrance on Egypt ! "

4. Handing back the territories to the families of the dispossessed Sultans is an act of justice both towards them and their people. The latter, at any rate, will no longer be at the mercy of foreign mercenaries, and if they are tyrannised over, it will be more or less their own fault. Handing back the districts to the old reigning families is also a politic act, as raising up a rival power to that of the Mahdi.

5. As it is impossible for Her Majesty's Government to foresee all the eventualities that may arise during the evacuation, it seems to me as the more judicious course to rely on the discretion of General Gordon and his knowledge of the country.

6. I, of course, understand that General Gordon is going to the Soudan with full powers to make all arrangements as to its evacuation, and that he is in no way to be interfered with by the Cairo Ministers. Also that any suggestions or remarks that the Cairo Government would wish to make are to be made directly to him and Her Majesty's Minister Plenipotentiary, and that no intrigues are to be permitted against his authority. Any other course would, I am persuaded, make his mission a failure.

(Signed)   D. H. Stewart,
Lieutenant-Colonel, 11th Hussars.

Steamship Tanjore, at sea, January 22nd, 1884.

No. 4A.

MAJOR-GENERAL GORDON TO SIR E. BARING.

(Extract.) ABU HAMED, *February 8th*, 1884.

I have the honour to state that, from the various telegrams soliciting appointments, and from other signs of confidence in the Government, it is evident that the country is far less disturbed than has been reported, and that very probably the mass of civil employés will refuse to leave the Soudan, even if dismissed, and their expenses paid to Cairo.

Both with a view to eventual evacuation and also economy, it will be absolutely necessary to reduce all establishments to a minimum, and should the dismissed employés refuse to leave the country, I propose making them sign a paper releasing the Egyptian Government from all future responsibility on their behalf.

I consider that on my arrival at Khartoum my first object should be to send to Cairo the families of all deceased employés, soldiers, etc., and to attempt the pacification of the country, and the re-opening of the communications. When these objects are fulfilled, I would wish your Excellency to consider what is to follow.

You are aware that a regular system of posts and telegraphs exists; legal Courts, financial and other Departments, are established, and that, in short, the country has, during a considerable time, been accustomed to a more or less controlling and directing government.

To disturb, if not annihilate, this system at a moment's notice would appear to me to hand over the country to complete anarchy. Consider what the situation will be.

Let it be supposed that the Soudan, or at least the Eastern Soudan, is tranquillised, its administration " Soudanised," native Mudirs appointed, refugees all sent to Cairo, the Equatorial and Bahr Gazelle Provinces evacuated, and the Egyptian troops ready to leave. Suppose that the firman dissolving the connection between Egypt and the Soudan is read; and the result will inevitably be that each Mudir will aim at securing his own independence, and that a period of violent and protracted commotion will ensue, which may very possibly re-act prejudicially on Egypt, owing to the intimate connection which has for so long obtained between the two countries.

Hence I would suggest that the Government of Egypt should continue to maintain its position as a suzerain Power, nominate the Governor-General and Mudirs, and act as a Supreme Court of Appeal.

Its controlling influence should, however, be a strictly moral one, and limited to giving advice.

In spite of all that has occurred, I feel satisfied that the prestige of the Cairo Government, except in so far as the conduct of its troops in the field is concerned, is not seriously shaken, and that the people still continue to look up to the Cairo Government as the direct representative of the Sultan as Khalif, and would look with horror on a complete separation.

Should a nominal control, such as I advise, be maintained, it is evident that it could in no way involve the Egyptian Government, and that the prestige, which the Governors, Mudirs, etc., would acquire from being nominated by Cairo, would most probably secure them against rivals. On the other hand, in the event of the Mudir becoming unpopular, an order for his removal from Cairo would carry great weight and most probably ensure his dismissal.

I would therefore earnestly beg that evacuation, but not abandonment, be the programme to be followed, and that the firman with which I am provided be changed into one recognising moral control and suzerainty.

In offering this suggestion, I must, however, premise that the moral control will be exercised by the Egyptian Government as a responsible body, and that all nominations will be made by the Ministry uninfluenced by any individual, however exalted may be his position.

I am persuaded that, by following the above policy on the lines I have drawn, neither Her Majesty's Government, nor yet the Egyptian Government, would incur any risk, and that they would be able to secure, in a greater or less degree, the future of the Soudan.

———

COLONEL STEWART'S REMARKS ON MAJOR-GENERAL GORDON'S DESPATCH OF FEBRUARY 8, 1884, TO SIR E. BARING.

Although it cannot be denied that anarchy and bloodshed would ensue were the policy of abandonment carried out in its entirety, still I think a solution in the direction as pointed out by

General Gordon will altogether depend upon what policy Her Majesty's Government intend to pursue towards Egypt.

Should they decide to evacuate Egypt, and to cease having a controlling and directing voice in the affairs of that country, then I am decidedly of opinion that it would be far better, in the interests of both countries, to abandon the Soudan. To allow, in such a case, Egypt to maintain even a nominal control over the Soudan would only tend to insure further attempts at active interference, with their accompaniment of misgovernment, oppression, venality, and Cairene intrigue.

In the event of Her Majesty's Government retaining a directing voice in Egyptian affairs, then I think that General Gordon's advice might be followed with considerable advantage.

Although I do not quite agree with him that the prestige of Cairo has not been greatly diminished, still I think sufficient of it remains to enable the Egyptian Government to exert a beneficial influence towards curbing the forces of disorder in the Soudan. Whether, or for how long, such an influence may last, it is impossible to say. Probably, in time, unless the Egyptian Government takes a more active part in the government of the country than that of giving advice, and the appointing and removing Mudirs at the request of the people, it will gradually wane and wear out; but, at any rate for some time to come, it will probably be strong enough to act usefully as a moral support to the Soudanese Government and to diminish the extent of the change.

(Signed)   D. H. STEWART,
Lieutenant-Colonel, 11th Hussars.

ABU HAMED, *February 11th,* 1884.

No. 5.

MAJOR-GENERAL GORDON TO SIR E. BARING.

KHARTOUM, *February 18th,* 1884.

In a previous Memorandum I alluded to the arrival of an epoch when whites, fellaheen troops, civilian employés, women and children of deceased soldiers—in short, the Egyptian element in the Soudan—will be removed; when we shall be face to face with the Soudan administration, and when I must withdraw from the Soudan. I have stated that to withdraw without being able to place a successor in my seat would be the signal for general anarchy throughout the country, *which, though all Egyptian* element was withdrawn, would be a misfortune, and inhuman.

Also, I have stated that even if I placed a man in my seat unsupported by any Government, the same anarchy would ensue.

Her Majesty's Government could, I think, without responsibility in money or men, give the Commission to my successor on certain terms which I will detail hereafter. If this solution is examined, we shall find that a somewhat analogous case exists in Afghanistan, where Her Majesty's Government give moral support to the Ameer, and go even beyond that in giving the Ameer a subsidy, which would not be needed in the present case.

I distinctly state that if Her Majesty's Government gave a Commission to my successor, I recommend neither a subsidy nor men being given. I would select and give a Commission to some man, and promise him the moral support of Her Majesty's Government and nothing more.

It may be argued that Her Majesty's Government would thus be giving nominal and moral support to a man who will rule over a Slave State; but so is Afghanistan, as also Socotra.

This nomination of my successor must, I think, be direct from Her Majesty's Government.

As for the man, Her Majesty's Government should select one above all others, namely, Zebehr. He alone has the ability to rule the Soudan, and would be universally accepted by the Soudan. He should be made K.C.M.G., and given presents. The terms of nomination should be as follows :—

1. Engagement not to go into Equatorial or Bahr Ghazelle Provinces, and which I should evacuate.

2. Engagement not to go into Darfour.

3. Engagement, on payment of £200 annually, to telegraph height of Nile to Cairo.

4. Engagement to remain at peace with Abyssinia.

5. Engagement not to levy duties beyond 4 per cent. on imports or exports. Of course he will not have Suakin or Massowah.

6. Engagement not to pursue anyone who was engaged in suppressing his son's revolt.

7. Engagement to pay the pensions granted by the Egyptian Government to old employés.

To the above may be added other clauses as may seem fit.

P.S.—I think the decision of any Council of Notables for the selection of candidates for the post of my successor would be useless.

Zebehr's exile at Cairo for ten years, amidst all the late events, and his mixing with Europeans, must have had great effect on his character. Zebehr's nomination, under the moral countenance of Her Majesty's Government, would bring all merchants, European and others, back to the Soudan in a short time.

Despatch as above by post.

I have asked Stewart to give his opinions independently of mine, in order to prevent a one-sided view.

He is a first-rate man.

LIEUTENANT-COLONEL STEWART TO SIR E. BARING.

KHARTOUM, *February* 18*th*, 1884.

With reference to Gordon's telegram of to-day, I think that the policy he urges would greatly facilitate our retirement from the country.

The Turco-Arabian view of the question I would suggest as one demanding serious consideration. As to whether Zebehr Pasha is the man who should be nominated, I think we have hardly yet a sufficient knowledge of the country to be able to form an opinion. It is, however, probable whoever is nominated will be accepted for a time.

SIR E. BARING TO EARL GRANVILLE.

CAIRO, *February* 19*th*, 1884.

MY LORD,—With reference to my despatch of this day's date, I have the honour to submit to your Lordship my views upon General Gordon's proposals.

As regards the choice of his successor, there is, as Colonel Stewart says in his telegram, no necessity to decide at once ; but I believe Zebehr Pasha to be the only possible man. He undoubtedly possesses energy and ability, and has great local influence.

As regards the Slave Trade, I discussed the matter with General Gordon when he was in Cairo, and he fully agreed with me in thinking that Zebehr Pasha's presence or absence would not affect the question in one way or the other. I am also convinced, from many things that have come to my notice, that General Gordon is quite right in thinking that Zebehr Pasha's residence in Egypt has considerably modified his character. He now understands what European power is, and it is much better to have to deal with a man of this sort than with a man like the Mahdi.

I should be altogether opposed to having General Gordon and Zebehr Pasha at Khartoum together. As soon as General Gordon has arranged for the withdrawal of the garrison and the rest of the Egyptian element, he could leave Khartoum, and Zebehr Pasha might shortly afterwards start from Cairo. One of my chief reasons for allowing the interview between the two men to take place was, that I wished to satisfy myself to some extent of the sentiments entertained by Zebehr Pasha towards General Gordon. I would not on any account run the risk of putting General Gordon in his power.

If Zebehr Pasha is nominated, it will be very necessary to lay down in writing and in the plainest language what degree of support he may expect from Her Majesty's Government. I cannot recommend that he should be promised the " moral support " of Her Majesty's Government. In the first place, he would scarcely understand the sense of the phrase ; and, moreover, I do not think he would attach importance to any support which was not material. It is for Her Majesty's Government to judge what the effect of his appointment would be upon public opinion in England, but except for that I can see no reason why Zebehr Pasha should not be proclaimed ruler of the Soudan, with the approbation of Her Majesty's Government. It should be distinctly explained to him in writing that he must rely solely upon his own resources to maintain his position. He might receive a moderate sum of money from the Egyptian Government to begin with. His communications with that Government might be conducted through Her Majesty's representative in Cairo, as General Gordon suggests.

With regard to the detailed conditions mentioned by General Gordon, I think they might form the subject of further consideration and discussion, both with General Gordon and with others in authority here. I am inclined to doubt whether such conditions would be of any use ; they would probably not long be observed.

In conclusion, I may add that I have no idea whether Zebehr Pasha would accept the position which it is proposed to offer him.—I have, etc.,

(Signed)   E. Baring.

No. 6.

SIR E. BARING TO EARL GRANVILLE.

CAIRO, *February* 27*th*, 1884, 3.30 P.M.

Gordon has issued following proclamation to inhabitants of Soudan :—

"Since my arrival I have constantly assured you of good treatment and justice, and advised you to desist from rebellion, which leads to war and bloodshed; but, finding that this advice had no effect on some people, I have been compelled to use severe measures, so much so that British troops are now on their way, and in a few days will reach Khartoum; then, whoever persists in bad conduct will be treated as he deserves. Therefore upright men should have no intercourse with rebels, or they will share the same fate. I am watching things closely, and you should not think I am ignorant of what goes on. The present rebellion will bring ruin on a country and much loss of life. The wise man is his own guardian."

No. 7.

MAJOR-GENERAL GORDON TO SIR E. BARING.

KHARTOUM, *February* 24*th*, 1884.

It is quite possible that in a short time the whole Soudan, comprising Dongola, Berber, Khartoum, Senaar, Kassala, will be quieted, and Bogos evacuated. This will leave us with a large and expensive force with a diminished revenue, as hardly even the half of the tax is likely to be realised for a year or so. We will allow that all Egyptian employés have left, and also the white troops; what are we next to do? We will not have funds to pay the forces requisite for the defence of the towns mentioned, for longer than the allowance of the £100,000 lasts. Then comes a deadlock. To this question I can offer no solution. It is obvious that not the least self-reliant spirit exists among the wealthy people of the towns, and that nothing can be expected of them. The difficulty above alluded to, namely, how to pay for the Soudan garrisons of these towns, is one which whoever may be named Governor must face. How he is to do so without funds I do not see. I can only see a slight hope against anarchy, which is this, namely, to place 1000 Soudan troops in Khartoum, 500 ditto in Berber, 500 ditto in Dongola, 500 ditto in Kassala, 500 ditto in Senaar. Total 3000, and costing about £70,000 a year. I would then place in each town a Governor and a Meglis, and hand over to him the whole administration of taxes and of government. I would keep the £70,000 a year apart for the payment of the 3000 men, and I would place a supreme officer over them. By this means anarchy would be prevented, at any rate for a time, and if it did occur it would be the fault of the native government. Should an outbreak occur, as the troops will be natives, there would be no chance of their being massacred ; the only risk would be for the European commander. The question therefore is now before you. Do you approve this scheme, can you find the £70,000, or will you suggest some other? It is a most serious matter when one considers the state of the people of these towns. It must be remembered that revenue is taken by the separation from the Soudan of Suakin and Massowah and customs duties now taken at Suez.

No. 8.

Sir E. Baring to Earl Granville.

(*Received by telegraph February 28th.*)

Cairo, *February 28th*, 1884.

My Lord,—I communicated to General Gordon your Lordship's telegram of the 22nd instant, asking him at the same time whether he could suggest anyone besides Zebehr Pasha to succeed him at Khartoum.

I have the honour to enclose copy of my telegram to General Gordon on the subject, and of his reply. I also forward herewith another telegram from General Gordon, in the course of which he recommends that 3000 black troops should be kept in the Soudan, and that the cost of their maintenance, which he estimates at £70,000 a-year, should be defrayed by the Egyptian Government.

Besides these telegrams, I have before me a Report addressed to me by General Gordon from Abou-Hamad on the 8th instant, a copy of which was forwarded to your Lordship in my despatch of the 25th instant. Your Lordship will observe that this Report is dated ten days before his long telegram respecting the future government of the Soudan, which will be found in my despatch of the 18th instant.

I will now submit to your Lordship my views upon the main points at issue, after having carefully considered the different proposals made by General Gordon. There are obviously many contradictions in those proposals; too much importance should not be attached to the details. But I venture to again recommend to the earnest attention of Her Majesty's Government the serious question of principle which General Gordon has raised.

Two alternative courses may be adopted. One is to evacuate the Soudan entirely, and to make no attempt to establish any settled government there before leaving; the other, to make every effort of which the present circumstances admit to set up some settled form of government to replace the former Egyptian administration.

General Gordon is evidently in favour of the latter of these courses. I entirely agree with him. The attempt, it is true, may not be successful, but I am strongly of opinion that it should be made. From every point of view, whether political, military, or financial, it will be a most serious matter if complete anarchy is allowed to reign south of Wadi Halfa. And this anarchy will inevitably ensue on General Gordon's departure, unless some measures are adopted beforehand to prevent it.

With regard to the wish of Her Majesty's Government not to go beyond General Gordon's plan, as stated in his Memorandum of the 22nd ultimo, I would remark that he appears to have intended merely to give a preliminary sketch of the general line of policy to be pursued. Moreover, in that Memorandum he makes a specific allusion to the difficulty of providing rulers for Khartoum, Dongola, and other places where there are no old families to recall to power.

It is clear that Her Majesty's Government cannot afford moral or material support to General Gordon's successor as ruler of the Soudan, but the question of whether or not he should be nominally appointed by the authority of Her Majesty's Government appears to me to be one of very slight practical importance.

Whatever may be said to the contrary, Her Majesty's Government must in reality be responsible for any arrangements which are now devised for the Soudan, and I do not think it is possible to shake off that responsibility.

If, however, Her Majesty's Government are unwilling to assume any responsibility in the matter, then I think they should give full liberty of action to General Gordon and the Khedive's Government to do what seems best to them.

No. 9.

Earl Granville to Sir E. Baring.

Foreign Office, *February 29th*, 1884.

Sir,—The arguments advanced by General Gordon and yourself in favour of the appointment of Zebehr Pasha as Governor-General of the Soudan are under the consideration of Her Majesty's Government; and I have to point out to you the principal grounds upon which they apprehend danger from such an appointment.

In the first place, it would appear not unlikely that he might, either by allying himself with the Mahdi, with whom he is already supposed to have some connection, or in some other manner, become himself a source of increased danger to Egypt from the Soudan, instead of a security against them.

Secondly, his reputation as a slave-trader, and the absence of any reason for supposing that he would find in his new position an object of ambition sufficient to induce him to give assurances in the fulfilment of which reliance could be placed, might raise grave doubts as to whether his power and influence after his appointment would be used for the prevention, or, at all events, for the discouragement of the Slave Trade.

In the third place, it is impossible to overlook the danger in which General Gordon might be placed, owing to Zebehr Pasha's hatred of that officer, if they should both be in the same region at a time when Zebehr had the supreme control.

I shall be glad to receive your observations upon these points. —I am, etc.,

(Signed) Granville.

No. 10.

Major-General Gordon to Sir E. Baring.

(Telegraphic.) Khartoum, *March 8th*, 1884.

The sending of Zebehr means the extrication of the Cairo employés from Khartoum, and the garrisons from Senaar and Kassala.

I can see no possible way to do so except through him, who, being a native of the country, can rally the well-affected around him, as they know he will make his home here.

I do not think that the giving a subsidy to Zebehr for some two years would be in contradiction to the policy of entire evacuation.

It would be nothing more than giving him a lump sum in two instalments under the conditions I have already written.

As for slave-holding, even had we held the Soudan, we could never have interfered with it.

I have already said that the Treaty of 1877 was an impossible one, therefore, on that head, Zebehr's appointment would make no difference whatever.

As for slave-hunting, the evacuation of the Bahr Gazelle and Equatorial Provinces would entirely prevent it.

Should Zebehr attempt, after his two years' subsidy was paid him, to take those districts, we could put pressure on him at Suakin, which will remain in our hands.

I feel sure that Zebehr will be so occupied with the Soudan proper, and with consolidating his position, that he will not have time to devote to those provinces.

As for the security of Egypt, Zebehr's stay in Cairo has taught him our power, and he would never dream of doing anything against Egypt. He would rather seek its closest alliance, for he is a great trader.

As to progress made in extrication of garrisons, all I have done is to send down from Khartoum all the sick men, women, and children of those killed in Kordofan.

Senaar, I heard to-day, is quite safe and quiet.

Kassala will hold out without difficulty after Graham's victory, but the road there is blocked, as also is the road to Senaar.

It is quite impossible to get the roads open to Kassala and Senaar, or to send down the white troops, unless Zebehr comes up.

He will change whole state of affairs.

As for the Equatorial and Bahr Gazelle Provinces, they are all right, but I cannot evacuate them till the Nile rises, in two months.

Dongola and Berber are quiet; but I fear for the road between Berber and Khartoum, where the friends of the Mahdi are very active.

A body of rebels on the Blue Nile are blockading a force of 1000 men, which have, however, plenty of food; till the Nile rises I cannot relieve them.

Darfour, so far as I can understand, is all right, and the

restored Sultan should be now working up the tribes to acknowledge him.

It is impossible to find any other man but Zebehr for governing Khartoum. No one has his power. Hussein Pasha Khaleefa has only power at Dongola and Berber.

If you do not send Zebehr you have no chance of getting the garrisons away; this is a heavy argument in favour of sending him.

There is no possibility of dividing the country between Zebehr and other Chiefs; none of the latter could stand for a day against the Mahdi's agents, and Hussein Pasha Khaleefa would also fall.

The Chiefs will not collect here, for the loyal are defending their lands against the disloyal.

There is not the least chance of Zebehr making common cause with the Mahdi. Zebehr here would be far more powerful than the Mahdi, and he would make short work of the Mahdi.

The Mahdi's power is that of a Pope, Zebehr's will be that of a Sultan. They could never combine.

Zebehr is fifty times the Mahdi's match. He is also of good family, well known, and fitted to be Sultan; the Mahdi, in all these respects, is the exact opposite, besides being a fanatic.

I dare say Zebehr, who hates the tribes, did stir up the fires of revolt, in hopes that he would be sent to quell it.

It is the irony of fate that he will get his wish if he is sent up.

––––––

SIR E. BARING TO EARL GRANVILLE.

(*Received by telegraph March 9th.*)

(Extract.)   CAIRO, *March 9th*, 1884.

Having forwarded to your Lordship General Gordon's reply to your telegram of the 5th instant, I have now the honour to submit my own views upon the points raised therein.

I think that the policy of sending Zebehr Pasha to Khartoum, and giving him a subsidy, is in harmony with the policy of evacuation. It is in principle the same policy as that adopted by the Government of India towards Afghanistan and the tribes on the North-West Frontier. I have always contemplated making some arrangements for the future government of the Soudan, as will be seen from my despatch of the 22nd December 1883, in which I said that it would be " necessary to send an English officer of high authority to Khartoum with full powers to withdraw all garrisons in the Soudan, and make the best arrangements possible for the future government of that country."

As regards slavery, it may certainly receive a stimulus from the abandonment of the Soudan by Egypt, but the despatch of Zebehr Pasha to Khartoum will not affect the question in one way or the other. No middle course is possible as far as the Soudan is concerned. We must either virtually annex the country, which is out of the question, or else we must accept the inevitable consequences of the policy of abandonment.

Your Lordship will see what General Gordon says about the question of the security of Egypt. I believe that Zebehr Pasha may be made a bulwark against the approach of the Mahdi. Of course there is a risk that he will constitute a danger to Egypt; but this risk is, I think, a small one, and it is in any case preferable to incur it rather than to face the certain disadvantages of withdrawing without making any provision for the future government of the country, which would thus be sure to fall under the power of the Mahdi.

No. 11.

SIR E. BARING TO EARL GRANVILLE.

(*Received April 16th, 5.30 P.M.*)

(Telegraphic.)   CAIRO, *April 16th*, 1884, 5.30 P.M.

Urgent demands for aid continue to come from Berber. Inhabitants of Berber have telegraphed to Egyptian Government earnestly begging for assistance. Governor of Berber says that some people are kept loyal on account of frequent rumours that English troops are coming from Suakin, but that if these rumours turn out to be false, the Bedouins who are about to be sent to him will not constitute a force sufficient to enable him to maintain his position.

SIR E. BARING TO EARL GRANVILLE.

(*Received April 20th, 5 P.M.*)

(Telegraphic.)   CAIRO, *April 20th*, 1884, 2 P.M.

Hassan Khalifa telegrams that Bishareen are ready to join rebels, and that he fears that in two days Berber will be surrounded. He also confirms the news that the garrison of Shendy is surrounded at Aliab.

Nubar Pasha has sent me his telegram with a semi-official note, in which he says that the conduct of the retreat from the Soudan having been taken in hand by Her Majesty's Government, the Council of Ministers requested him to ask me what answer shall be sent. The matter is serious. Please send early reply. Unless some prospect of help can be held out to Hassan Khalifa, there is some risk that he will be thrown into the arms of the rebels. This would seriously affect Gordon's position.

Sir E. Baring to Earl Granville.

(*Received April 20th*, 5.40 P.M.)

(Telegraphic.)   Cairo, *April 20th*, 1884, 5.20 P.M.

There is a panic at Berber. Everyone who can do so is leaving. If any message is to go to General Gordon, it should be sent at once. The telegraph clerks at Berber want to leave, and it will be difficult to keep them to their post.

No. 12.

Earl Granville to Sir E. Baring.

Foreign Office, *March 28th*, 1884.

Sir,—It is desirable that I should explain at greater length than is possible in telegraphic despatches, the reasons which have influenced Her Majesty's Government in declining to sanction the proposals made to them by General Gordon, with your support, that Zebehr Pasha should be despatched to assist him at Khartoum, and to succeed him there as Governor.

For this purpose it is necessary to advert shortly to the previous history of Zebehr Pasha, which is to be found in the account of General Gordon's proceedings in Central Africa, written by Dr. Birkbeck Hill in 1881, and in the journals of General Gordon published in that volume. Zebehr was a kind of king of the slave-hunters who devastated the countries bordering the White Nile. His court, his wealth, his troops of slaves, and his fortified stations were graphically described by Dr. Schweinfurt. In 1869 the Khedive Ismaïl made an ineffectual effort to curb his power, and he was subsequently employed to conquer the kingdom of Darfour.   Zebehr next claimed the appointment of Governor-General of the Soudan ; but he was induced to visit Cairo, where he was detained, and has since remained under surveillance.

When General Gordon was Governor-General of the Soudan, Zebehr's son Suleiman was at Shaka with his father's forces, some 10,000 strong, consisting of murderers and robbers, who made raids upon the negro tribes for slaves.   General Gordon tried to dissolve these forces by peaceful means, and succeeded for a time ; but in 1878 Suleiman raised a formidable insurrection, which was put down by Gessi Pasha with great difficulty, under the instructions of General Gordon, who tried and executed the emissaries sent to him by Suleiman, among whom was Zebehr's chief secretary.   Suleiman himself was captured and executed by Gessi in July 1879, an action which General Gordon subsequently approved.

The language of General Gordon as to the power of Zebehr and his responsibility for the worst abuses of the Slave Trade is clear and decided.   "Zebehr," he says, "alone is responsible for the Slave Trade of the last ten years," and he notices with indignation a proposal made to him from Cairo in 1879, that Zebehr should be sent back to the Soudan.

Such being the antecedents of Zebehr, it is not surprising that, when General Gordon accepted the mission to proceed to Khartoum, one of his first requests should have been that Zebehr should be carefully watched.   Chérif Pasha had proposed to employ him at Suakin, and General Gordon, in a Memorandum of the 22nd January, written on his voyage to Alexandria, expressed the following opinion in respect to his employment :—

"My objection to Zebehr is this.   He is a first-rate General, and a man of great capacity, and he would in no time eat up all the petty Sultans and consolidate a vast State, as his ambition is boundless.   I would therefore wish him kept away, as his restoration would be not alone unjust, but might open up the Turco-Arabic question.   Left independent, the Sultans will doubtless fight among themselves, and one will try to annex the other ; but with Zebehr it would be an easy task to overcome these different States and form a large independent one."

Colonel Stewart observed upon the same subject :—

" Zebehr's return would undoubtedly be a misfortune to the Soudanese, and also a direct encouragement to the Slave Trade.

As he would be by far the ablest leader in the Soudan, he could easily overturn the newly-erected political edifice, and become a formidable power."

On his arrival at Cairo, General Gordon had a remarkable interview with Zebehr, who complained vehemently of the execution of his son and the confiscation of his property. At a Council, consisting of yourself, Nubar Pasha, Sir Evelyn Wood, General Gordon, and Colonel Stewart, held immediately after the interview, Lieutenant-Colonel Watson, Egyptian army, was asked what he thought of sending Zebehr and Gordon together to the Soudan. He answered that, not alone he himself, but natives thoroughly conversant with both men, were of opinion that such a policy would entail the death of one or other of them. A letter was then read from General Gordon, in which he gave it as his opinion that Zebehr was far the ablest man in the Soudan; that if he were sent up, the Mahdi would probably soon disappear; and that, if it were thought advisable, he would go up with him, though thoroughly convinced that he was no friend of his.

At General Gordon's suggestion, you informed Zebehr that he would be allowed to remain at Cairo, and that the future treatment he would receive at the hands of the Egyptian Government depended in a great measure upon whether General Gordon returned alive and well from the Soudan; and upon whether, whilst residing at Cairo, Zebehr used his influence to facilitate the execution of the policy upon which the Government had determined.

Notwithstanding this decision, General Gordon appears to have reconsidered the subject on his journey to Khartoum, and on his arrival at that place, on the 18th February, he proposed that, on his withdrawal from Khartoum, the British Government should appoint Zebehr as Governor of the Soudan, and give him "their moral support, but nothing more," taking from him certain engagements, and particularly one binding him not to go into Darfour or the Equatorial and Bahr Gazelle Provinces.

In forwarding this recommendation for the consideration of Her Majesty's Government, you expressed your concurrence in General Gordon's opinion, that it was desirable that he should leave behind him the man most likely to preserve some settled form of government at Khartoum; and that, although there was no necessity to decide at once, you believed Zebehr to be the only possible man. You described him as undoubtedly possessing energy, ambition, and great local influence; that you "would not on any account risk putting Gordon in his power"; and you did not recommend his being promised the moral support of the British Government.

Your conclusion was that, save from the point of view of English opinion, you saw no reason why Zebehr should not be proclaimed ruler of the Soudan, after General Gordon had arranged for the withdrawal of the garrisons and had left Khartoum, it being distinctly explained to him, in writing, that he must rely upon his own resources to maintain his position.

Her Majesty's Government at that time had no reason to suppose that there was any pressing necessity for the announcement of a successor to General Gordon, whose arrival at Khartoum had been welcomed by the people; and you were informed on the 22nd that there were the gravest objections to General Gordon's proposal that a successor to him should be appointed by the British Government; that Her Majesty's Government did not, as yet, see the necessity of a special provision for the government of the country beyond the policy indicated in General Gordon's Memorandum of the 22nd January, wherein he proposes to make over the country to the representatives of the different petty Sultans who existed at the time of Mehemet Ali's conquest; and that public opinion in England would not tolerate the appointment of Zebehr.

You communicated in reply to Her Majesty's Government to General Gordon, who in his answer expressed a decided opinion that, in order to secure the future quiet of Egypt, it was necessary to subdue—or, to use his own expressive phrase, to "smash up" —the Mahdi; and that he could not suggest any other successor than Zebehr. In forwarding, on the 28th February, these opinions, you thus summed up the situation :—

"There are two courses to pursue. Either the Soudan may be evacuated, and no attempt made to establish any settled government there, or the best measures of which the circumstances admit may be taken to set up some form of government. General Gordon is evidently in favour of the latter course. I entirely agree with him. The attempt may not succeed, but I am very strongly of opinion that it should be tried. It will be a serious matter from every point of view, political, military, and financial, if complete anarchy reigns at Wady Halfa; and anarchy will certainly ensue when Gordon comes away, if some measures be not taken beforehand to prevent it."

Your conclusion, in which Nubar Pasha agreed, was that the

objections to Zebehr were overrated, and that he should be
allowed to succeed Gordon, with a sum of money to start with,
and an annual subsidy for five years dependent upon his good
behaviour, so that he might be able to maintain a moderate
military force.

Her Majesty's Government, on the perusal of General Gordon's
advice, were under the impression that he gave undue weight to
the assumed necessity of an immediate evacuation of Khartoum,
and they inquired whether it was urgent to make an arrangement
at once to provide for his successor, expressing a hope that General
Gordon would remain for some time. They were unwilling hastily
to negative the proposal to employ Zebehr, and you were therefore
informed that the opinion you had expressed would be carefully
weighed before deciding upon the subject.

You replied on the 4th March, that General Gordon strongly
pressed that Zebehr should be sent to Khartoum without delay,
and that the combination at Khartoum of Zebehr with himself
was an absolute necessity. "My weakness," he said, "is that of
being foreign, and Christian, and peaceful, and it is only by sending
Zebehr that this prejudice can be removed."

In consequence of the confidence expressed by General Gordon
that Zebehr would not injure him, you withdrew the objection
you had previously expressed to Zebehr being sent to join General
Gordon at Khartoum, and supported his recommendation.

Up to this time Her Majesty's Government had entertained
a hope that some other arrangement might have been made
by General Gordon; but, having to determine whether Zebehr
should be sent or not, and looking to the opinions so recently
expressed by General Gordon and Colonel Stewart as to the
danger of making use of him, which it is not necessary to re-
capitulate here, they replied on the 5th March that they had no
information in their possession which led them to alter the
impressions produced by those opinions, and that unless those
impressions were removed, they would not be able to take the
responsibility of authorising the mission of Zebehr.

The telegrams subsequently received from you conveying
further messages from General Gordon did not materially add to
the considerations which had already been placed before Her
Majesty's Government. The arguments in favour of employing
Zebehr were stated with great force and ability by yourself and
General Gordon. A strong conviction was expressed that his
interest would prevent him from injuring General Gordon; that,

although he might have been concerned in stirring up the revolt of the tribes, there was no probability of his joining the Mahdi; and that his stay in Cairo must have taught him sufficient respect for British power to prevent him from entertaining any designs hostile to Egypt.

If reliance could safely have been placed upon Zebehr to serve loyally with General Gordon, to act in a friendly manner towards Egypt, and to abstain from encouraging the Slave Trade, the course proposed was undoubtedly the best which could have been taken under the circumstances; but upon this most vital point General Gordon's assurances failed to convince Her Majesty's Government. They felt the strongest desire to comply with his wishes, but they were bound, at the same time, to exercise their own deliberate judgment upon a proposal the adoption of which might produce such serious consequences.

They could not satisfy themselves of the probability that the establishment of Zebehr's authority would be a security to Egypt: on the contrary, his antecedents, and the opinions expressed only a few weeks ago by General Gordon and yourself as to his character and disposition, led them to the conclusion that it would probably constitute a serious danger to Egypt. There seemed to Her Majesty's Government to be considerable risk that Zebehr might join with the Mahdi, or, if he fought and destroyed him, that he would then turn against Egypt. The existence of an outbreak of Mussulman fanaticism was undoubted; but the Mahdi had not shown any personal qualifications which threatened to convert it into a military power and organisation. To have let loose in the Soudan a Mussulman of undoubted ability and ambition, possessed of great military skill, and with a grievance against the Egyptian Government, appeared to Her Majesty's Government to be so perilous a course that they were unable to accept the responsibility of adopting it.

They were unable to share General Gordon's confidence, that Zebehr's blood feud with him involved no serious danger, and they felt that the opinion originally expressed by General Gordon, by the Council at Cairo, and by yourself, was more likely to be correct than the subsequent one. The chivalrous character of General Gordon appeared to be likely to lead him into the generous error of trusting too much to the loyalty of a man whose interests and feelings were hostile to him.

Besides these considerations affecting the interests of Egypt and the safety of General Gordon, Her Majesty's Government had further to consider how far it was probable that his authority might be exercised to renew the slave-hunting raids for which he was notorious.

The temptation to embark in such lucrative transactions would be great to himself, and there would be the additional risk that, having to rely on the support of his former friends and dependents, the slave-hunters, he would be obliged to purchase their support by connivance at their nefarious practices.

Her Majesty's Government understand the reasons which compelled General Gordon to announce that the property in slaves in the Soudan would be recognised; but this is a very different thing from using the authority of Great Britain to establish a notorious slave-hunter as ruler over that country. General Gordon indeed proposed that the Bahr Gazelle and Equatorial Provinces should be excluded from Zebehr's rule, but England would have possessed no power to secure his adherence to such a stipulation.

These were the considerations which led Her Majesty's Government to address to you the instructions of the 13th instant.

Since that time, General Gordon's apprehension that the tribes would rise between Khartoum and Berber has been realised, and the communication between those places has been interrupted. On the other hand, the power of Osman Digna, apparently the most dangerous leader of the fanatical movement, has received a serious check, if it has not been altogether destroyed, by the victories of Sir Gerald Graham, which must produce a sensible effect upon all the tribes of the Eastern Soudan. General Gordon, so far as is known, is not in any immediate danger at Khartoum; and Her Majesty's Government are glad to learn, from a communication addressed to you by General Gordon, that he is ready to proceed with his task, with or without the assistance of Zebehr.

The observations which I made in this despatch are not intended to imply the slightest blame upon the manner in which you have discharged the arduous and responsible task of advising Her Majesty's Government under circumstances of extraordinary difficulty. It was your obvious duty to communicate your opinions to them in the plainest manner. You have discharged that duty faithfully and well. Her Majesty's Government are deeply sensible of the courage, patriotism, self-sacrifice, and devotion to duty which actuate General Gordon. They have felt no disposition to criticise, in any narrow spirit, the suggestions which, with his characteristic frankness, he has made from day to day as the most effectual way of meeting difficulties as they presented themselves to him. But Her Majesty's Government had to decide upon those suggestions to the best of their ability. They are fully sensible of the difficulty of the task, and, while they have been unable to agree with General Gordon and yourself upon this particular question, they are satisfied that the interests of Egypt and of Great Britain could not be entrusted to abler hands.—I am, etc. (Signed) GRANVILLE.

No. 13.

COLONEL DUNCAN TO THE GENERAL OFFICER COMMANDING THE TROOPS IN UPPER EGYPT.

KOROSKO, *July 28th*, 1884.

SIR,—I have the honour to forward, for your information and that of his Excellency the Sirdar, a detailed statement of the evacuation of the Soudan, carried out under my control between the 10th March 1884, and the date of your arrival in Upper Egypt. I have during that period sent regular weekly Reports to Cairo, but in this, my final Report, I give a summary of the whole. This course will be convenient in case of reference.

1. *Instructions as to Procedure.*

My orders were briefly as follows, namely :—

(*a*) To discharge summarily and send to their homes all soldiers of the Egyptian army who might be sent from the Soudan, having first settled with them pecuniarily.

(*b*) To send away all army officers to Cairo, with letters of explanation, and, as far as possible, to settle all their claims for arrears of pay.

(*c*) To settle with and send to their homes all officers and men of the Bashi-Bazouks.

(*d*) To settle with and send to Cairo all civil Government officials, with explanatory letters to the Bureau du Soudan.

(*e*) To assist with biscuit and conveyance to their homes all poor refugees from the Soudan not in the service of Government.

(*f*) To assist with passages to Cairo or their homes, but not with food, all refugees able to subsist themselves, but not able to obtain passages.

To these I added a self-imposed regulation, namely, of registering the names and numbers of all refugees from the Soudan who required no assistance in any way from Government. By this means I am able to give with accuracy the numbers who passed by the Nile from the Soudan into Egypt proper, before the evacuation was suspended owing to the closing of the desert road between Abu Hamad and Korosko.

2. *Method of Conducting the Evacuation.*

The first link in the chain was his Excellency Gordon Pasha at Khartoum, who despatched the refugees, with all the available information, to Berber.

The second link was his Excellency the Governor of Berber, assisted by Signor Cuzzi, Acting English Consular Agent, the latter of whom was very painstaking.

Next came my representative at Korosko, his Excellency Giegler Pasha, to whom I am greatly indebted ; and lastly, at Assouan I myself carried out all the final details.

I was in telegraphic communication for a long time with Berber, and during the whole time with Korosko, thus being able to have ships, etc., ready, and to avoid all delay or congestion of traffic.

During the whole period I was very ably assisted by my Egyptian Brigade Major, Ahmed Effendi Fadhly, and a very excellent staff of Arab clerks from the Bureau du Soudan. I had also the co-operation, for a short time in succession, of the following English officers of the Egyptian army, namely, Captain Daubeny, Major Rundle, and Major Molyneux. I had depôts of biscuits at Korosko, Philœ, and Assouan.

I had full powers given me to issue passages by all the Government steamers on the Nile, and to give railway warrants on the Egyptian railways. I was also able, fortunately, to avail myself of returning troopships and barges for the conveyance of refugees as far as Assiout, where I found it cheaper. I hired dahabeahs between Assouan and Assiout, rationing the refugees with biscuit for the voyage.

Credits were opened for me at Assouan and Esneh to enable me to defray all the expenses of the evacuation, and a large sum of money having reached me to forward to his Excellency Gordon

Pasha, after the road to Khartoum was closed, I obtained permission to send it to Esneh as a further source on which I might draw if necessary.

3. *Number of Refugees* (2138).

The number of people of all professions and ages, and of both sexes, who have been passed through Assouan from the Soudan to their homes or to Cairo, since the date of my arrival up to my leaving for Korosko, has been 2138 ; should the evacuation, which is now suspended, be resumed, you will be able, by means of this Report, to continue similar tables of statistics to those which I have kept. I kept duplicate and very exhaustive tables in Arabic, which you will find in possession of the Arab clerks left by me in Assouan. I would strongly recommend that you keep precisely similar tables, as their value has been satisfactorily tested by references and inquiries made by the various Government Departments in Cairo.

The following table may be found interesting, as showing the weekly rate of the evacuation up to the 27th May, when it practically terminated, the few who came from the Soudan since that date having escaped by Dongola and Wady Halfa, irrespective of any organisation, until they reached me at Assouan.

Number of refugees passed through Assouan :—

March 11 to 21	92
,, 21 to April 1	114
April 2 to 13	410
,, 14 to 19	203
,, 20 to 25	322
,, 26 to 30	209
May 1 to 8	240
,, 9 to 14	215
,, 15 to 20	114
,, 21 to 27	201
,, 28 to June 8	18
Total	**2138**

4. *Proportion of Sexes among Refugees.*

Men and boys	1178
Women and girls	960
Total	**2138**

Not a single death occurred among the female refugees, which, considering the hardships of the journey, speaks well for the care of the Executive.

Three deaths were reported of male refugees in the Korosko desert.

5. *Proportion of Military and Civilian Elements.*

Officers and men of Egyptian Soudan army passed through   185
Bashi-Bazouks   155
Civilians and families of officers and of soldiers   .   .   1798

Total   .   .   .   2138

The number of soldiers would have been greater if his Excellency Gordon Pasha had not recalled from Berber all the men who had started for Egypt and who were fit for service.

The soldiers given in the table were nearly all invalids, and a more wretched, broken-down set of men it would be hard to conceive.

6. *Number of Civilian Officials.*

Number of Government civilian officials, telegraph clerks, etc., passed through   66

Three Pashas in civil office, but with military rank, have been included among the 185 officers and men mentioned in the previous table.

7. *Special Remarks on Proportion of Sexes, and Civil and Military Refugees, etc.*

Among refugees not mentioned in paragraphs 4, 5, 6, were a good many merchants, some Copts and teachers, a few European priests and converts, and some prisoners released by Gordon Pasha at Khartoum.

But the most striking feature, to my mind, was the large family and retinue I generally found with Government officials.

Many had undoubtedly been slaves, but most had obtained their letters of freedom before they reached Assouan.

For those who had not, I procured these letters from the civil authorities.

I observed that the letters were always in the possession of the masters, and never of the servants, and I doubt if many of the latter knew of their existence, and they were quite indifferent when told of it.

But the size of the families and retinues was suggestive of very large incomes which must have been enjoyed by the Egyptian officials in the Soudan.

8. *Local Arrangements at Assouan.*

I adopted the following system on arrival of the refugees from Korosko, from which place Giegler Pasha used to telegraph to me their departure :—

The vessels arrived at the village of Shellal, opposite Philœ Island, and at the south end of the Assouan Railway. Here I had a biscuit depôt, and some large marquees for the women and children.

The men who wished might remain on board the boats till the vessels for Assiout were ready. If any (except soldiers and Bashi-Bazouks) wished to stay in Assouan at their own expense till the vessels were ready, I allowed them to do so. I did not allow the soldiers and Bashi-Bazouks to go to Assouan, as I did not wish them to have any intercourse with my young soldiers.

As soon as I had enough refugees to fill a steamer or dahabeah, I despatched it down the river, with necessary orders to each for the railway at Assiout, to insure their conveyance home.

I had no trouble with the refugees, who all seemed most grateful, and anxious to save me any labour. Although to some the evacuation was a happy release, yet to most it was the breaking up of their professional lives, and perhaps the beginning of a hard struggle for existence, and their cheerfulness and complacency cannot be too highly praised.—I have, etc.,

(Signed)   F. DUNCAN, *Colonel,*
Commanding Troops in Wady Halfa and Korosko.

No. 14.

FURTHER DETAILS OF THE WRECK OF THE STEAMER FROM KHARTOUM, AND DEATH OF COLONEL STEWART.

The steamer struck a rock at the entrance to the Monassir cataracts, just below the island of Kanaiett, on the small island of Um-Dewermat. Stewart, Power, and the French Consul were on board. Stewart ordered the spare ammunition to be thrown into the river, and, after spiking the small gun, threw it also into the river.

The inhabitants were at first much alarmed, and ran away, but Stewart sent the raïs Mohammed on shore to reassure them, and promised them peace. The natives sent word at once to Suleiman Wad Gamr, who came to the house of Etman Fakri, a blind man, living on the right bank of the river, who has considerable influence over Suleiman, and was his principal adviser during the subsequent proceedings.

Stewart ordered camels to be brought to take him and his party to Merawi. The camels were brought, and the baggage was brought on shore by the soldiers in a small boat, and the camels were being loaded, when Stewart ordered the Sheikh to come and receive full payment for them as far as Merawi.

Suleiman Wad Gamr had previously seen the raïs Mohammed, and found out from him who the party consisted of. He then promised him that his life should be spared if he would bring Stewart and the Consuls, unarmed, to his house.

On the receipt of the message from Stewart to come and receive the hire of camels, he replied to the effect that he was the ruler of that part of the country, that he considered Stewart as his guest, and that if he would come and pay him a visit in his house, he would be very glad to receive him, and would then receive half the price of the camels as far as Merawi, the remainder to be paid on their safe arrival at Merawi.

Stewart started to go to the house, when he was met by a messenger to say that if he came with an armed party, or with arms, the Sheikh's people would run away, and requesting him to leave soldiers and arms behind. This was accordingly done, and Stewart, with Power and the French Consul, accompanied by their interpreter, the telegraph clerk Hussein, went alone to the house of Etman Fakri.

They were well received, and supplied with dates and coffee. Suleiman went out and called in his men, who rushed in, shouting "Surrender." Stewart gave up his pistol, and said he surrendered. The Consuls were then immediately attacked with swords. Stewart fought hard with only his fists, but was overcome. Hussein, the interpreter, caught hold of Etman and protected himself with his body from the blows made at him. He was severely wounded, but not killed. After Stewart and the Consuls had been killed, the party sallied out and surprised the soldiers, who were busy loading their camels. They rushed for the boat, which was upset. Two men of the Monassir were shot, and the Turkish soldiers were then despatched as they came to the bank; the blacks and Dongolawi men being taken prisoners. The steamer was then looted, but was not otherwise damaged. The prisoners and papers found were sent to Berber.

Suleiman paid 400 of his men $1\frac{1}{4}$ dollars each, out of the money taken on the steamer, for their work.

(Signed) H. H. KITCHENER, *Major*,
Deputy Assistant Adjutant-General.

No. 15.

LETTER FROM GORDON TO LORD WOLSELEY.

DONGOLA, *November* 14*th*, 1884.

" KHARTOUM, 4/11/84.

" Post came in yesterday from Debbah, Kitchener, dated 14th October, cipher letter from Lord Wolseley, 20th September last, which I cannot decipher, for Colonel Stewart took the cipher with him.

" No other communications have been received here since 31st, letter which arrived 17th September, a week after Colonel Stewart's steamer left this. On other side are names of Europeans who went with Colonel Stewart in steamer. At Metammah, waiting your orders, are five steamers with nine guns.

" We can hold out forty days with ease; after that it will be difficult.

" Terrible about loss of steamer.

" I sent Colonel Stewart, Power, and Herbin down, telling them to give you all information.

" With Colonel Stewart was the journal of all events from 1st March to the 10th September. The steamer carried a gun, and had a good force on board.

" The Mahdi is here, about eight miles away. All north side along the White Nile is free of Arabs; they are on south and south-west and east of town some way off; they are quiet.

" Senaar is all right, and knows of your coming.

" With steamers are my journals from 10th September to date, with all details, and map of Berber.

" We have occasional fights with Arabs.

" Mahdi says he will not fight during this month, Moharram.

" With him are all the Europeans, nuns, etc.; rumoured all

are become Mussulman. Slatin is there; Lupton, Mahdi says, has surrendered.

"Since 10th March we have had up to date, exclusive of Kitchener's, 14th October, only two despatches; one, Dongola, with no date; one from Suakin, 5th May; one of some [? same] import, 27th April.

"I have sent out a crowd of messengers in all directions during eight months.

"Get the newspapers to say I received letters through Kitchener from Sir S. Baker, my sister, Stanley, from Congo. Do not send any more letters private, it is too great a risk. Do not write in cipher, for I have none, and it is of no import, for Mahdi knows everything, and you need not fear him.

"I should take the road from Ambukol to Metammah, where my steamers wait for you. Leontides, Greek Consul-General, Hanswell, Austrian Consul, all right.

"Stewart, Power, and Herbin went down in the *Abbas*.

"A letter came from Mitzakis, the 31st July, from Adowa.

"The messenger had a letter from King for me, but Mahdi captured it. Please explain that to His Majesty.

"If journal is lost with Stewart we have no record of events from the 1st March to the 10th September, except a journal kept by doctor.

"Your expedition is for relief of garrison, which I failed to accomplish. I decline to agree that it was for me personally.

"Stewart's journal was a gem, illustrated with all the Arabic letters of Mahdi to me, etc.

"You may not know what has passed here.

"The Arabs camped outside Khartoum on the 12th March. We attacked them on the 16th March; got defeated, and lost heavily, also a gun. We then from that date had continual skirmishes with Arabs. Stewart was wounded slightly in arm.

"On one occasion, when river rose, we drove off Arabs in three or four engagements, and fired their towns. Sent up to Senaar two expeditions; had another fight, and again was defeated with heavy loss, the square was always broken; this last defeat was on the 4th September; since then we have had comparative quiet. We fired 3,000,000 rounds.

"The palace was the great place for the firing. Arabs have the Krupps here, and often have hulled our steamers. Arabs captured two small steamers at Berber, and one on Blue Nile. We have built two new ones, steamers. The steamers had bulwarks, and were struck with bullets 1090 times each on an average, and three times with shot each. We defended the lines with wire entanglements, and live shells as mines, which did great execution. We put lucifer matches to ignite them.

"The soldiers are only half a month in arrears. We issue paper money, and also all the cloth in magazines. All the captives with Mahdi are well; the nuns, to avoid an Arab marriage, are ostensibly married to Greeks. Slatin is with Mahdi, and has all his property, and is well treated; but I hear to-day he is in chains. A mysterious Frenchman is with Mahdi who came from Dongola.

"We have got a decoration made and distributed, with a grenade in centre; three classes—gold, silver, pewter.

"Kitchener says he has sent letters and got none in reply. I have sent out during last month at least ten. Steamer with this leaves to-morrow for Metammah.

"Do not let any Egyptian soldiers come up here; take command of steamers direct, and turn out Egyptian fellaheen.

"If capture of steamer with Stewart is corroborated, tell French Consul-General that Mahdi has the cipher he gave Herbin.

"Hassan Effendi, telegraph clerk, was with Stewart. You should send a party to the place to investigate affairs, and take the steamer."

On back, plan and following list of Greeks who were with Stewart in *Abbas* :—

Dimitri Kapnoulos.	Demosthenes Kapilos.
George Kepetzakos.	Dimitri Gourgo.
Herakli Bolonaki.	Paulos Xenophon.
Alex. Gemari.	Apostolios Georgios Tanizos.
Nazham Abogiri.	Jean Strizion.
Neseem Morines.	Nicolas Konbaros.
Dimitri Pediakis.	Jean Derentzakis.
Matuk Nomikos.	Michel Chatzi.
Stavros Papadakis.	Christo Doulkon.
Jean Proispireu.	

www.ingramcontent.com/pod-product-compliance
Lightning Source LLC
Chambersburg PA
CBHW022346280326
41935CB00007B/96